D0264907

Fatherhood

RESEARCH ON MEN AND MASCULINITIES SERIES

Series Editor:
MICHAEL S. KIMMEL, SUNY Stony Brook

Contemporary research on men and masculinity, informed by recent feminist thought and intellectual breakthroughs of women's studies and the women's movement, treats masculinity not as a normative referent but as a problematic gender construct. This series of interdisciplinary, edited volumes attempts to understand men and masculinity through this lens, providing a comprehensive understanding of gender and gender relationships in the contemporary world. Published in cooperation with the Men's Studies Association, a Task Group of the National Organization for Men Against Sexism.

Volumes in this Series

1. Steve Craig (ed.)
   MEN, MASCULINITY, AND THE MEDIA
2. Peter M. Nardi (ed.)
   MEN'S FRIENDSHIPS
3. Christine L. Williams (ed.)
   DOING WOMEN'S WORK: Men in Nontraditional Occupations
4. Jane C. Hood (ed.)
   MEN, WORK, AND FAMILY
5. Harry Brod and Michael Kaufman (eds.)
   THEORIZING MASCULINITIES
6. Edward H. Thompson, Jr. (ed.)
   OLDER MEN'S LIVES
7. William Marsiglio (ed.)
   FATHERHOOD

Fatherhood

Contemporary Theory, Research, and Social Policy

Edited by
William Marsiglio

*Published in cooperation with the Men's Studies Association,
A Task Group of the National Organization for Men Against Sexism*

SAGE Publications
International Educational and Professional Publisher
Thousand Oaks   London   New Delhi

For information address:

SAGE Publications, Inc.
2455 Teller Road
Thousand Oaks, California 91320
E-mail: order@sagepub.com

HQ
756
F393

SAGE Publications Ltd.
6 Bonhill Street
London EC2A 4PU
United Kingdom

SAGE Publications India Pvt. Ltd.
M-32 Market
Greater Kailash I
New Delhi 110 048 India

Printed in the United States of America

Library of Congress Cataloging-in-Publication Data

Main entry under title:

Fatherhood: contemporary theory, research, and social policy / edited
   by William Marsiglio
         p.   cm. — (Research on men and masculinities series; 7)
   Includes bibliographical references and index.
      ISBN 0-8039-5782-3 (acid-free paper). — ISBN 0-8039-5783-1 (acid-
   free paper)
      1. Fatherhood—United States.   I. Marsiglio, William.
   II. Series.
   HQ756.F3744   1995   3949/4
   306.874'2—dc20   95-5107

This book is printed on acid-free paper.

97   98   99   00   01   02   03   04   9   8   7   6   5   4   3   2

Sage Project Editor: Susan McElroy

Contents

Foreword   vii
    MICHAEL S. KIMMEL

Preface   xi

**Part I: Overview of Fatherhood Scholarship,
          Theory, and Social Policy**

1. Fatherhood Scholarship: An Overview and Agenda
   for the Future   1
   WILLIAM MARSIGLIO

2. Reshaping Fatherhood: Finding the Models   21
   KERRY J. DALY

3. Rethinking Fathers' Involvement in Child Care:
   A Developmental Perspective   41
   ALAN J. HAWKINS, SHAWN L. CHRISTIANSEN,
   KATHRYN POND SARGENT, and E. JEFFREY HILL

4. Developing a Middle-Range Theory of Father
   Involvement Postdivorce   57
   MARILYN IHINGER-TALLMAN, KAY PASLEY,
   and CHERYL BUEHLER

5. Fathers' Diverse Life Course Patterns and Roles:
   Theory and Social Interventions   78
   WILLIAM MARSIGLIO

Part II: Fatherhood Research and Prospects for the Future

6. Paternal Involvement and Perception Toward Fathers' Roles:
   A Comparison Between Japan and the United States   102
   MASAKO ISHII-KUNTZ

7. Fathering in the Inner City: Paternal Participation and
   Public Policy   119
   FRANK F. FURSTENBERG Jr.

8. Fathering Behavior and Child Outcomes: The Role of
   Race and Poverty   148
   JANE MOSLEY and ELIZABETH THOMSON

9. What Fathers Say About Involvement With Children
   After Separation   166
   JUDITH A. SELTZER and YVONNE BRANDRETH

10. Single Fathers With Custody: Do They Change
    Over Time?   193
    GEOFFREY L. GREIF and ALFRED DeMARIS

11. Stepfathers With Minor Children Living at Home:
    Parenting Perceptions and Relationship Quality   211
    WILLIAM MARSIGLIO

12. The Fathers' Rights Movement: Contradictions in
    Rhetoric and Practice   230
    CARL E. BERTOIA and JANICE DRAKICH

13. The Future of Fatherhood: Social, Demographic, and
    Economic Influences on Men's Family Involvements   255
    SCOTT COLTRANE

    References   275

    Author Index   302

    Subject Index   310

    About the Authors   316

Foreword

If opinion polls are to be believed, American men speak with a single voice on the subject of fatherhood: We all want to be good fathers—caring, nurturing, involved with our children in ways our own fathers never were with us. Such desires cut across lines of race, of class, of ethnicity, of region or the country. Fatherhood is also political. Some right-wing groups support fathers' rights (as against mothers or experience-wives), while others, like the PromiseKeepers (a conservative evangelical Christian organization founded by the football coach at the University of Colorado) promote a responsible fatherhood based on traditional Christian values, in which the father works to provide for his intact nuclear family and his wife stays home with the children. Each weekend, thousands of men troop off to the woods for a therapeutic "mythopoetic" experience, there to "heal the father wound"—to reconnect with fathers who were inexpressive, unloving, abusive, or simply absent—and thereby discover their own ability to nurture and care for their children.

Profeminist men often take a different tack altogether, placing men's experience of fatherhood within a larger social, economic, and political context. What are the structural barriers to men's ability to be more active fathers? How does the structure of the workplace—the radical spatial and temporal separation from the home, workplace demands, career aspirations—affect men's experience of fatherhood? Structural reforms—on-site child care, flexible work hours, parental leave—are necessary innovations for men to become more active and nurturing fathers. Currently, we see these reforms as "women's issues," desired by women so that they can balance work and family. Obviously, these are not "women's" issues; they are *parents'* issues, and to the extent that men seek to be active and involved parents, they will support these innovative changes as well.

Which, of course, leaves us with the question of motivation. What kinds of interpersonal obstacles do men face in their efforts to become more active and engaged fathers? What types of personal challenges do men face if they attempt to be the fathers that they say they want to be? Most important, how are men faring in the midst of this sea of change in the way we parent? What are the differences among groups of men as we attempt to chart our ways through what appear to be totally uncharted waters?

These are the kinds of questions raised in this, the seventh volume in the **Sage Series on Research on Men and Masculinities**. The purpose of this series is to gather the finest empirical research and theoretical analysis in the social sciences that focuses on the experiences of men in contemporary society.

Following the pioneering research of feminist scholars over the past two decades, social scientists have come to recognize gender as one of the primary axes around which social life is organized. Gender is now seen as equally central as class and race, both at the macro, structural level of the allocation and distribution of rewards in a hierarchical society, and at the micro, psychological level of individual identity formation and interpersonal interaction.

Social scientists distinguish gender from sex. Sex refers to biology, the biological dimorphic division of male and female; gender refers to the cultural meanings that are attributed to those biological differences. Although biological sex varies little, the cultural meanings of gender vary enormously. Thus we speak of gender as socially constructed; the definitions of masculinity and femininity as the products of the interplay among a variety of social forces. In particular, we understand gender to vary spatially (from one culture to another), temporally (within any one culture over historical time), and longitudinally (through any individual's life course). Finally, we understand that different groups within any culture may define masculinity and femininity differently, according to subcultural definitions; race, ethnicity, age, class, sexuality, and region of the country all affect our different gender definitions. Thus it is more accurate to speak of "masculinities" and "femininities" than positing a monolithic gender construct. It is the goal of this series to explore the varieties of men's experiences, remaining mindful of specific differences among men and also aware of the mechanisms of power that inform both men's relations with women and men's relations with other men.

The articles in this book help us to consider the issues facing the contemporary American father as well as a variety of his experiences. This volume thus helps to fill a deep need among American scholars and students—not to see fatherhood bathed in the rosy glow of some mythic past, or idealized through some vague notions of quality time and self-fulfillment, but through the clear lens of research on the experience of fathers, the construction of fatherhood, both as ideology and as a set of practices.

MICHAEL S. KIMMEL
Series Editor

Preface

Fatherhood: Contemporary Theory, Research, and Social Policy evolved out of my earlier guest editorship of the December 1993 and March 1994 volumes of the *Journal of Family Issues (JFI)*. Both of these "special issue" volumes were devoted to fatherhood. I received a large number of high-quality proposals in response to my initial call for papers for the *JFI* project. After reviewing 55 proposals, I decided to include five theoretical essays and two empirical studies in the December issue and seven studies based on national survey data in the March issue.

Given the quality of these manuscripts and the growing interest in fatherhood topics among scholars, policymakers, and the general public, I decided to use some of the articles as the foundation for this edited *Fatherhood* book. The introductory chapter is a revision of the thematic essay I prepared for the *JFI* series. I have updated the thematic essay by incorporating some of the most recent sociological literature on fathers and I deleted my previous discussion of social policy issues from this chapter (I include a discussion of fatherhood and social policy in Chapter 5). Chapter 1 provides an overview of sociologically relevant scholarship on fatherhood. Because this chapter reviews much of the material from the other 12 chapters in this volume, I only mention them briefly here.

In addition to the opening chapter, this book includes six chapters (2, 3, 4, 6, 9, and 12) that were originally published in the two-volume *JFI* series (with a few very minor editorial changes in some cases). I chose these six articles because they dealt with important theoretical and substantive issues that I felt should be represented in an edited volume and they also seemed to be the most accessible to scholars, policymakers, and students interested in fatherhood issues from a sociological or social psychological perspective. The three chapters by Daly; Hawkins, Christiansen, Sargent, and Hill; and Ihinger-Tallman, Pasley, and Buehler focus on theoretical issues pertaining to paternal modeling, fatherhood and adult development, and fathers' postdivorce identity. Ishii-Kuntz, Seltzer and Brandreth, and Bertoia and Drakich add to the breadth of this volume by providing a cross-cultural analysis of paternal involvement, a methodologically oriented analysis of fathers' involvement with their children after separation, and a qualitative analysis of the disparities between fathers' rhetoric and behavior within the fathers' rights movement.

This book also includes five new chapters. Four of these chapters (7, 8, 10, and 13) were solicited from other authors. Because fathers' perceptions and circumstances vary dramatically within U.S. society, I solicited new empirical studies that examined concerns relevant to African American, disadvantaged, and single fathers. Furstenberg's qualitative study explores the firsthand accounts of how parenthood is negotiated and what it represents to a small sample of young inner-city African American young men and women. Mosley and Thomson, on the other hand, use a quantitative approach and national survey data to consider how fathers' race and poverty status are related to their children's academic performance and school behavior problems. Greif and DeMaris's Chapter 10 focuses on the growing population of single fathers by using longitudinal data to consider some of the ways these fathers may change over time. Coltrane provides the conclusion for this book in Chapter 13 by speculating about the prospects for fathers' involvement in family life in the future. I prepared the remaining new manuscript (Chapter 5) to underscore the connections between theoretical issues and social interventions germane to fatherhood. Finally, the growing visibility of stepfathers in U.S. society led me to include a slightly updated version of an article on stepfathers I published in *JFI* in 1992.

Given that a number of these articles were first conceived and written independent of the Research on Men and Masculinities series, most do not explicitly emphasize gender or masculinity themes. Nonetheless, I believe this collection of chapters informs the emerging body of scholarship that addresses men's fatherhood experiences in their gendered family and social environments. I also hope that this book will raise numerous questions for those who are interested specifically in the gender-related aspects of fatherhood.

I would like to thank a number of people who have played a role in bringing this book to fruition. I would first like to thank Patricia Voydanoff, the recent editor of *JFI*, who solicited and supported my guest editorship of the *JFI* two-volume series on fatherhood. Moreover, I am indebted to a number of colleagues who graciously assisted me in reviewing the manuscripts that were reprinted from the *JFI* series. These persons include Terry Arendell, Theodore Cohen, Scott Coltrane, Philip A. Cowan, Frank F. Furstenberg, Jr., Patricia Freudiger, Marilyn Ihinger-Tallman, Michael Lamb, S. Philip Morgan, Frank L. Mott, Sheldon Stryker, and Merry White. I would like to express my appreciation to the editors of this book, Mitch Allen (Executive Editor for Sage) and Michael Kimmel (Series Editor) for their support. They have encouraged me for the past 6 or 7 years to undertake a project of this nature; their persistence paid off. I would also like to thank Stacy Smith for helping me compile the indices for this volume. The last person I would like to acknowledge is my father, Domenick Marsiglio. It is unlikely that this project would have seen the light of day if I had not adopted the disciplined and hardworking lifestyle he modeled for me. It brings me much pleasure, then, to dedicate this volume on fatherhood to my own loving father. Thank you Dad!

PART I

OVERVIEW OF FATHERHOOD SCHOLARSHIP,
THEORY, AND SOCIAL POLICY

1

Fatherhood Scholarship

An Overview and Agenda for the Future

WILLIAM MARSIGLIO

Fatherhood remains a hot topic in the 1990s as is evidenced by the extensive public debate and scholarly inquiry it has generated in recent years in North America and Europe.[1] This edited volume reinforces this pattern by illustrating social scientists' current theoretical and empirical work on a range of issues related to fatherhood in contemporary North America.[2] The interest in fatherhood has been facilitated by recent interrelated changes in the demographic profile of modern families (Ahlburg & De Vita, 1992; Bumpass, 1990; Griswold, 1993), women's increased labor force participation and the accompanying questions this shift has raised in terms of parents' household division of labor, and the intensified policy debates over the well-being of children (Cherlin, 1988a), especially those residing in single-parent households. The developing field of men's studies that has emerged during the past 20 years (Brod, 1987; Brod & Kaufman, 1994; Kimmel, 1987b), with its principal critique of men and masculinity issues, has also facilitated a family policy debate and research agenda that addresses fatherhood topics more extensively, often in qualitatively new ways.

AUTHOR'S NOTE: This chapter is a revised version of my article, "Contemporary Scholarship on Fatherhood: Culture, Identity, and Conduct," that appeared in *Journal of Family Issues* (1993, Vol. 14, No. 4, 484-509).

In reviewing the burgeoning literature germane to fatherhood issues, it is helpful to identify and discuss several sociological and social psychological foci representative of much, although by no means all, of the recent scholarship in this area. Some scholars have explored the meaning and changing nature of the symbolic representations, ideologies, and cultural/subcultural images of fatherhood (e.g., Bozett & Hanson, 1991; Drakich, 1989; Ehrenreich, 1983; Furstenberg, 1988b; Gerson, 1993; Griswold, 1993; Knijn, in press; LaRossa, 1988; Pleck, 1987; Rotundo, 1985; Segal, 1990; Sullivan, 1989). Others have attempted to conceptualize and study the nature and consequences of men's perceptions about their father role identities (Hyde, Essex, & Horton, 1993; Ihinger-Tallman, Pasley, & Buehler, Chapter 4, this volume; Marsiglio, 1991a, and Chapter 11, this volume). Finally, a large number of studies have investigated the ways and extent to which both resident (Harris & Morgan, 1991; Marsiglio, 1991b; Mosley & Thomson, Chapter 8, this volume; Nock & Kingston, 1988; Starrels, 1994) and nonresident fathers (Furstenberg & Harris, 1993; Furstenberg, Morgan, & Allison, 1987; Furstenberg & Nord, 1985; King, 1994; Mott, 1990, 1993; Seltzer, 1991; Seltzer & Brandreth, Chapter 9, this volume; see also Arditti, 1990; Fox & Blanton, 1995; Marsiglio, 1995) interact with their children and demonstrate their sense of responsibility to them. Some of these studies have considered the extent to which paternal activities are related to aspects of children's well-being.

In this introductory thematic chapter, I elaborate on these foci, discuss the important linkages between them, and highlight how various chapters in this book advance work in these areas. I frame many of my observations within the context of identity theory and structural symbolic interactionism more generally (see Burke & Reitzes, 1981, 1991; Stryker, 1980, 1987; Stryker & Serpe, 1982). I specifically focus on how the *commitment* concept is related to paternal conduct, including aspects of father-child interaction and child support. My concluding remarks delineate avenues for future theory development and research in these areas. I extend this discussion in Chapter 5 by showing how theoretical issues can inform social interventions designed to promote responsible fatherhood.

Cultural Images of Fatherhood

As noted earlier, numerous scholars have already provided excellent discussions of the symbolic representations and ideologies of fatherhood as well as the cultural images of fatherhood—the norms, values, and beliefs surrounding the social status of father and its associated roles that are shared by the general population or a sizable segment of it. These images include both *stereotypes*—people's perceptions of how typical fathers think, feel, and act—as well as *ideal* images—how people think fathers should think, feel, and act. Several of these authors' insights warrant mention here because of their relevance to how scholars have conceptualized and researched fatherhood issues to date and how they are likely to do so in the future.

Historical analyses reveal the socially constructed nature of fatherhood images. They suggest that, although the breadwinner role has represented the dominant ideal image of fatherhood throughout U.S. history, its relative importance has varied and it has been complemented at various times with other roles such as a "moral overseer," "sex role model," and "nurturer" (Furstenberg, 1988b; Griswold, 1993; Pleck, 1987; Wilkie, 1993). A social constructionist perspective invites analyses of both the specific types of fatherhood images individuals are exposed to in their everyday lives and how these images vary according to sociohistorical context, culture, and individuals' social background (e.g., race, class, religious affiliation). This perspective suggests that particular images are shaped by social factors (e.g., increased rate of women's labor force participation and the shift to a service-based economy). LaRossa (1988) posits, for example, that current expectations commonly associated with mainstream ideal images of the "good father" are typically not consistent with fathers' actual behaviors and that part of this asynchrony is due to the public's erroneous assumptions about who is caring for working mothers' children (see Pleck, 1993, for a somewhat less pessimistic interpretation of recent paternal involvement trends).

Unlike LaRossa (1988), whose discussion of the culture of fatherhood tends to focus specifically on positive images, Furstenberg (1988b) examines the "good dad-bad dad" dichotomy that may have been precipitated by the declining division of labor in family life (see also Gerson, 1993; Griswold, 1993). He suggests that the public has been inundated with coexisting, competing images of fatherhood—the involved, nurturing father versus the uninvolved, "deadbeat" father who ignores his paternal obligations. These opposing images have been reinforced by fathers' rights and mothers' groups in their efforts to shape public discourse and legislation associated with fathers' rights and obligations (Bertoia & Drakich, Chapter 12, this volume; Coltrane & Hickman, 1992). Although negative images of fathers are not new to the cultural landscape (LaRossa, Gordon, Wilson, Bairan, & Jaret, 1991), they may have become more prominent in recent years partly because of greater media exposure. Furthermore, problems associated with the high rates of divorce and out-of-wedlock childbearing (Ahlburg & De Vita, 1992) have meant that narrow stereotypical images of nonresident fathers may have become more common and pejorative. Is it possible too that the image of fatherhood is being tainted by greater public awareness of the pervasiveness and magnitude of fathers' sexual abuse of children (Griswold, 1993; Segal, 1990)?

Unfortunately, reliable data are not available to document the extent to which the general public embraces these negative (or positive) images. Moreover, the difficulty in determining whether media representations of fatherhood alter people's perceptions or merely reflect and reinforce preexisting ideals and stereotypes is a classic dilemma common to media research (McGuire, 1986). Researchers presently can only speculate about how media affects the types and strength of individuals' fatherhood images. Knijn (in press) suggests, for example, that the widespread visualization of new and positive images of fatherhood through advertisements may have prompted growing numbers of men to "go public" with their children to satisfy their emerging need to be known as good fathers.

If Furstenberg's (1988b) thesis about the polarization of fatherhood images is accurate, such a cultural climate could facilitate a social comparison process whereby individuals (men, women, and children) develop perceptions about their own or someone else's fathering behaviors by comparing themselves (or others) with the ideal and stereotypical images with which they have become familiar. On the one hand, individuals who internalize the norms, values, and beliefs associated with the positive image of the nurturing "new father" may base their evaluation of specific fathers on higher than average role expectations and conclude that their expectations are not being fulfilled. On the other hand, individuals may maintain a positive perception of themselves (or a referent father) if they perceive that they (or a referent father) are more involved than the publicly disparaged "deadbeat" fathers who show little if any interest in their children.

Two important factors that may affect the "good dad-bad dad" imagery are race and social class. Although no data address this issue directly, most would agree that public perceptions of black fathers in general tend to be more negative than those of white fathers. Everyday observation suggests that many whites stereotypically perceive of black fathers as inner-city, hypermasculine males who are financially irresponsible and uninvolved in their children's lives. Researchers have also been accused of perpetuating this stereotype by studying primarily poor black fathers at the expense of their middle-class counterparts (McAdoo, 1986a). Ironically, one possible consequence of the pervasiveness of these negative images is that both whites and blacks may develop a favorable and exaggerated view of individual black fathers who act responsibly toward their children.

The extent to which class, independent of race, is related to fatherhood images and individuals' evaluation of fathers' behaviors is less clear (see Entwisle & Doering, 1988). Historically, males who rejected their fatherhood roles were more likely to be economically disadvantaged, but the significance of class in this respect appears to have declined in recent years, partly because of middle-class men's growing emphasis on individualism (Ehrenreich, 1983; Furstenberg, 1988b). Meanwhile, Griswold (1993) has observed that social class has played and continues to play a major role in shaping fatherhood imagery. In observing how the "new father" image is decidedly middle class, he notes:

> The new fatherhood thus becomes part of a middle-class strategy of survival in which men accommodate to the realities of their wives' careers and the decline of their breadwinning capabilities. For these men, pushing a pram [baby carriage] becomes less the sign of a wimp than a public symbol of their commitment to a more refined, progressive set of values than those held by working-class men still imprisoned by outdated ideas of masculinity. (p. 254)

Finally, the generic cultural image of fatherhood tends to assume that the father and child are related biologically—or at least through adoption. Although these models can be extended to stepfathers to some extent, the public's perceptions of and expectations for stepfathers appear to be ambiguous and different from those applicable to biological/adoptive fathers (Cherlin, 1978; see also Schwebel, Fine, & Renner, 1991). The ambiguity of the stepfather status is illustrated by the finding, based on data from the National Survey of Families and Households (NSFH), that 31% of stepfathers felt that it was at least "somewhat true" that it was hard to get relatives to treat stepchildren the same as their own children (Marsiglio, Chapter 11, this volume). Issues pertaining to being a stepfather have become more salient as growing numbers of men have assumed the culturally ill-defined stepfather status in response to changing marriage, divorce, remarriage, and out-of-wedlock childbearing patterns (Hernandez, 1988).

The Social Psychology of Fatherhood

The practical significance of the culture of fatherhood is expressed through individuals' everyday life experiences. Although numerous studies during the past few decades have focused on aspects of paternal conduct, relatively little has been done to advance our conceptualization of the diverse social psychological aspects of fathers' lives (Marsiglio, 1991a). Several notable exceptions to this pattern are featured in other chapters in this volume. Efforts to develop and apply identity theory to fatherhood issues seem especially fruitful. Ihinger-Tallman et al. (Chapter 4, this volume) and Marsiglio (1995) discuss at length how identity theory can be applied to divorced fathers and young nonresident biological fathers, respectively. Consequently, I discuss this theory only briefly here and then clarify in Chapter 5 how it is compatible with viewing fatherhood from a scripting perspective.

Identity theory maintains that the individual's "self" consists of dynamic self-perceptions that stem from interactions and negotiations occurring within structured role relationships. It posits that fathers' self-perceptions are organized in an ordered fashion so that fathers will experience some of their statuses (e.g., worker, friend, son) and father roles (e.g., breadwinner, nurturer, companion) as more important than others at any given point in time (Ihinger-Tallman et al., Chapter 4, this volume). *Identity saliency* and *commitment* (the latter has been defined in several ways) are two of the key theoretical concepts that clarify how individuals' perceptions are shaped. The consequence of greater saliency is that fathers will be more apt to engage in specific father-related behaviors and emphasize their father roles when competing demands for their time and energy occur. According to some theorists (Stryker, 1980), fathers' sense of commitment involves the extent to which maintaining particular role relationships requires them to be a particular kind of father (e.g., breadwinner, nurturer), the strength of their conviction to maintain these relationships, and the number of relationships fathers have based on their identity. Burke and Reitzes's (1991) version of identity theory suggests that fathers establish identity standards and their commitment is represented by their efforts to maintain congruity between their personal "identity setting" and the reflected appraisals they receive from others (Burke & Reitzes, 1991). Although their approach links fathers to social structure, they do not explicitly consider the ways in which standards about fathers' role behavior are established, disseminated, or processed. Examples of other recent efforts to theorize about the poorly understood subjective aspects of fatherhood include a developmental perspective (Hawkins, Christiansen, Sargent, & Hill, Chapter 3, this volume; see also Pedersen, 1985) and a model based on object relations and self-psychology theory (Krampe & Fairweather, 1993). Hawkins et al., for example, register their concern that most research does not address the dynamic and reciprocal aspects of the fathering experience. In response, they conceptualize fatherhood within the theoretical context of adult development and identify several processes, relying heavily on social learning theory, by which fathers are able to develop a sense of generativity—the developmental task of caring for younger generations. In addition, they speculate on how the quality of spousal relationships may suffer because of men's and women's "divergent developmental trajectories" associated with parenting. Their approach is consistent with the emerging interest in studying the interconnection between individual and relationship development (Scanzoni, Polonko, Teachman, & Thompson, 1989) and provides a number of fresh avenues for future research.

Paternal Conduct, Relationship Quality, and Child Outcomes

Sociological analyses of paternal conduct, the third foci of recent fatherhood scholarship, have primarily considered resident fathers' engagement activities (one-to-one interaction) with their minor children and nonresident fathers' level of contact with, closeness to, and financial support for their children.[3] One of the most important reasons for studying fathers is to examine how their level and particular type of conduct are related to children's emotional, psychological, and financial well-being. Most scholars agree that, although fathers typically interact with their children differently than do mothers, men are not inherently deficient in their ability to parent and a father's gender is far less important in influencing child development than are his qualities as a parent (M. E. Lamb, 1987; Russell, 1986; Starrels, 1994; see also Griswold, 1993; Rossi, 1985).

Researchers have sought to identify factors that account for fathers' varying levels of involvement in doing numerous activities (e.g., playing, doing projects, having private talks, reading, and going on outings) with their children. This question is often framed in terms of the relative importance of characteristics associated with fathers, mothers, and children. From this perspective, paternal involvement is seen as a function of enabling as well as constraining factors. One noteworthy and disconcerting finding for liberal feminists has been that paternal involvement levels, as assessed by multivariate models using different data sources, are seemingly affected very little if at all by mothers' employment status or work schedule (see Marsiglio, 1991b, for a review). Although some evidence suggests that fathers tend to be more involved if their partner works evening and/or weekend hours, this finding may be conditional on their own work schedules (Presser, 1988, 1989; see also O'Connell, 1993). Clearly, recent increases in mothers' workforce participation have far outstripped fathers' increased involvement in all aspects of child care.

One common purpose of sociodemographic research conducted during the past decade, using data from three distinct and varied (i.e., parents represented different age groups) national samples—the youth cohort of the National Longitudinal Survey of Labor Market Experience (NLSY), the National Survey of Children (NSC), and the NSFH—has been to document patterns of biological fathers' and other father figures' household presence and absence during children's early years of life (Furstenberg & Harris, 1992; Mott, 1990, 1993, 1994; Seltzer, 1991). This research has also considered the extent to which nonresident fathers maintain contact with their minor children of varying ages. It is well documented that a large proportion of nonresident fathers have no or very little contact with their children and that the level of father-child contact tends to decline appreciably over time (see Fox & Blanton, 1995). Mott's (1990) longitudinal analysis reveals the complex nature of the dynamic flows of biological and other father figures in and out of households with young children. He clarifies how these patterns, without controlling for social class, are significantly related to the mother's age at first birth and whether the father was black. He concludes that traditional notions about discrete family transitions do not reflect the experiences of many children (and fathers), especially blacks, and that traditional definitions of residential status may underestimate the extent to which black fathers (biological and surrogate) play an important role in children's lives.

Some researchers have examined the manner and extent to which aspects of nonresident fathers' conduct (e.g., frequency of contact, father-child closeness, child support) are related to children's well-being. Most of the research examining the relationship between contact and child's well-being has been based on small observational studies and has produced mixed findings. Several recently published studies using survey data also inform this debate. One study using NSC data (sample of 11- to 16-year-olds) found that nonresident fathers' frequency of contact (mother's report) and level of closeness with their child (child's report) were not related to various measures of their child's well-being (Furstenberg et al., 1987). Furstenberg and Harris (1993) reported a similar pattern between nonresident fathers' contact and several outcome measures (e.g., educational and work attainment, imprisonment, depression) using data for children 18 to 21 years of age who were born primarily to black teenage mothers who participated in the longitudinal Baltimore study. They found, however, that children who were more attached to their biological father (as well as other surrogate father figures) were significantly less likely to have experienced negative outcomes. Finally, Crockett, Eggebeen, and Hawkins (1993) used data from the 1986 Child Supplement of the NLSY to examine the relationship between father presence during the first 3 years of their children's lives and children's cognitive and behavioral outcomes when they were aged 4 to 6. They found that father presence was positively related to child outcomes for white and Hispanic children in bivariate analyses, but father presence did not make a unique contribution to explaining child outcomes in a multivariate context.

Two other researchers, King (1994) and Mott (1993), used data from the 1988 Child Supplement of the NLSY (sample of children 5-9 years of age who were born to mothers aged 14-21 in 1979) to examine in great detail the relationship between facets of nonresident fathers' contact with their children (e.g., frequency of visitation, previous co-resident status) and a wide variety of standardized measures for children's emotional, cognitive, psychological, and behavioral well-being. In short, King found no association between frequency of nonresident father-child contact and children's well-being. Meanwhile, Mott's extensive report considered several configurations of biological "father absence" from the child's perspective by taking into account the frequency of visits and whether the child was living with a surrogate father figure. In general, his analyses revealed that children are in some ways disadvantaged in situations where fathers are not present, but even in those instances where children's well-being is affected, patterns are only significant for selective categories of children based on their gender and mother's race. Furthermore, these patterns are often attenuated when factors associated with children's home environment are controlled. Mott (1993) concluded that

> perhaps our most generalizable finding, particularly for white children, is that the presence of a father in the home makes more of an emotional than a cognitive difference; specific characteristics of the home environment do not seem to make as much of a difference emotionally for white children as does the presence or absence of a father *per se*. In contrast, the presence or absence of the father matters less for cognitive development for black and white children than does the quality of the child's environment—the presence of caring individuals, and the extent to which they are willing to work with or stimulate their children. (p. 213)

Although fathers' greater involvement with their resident or nonresident children does not necessarily enhance children's well-being when examined at the aggregate level, this pattern may be sustained to some extent by fathers who are abusive and/or intensify friction within their children's home through their negative interactions with the mother. Some scholars have also suggested that children who have grown attached to a father who subsequently retreats from his father roles, compared with children who never bonded with their father, may be more vulnerable to experiencing negative consequences when their father is no longer able or willing to maintain the same level of contact with them (Hawkins & Eggebeen, 1991; Mott, 1990). Mott (1993) found no support for this hypothesis in his own research with children 5 to 9 years of age, but child outcomes were frequently measured a number of years after fathers' coresident status with their children had changed.

Nonresident fathers' financial contributions, or lack thereof, can clearly affect children's standard of living (Furstenberg, 1989; Weitzman, 1985). The relationship between fathers' child support and children's financial well-being is especially critical in low-income, female-headed households (Garfinkel & McLanahan, 1986). Unfortunately, many nonresident fathers provide only partial or no child support (Meyer & Garasky, 1993; Seltzer, 1991; U.S. Bureau of the Census, 1991). Census data reveal too that the probability of nonresident fathers meeting their child support obligations is clearly related to their legal relationship with their child. Fathers with joint custody pay 90% of their support, fathers with visitation rights pay 79%, and fathers with neither joint custody nor visitation pay only 44.5% (Zill, 1993). It is surprising that research has found that child support is either a nonsignificant or only a weak predictor of other indicators of children's well-being (King, 1994; McLanahan, Seltzer, Hanson, & Thomson, 1994).

Another approach to examining the processes by which fathers affect their child's well-being is to compare child outcomes among single-father and single-mother households (Downey, 1994; Mulkey, Crain, & Harrington, 1992). Downey (1994), using data from the National Longitudinal Study of 1988, found that children's school performance was basically the same for those living in single-father or single-mother households but was lower in both cases when compared with children from families with two resident parents. Downey also concluded that children's difficulties were related to fathers' lower interpersonal resources in single-father households, whereas it was related to women's lower economic resources in households headed by single mothers. In other analyses with these data, Downey and Powell (1993) found that living with the same-sex parent did not significantly enhance how well children fared.

A final issue focuses on how formal and informal stepfathers affect children's lives. Data from the NSFH indicate that stepfathers who report feeling more like a real father to their minor children also report having a better relationship with them; however, it is not known how the quality of this relationship affects stepchildren (Marsiglio, Chapter 11, this volume). Hawkins and Eggebeen's (1991) study of children 4 to 6 years of age from the 1986 Child Supplement to the National Longitudinal Survey of Youth (NLSY) found that the presence or absence of different types of coresident father figures was not related to young children's verbal-intellectual functioning. Likewise, Mott (1993) found, using data from the 1988 NLSY Child Supplement and controlling for maternal characteristics and other background factors, that children's cognitive abilities did not significantly differ among children categorized in one of three ways (living with biological father, at least weekly contact with a nonresident biological father or living with a resident nonbiological father figure, and no significant contact with a male father figure). Separate comparisons between children with frequent contact with a nonresident father and those living with a father figure also revealed no significant differences. However, a father's absence from the home was associated with children's (white boys in particular) tendency to engage in problem behaviors. This relationship was statistically significant, although much weaker after controlling for a variety of other factors. As Mott notes, these types of analyses reveal aggregate patterns among categories of children, but they do not clarify the social psychological mechanisms by which individuals respond to similar (or different) life circumstances.

Directions for Future Fatherhood Scholarship

Future attempts to advance fatherhood scholarship should be initiated on several fronts and explore how the foci discussed here are interrelated. These efforts will prove most fruitful if a concerted attempt is also made to refine the conceptualization and measurement of conventional and novel concepts relevant to this area, such as (a) fatherhood stereotypes, ideals, and symbolic representations, (b) father role identity salience and commitment, (c) father-child closeness and relationship quality, (d) various forms of paternal involvement (e.g., accessibility, engagement, and responsibility), (e) financial and other forms of child support, and (f) aspects of fathers' adult development (e.g., generativity). New data collection efforts that focus systematically on fatherhood issues and include extensive reports from fathers, children, and, ideally, mothers too are needed if researchers are to generate a more complete understanding of the key concepts and processes in this area.

New scholarship that attempts to link these foci should be sensitive to two additional issues (F. F. Furstenberg, personal communication, June 1993). First, it is important to view fathers' commitment to various identities and their paternal involvement as being both socially patterned and individualistic in nature. Large-scale social processes often shape the opportunities and constraints that fathers experience as they attempt to embrace specific fatherhood roles. Thus discussions of fathers' type and level of conduct ideally should consider their behavior within the larger social context that *is partly* responsible for relegating fathers to roles such as nonresident father, breadwinner, playmate, and so on. The gendered and class dimensions of these sorting processes are particularly important. These processes, although powerful, are by no means determinant. Individual fathers, in conjunction with other family members, can and do sometimes challenge the typical patterns that occur as a result of these sorting processes. For instance, a young man who becomes a father unexpectedly and who has successful, self-employed, entrepreneurial parents would probably be able to assume the breadwinner role more easily than a counterpart whose parents were unemployed (or employed by others). However, if he lacks the desire to do so, he will probably assume less responsibility than a less affluent but more motivated peer. Second, analyses of fatherhood should consider how men's and women's diverging perspectives on relationships and family life color the symbolic meaning and description of paternal activities. To the extent that fathers and mothers develop gendered perspectives on parenthood, they may be inclined to distort and discount each other's sense of reality as well as their parental practices. This means that the theoretical issues associated with how fathers and mothers come to define and interpret their own and others' realities are linked with the methodological issues of gathering data on fatherhood from multiple persons with potentially very different perspectives.

Methodological Issues

A basic methodological shortcoming of large-scale sociological research on fathers to date is that much of it has relied on mothers' reports of fathers' attitudes, paternal conduct, and father-child relationship quality. The nature and magnitude of the problems associated with mothers' reports depend, in part, on whether mothers are reporting on resident or nonresident fathers, or if they are reporting on objective or subjective phenomena. Recent surveys such as the NSFH are beginning to address this concern by gathering data directly from fathers. However, the quality of fathers' self-report data, especially nonresident fathers, is questionable for at least two reasons (see Seltzer & Brandreth, Chapter 9, this volume, for a discussion). First, nonresident fathers often report that they provide more financial child support than mothers report receiving, a discrepancy that is probably only partially due to mothers' lack of knowledge about money fathers spend on their children directly. Seltzer and Brandreth do show, using NSFH data, that this discrepancy can be reduced by comparing unmatched samples of resident mothers and nonresident fathers who describe the father's relationship with a child born in the parents' first marriage. Second, sampling biases restrict the representativeness of specific subsamples of fathers, nonresident fathers in particular, because nonresident fathers are much less likely than resident mothers to participate in survey research. Although creative strategies that identify comparable samples of resident mothers and nonresident fathers should produce more reliable estimates, some questions can only be answered adequately by using data from father-mother pairs.

Another complex measurement issue arises when different respondents provide discrepant reports for subjective phenomena such as father-child closeness. Smith and Morgan (1994) examine this issue by using data from the NSC to assess mothers' and children's reports of father-child closeness. After applying Rasch's (1966) measurement model to these data, they discover that, when fathers coreside with their children, "mothers' and children's (both sons and daughters) responses are consistent with the perceived existence of a common underlying *closeness* dimension" (p. 26). Mothers' and children's reports both indicate that sons are closer than daughters to their resident father, but when reports about nonresident fathers are examined, they find that mothers and children appear to base their evaluation of closeness on different dimensions. Smith and Morgan speculate that mothers' reports may in some cases incorporate their negative feelings toward their nonresident former partner. This type of research reinforces the notion that the advancement of knowledge in this area depends a great deal on researchers' ability to scrutinize and refine their measures. In addition, it is consistent with the notion that scholars' ability to unveil the more elusive features of fatherhood will require them to consider the theoretical and empirical implications of separate gender perspectives on parenthood.

Substantive Issues

The advancement of this field of study will also rest on researchers' ability to address the substantive foci discussed earlier. At the broadest level, research needs to document the types of cultural scenarios or messages the general public and specific groups (e.g., young urban black men, single fathers) are exposed to today (Marsiglio, Chapter 5, this volume). Researchers should first examine how fathers are portrayed in formal media such as movies, television, novels, and advertising (see Coltrane & Allan, 1993). They should then consider how these images are processed and reinforced through informal, interpersonal communication sources (e.g., family, friends, coworkers). A complementary type of analysis would assess fathers' rights groups' efforts to alter public perceptions about fathers in general and fathers' legal rights and obligations toward their children in particular.

Berry's (1992) analysis of 54 black adolescents' perceptions about main father figures portrayed on television sitcoms such as *The Cosby*

Show and *Good Times,* although limited, represents a preliminary attempt to study the relationship between the media's representation of different fatherhood images and viewers' beliefs. Likewise, studies similar to LaRossa et al.'s (1991) trend analysis of cartoons depicting incompetent fathers between 1924 and 1944 would be instructive. In addition to these types of analyses, detailed surveys are needed that examine the general public's beliefs and attitudes regarding father roles as well as possible shifts in the cultural messages people assimilate. Innovative methodologies designed to determine the extent to which individuals' perceptions are actually altered, rather than simply reinforced, by various types of media representations and interpersonal experiences could provide valuable insights.

Research should examine, then, the processes by which men, as well as women and children, internalize or reject particular fatherhood images. One of the central questions is this: How do males develop their perception of their father status and its accompanying roles? Fathers' perceptions may be based partially on cultural images they encounter through the popular culture as well as their direct contact with a specific father figure(s), their friends, and/or acquaintances who are fathers. It is also possible that men may attempt to emulate their female partner's level of commitment and parenting style. Daly's (Chapter 2, this volume) qualitative study of "father models" represents a preliminary attempt to assess the importance of role models for new fathers. Unexpectedly, this exploratory analysis found that new fathers frequently did not use specific fathers, even their own, as role models. Instead, they tended to model their fathering behaviors after a fragmented set of behaviors displayed by a variety of persons. Researchers need to pursue this line of inquiry further and draw on these qualitative studies to design research using larger and more diverse samples. Determining how fathers with more narrowly defined identities (e.g., single father, stepfather) develop their fathering style is critical given fathers' diverse life course patterns (Marsiglio, Chapter 5, this volume). Furthermore, cross-cultural studies that examine the nature and consequences of paternal involvement, and compare fathers', mothers', and children's perceptions about father involvement within the United States and other countries, such as Japan, afford scholars the opportunity to consider aspects of fatherhood in North America within a broader context (Ishii-Kuntz, Chapter 6, this volume).

One promising approach to studying fathers' perceptions about their father roles is based on identity theory. Ihinger-Tallman et al.'s (Chapter 4, this volume) work is significant in this regard because their pilot study uses this theory to focus on social psychological factors that enhance divorced fathers' paternal involvement and, in turn, children's well-being. Their theoretical model is also consistent with a dynamic image of fathers' commitment to their role identity—that is, it is likely to fluctuate in response to changing social/economic opportunities and constraints as well as to interpersonal pressures. This approach can be developed further by focusing on several issues. First, it could be modified and expanded to apply to a more diverse group of fathers (e.g., all fathers who are aware that they have fathered a child irrespective of their previous or present relationship with the child's mother). Second, the theory could be enhanced if it accounted more clearly for the different aspects of fathering, for example, financial provider, nurturer, and disciplinarian. Third, it should expand on Burke and Reitzes's (1991) discussion of reflected appraisals and incorporate a more explicit discussion of the specific processes by which fathers develop and maintain their self-perceptions and role identity commitments (e.g., Bandura's, 1977, social learning theory's emphasis on modeling and response consequences). Part of a related, but broader, theoretical project would involve attempts to specify how macro- and middle-range social processes/structures enhance or restrict the opportunities fathers have to develop and sustain particular father roles. Fourth, the theory should take into account the interrelationship between father role identities and those associated with being a partner, worker, and masculine male (Marsiglio, 1991a). This last issue could be addressed by considering how the scripting perspective provides a context within which fathers interpret, negotiate, play, and reprioritize their identities and paternal roles (Marsiglio, Chapter 5, this volume).

The role relationship a father has with his partner is likely to influence his perceptions about the salience of his father role identity as well as his commitment to aspects of it. If he is aware that his relationship with his partner requires him to be a particular type of father and he values his relationship with his partner, he will probably be more committed to at least some facets of his father role identity. Thus researchers should examine how fathers develop and/or lessen their commitment to specific aspects of their father identity as a function of the nature and quality of their relationship with their partner. An analysis such as this should control for whether fathers have ever lived with and enjoyed being with their children, because children's needs and personality characteristics can either encourage or discourage fathers' involvement.

Fathers' work identity may often be related to their perceptions about their father role identity. Research that explores this relationship needs to be sensitive to the sometimes competing expectations associated with particular father roles. Fathers who feel that their primary responsibility is to be a dependable financial provider may think very differently about their work than those who place greater emphasis on father roles that are based on father-child interaction (Hyde et al., 1993). Although each may be very committed to being a father, they may perceive their primary responsibilities differently. In their recent longitudinal study of 550 men whose wife/partner was pregnant, Hyde et al. found that work identity was not related to fathers' parental leave, although those who had egalitarian gender role attitudes and were high in family salience were more likely to take longer leaves—even though they were still quite short.

Having a strong commitment to a work identity does not necessarily preclude men from having a similar commitment to nonprovider father roles too. Being committed to nonprovider aspects of fathering may not always be apparent, however. For instance, fathers' public presentation of self may be inconsistent at times with their perceptions about their actual work and father role identities. Pleck (1993) and Levine (1991) observe that some fathers attempt to portray themselves as abiding by workplace norms that emphasize a strong commitment to work/career while at the same time attempting to honor their commitment to father roles other than financial provider. Research is needed that explores the typical practices and impression management strategies that these fathers use in an effort to accommodate themselves to a workplace culture that typically emphasizes work over family responsibilities.

A related transitional issue involves the timing of a first child relative to men's (and their partners') occupational experiences. The timing of a child may affect fathers' orientation toward assuming responsibility for housework—including parenting (Coltrane & Ishii-Kuntz, 1992; May, 1982; see also Cooney, Pedersen, Indelicato, & Palkovitz, 1993). Under certain conditions, for example, older men who have already established themselves in their respective careers may be more willing than younger men to assume the time-intensive nonbreadwinner roles associated with fatherhood.

The analyses discussed above should emphasize the transitional nature of men's commitment to father roles created and played in connection with both their sexually based primary relationship with the mother of their child (or stepchild) and their work identity (Marsiglio, Chapter 5, this volume). The transition theme will tend to be most relevant for newly separated or divorced fathers as well as for first-time fathers. Qualitative studies of the socioemotional aspects of fathers' transitional experiences could be quite useful in this area. They could focus on the negotiated processes that affect fathers' (or prospective fathers') roles within the context of their identity salience hierarchy (Backett, 1987; Furstenberg, Chapter 7, this volume). Resident and nonresident partners may demand, cajole, and inspire fathers to develop a particular fathering style or partners may attempt to restrict fathers' efforts (Haas, 1988). The race differences in household structure and family transition patterns noted earlier underscore the need for additional research that examines nonresident black fathers' perceptions about nonresident paternal roles after controlling for social class. Mothers' perceptions of nonresident fathers' roles should also be considered, for blacks as well as others.

Fathers' perceptions about the "masculine male role," in combination with their views about specific role identities, may also affect their fatherhood experiences if they are responsive to others' expectations of them as men. For instance, if male gang members perceive that to prove their masculinity and worthiness as a gang member they must demonstrate their independence from women and avoid domestic activities, those members who become fathers will be reluctant to be involved in child care and they may shirk their financial responsibilities as well. On the other hand, men who appreciate more modern versions of masculinity, or are at least sensitive to a feminist position on parenting, may attempt to interact with their own children (or their partner's children) in a sensitive way if they assume such behavior will enhance their "sex appeal" (Knijn, in press; Segal, 1990).

Although negotiation issues will be relevant to the intersection of father and other role identities for many fathers, the need to focus on the negotiated aspects of father roles is especially keen when studying stepfathers. Research that examines the relationship between fathers' commitment to specific father roles and their paternal behaviors should compare stepfathers and biological fathers. I found, in one study using a subsample from the NSFH of biological fathers living with at least one biological child, that fathers reported more involvement in playing and project activities and private talks with their biological children than with their stepchildren (Marsiglio, 1991b). Moreover, I found in a study restricted to stepfathers in the NSFH that stepfathers were more likely to perceive that they felt like a father to their stepchildren if one or more of their biological children lived with them (Marsiglio, Chapter

11, this volume). These findings suggest that researchers should examine why some stepfathers develop "fatherlike" perceptions and others do not. It is important to understand the processes by which stepfathers come to define their relationship with their children as being based on the moral norm of univocal reciprocity—a norm that is typically associated with biological parents (Ekeh, 1974; Scanzoni & Marsiglio, 1993). Adhering to this moral norm occurs when stepfathers do not expect to be reciprocated immediately or directly for their paternal investment and they express fundamental obligations toward their stepchildren as if they were their own. Researchers should also consider the ways in which children benefit (or suffer), both in the short and the long term, when stepfathers develop this orientation. In sum, it has become increasingly important in the light of changing family structure patterns to examine how men perceive their formal and informal stepfathering experiences, how others perceive stepfathers, and the relationship between perceptions, paternal conduct, and child outcomes.

Meanwhile, research with biological fathers should consider the association between their orientation toward their father, work, partner (or ex-partner), and masculine male roles and their actual paternal conduct. One key question focuses on how biological fathers' commitment to aspects of father roles are related to their (a) type and level of involvement with their resident and nonresident children and (b) provision of child support to their nonresident children. In some instances, it may be important to identify the factors that tend to curtail or strengthen their relationship (e.g., father's employment opportunities, resident mother's role in restricting or facilitating paternal involvement).

A final neglected area of research on paternal involvement deals with what Pleck, Lamb, and Levine (1986) refer to as "responsibility" types of activities. Fathers spend very little time organizing or managing their children's lives (e.g., scheduling medical appointments, buying clothes) yet we know little about the factors that are related to fathers' lack of involvement in this area. Studying fathers who have primary or exclusive custody of their children may provide researchers with some clues in this regard.

Summary and Conclusion

As we approach the twenty-first century, social scientists will continue to play a vital role in the public discourse concerning the changing nature of families and father roles. This debate, fueled by the diverse interests of those associated with the feminist movements, men's rights organizations, gay/lesbian organizations, and the new right, is likely to remain heated for the foreseeable future. The politics of fatherhood have clearly become a fascinating feature of the sociopolitical landscape in recent years (Griswold, 1993). Social scientists' contributions to this discourse that implicates fathers, mothers, and children are likely to be varied and extensive. Their theoretical and empirical work will continue to provide the foundation for making informed predictions about the future of fatherhood (Coltrane, Chapter 13, this volume).

I attempted in this introductory chapter to identify several of the major foci that have guided the growing theoretical and empirical sociological literature relevant specifically to fathers. It also discussed how these foci address fatherhood in terms of the cultural, social psychological, and behavioral levels while suggesting ways in which researchers can improve their understanding of how these foci intersect. It is encouraging that scholars appear eager to forge ahead in their quest to develop a better understanding of fatherhood in contemporary North America and elsewhere. However, the extent to which scholars can address these issues in a meaningful fashion will be affected considerably by the general public's and policymakers' level of interest in fatherhood issues. At this moment in history, public intrigue with the positive and negative aspects of fatherhood is likely to provide scholars with a supportive environment to explore various dimensions of fatherhood.

Notes

1. Although this thematic chapter focuses primarily on scholarship within a North American context, European scholars and policymakers have increasingly shown an interest in fatherhood issues as is reflected in the foci of two recent special international conferences (the "Conference on Changing Fatherhood" organized by the Faculty of Social Sciences at the University of Tilburg, the Netherlands, May 1994, and "Fathers in Families of Tomorrow" coordinated through the Danish Ministry of Social Affairs and held in Copenhagen, June 1993). A similar U.S. conference, "America's Fathers and Public Policy," was sponsored by the National Science Foundation in October 1993 (see Crowell & Leeper, 1994).

2. This volume evolved out of my editorship of the *Journal of Family Issues*'s two-volume series devoted to fatherhood issues (December 1993 and March 1994).

3. My discussion of this general area focuses only on recent sociological analyses that use large-scale survey data. As Lamb (1994) recently noted, roughly 10,000 articles have been published on how fathers influence child development, most of which are based on small-scale samples.

2

Reshaping Fatherhood

Finding the Models

KERRY J. DALY

There is a belief that the "culture" of fatherhood (LaRossa, 1988) has changed dramatically insofar as there are heightened expectations for how fathers should act (Lamb, 1986; Pleck, 1984, 1987). However, the "conduct" of fatherhood (LaRossa, 1988), as marked by men's active participation in child-rearing activities, has been relatively slow to change (Lamb, Pleck, & Levine, 1985; Thompson & Walker, 1989), even though recent evidence suggests that men may be doing more than has been previously reported (Pleck, 1993). One of the major reasons given for why fathers have been slow to change is lack of exposure to appropriate paternal role models (Palkovitz, 1984). Traditionally, mothers have acted as a central parental role model for their adult children (Chodorow, 1978), with one consequence being that small boys often do not have a clear picture of who father is. He is "often a shadowy figure at best, difficult to understand" and typically unavailable to "provide a confident, rich model of manhood" (Osherson, 1986, p. 6). In addition, some have argued that males have not had the education, social services, or support necessary to foster more involvement with their children

AUTHOR'S NOTE: This chapter previously appeared as an article, with the same title, in *Journal of Family Issues* (1993, Vol. 14, No. 4, 510-530). An earlier version of the article was presented at the Canadian Sociology and Anthropology meetings in Charlottetown, P.E.I., May 31, 1992.

(Berman & Pedersen, 1987; Bolton, 1986; Klinman, 1986; Levant, 1988). As Dickie (1987) has suggested, men are attempting to meet heightened cultural expectations for fatherhood with a set of preparations that are rooted in the 1950s. The result of this lack of preparation appears to be an increased level of stress for fathers (McBride, 1989).

As the preceding discussion would suggest, the absence of preparation for fatherhood and its consequences have been well documented. However, there is little research that examines how role models influence the ongoing construction of the fatherhood identity in the absence of these preparatory experiences. This research was designed to examine how fathers of young children socially construct and define the fatherhood identity. Of particular interest in this chapter is the way that men shape fatherhood roles according to various models in their lives. Do fathers have role models that they follow? To what extent do their own fathers, mothers, wives, friends, and others play a part in the way that they construct their fatherhood identity? Moreover, in the light of changes in gendered experience in recent years, how do men reconcile the "good provider" model (Bernard, 1983) of their father's generation with the current societal expectation that they be the "new, nurturant father" (Giveans & Robinson, 1985)? Although there is a danger of oversimplifying the history of fatherhood into "then" and "now" categories (LaRossa, Gordon, Wilson, Bairan, & Jaret, 1991), it would appear that these ideological constructions of what fatherhood should be are well established in the literature (see Marsiglio, Chapter 1, this volume, for a review). Paramount among these is the expectation that fathers *should be* more involved with their children (Backett, 1987).

There has been a growing literature on men and masculinity that reflects a need to understand the changes and conflicts that men experience at home, on the job, and in their personal lives (see, e.g., Daly, 1993; Hanson & Bozett, 1985; Kimmel, 1987a; Lewis & O'Brien, 1987; Lewis & Salt, 1986; Lewis & Sussman, 1986; Thompson & Walker, 1989). As Doherty (1986) reminds us, it is important that we not reify these experiences but that we adopt a scientific posture that respects the contextual and fluctuating nature of these changes and conflicts. Historical analyses have suggested that there have been radical shifts in the way that fatherhood roles have been conceptualized (Demos, 1982). Lamb (1986) summarizes these changes, suggesting that over the last two centuries the "dominant motif" of fatherhood has shifted from "moral teacher" to "breadwinner" to "sex role model" to "new nurturant father" (pp. 4-6). In acknowledgment of the changing and emergent nature of paternal roles, Parke (1985) has suggested that researchers must take a series of continuing pictures across time. This research is intended to provide one such picture of men's experiences. It does not presume to represent the full spectrum of men's experiences as fathers, nor does it pretend, on its own, to capture the process of historical change. Other pictures will need to be taken, which, when pieced together, will offer some insight into these historical shifts.

This research focuses on a small sample of relatively new fathers who have young children. Consistent with the assumptions of qualitative family research (Gilgun, Daly, & Handel, 1992), the goal of this study is to provide insight into the interactional and interpretive meanings of fatherhood identity as they emerge from the experiences of fathers themselves. The intent, then, is not to generalize about all fathers but to elaborate on the "idiographic" (Allport, 1942) experiences of some fathers.

Theoretical Perspectives

Historically, several theoretical approaches have dominated the analysis of fatherhood identity: socialization theories, microstructural theories, psychoanalytic explanations, and social learning theory. In its most rigid form, socialization theory is represented by the work of structural functionalists such as Parsons and Bales (1955), who suggest that becoming a father involves the internalization of a set of role prescriptions and requirements for what a father should be. These prescriptions are rooted in cultural values and stereotypes that have reinforced the breadwinner role of fathers with their families. Although structural functionalist explanations have largely fallen into disfavor, notions of instrumental roles and the provider function continue to have a residual impact on our way of thinking about fatherhood.

Other sociological models have been used in the study of fatherhood. For example, Risman and Schwartz (1989) advocate for a "microstructural" approach that deemphasizes the power of early socialization and focuses instead on how men and women "are continually re-created during the life cycle by the opportunities available to them and their interactions with others" (p. 1). According to this view, single fathers can become "competent as primary parents" when the situation demands it of them, in spite of being poorly socialized for parenthood (Risman, 1989, p. 163). In a similar vein, LaRossa and LaRossa (1989) accentuated the "sociocultural forces and interactional contexts" that men experience as they negotiate the transition to fatherhood. Cohen (1989) suggests that men are having to "remake" fatherhood because their "opportunities for participation in their familial roles fell short of their preferred levels of involvement" (p. 229). As these ideas would suggest, fatherhood is changeable and reflects the shifting context within which it is experienced.

Psychoanalytic explanations of fatherhood identity gained a resurgence of momentum with Chodorow's (1978) feminist writings, which focused on the inadequacy of fathering role models and the corresponding power that women have in shaping male identity. From this perspective, sex role identity (including a predisposition to parent) is established early on through repeated experience and differential reinforcement. The consequences for the fatherhood identity are profound: "Women come to mother because they have been mothered by women. . . . By contrast, that men are mothered by women reduces their parenting capacities" (Chodorow, 1978, p. 211). The psychoanalytic approach suggests that men are handicapped in their effort to become committed fathers by the absence of early identification experiences with their own fathers. Following in this vein, Osherson (1986) suggests that a little boy naturally seeks to separate from his mother around the age of 3 but is left without "a clear and understandable model of male gender upon which to base his emerging identity" (p. 6). From this perspective, men develop a conflicted sense of masculinity that stems from the rejection, incompetence, or absenteeism of their own fathers. Although this approach is a useful one for highlighting the implications of the traditionally closer mother-child bond in the early years of childhood, it is limited by its inattentiveness to the complex interactive effects of the father's multiple roles as provider, parent, and support for the mother. The failure of Chodorow's theory to account for these effects is most evident when one turns to the father-absence research (Adams, Milner, & Schrepf, 1984). This research indicates that boys growing up without their fathers are more likely to experience problems in the development of appropriate sex roles and gender identity, suggesting in turn that boys who do grow up with their fathers have a more "normal" sex role development. The applicability of Chodorow's theory is further tempered by historical changes in family experience (Lorber, Coser, Rossi, & Chodorow, 1981). Chodorow seems to focus on the traditional nuclear family and, as a result, does not adequately account for historical changes, such as increased maternal employment in the preschool years

(Hoffman, 1989) or single custodial fathers (Hanson, 1985; Meyer & Garasky, 1993; Risman, 1989).

Social learning theory has focused on the way that individuals develop gender-appropriate behaviors through the observation and imitation of models (Mischel, 1966). Although there is little research on how men have learned to be fathers, there has been a long research tradition that looks at the implications of differential reinforcement of boys' and girls' behavior (Salamon & Robinson, 1991). Of particular relevance for this study is the observation that children do not appear to imitate people of their own gender more than the other gender (Maccoby & Jacklin, 1974), nor do they typically end up resembling the same-sex parent more than the other (Losh-Hesselbart, 1987). As this would suggest, men are unlikely to construct their fatherhood identity on the basis of only male models. Furthermore, there are at least three important types of modeling situations for the development of gender roles: (a) symbolic presentations, including media models; (b) concrete figures, including parents and peers; and (c) the patterning of behavior in social situations (Losh-Hesselbart, 1987). According to Losh-Hesselbart (1987), the first two types of modeling have received more attention than the third.

The proposed research will address some of the issues arising from these theoretical approaches but will do so within a symbolic interactionist theoretical framework. In accordance with the fundamental premise that identity is an ongoing process of social construction (Berger & Luckmann, 1966), fatherhood will be examined as it is interpreted and negotiated from situation to situation. In their classic work titled *Family Worlds*, Hess and Handel (1959) convincingly argue that patterns of family action can never be complete, "since action is always unfolding and the status of family members is always undergoing change" (p. 8). In this regard, fatherhood is an emergent identity that is continuously being reshaped and reinterpreted as one encounters new circumstances, challenges, or obstacles.

This focus on the changing nature of the fatherhood identity differs from socialization and psychoanalytic views that emphasize identity as *product* that is, in varying degrees of "success," shaped early on. Nevertheless, the interpretation, and reinterpretation, of these modeling influences represents an important dimension in the process of socially constructing the fatherhood identity. Hence participants in this study were prompted to discuss who the salient actors were in their ongoing construction of fatherhood. They were asked to identify not only who these models were but to discuss why and how they came to be important.

Method

Following the qualitative research principles of grounded theory and comparative analysis (Glaser & Strauss, 1967), this research focused on identifying the key elements in the process of socially constructing the fatherhood identity. In keeping with this method, the data were categorized and analyzed for emergent themes.

Although, in its purest form, a grounded theory approach involves suspending preconceived notions about what to expect in the data, the reality is that the researcher's experience with the phenomenon in question and the existing literature give some shape and direction to the interview. In this study, my experience as a father of two children aged 8 and 6 has had a strong impact on my motivation to do the study and my way of thinking about fatherhood. This experience had both positive and negative implications for the research. On a positive note, it was a source of "theoretical sensitivity" that stimulated the generation of concepts and their relationships (Strauss & Corbin, 1990). Conversely, such experience can also be seen as having a biasing effect on the research. In acknowledgment of this, I made an effort at the outset to get some perspective on my personal issues as a way of gaining some control over their impact on the research. For example, I attended a weekend workshop dealing with men's relationships with their fathers, and I interviewed my own father. Although my personal experiences still shaped the interpretive course of the research in countless ways, these activities were extremely valuable for separating personal needs from the research agenda.

Men have traditionally been difficult to recruit for research studies (Daly, 1992) and this was no exception. A sample of 32 fathers from intact families was obtained through two sources: a children's recreational program at the YM-YWCA and a large corporation. In the first setting, 5 fathers participated, and in the second, 27 were interviewed. Only two criteria were used in the selection of the sample: Fathers had to be in an intact family (to avoid issues of stepparenting or divorce), and, second, they had to have at least one child who was age 6 or under. The second criteria was intended to create some homogeneity in the sample with respect to the fathering experience. This is in keeping with

Goffman's (1974) notion of "framing" a time period to define some experiential boundaries. The young age of the children was chosen on the assumption that the process of constructing the fatherhood identity would be more salient at this early stage of the parenting career than later on. Furthermore, there is some evidence to suggest that fathers spend less time with their children as they get older (Lamb, Pleck, Charnov, & Levine, 1985). Although the sample is nonrandom and therefore limited in its generalizability, the goal of qualitative research is not to discover how many or what kind of people share a fatherhood characteristic but, instead, to capture the complex assumptions, meanings, and contradictions that enter into the process of experiencing and constructing the fatherhood identity.

The interviews were audiotape-recorded and later transcribed verbatim. The researcher conducted all the interviews. Interviews were analyzed using *The Ethnograph*, a software program for computer-assisted analysis of text-based data.

All interviews started out in a general, nondirective way. Questions were asked about how respondents decided to have children, what was important about being a father, what they disliked about being a father, what it meant to be a "good father," and how important fatherhood was to them in relation to other identities. Following from these questions, the interview was organized into three general classes of questions. These classes are suggested by identity theory and include the role of significant others, definitions of relevant situations, and the influence of relationships. For example, with respect to relationships, questions were asked about the influence of the respondents' own parents on their fathering roles, their relationships with their wives and their children, and whether there were other relationships that affected how they saw themselves. They were also asked questions about their preparation to become a father, whether they compared themselves with others, and who their role models were.

Providing some structure to the interview beforehand had the pragmatic advantage of "diminishing the indeterminacy and redundancy" of unstructured interviews, thereby making the data-gathering process more efficient (McCracken, 1988). However, consistent with the qualitative aim of discovering the participant's view and avoiding the "passive-compliance" that stems from a highly structured interview format (Cicourel, 1967, p. 58), questions within these broad classes were as nondirective as possible. Furthermore, the researcher was quite happy to wander into areas that were outside of these general classes.

The average age of the sample was 34. Participants were married for an average of 8 years; 56% had two children, 31% had one child, and 12% had three or more children. The sample represented a good range of educational and occupational experiences: 16% held a master's degree, 28% a bachelor's degree, 28% had attended community college, 25% had completed high school, and 3% had not completed high school. In terms of occupation, 25% held senior management or semi-professional positions, 22% held a middle-management position, 25% were in skilled trades, 25% were laborers, and one participant was a student; 19% worked shifts. Most wives were employed outside the home: 41% worked part time, 28% worked full time, and 31% worked as homemakers.

Discussion

When the men in this study were asked about who served as important role models for their own fatherhood identity, there was a wide range of responses. Three key themes emerged. First and foremost, when they were asked about who had influenced how they played out fatherhood roles, they had great difficulty identifying specific individuals as models. However, they typically ended up talking about their own fathers—not as role models but as a point of reference for describing how they were different. A second major theme to emerge was that these fathers tended not to model their behavior after a particular individual but selected particular behaviors to incorporate into their roles from a wide purview of choices. The women in their lives—namely, mothers and wives—tended to be significant in this regard. A third theme to emerge was the emphasis that was placed by these men on providing a role model to their children, in the absence of role models in their own lives. Although there was variation in the background characteristics of the sample (e.g., occupation), this appeared not to affect the emergence of these themes.

The Absence of Father Models

One of the most striking findings was that these fathers perceived that they had no specific role models. Jonathon's[1] response was typical. He talked about the absence of any significant role models in the anticipatory stage of becoming a father:

I really didn't have a lot of people around me—at least when I was growing up or before I became a father—who really stick in my mind to say, "Yeah, I'd like to be a father like this one." I can't say that there was a figure that influenced me.

Of course, the most obvious candidate for modeling fatherhood roles would be one's own father. Although respondents frequently talked about their own fathers in response to the question about models, their fathers served only as a negative role model or a reference point for what respondents wanted to change in their own lives. While talking about his own father, one man succinctly suggested that "I was influenced more by the bad examples I had around me than the good." Fathers were perceived as a powerful influence but only insofar as they had done a poor job of fathering by today's standards. This is consistent with other reports that fathers perceive themselves to be more involved in their children's care than were their own fathers (Kennedy, 1989) and that this seems to be expressed by each new generation of fathers (Lewis, 1986). Stephen explains:

I don't want to be like him as far as his parenting goes. We don't see that much of my father since Mom passed away, but usually there's a period in summer of 6 weeks or so, when he spends part of his time with us. We see him on a very regular basis during this 6-week period, and we look forward to the end of it. It's not that I don't love him and I respect him as a father, but he's not a family person. He feels the children are to be seen and not heard. We don't have that same feeling.

For Stephen, there was a need for a complete departure from the kind of father model that was presented to him. Although maintaining a level of deferential "respect," he does not want to be like his father because his father is not a "family person."

For many men in this study, the failure of their own fathers to serve as adequate role models was the result of generational differences in the expectations for how one should father. The emphasis that their own fathers placed on work, at the cost of their family experiences, was something that concerned these men. Charlie described how his attitude toward work and family was very different from his own father's:

My dad was in business for himself. If I could fault my dad in any way, he didn't spend the time with us; he was always working. My dad didn't play ball with me; he didn't play hockey with me or anything like that. If I wanted to go and be with my dad, I would go to the construction site with him and I would wear my little hard hat, my little nail bag, and I would go around with him and look at construction sites and drive around in the truck with him because he was just always very busy. I think he regrets that. . . . I told him that I regretted that we didn't get to spend enough time together when I was little. He feels bad about that, but I think we have a lot more freedom to spend time with our kids today than maybe our parents did. And maybe it was the values of society at the time but dad was supposed to work and mom was to look after the kids. And that has sort of changed; nowadays, dads are also supposed to participate in raising a kid.

The mutual regret expressed by Charlie and his father in the preceding passage reflects a co-constructed awareness by both generations that the father models of the past were deficient. At the same time that Charlie held his father accountable for this by expressing his regret, he readily attributed his father's failure to spend time with him to the cultural expectations of the time, claiming that his father was "supposed to work," but he is "supposed to participate in raising a kid."

In light of the different ideological forces that affected the generations, the models provided by the respondents' fathers no longer worked. The inadequacy of these models was not tied solely to changes in the expectations for fatherhood but were also a function of changing patterns of work in the parental subsystem. With more women in the paid labor force, the distribution of parenting responsibility was necessarily different from that of the previous generation. Gerry described how different work patterns between spouses necessitated new fathering patterns:

Well, I think a lot of the traditional sort of functions that were divided between mother and father are not there any more or are certainly disintegrating very quickly. I know looking back to my childhood, you know, usually the functions were very distinct. Now I find it was a little bit different, but you know, looking at my friends, their fathers went off to work from 9 to 5, got home, did this, and the mothers were there to take care of the kids. Now it's more parents both working or some working full time or part time—there's a more shared responsibility. Now whether that means getting the kids ready in the morning for preschool or putting them to bed at night, or making them dinners—I think fathers are starting to play more of a role in that and starting to play more of a role in deciding how their kids are going to be brought up instead of leaving most of that responsibility to the mother nowadays.

Some men perceived their own parents as simply being unable to provide them with the modeling that they needed. From this perspective, it would appear that parents operated under a different set of assumptions for what their children should do. With the clarity of historical hindsight, Jonathon was ready to excuse his own parents because they were simply unaware, according to the standards of the time, that they should try to get more from kids:

> The parents' role should be to get the best out of their kids, to help them be the best that they can be. Again, maybe that's partly because I think my parents didn't do that. Not because they didn't want to; they didn't know any better.

Some men were more equivocal about the modeling influence of their own fathers. Although they expressed the view that their fathers were largely unavailable to them as models, they did identify aspects of the relationship that had some influence. Of interest, the memorable aspects of the relationship had to do with the imposition of standards for proper behavior. These were standards that conveyed a set of values and expectations for how the son should act. For Gary, these standards were rooted in his father's commitment to his work and, perhaps, reflected his father's influence on him as a model worker and not a model father. Although the communication of standards did influence Gary, the standards were overshadowed by the perception that his father "never once" made the effort to spend time with him doing an activity Gary enjoyed:

> My father was a medical doctor, and because of his training, or his profession, he had an air of responsibility about him. You know, you were responsible to people, you were responsible to your community, and when you said you were going to do something, you did it. I think from him, I got a sense of responsibility, that, you know, you make a decision to have kids, then you don't walk out, that's it, you made a commitment. . . . He taught me all those values, but in terms of quality time, I don't think he spent as much quality time with me as I think was reasonable. As a teenager, I used to sail a lot—I taught sailing, I loved sailing, and you know, he never once would have met me on my grounds and said, "Let's take . . . a boat for the day." Those are the little things we could have done. So I'm sensitive to that because I think I missed those thing.

As this passage would suggest, there is an important distinction between the way that Gary's father successfully modeled the work values of responsibility to patients and the community and the way that his father failed to serve as a positive parental model who could give time and meet his son on his own ground.

As another expression of their equivocating attitude toward their fathers, some men commented on how they did not like their fathers or what they did to their sons but that they were willing to accept the good intentions that appeared to motivate their fathers' behavior. Again, "doing what was right" or the communication of proper standards seemed to override other aspects of the relationship. In reflecting back on his experience of being fathered, Charlie recalls "respecting" but not "liking" his father because of his authoritarian nature:

> When I was growing up, my dad was law and order. I think he wanted to instill certain values in me; whether I liked it or not, that was what he was going to do because it was good for me. And I think it was a good choice because I look back and I did not appreciate all the things he did to me when I was a teenager or when I was a child for that matter, but, I look back now and I realize it was for my own good. . . . I didn't always like my dad and a lot of times we had terrible fights and that kind of thing, but I respected him, and I respected his values.

The respect that Charlie afforded his authoritarian father reinforces the idea that, when fathers were seen as models at all, it was in the context of establishing "respect" or preserving "law and order." From this perspective, fathers serve as a kind of a constabulary model that ensures that children do not get out of line or do something that "is not for [their] own good." Once again, the model of father is immersed in a set of external societal standards of proper behavior, at the cost of other kinds of modeling influences, whether spending time together, expressing affection, or showing interest. In this sense, what was striking was the absence of loving modeling influences because of the apparent fixation on proper codes of conduct. Although family theory has been quick to dismiss Parsons's ideas about instrumental and expressive roles (Broderick, 1992), it would appear that the men in this study were very strongly influenced by the role of their fathers as instrumental ambassadors of the outside world. Charlie's relationship with his father was echoed in his role with his own daughter, when he suggested again that it was more important for her to respect him than to like him:

[My father] tried to do what was in my best interests, and that is an influence on me when I am raising my kids. I may make mistakes and that kind of thing, but as long as I explain to my kids this is why I want you to do these things and explain to them they may not like it, but it is in their best interests to do what I ask them to. I'm not so concerned about my daughter liking me at this point, because I respected my father as I was growing up because dad was the authority figure.

Those men who held their fathers in high regard and tried to imitate them emerged as the "negative case" (Strauss & Corbin, 1990, p. 109). The discovery of isolated segments of data that run contrary to the general trend not only serve to reinforce the predominance of that trend but reflect the expectable variation in behavior. Only rarely did the fathers in this study talk of their own fathers with a sense of contentment or pride. Yet, for Sam, his father was decisively the silent guiding beacon:

I would say that with my father, we don't discuss parenting—with [him and me] it's other matters, conversations. I don't go to him so much for advice on parenting, although I think that much of what I base my parenting practices on are his model. The type of father that he was, I am trying to emulate. He was very solid, always around and was never not there. At the same time, we were always, my brothers and myself, proud of his accomplishments.

As Sam's comments suggest, the father is identified as a model of heroic proportions: He is solid, always there, and a source of great pride. Yet, like most relationships that boys have with heroic figures, there is distance that fosters "emulation" but not "discussion" or direct "advice." As this would suggest, not only is Sam's view of his father as a paragon somewhat unique, it also suggests that when the father is presented in this way it is a "model-at-a-distance."

For many men, the absence of role models existed not only with respect to their predecessors but also in relation to their contemporaries. In the absence of good role models in their fathers' generation, there was a perception that there was no one to whom they could turn to monitor their progress as fathers. Reflecting this experience of being part of a "new generation" of fathers without clear guidelines, Charlie talked about "no one being around" who might otherwise provide a basis for "judging" how he was doing as a father:

Very few people are experts the first few times they try and do anything. Get up and try to water ski and you are going to fall down. It is not until you have been doing it for a while [that you get better]. I would say that as we get a little bit older we will be able to say, "So and so is a good dad—so and so is sort of missing the boat in this area." Right now, it is a little hard to tell because a lot of our friends don't have kids yet or their kids are very small and we are not constantly exposed to them. We don't really see how they relate to their kids when there is no one around.

The absence of influential father figures in their day-to-day lives made the social construction of the fatherhood identity extremely difficult. For these men, there was no reference group that could serve as a point of comparison for shaping their identity formation. Instead of having access to these reflective beacons, there appeared to be a hazy horizon that seemed only to absorb their searching gaze.

One of the implications of feeling that they had no models was to feel unprepared for parenthood and uncertain about what was required in the job of being father. Bill talked about his uncertainty about what to do when he first became a father, which was related to the absence of any figure who could tell him whether he was "doing it right":

I think showing tenderness was hard at first. Emotionally, it was a drain, because you have this little tiny baby, and you have to do everything for it. "Was I doing it right?" "Is this the way to do it?" It's very difficult to know if I was doing it right; that was one of the harder parts.

Fragmented Models of Fatherhood

One of the responses to the absence of father models was to take a more piecemeal approach to the imitation of fathering behavior. Rather than trying to imitate one person who might serve as a kind of mentor, Allan talked about trying to emulate desirable behaviors from many fathers, not one:

No, I don't think I try to emulate anybody, saying, "This person is a good father, I want to be more like him." You know I look at the people I know and I say, "Well, he does that well with his kids," or "He handles these sorts of situations well with his kids"—maybe draw on that, and someone else, but I can't say that I've pointed to anyone and said, "Yeah, I want to be a father just like they are."

From this perspective, learning to be a father is somewhat akin to the process of a thoughtful consumer who stands before the shelves making a careful selection of products that are to be added to the cart. For these fathers, there was a quiet observance of other fathers from whom they were able to cull desired skills or techniques to add to their repertoire. Ed talked about the importance of being alert to other parents who had to deal with the same kinds of problems that he did. Like the consumer who sorts out the good buys from the junk, he was selective in what he chose to add to his parenting role:

> In just observing other people and what they do and how they do it, I've seen good and bad, and I think that helps more than anything else, watching how other people have gone through their problems and how they dealt with them and how they act with their children and things like that. It is a very important thing to keep your eyes open to how other people are doing things.

In the light of the perception that parenthood had changed so dramatically from the previous generation, there was a tendency to search for specific instances of good fathering behavior among one's peers. Although there was variation in what constituted good fathering behavior when looking at friends, one of the hallmark values to emerge was the importance of having children respect these men as fathers. Ironically, this concern with respect had a striking resemblance to the respect that their own fathers demanded from them. In his observations of a friend, Stephen talked about respect as something he would like to achieve in his own parenting:

> I have a very close friend whose . . . upbringing wasn't as restricted as what mine was. My parents were fairly strict, and he had a lot more liberties. I sometimes look towards him, you know, like his life—not that I ask him advice on bringing up kids—but I just look towards him because his kids have a tremendous amount of respect for him and they're well-behaved, well-mannered, well-disciplined children. . . . I look towards him and I don't want to give my kids all the liberties he has given his kids but still I want to try and find a happy medium there. So I kind of try to make a compromise between the way I was brought up and the way he was brought up so that the kids can understand that you love them and care for them.

In this passage, finding the compromise between his own strict upbringing and the more liberal experience of his friend suggests that Stephen is selecting parts from the fathering activity around him. Although each of the models was instructive in some way, they were also limited and required that he package together the pieces of what a father is to "find a happy medium." When Stephen qualified his comments with "not that I ask him for advice," he expressed a common sentiment among men, which is that fatherhood should be done and not talked about. As this would suggest, the process of role modeling for fatherhood appears to be characterized by a quiet absorption rather than deliberate and interactive pursuit.

Frank also talked about being uneasy when he was with a friend who was not strict enough with his children. Although his friend did not serve as a model per se, he did serve as a point of reference for defining Frank's own standards and limits for how to father. When asked to comment on his perceptions of how his friends father, he focused on control issues:

> Well, maybe the discipline end of it—like you can only say "no" so often, and if you don't do anything about it—whatever—whether you make them sit in the corner or not, the child is going to get away with murder and it's like, "No, don't do this, no, Johnny, no, no, no." Johnny just keeps doing it and they don't do nothing. What's the point of even saying no?

In contrast to their perceptions of their fathers, the men in this study viewed their mothers and wives as providing some of the more practical and tangible guidance on how to provide care for children. Although these men did not talk about emulating their mothers as models, they did talk about learning how to deal with specific situations. This is consistent with the work of Chodorow (1978), who has suggested that the absence of father models has resulted in a stronger focus on mothers for guidance. Bill talked about the greater salience of his mother in shaping his fathering actions:

> I think my mom for the most part did the better job of getting me ready to be a father. When the child came home, there was more input from my mother in helping me out on how to handle things; where my father was pleased for me, you know, "it's your child" and that's what I got from my dad.

In the same way that mothers had an impact on their sons, wives had an important modeling effect on their husbands when it came to the day-to-day decisions of parenting. The centrality of the modeling effect of wives is consistent with the literature that suggests that mothers are the primary parent, whereas fathers will often play the role of the helping or marginal parent who fills in or baby-sits in the mother's absence (Geerken & Gove, 1983; LaRossa, 1986; LaRossa & LaRossa, 1981). Jonathon explained how his wife's mothering "standards" and "expectations" are a central focal point for his own definitions of "raising kids":

> My wife's ideas about being a parent are even more centered around kids than mine so she is even more focused on raising the kids. Her standards, her expectations are higher, and she has certain ideas as we were married before we had kids and also as we raised them, certain things she says and does—and we talk about those things—influence me and some of which were different from what I encountered at home.

Being a Model Without a Model

Without strong models to guide their behavior, these men were in a position of creating new models for what it meant to be a father. For most, the intergenerational continuity of fathering ideals and practices was being consciously severed. In the light of this, they spoke about being role models to their children in a way that represented a departure from previous generations of fathers. Instead of presenting an inherited model of fatherhood to their children that is rooted in the past, these fathers appeared to be focused on the construction of a fatherhood model from the values of the present. Ed talked about this process:

> I think what we're looking to do is be what we tell the kids we are, and in that sense become the role model for them. You know, we have quite high values, and if we exercise those values within ourselves and become the role model for them, then I think they will see the value in what we are doing. The idea of the father having license to do whatever he wants because he is the father, I think is wrong, and I think the father must be what he wants his children to grow up to be.

For Ed, there was a clear departure from the traditional entitlement of the father "to do whatever he wants because he is the father." As this would suggest, the legacy of power that has given father "license" must be abandoned to infuse a different set of values into what it means to be a father. These new values reflect these men's hope of establishing a new line of generational continuity that their children will want to imitate. Randy, who was a shift worker, expressed his hopes in this regard:

> Um, I think being the role model is most important. I want my children to be what I am, not what I say I am. Having children carry on your name is one thing, but that isn't really my idea [of what is important]—it's having somebody to look after and to see myself in my children.

When Randy suggested that he wanted his children to "be what I am," he expressed the desire to be an active and influential force in the lives of his children. This is distinct from the perception of fathers in the previous generation who were concerned with "having children carry on your name" and who were likely to be seen as absent and aloof. For Randy, like other men in the study, the conscious and deliberate effort of *being* a model to their children was paramount in a context that was devoid of usable fatherhood models from the past.

Conclusion

From a social constructionist perspective, fatherhood is an ongoing project of action that involves the creation and reformulation of roles through observation, communication, and negotiation. Although this perspective places a primary emphasis on the importance of fathers actively shaping fatherhood roles, it must also be attentive to the structural context of parenthood, which imposes institutional constraints on how these roles are exercised. Hence, although there is wide latitude for how men mold fatherhood roles for themselves, there are traditions, values, norms, and standards that are socially present that can limit the way these roles are formulated.

At the same time, postmodernist analyses of families (see Cheal, 1991, 1992) would suggest that structural uniformity is undergoing a process of emulsification that is blurring the boundaries between what should be and what simply is. For fathers, there is an angst that accompanies this new postmodernist pluralism in which the ideological structures of the past appear to have loosened their hold on who they should be as fathers. History, from a postmodernist perspective, is not an erasure of traditions but is "that of re-use and collage, taking up elements of tradition and re-cycling them in new contexts" (Kvale, 1992, p. 7). These traditions were present in the lives of these fathers as they actively sought to reshape the meaning of fatherhood in a radically different context.

The resulting angst was expressed most directly in the form of a concern about "doing it right." In the absence of strong and relevant role models, these men appeared to express a fundamental anxiety about who they should be or how they should act as fathers. Their own fathers, although identified as influential, seemed to serve as the antithesis of who they wanted to be as fathers. Their uncertainty was compounded by generational changes in the standards for being a good father, which appeared to prevent many men from making reference to models in the previous generation. As this would suggest, men do not have a "clear job description of their parental roles within the home" (Lewis & O'Brien, 1987). Instead, without the benefit of a relevant comparison group, fatherhood was opaque and nebulous.

There were a variety of contradictions that emerged for these fathers as they sought to reshape fatherhood into a form quite different from that of their own fathers. For example, although the men in this study typically held their fathers accountable for not spending more time with them when they were growing up, they were usually quite willing to excuse their fathers' absenteeism on the basis of the work demands that their fathers experienced during that historical period. Similarly, although these men were clear about not wanting to be like their fathers, they frequently expressed respect for the way that their fathers carried out their roles. At the same time that they deliberately sought to construct for themselves fatherhood roles that were different from their own fathers', they were frequently preoccupied with some of the same symbols of good parenting, such as standards of conduct and control over their children. Moreover, in the rare instance when fathers did serve as a modeling influence, it was across a great distance insofar as their sons sought to emulate rather than "discuss with" their fathers.

Losh-Hesselbart (1987) has suggested that "symbolic presentations" and "concrete figures" have received more attention than the "patterning of behavior in social situations." For the fathers in this study, the patterns of behavior in specific social situations are the key mechanism by which models are experienced. Most of the fathers in this study had difficulty identifying either symbolic presentations or concrete figures whom they would like to emulate, yet they were more readily able to identify actions, values, or standards that they sought to incorporate into their fathering repertoire. Whether it was expressing admiration for the way that a fathering peer had managed to have well-behaved children or being receptive to the advice of a mother or wife on how to carry out a particular task, their models came in a segmented rather than a holistic form. Although we more often think of role models as being embodied in a singular, significant other, for these men, their models, when there were any at all, were fragmented and disjointed.

As this would suggest, men appear to have disparate reference points, which put them in the position of having to creatively forge new rules for themselves. Without a clear sense of direction from the traditions of the past, they were in a position of sorting through the good and bad examples of fathering behavior among their contemporaries. What was missing in their lives was the father mentor who could help them read the map for how the work of fathering should be done. Like any map, however, it would appear that history quickly dates the information about the best way to reach the destination. For these fathers, not only were they without a map-reading guide, the contours of the map had changed in that they were faced with the challenge of putting together in a balanced way the competing demands of the residual provider role and the emergent cultural demands that they be a different kind of father from their own fathers.

Without a readily available set of fatherhood models, these men have tended to focus on being a model to their own children to create for them a new set of standards for *who father is*. They seek to fill the space left by their own fathers with a fuller and more committed presence that they hope will be experienced and remembered by their own children. In the resonant silence of their own fathers' voices, they seek to proclaim a new expression of fatherhood. Nevertheless, as Lewis (1986) has suggested, this is a sentiment that seems to echo down through generations. In the light of this, the degree to which this new fatherhood presence is experienced differently by the next generation of fathers remains to be seen.

Note

1. The names used are fictitious, to protect the anonymity of the participants.

3

Rethinking Fathers' Involvement in Child Care

A Developmental Perspective

ALAN J. HAWKINS
SHAWN L. CHRISTIANSEN
KATHRYN POND SARGENT
E. JEFFREY HILL

In this chapter, we critique current thinking about fatherhood, in general, and men's involvement in child care, specifically. Scholarly literature portrays fathers nondevelopmentally; fathers are viewed as incumbents of a changing social role rather than as developing individuals. A nondevelopmental portrait of fathers, we argue, is incomplete. Analyses of fathers' relative lack of participation in domestic labor particularly exemplify the above critique (Hardesty & Bokemeier, 1989; Hochschild, 1989; Pleck, 1985; Rexroat & Shehan, 1987; Shelton, 1990). The "second shift" (Hochschild, 1989) remains primarily women's work (Thompson & Walker, 1989). Undergirding this literature on fathers' underinvolvement in housework and child care are conceptions of fatherhood influenced by exchange, conflict, resource, and feminist theories (e.g., Barnett & Baruch, 1988; Berk, 1985; Blair & Lichter, 1991; Coverman, 1985; Ferree, 1988; Harris & Morgan, 1991; Hiller &

AUTHORS' NOTE: This chapter previously appeared as an article, with the same title, in *Journal of Family Issues* (1993, Vol. 14, No. 4, 531-549).

Philliber, 1986; LaRossa, 1988; Mederer, 1993; Moen & Dempster-McClain, 1987; Perry-Jenkins & Crouter, 1990; Peterson & Gerson, 1992; Russell, 1986; Thompson & Walker, 1989). This literature depicts fathers as weighing the personal costs and benefits of increased involvement, using power to avoid doing more in the home, paralyzed by structural changes in the economy and the family that call for new gender role ideologies, or simply responding minimally to family structural demands (e.g., more and younger children, wives' work hours).

Scholarly investigations of fathers' underinvolvement in daily family work in the light of exchange, conflict, resource, or feminist theories have focused our attention on fairness. When family work is not shared equitably, these theories lead us to anticipate that wives will feel a sense of unfairness and that this will negatively affect their well-being and the quality of marital relationships. The problem with a focus on fairness, however, is that judgments of fairness in this context are highly complex; seemingly inequitable situations may not be judged so by many wives (Thompson, 1991). Moreover, the empirical link between men's underinvolvement in domestic labor and women's perceptions of fairness is equivocal (Benin & Agnostinelli, 1988; Berk, 1985; Ferree, 1988; Hochschild, 1989; Pleck, 1985; Thompson, 1991). Thus, although research focused on fairness is valuable, it should not be the sole focus. What is sacrificed by fairness-focused studies of family work is attention to the developmental tasks that adult men and women face while building a life together (C. Cowan & Cowan, 1992; P. Cowan, 1988; P. Cowan & Cowan, 1988). There is ample room for other perspectives to further our understanding of men's participation in daily family work.

Accordingly, this chapter attempts to reconceptualize men's involvement in child care from a developmental perspective rather than from social structural perspectives that emphasize the issue of fairness. Our discussion here targets specifically fathers' participation in child care because the dyadic interaction between children and fathers when men care for their children can be a potent developmental force (Bronfenbrenner, 1979). After reviewing basic developmental concepts, we will discuss Erik Erikson's (1963) theory of human development, focusing on his concept of generativity. Then, we examine ways in which fathers may develop generativity, a task hypothesized to be critical to healthy adult development. We devote the remainder of the chapter to exploring the implications of a developmental perspective on fathers' involvement in child care. We argue that the transition to parenthood often sets mothers and fathers on divergent developmental trajectories that eventually leave them in different developmental positions. This can have a negative impact on marital quality. Further, we argue that men's intimate involvement in daily domestic work may help keep men's and women's development parallel and hence help maintain satisfying relationships.

Developmental Definitions

First, it is important that we clarify our use of the term *developmental perspective*. We conceptualize development as consisting of systematic and successive changes over time in the organization of an organism that serve an adaptive function (Lerner, 1986). Moreover, development is change from global to differentiated, more integrated behavior and skills and from simple to more complex and adaptive behavior. Another important concept is that development is marked by qualitative change, or developmental transitions, as well as by quantitative change (Lerner, 1986). In addition, these transitions are critical times for development. Transitions are detected by a reorganization of an individual's inner psychological world and external behavior (Cowan, 1991). In other words, a developmental transition involves a "qualitative shift in perceptions of oneself and the world" (Cowan, 1991, p. 15) and concomitant behavioral shifts that can be observed by others. It follows, then, that developmental transitions produce periods of significant disequilibrium for individuals as their inner, psychological worlds are reorganized and behavior patterns are altered accordingly. This disequilibrium and the accompanying stress stimulate individuals to achieve higher levels of functioning. Of course, not all transitions are successful. For numerous reasons, transitions can be short-circuited, disrupted, or avoided. The result is an individual less than optimally adapted to his or her social world. Thus, despite age similarities, individuals frequently are in different developmental places. Finally, as a result of active interaction with a changing environment, humans are open to change across the life span; development is not limited to preadult years (Kreppner, 1989).

Levinson's and Erikson's Conceptions of Adult Development

Probably the most important reason that a developmental perspective does not permeate the literature on father involvement is that adult development theories remain underdeveloped. Developmental research has concentrated on childhood and adolescence. Although most scholars accept the notion that development occurs throughout adulthood, conceptual expeditions to map the developmental terrain of adulthood have been limited (Levinson, 1986).

Daniel Levinson, one of the most prominent theorists of adult development (Levinson, 1986; Levinson, Darrow, Klein, Levinson, & McKee, 1978), centers his conception of adult development on a construct he labels *life structure*. Life structures are defined as an answer to the question: What are my most important relationships with various others in the external world? The other may be a person, group, institution, culture, object, or place. An individual invests a significant amount of time, energy, and commitment in this relationship with the other. Levinson (Levinson et al., 1978) argues that there is a universal rhythm to the evolution of one's life structure over the course of adulthood. Life structures are built, maintained, then questioned, and other life structures evolve to take their places. He argues that this occurs in an age-graded sequence for all humans. Levinson's theory, however, does not prescribe specific, normative tasks and qualitative psychological transitions that one must go through to become a healthy person, as many developmental theories do.

A more classical developmental conception of adulthood comes from Erikson (1963), who prescribes normative developmental tasks for adults as well as for children and a clearer notion of what psychosocial health looks like across the life span. Erikson (1982b) argues that three psychosocial strengths—hope, fidelity, and care—must be achieved to become a healthy, functional person; these strengths correspond to the developmental struggles of the three major life stages of childhood, adolescence, and adulthood. Basic trust and hope need to be gained in childhood, and a sense of faith in oneself and fidelity to an identity are required in adolescence. We concentrate here on the primary developmental tension of adulthood, which according to Erikson is learning to care for others, a process he labeled *generativity*.

Generativity, or care, is defined as an interest in establishing and guiding the next generation (Erikson, 1982a). Erikson believed that nurturing one's offspring was the primary locus of this developmental task, although generativity could also be accomplished by investing in other productive, creative, or altruistic endeavors that make the world a better place in which the next generation can live. Whatever the source, the necessary virtue that is developed in adulthood is care, or a

widening commitment beyond self to nurture the next generation—
one's own children, other children, and the environment in which they
will grow up.

Successful achievement of this developmental task, like all other
tasks, is not guaranteed, and failure to achieve generativity possessed
discernible consequences for Erikson. He argued that failure to achieve
generativity results in self-indulgence and "an obsessive need for pseudo
intimacy . . . often with a pervading sense of stagnation and interpersonal impoverishment" (Erikson, 1982a, p. 103).

According to Erikson, then, becoming fully human is to invest in,
commit to, and care deeply for others. "Mature man needs to be needed,
and maturity needs guidance as well as encouragement from what has
been produced and must be taken care of" (Erikson, 1963, pp. 166-167).

Despite scholars' familiarity with Erikson's theory of human development, we are struck by the lack of attention to the concept of generativity and its importance to adult development. Erikson himself lamented
our scholarly blindness "to the dependence of the older generation on
the younger one" (Erikson, 1963, p. 166). It seems that 30 years have
done little to remove this blind spot. (Some notable exceptions exist;
see Daniels & Weingarten, 1982; Farrell & Rosenberg, 1981; Franz,
McClelland, & Weinberger, 1991; Gutmann, 1987; McAdams, 1985;
Snarey, 1993; Snarey, Son, Kuehne, Hauser, & Vaillant, 1987.)

We believe that scholars need to devote more attention to the importance of developing generativity and to the role that nurturing children
plays in achieving psychosocial health in adulthood. At least one study
(Snarey, 1993; Snarey et al., 1987) provides support for the importance
of parenting to developing psychosocial health in midlife, and greater
attention to Erikson's concept of generativity seems particularly valuable for studies of fathers' involvement in child care. The remainder of
this chapter, then, attempts to integrate generativity into our thinking
about men's involvement in child care.

Developing Generativity in the Familial Context

If developing generativity is essential to adults' psychosocial development, then men's levels of involvement in child care take on added
significance. In this section, we address the issue of how familial
processes facilitate the development of generativity, outlining four
processes that may operate to produce change in fathers in the family

context: socialization (child → father), striving to achieve the possible self, role-person merger, and modeling and reinforcement. Each of these processes emphasizes that the strength of the developmental force acting on men is directly proportional to their involvement in their children's daily lives.

Socialization (Child → Parent)

Lerner and Kreppner (1989) argue that we underestimate and give inadequate attention to the developmental influence of children on their parents; we have been fixated on parents' influences on their children. Yet an axiom of developmental theory is that, when one part of a dyad develops, the other part develops as well (Bronfenbrenner, 1979). After the birth of a child, fathers are often confronted with experiences that cannot be assimilated into their present model of the world. The result is a developmental disequilibrium; fathers often feel "mixed up" (Lewis, 1986, p. 151) or "scared" (Greene, 1984, p. 7) because they sense that one stage of their lives, a more egocentric and instrumental one, is coming to an end and they are unprepared for the next stage. Fathers can accommodate this disequilibrium by creating new expressive cognitive structures. These structures will vary from father to father but generally include elements of what Ruddick (1984) refers to as an ethic of care. Thus children's entry into the family system, and father-child interaction, becomes a potential stimulus of fathers' development of generativity.

Striving to Achieve the Possible Self

Markus and Nurius's (1986) concept of "possible selves" provides a second potential process by which fathers develop in the family context. They argue that people maintain a conceptualization of themselves as they might become or would like to become. They call this conceptualization a person's possible self. A view of one's possible selves can be an incentive for engaging in or changing certain behaviors. For example, when the *actual* fathering self is evaluated against the *possible* fathering self, there may be dissonance. Thus, if a father's ideal is to be involved in his children's lives, he may engage in generative behaviors that match his perceptions of his ideal self. Of course, if the dissonance between the real self and ideal self is too great, a father may flee from involvement and discard the ideal. This happens frequently. On the other hand, when fathers struggle to meet the ideal, it stimulates generativity. Those who hold an intrinsic ideal of being involved and nurturant, or those influenced by the changing culture of fatherhood that stresses greater paternal involvement (LaRossa, 1988), may embrace the fathering role by behaving consistently with their fathering ideal.

Role-Person Merger

Similar to the idea of possible selves, Turner (1978) provides a theory of role-person merger to provide a third explanation of how one's investment in a role can be a potent developmental force. Turner believes roles that require the most investment will be merged with the person. When a person merges with a role, attitudes and beliefs appropriate to the role are acquired. A number of scholars (Antonucci & Mikus, 1988; Beutler, Burr, Bahr, & Herrin, 1989) have argued that caring for young children is a unique, labor-intensive effort that requires enormous amounts of time and energy. In addition, the physical activity is paralleled by the emotional intensity of being a parent. Turner also states that the merger of role and person is a process that takes place over an extended period of time, building on many episodes and experiences. The extended and permanent relationships between parents and children in intact families provide a powerful context in which fathers can be transformed through involvement in their children's lives.

Modeling and Reinforcement

Social learning theory (Bandura, 1977) concepts such as modeling and reinforcement also can be used to explain how men learn generativity in the family context. Fathers may observe mothers modeling child care skills and attitudes and use this as a basis for learning how to be an effective caregiver. However, people encode modeling only if they see the behavior as important to their future behavior. This is why it is important for fathers to have an image of themselves as they would like to be that is supported by their partners and the culture. In addition, fathers are more likely to persevere in new caregiving behavior if they are reinforced for their efforts at least some of the time. If mothers respond in supportive ways to fathers' initial attempts at caregiving rather than critiquing or demeaning their efforts, fathers are more likely to continue caregiving behavior. According to social learning theory, however, most human behavior is motivated out of anticipated rather than immediate benefits. Thus fathers who hold an involved ideal-father self would be more likely to persevere in the face of early struggles to become an effective caregiver. Then, as a father's "involvement and skills in the activities increase, social, symbolic, and self-evaluative rewards assume the incentive function" (Bandura, 1977, p. 113).

Implications

Diverging Developmental Paths for Fathers and Mothers

Fathers who involve themselves deeply in the process of nurturing children facilitate the development of generativity. However, because fathers are significantly less involved in the care of dependent children, men may face greater struggles to achieve generativity than do women. Research on the transition to parenthood shows that, despite egalitarian plans of husbands and wives for sharing the domestic world, when the baby arrives there is a distinct traditionalization of family role behavior; mothers take on a greater proportion of daily family work, and fathers redirect time and energy to occupational pursuits (C. Cowan & Cowan, 1992; Cowan et al., 1985; P. Cowan & Cowan, 1988; LaRossa & LaRossa, 1981). From an Eriksonian perspective, then, fathers' under-involvement in caregiving during the early parenting years puts men at a disadvantage for achieving generativity.

The transition to parenthood is a time of both change and consistency. Men and women stay in pretty much the same rank order on a number of measures taken before and after the birth of a child (C. Cowan & Cowan, 1987). Despite the individual rank order consistency, however, the developmental trajectories of adult men and women face a significant risk at this time of going in different directions. Faced with the 9-month gestation of a child in her body and then the demands of caring for a newborn infant in the first few postpartum months, a mother is challenged to quickly develop a generative commitment to her dependent infant. Of course, not all mothers develop this bond, and the pace at which it develops varies, but the generative *potential* of this transition on women's development has been outlined by feminist scholars (Chodorow, 1978; Dinnerstein, 1976; Miller, 1976; Ruddick, 1984).

For fathers, however, the transition to parenthood is usually different. Whereas women's active participation in the daily care of their infants is virtually universal, men's involvement is still viewed as optional. From their research on men's and women's experiences of the transition to parenthood, Daniels and Weingarten (1982) contend:

> Biologically, men become fathers and women become mothers at the moment of their first child's birth. But only through daily care, and in sustained emotional engagement in their children's lives, do fathers and mothers become parents in the generative sense. Mothers are expected to become parents instantly, but fathers are not. *The translation of paternal identity into parental generativity, as we have seen, has been optional* [italics added]. (p. 161)

Transitions are qualitative changes that significantly reorganize both the inner psychological world and the external behavior of an individual. Whereas this happens rapidly for many women when a child is born, the process is more variant for fathers. For men, significant, direct involvement with their children may not occur right away or at all. Caring for newborns by fathers is limited by a confluence of factors: lactation, infant activity, employment/caregiving arrangements, the economics of unequal salaries, residual societal attitudes about men's roles, and some women's ambivalence about "making room" for fathers' participation in the domestic role (C. Cowan & Cowan, 1992). As a result, it is not difficult to see how fathers often come to view themselves as relatively inadequate caregivers compared with mothers. In addition, they often develop a view of the paternal role that is qualitatively different from that of the maternal role; fathers are physically stimulating playmates, substitute caregivers ("baby-sitters"), and, most important, primary providers. Defining the paternal role in this way is often a pragmatic, mutually agreed upon response to situational demands. Moreover, for many men, especially in the working class, working hard to provide for their families is the primary way they express interest in their children's lives (Doherty, 1991). Thus we must be cautious about preaching the secular doctrine that equal involvement from mothers and fathers is always best (Crouter, Perry-Jenkins, Huston, & McHale, 1987). Still, we should acknowledge that substantially unequal levels of participation in child care early on may contribute to challenging developmental differences between mothers and fathers over time.

Even if fathers become more involved with their children at a later point, the timing of increased involvement has important implications for the quality of marital relationships. When developmental changes occur on significantly different timetables for men and women, it suggests that spouses are in different developmental places (C. Cowan & Cowan, 1992). The process of achieving generativity may be well under way for mothers, but a large proportion of fathers will lag behind. Whereas some family theories (Parsons & Bales, 1955) would not view this as a problem, so long as roles were clear and agreed upon, we believe it may be a serious impediment to satisfying, intimate relationships. Most contemporary men and women put a premium on psychological intimacy. Thus asynchronous couples are likely to experience more barriers to building close relationships than couples who have matured to similar points in the life cycle.

Studies document the difficulties that relationships face as a result of a division of labor that promotes generativity in women more than it does in men. The most impressive longitudinal study to date of the transition to parenthood (C. Cowan & Cowan, 1992) provides evidence that men and women do indeed become more different from each other during this transition, and the larger the differences between them, the more their marital satisfaction declines. Other studies consistently confirm that more gendered arrangements of child care and housework have negative effects on both women's and men's perceptions of marital relationships and on the mental health of women (Belsky, Youngblade, Rovine, & Volling, 1991; Harris & Morgan, 1991; Hochschild, 1989; Hoffman, 1983; Huber & Spitze, 1983; Kessler & McRae, 1982; Pleck, 1985; Ross, Mirowsky, & Huber, 1983; Suitor, 1991). More equitable arrangements for child care that give fathers greater opportunity to develop generativity are conducive to dyadic intimacy because wives and husbands are on more synchronous developmental trajectories.

A developmental perspective on fathers' participation in child care also provides a valuable way to interpret recent discouraging findings that *increased* involvement in domestic work by fathers sometimes leads to greater dyadic conflict and decreased satisfaction with marriage (Barnett & Baruch, 1988; Baruch & Barnett, 1986; Crouter et al., 1987; MacDermid, Huston, & McHale, 1990; Russell, 1986; Stanley, Hunt, & Hunt, 1986; Volling & Belsky, 1991). Negotiating who does what, when, and how provides fruitful ground for disagreement and conflict. Often ignored, however, by focusing on the behavioral shifts required of fathers for shared domestic labor is the internal, psychological reorganization that accompanies greater participation in caregiving and its related household tasks. Like mothers, fathers also find it challenging to develop an enlarged identity that allows for more generative care of children. Fathers' struggles to do this may be even greater than mothers' because the biological and social forces that accelerate mothers through the difficult transition to parenthood appear to be weaker for men (Lamb, Pleck, Charnov, & Levine, 1987). For example, whereas pregnancy helps women adjust to their impending motherhood, fathers have little biological preparation. From infancy, girls are socialized for caregiving; fathers are socialized for providing. In addition, once the baby arrives, mothers often have numerous social supports to help them adjust to their roles, whereas society provides few supports for fathers.

It seems that men must make a more concerted, conscious effort to shift both their inner psychological worlds and external behavior to be more involved in daily family work. A shift like this will take time. Even for those men who successfully negotiate this challenging transition, there will be considerable disequilibrium, and they are likely to feel uncomfortable and ambivalent about the changes they are going through for a time. Thus there is the potential for more dyadic conflict and decreased marital satisfaction while fathers are increasing their participation in daily family work.

The point here is not that increased paternal participation in child rearing leads directly and quickly to happier families. In some instances, greater involvement presents its own challenges to individual and family well-being. But whatever the consequences, fathers' intimate involvement in caring for children can facilitate generativity. Caring for children can become a symbol of togetherness, even when sometimes it is the source of conflict. And wives and husbands can relate to each other better not only because the division of child care is "fair" but also because they are in similar developmental places, progressing along the adult path to generativity.

From Domestic Democracy to
Interdependent Development

A second use for a developmental perspective on fathers' involvement in child care is that it alters the way we think about changing men's underinvolvement in domestic labor. Typically, researchers have cast fathers' underinvolvement in daily family work in terms of personal and social injustice, with women bearing the burden of an inequitable, gendered family system. However, wives' calculations of fairness are complex and often fail to produce feelings of injustice, even when an "objective" appraisal suggests otherwise (Benin & Agnostinelli, 1988;

Berk, 1985; Ferree, 1988; Hochschild, 1989; Pleck, 1985; Thompson, 1991). Although a focus on personal and social injustice illuminates an important portion of the problem, we argue that it may be more useful to view the inequitable distribution of domestic labor as a developmental issue rather than as a demonstration of social power or a struggle for domestic democracy, especially if our objective is to help fathers change. The domestic-democracy perspective is a macro-level view of the problem of gendered family work. Accordingly, its application to the lives of specific individuals is problematic. Some women do not define their disproportionate involvement in domestic labor as oppression. As such, the domestic-democracy perspective may be effective only as a means of changing individual lives when women view their situations as oppressive.

In contrast, the more micro-oriented developmental perspective highlights the need for both men and women to be involved intimately in daily family work to further their own development. Greater paternal participation need not be a reluctant personal sacrifice of patriarchal privilege for the sake of social justice; instead, it can be viewed as an important step in one's personal growth. Similarly, a developmental perspective on fatherhood calls attention to the necessary interconnections between men and women rather than to their inevitable separateness. Although the domestic-democracy perspective seems to call for wives to assert their rights and demand equitable participation from their husbands, the developmental perspective encourages women and men to assist each other in the process of becoming more fully human. The developmental perspective suggests the possibility of something like a mentoring role for wives as their husbands go through the challenging process of achieving generativity, a process mothers have probably learned at a more rapid pace while receiving more support from others (C. Cowan & Cowan, 1992). Bly (1990) and others in the men's movement would have fathers turn to other adult men for nurturance and developmental help instead of to their female partners, because of the barrier that gender presents to understanding. In contrast, a developmental perspective suggests the opposite; wives understand the developmental difficulties of adulthood well and can be helpful partners in that process.

Of course, there is always the possibility that fathers are further down the path of generativity than mothers. Hence fathers too may function in the "mentoring" role. Given rapid increases in single-father households (Meyer & Garasky, 1993) and high rates of recoupling, this possibility may increase.

In addition, approaching the problem of fathers' underinvolvement in child care from a developmental perspective is more conducive to change than the domestic-democracy perspective because it emphasizes what fathers gain by greater participation in the daily work of the home rather than what they sacrifice. It also casts wives in a nonadversarial position that is more likely to motivate change in fathers than is a conflictual one. Moreover, sharing daily family work may be a more pragmatic course for changing men's lives within the family than strategies advocated by some men's movements. The painful emotional work to reconceptualize masculinity required by all-male retreats or individual psychotherapy is probably more threatening to men than changing diapers and bathing children. LaRossa (1988) and Cohen (1987) argue that most men now view a father's intimate involvement in the domestic sphere as compatible with masculinity. The same probably cannot be said about inner emotional journeys. "Doing things," like feeding and bathing the children, is consistent with most men's external orientation to the world; showing care by doing things for others is a traditional male value (Levant, 1991) that fits nicely with our developmental prescription for achieving generativity. In contrast, men traditionally have not been comfortable with exploring their emotional lives (Levant, 1991). Hence they are likely to resist interventions that require it.

Directions for Future Research

Studies of paternal participation in daily family work have been dominated by a focus on fairness, or domestic democracy. We have argued that a developmental perspective also is needed. A developmental perspective on fathering highlights the importance of caring for children to adult men's growth and maturity. We believe this perspective can fruitfully guide future research on fathering and men's involvement in child care. Accordingly, the next section outlines some suggestions for future studies based on a developmental perspective rather than a domestic-democracy perspective.

Methodological Directions

A developmental approach to the study of father involvement in child care suggests several methodological issues to which researchers should pay greater attention. First, longitudinal studies must be emphasized. Previous work with cross-sectional designs was able to discern the disparity in the division of labor between mothers and fathers. However, to capture the complex developmental issues that men face during the early stages of parenthood (and beyond), longitudinal designs will be needed. Further, these studies will need to observe developmental processes over periods of time longer than a year (see C. Cowan & Cowan, 1992). Fathers' transitions to the involved-parent role are more voluntary, are likely to proceed at a slower pace, and may be marked by longer periods of disequilibrium.

In addition, studies need to go beyond measures of temporal involvement in child care and structural or attitudinal correlates of that involvement. *Assessing generativity should be central to studies of paternal participation in child care.* Other measures that assess the internal changes fathers may experience, such as nurturance, affiliation, instrumentality, identity, and self-esteem (see Hawkins & Belsky, 1989), need to be included as well. Sophisticated quantitative instruments should be used, but we will also need to invest in qualitative methods to capture difficult-to-quantify constructs and to observe subtle but significant developmental change. It may be that narrative data from fathers will be a rich source that reveals important internal shifts for men (see Lewis, 1986). Furthermore, we need to collect these kinds of data from both fathers and mothers. It is a father's developmental position *in relation to his partner's* that may be crucial to understanding marital quality rather than his own developmental location per se.

Substantive Directions

Within the framework of the methodological directions suggested above, a number of substantive questions about men's involvement in caring for children are called for by a developmental perspective. For instance, how do differing levels of involvement affect fathers' development of generativity and other dimensions of personality? Is involvement in certain periods of childhood (e.g., infancy) more effective in terms of achieving generativity? Similarly, how is the timing of fatherhood for adult men related to generativity? Some studies suggest that men who become fathers for the first time in their late twenties or early thirties are more involved in child care than are early fathers (Coltrane, 1990; Cooney, Pedersen, Indelicato, & Palkovitz, 1993). Is late-timed fatherhood more conducive to generativity and, if so, why?

Similarly, are particular kinds of father involvement especially conducive to developing generativity? Some research suggests that fathers' caring for children when the mother is not present stimulates greater attitudinal and behavioral change (Pleck, 1985). Researchers might fruitfully employ the three-level taxonomy of parental involvement proposed by Lamb, Pleck, Charnov, et al. (1987) (i.e., availability, engagement or direct interaction, and responsibility or management) to assess which kinds of involvement are especially generative for men. Perhaps accepting full responsibility for a child's well-being and "managing" child care (as opposed to performing assigned tasks) is essential to generativity. In addition, differing household contexts also might provide weaker or stronger developmental stimuli for fathers. Researchers could compare fathers in various family structures to assess their impact on development. Even better, given current patterns of family formation and dissolution, studies could plot the course of generativity as individual fathers move through different household structures and assume different relationships to their children (e.g., biological versus stepfather).

Also, a developmental perspective suggests that fathers will experience some disequilibrium as they increase their involvement with children and proceed on the path toward generativity. What is the longitudinal course of this disequilibrium? What factors influence successful movement through this period of disequilibrium? How do wives or partners facilitate or obstruct reestablishing equilibrium at a higher level of functioning? What are the consequences of this disequilibrium if it is not resolved quickly enough?

Understanding the psychological processes that facilitate the development of generativity will form an important basis on which to build interventions to help fathers increase their involvement in child care. Thus we need to ask questions such as these: In what ways do children stimulate the development of generativity in fathers? To what extent does dissonance between the possible father self and the actual father self motivate change toward greater involvement? Does extensive temporal investment in the fathering role eventually lead to an incorporation of that role into the core of a father's identity? In what ways are mothers effective models for fathers to help them learn needed caretaking skills and attitudes? How do mothers (and children) effectively reinforce greater paternal participation?

A developmental perspective on father involvement in child care also suggests new directions for research on marital relationships. Development should be posed as a mediating factor that links paternal involvement to marital outcomes. Questions to be asked include the following:

Do the developmental trajectories of fathers and mothers diverge across the transition to parenthood, and, if so, is divergence associated with differing levels and kinds of involvement? Are developmental differences between fathers and mothers in generativity and other personality dimensions related to marital quality and satisfaction? In addition, development is discerned when individuals achieve higher levels of functioning. Thus other questions to be asked include these: Do couples communicate better when differences in generativity are minimal? Are developmentally synchronous couples better able to cope with stressful life events and daily hassles, and do they experience less stress at later individual and family transitions, such as the empty nest, or retirement?

Conclusion

Dorothy Dinnerstein eloquently summarizes the theme of this chapter: "The process of nurturing life is the most profoundly transforming experience in the range of human possibilities. Because women have this experience and men generally don't, we live and think and love across a great gap of understanding" (quoted in Blakely, 1983, p. 73). The marital difficulties faced by many fathers and mothers are as much incongruence in developmental location as they are struggles for domestic democracy. For many couples, then, the resolution to this problem is to find ways to help men accept greater responsibility for nurturing children.

4

Developing a Middle-Range Theory of Father Involvement Postdivorce

MARILYN IHINGER-TALLMAN
KAY PASLEY
CHERYL BUEHLER

A nation with an eye on its future values, nurtures, and cares for its children. At the end of the twentieth century in America, there are an increasing number of children who do not receive this necessary valuing and care from their fathers. Some of these children are born to unmarried mothers and have no father in their lives from the start (Mott, 1990). Others lose the financial and emotional support of their father after divorce. We are not arguing here that father-absent families are inherently deficient. Rather, we suggest that children whose fathers are functionally absent are at greater risk for developing problems. We propose that children's well-being is placed in jeopardy for two reasons. First, children benefit from the love, caring, and economic support a father can provide. Second, a father's involvement in the life of his child is important to a child's development.

For children who are born to married (or stably cohabiting) parents, divorce does not automatically jeopardize children; some fathers con-

AUTHORS' NOTE: This chapter previously appeared as an article, with the same title, in *Journal of Family Issues* (1993, Vol. 14, No. 4, 550-571). An initial draft was presented at the Theory Construction and Research Methodology Annual Pre-Conference Workshop, National Council on Family Relations, 1991. We wish to thank Lynn White, Sharon J. Price, Alicia Cast, William Marsiglio, and an anonymous reviewer for their very useful comments on an earlier draft.

Figure 4.1. The Relationship Between Father Parenting Role Identity, Father Involvement, and Child Well-Being

tinue to fulfill all their parental roles postdivorce; however, many do not. Recent longitudinal research shows that a significant number of fathers cease to nurture and provide for their children after divorce (Furstenberg, Morgan, & Allison, 1987; Furstenberg & Nord, 1985; Furstenberg, Nord, Peterson, & Zill, 1983). Although several recent studies with small, nonrepresentative samples have attempted to shed light on why this happens (see as examples Arendell, 1992a; Kruk, 1991), we do not as yet have an answer. In this chapter, a theoretical conceptualization is presented that is intended to help explain this phenomenon. Using the principles of identity theory, we develop a middle-range theory that accounts for the degree of father involvement with children postseparation, postdivorce, and, in some cases, postremarriage.

The theory presented here proposes that the key element in father involvement postdivorce is the degree of a father's identification with the status and roles associated with being a parent.[1] Father's *parenting role* identity is defined as the self-meanings attached to the status and associated roles of parenthood (Burke & Tully, 1977). We hypothesize that this parent identity is a major determinant of father involvement with children following marital separation. *Father involvement* is defined as behaviors that promote interaction with and reflect a commitment to a child, including, among other activities, face-to-face contact, phoning or writing, physical caretaking, and providing financial support. The consequence of father involvement is *child well-being*, which is defined as the degree to which children are able to engage successfully and appropriately in interpersonal relationships and in work or play activities with relative freedom from noxious social behavior, burdensome emotions, and poor physical health (Trotter, 1989, p. 16).[2] Figure 4.1 illustrates these relationships.

Our task here is to develop the rationale for using identity theory to explain father behavior and to show how identity principles help explain father involvement postdivorce. Therefore, in this chapter, we focus on the first half of the model depicted in the figure—the concepts and propositions responsible for the relationship between father identity and father involvement—rather than on those that make up the second half of the model.

Our interest in using identity theory as an explanation of fathering behavior is not unique. In a recent article, Marsiglio (1995) proposes the utility of this theory to explain parenting involvement/noninvolvement of young fathers who live apart from their children. Using the concept of commitment, he suggests that this framework is a fruitful tool for understanding the dimensions of meaning that young fathers and their significant others associate with father roles. He also suggests that identity theory could guide research that explores "the cultural sources and interpersonal processes that shape individuals' perceptions about fatherhood and the way young fathers in particular experience the emotional and psychological aspects of fatherhood" (p. 339).

Marsiglio (Chapter 11, this volume) also used identity theory to guide a discussion of the stepfather parenting role. In a study of 195 stepfathers, he found that stepfathers who hold fatherlike perceptions (indicating that role identity and role performance are fatherlike in nature) had more positive relations with their stepchildren. Several other variables that were entered into a simultaneous multiple regression model also were significant (socialization values that emphasized conformity, a wife/partner who had a positive relationship with the target child), but stepfathering perceptions were the strongest predictors.

The theory offered here attempts to link key variables associated with father parenting role identity and show how they affect father involvement. Because the real world (as contrasted to the scholar's theoretical world) is extremely complex, it is not always easy to distinguish cause from effect when observing behavior over time. For example, L. White (personal communication, October 1991) raised the question of whether, in our theory, identity salience causes involvement or involvement causes salience. Acknowledging this point, we suggest that father parenting role identity directly influences father involvement, but involvement in turn affects a *future* level of father parenting role identity. This nonrecursive relationship is reflected in the full theoretical model presented later in the chapter. Also, when delineating change over time, an "entry point" in the process must be chosen. We accept as given all experiences and events that shaped, maintained, and/or changed father parenting role identity up to the point of residential separation from a child. Thus the theory presented predicts change or stability in father parenting role identity beginning at the time when father's coresidence with a child ends.

Postdivorce Fathering

Most studies investigating postdivorce fathering find that the majority of fathers disengage from their parenting roles over time. Data from the National Survey of Children document the limited contact that children have with their fathers postdivorce (Furstenberg & Nord, 1985; Furstenberg et al., 1983; Furstenberg, Morgan, & Allison, 1987). In one report based on these data, 23% of fathers had no contact with their children aged 11 to 16 during the previous 5 years (Furstenberg, Morgan, & Allison, 1987). Only 26% of children averaged at least bimonthly contact with their fathers (Furstenberg et al., 1983). However, in spite of limited contact, the conclusion drawn from these data was that the children who were surveyed showed no negative effects from paternal absence. Because of the quality of the research design and the fact that it is based on a national probability sample, considerable weight is given to these findings by scholars interested in the effects of divorce on children.

Studies using multimethod and/or qualitative techniques also document the limited involvement of fathers after divorce but produce different findings regarding the effects of lack of contact on children's well-being postdivorce (Hess & Camara, 1979; Hetherington, Cox, & Cox, 1976, 1979; Wallerstein & Kelly, 1980b). These studies conclude that fathers are important to children's postdivorce adjustment because father contact is associated with fewer behavioral problems, higher self-esteem, and other positive indices of children's development.

Thus the extent of the problem of limited father involvement postdivorce is well documented, even though the consequences of father absence as reported in the literature are inconsistent. More important, what the extant studies do not explain is *why* so many fathers remove themselves from active participation in their children's lives after divorce. We argue that at least part of the explanation lies in the potential for change in the salience of a man's identity as a father. Role ambiguity in fathering identity is introduced when the husband position and roles are relinquished after marital separation and divorce. A change occurs in the meaning of parenthood and self-conception as a parent of the child(ren) from the dissolved marriage.[3] This identity change may be represented by an increase or a decrease in the importance of fathering. We emphasize that the focus of the model is on process, change, and degree, not merely presence or absence of participation.

The Role of Identity

Key Concepts

Identity. At a time when scholars were less aware of sexist language, Manford Kuhn (1960) emphasized Mead's contributions to what we now call identity theory. He wrote: "George Herbert Mead suggested that a person's behavior is a function of his conception of his identity, and further, that his conception of his identity derives from the positions he occupies in society" (pp. 53-54). According to this conceptualization, identity has a cognitive dimension and is linked to social structure through status and associated roles. For Stryker and Serpe (1982), identities are defined as

reflexively applied cognitions in the form of answers to the question "Who am I?" These answers are phrased in terms of the position in organized structures of social relationships to which one belongs and the social roles that attach to these positions. (p. 206)

In this same tradition, Burke and Tully (1977) conceptualize identity as

a major component of the self. Indeed the self as a whole is a collection of identities, each of which is experienced indirectly through interactions with others (Stryker, 1981). These identities are the meanings one attributes to oneself as an object. Each identity is associated with particular interactional settings or roles. (p. 883)

The origin of these definitions of identity is the symbolic interaction perspective. Each conceives of identity as composed of meanings and cognitions associated with a specific status that is formed and maintained through interaction with others. According to this perspective, the social situation is the context in which identities are established, and they are maintained through the process of negotiation (Becker, 1964; Stone, 1962). The idea of negotiation brings to identity theory the importance of significant others in identity formation, maintenance, and change. For the specific theoretical model we develop here, parent identity is defined as the self-meanings and cognitions attached to the status and roles of parent.

Saliency. Identity theorists contend that identities are organized into salience hierarchies. As Stryker and Serpe (1982) explain:

> This hierarchical organization of identities is defined by the probabilities of each of the various identities within it being brought into play in a given situation. Alternatively, it is defined by the probabilities each of the identities have of being invoked across a variety of situations. The location of an identity in this hierarchy is, by definition, its salience. Implied in this conceptualization and definition is the general proposition that an identity's location in a salience hierarchy will affect its threshold for being invoked in situations and thus the likelihood that behavior called for by the identity will ensue. Whether or not that behavior will, in fact, occur will clearly depend on the way that salience of an identity interacts with (1) defining characteristics of situations (such as the degree to which the situation permits alternative identities to be expressed behaviorally), and (2) other self characteristics (such as self-esteem or satisfaction). It is worth emphasizing that, from the viewpoint of identity theory, the organization of identities in a salience hierarchy is a specification of the sociological conceptualization of personality as a structure reflecting the roles persons play. (p. 207)

From this definition and discussion, we expect to find that, when the parent identity is more salient vis-à-vis other identities, fathers will value the status and roles associated with fatherhood above other statuses and roles. Fathers also will choose to enact parenting behaviors in specific situations appropriate to those behaviors or across situations, taking into account the characteristics of the situation. This might be exemplified with the decision by a father to attend a child's musical recital instead of taking the opportunity to go out with friends when the characteristics of the situation are an evening free of other obligations and both child and friends are equally persuasive in their appeal.

One further point concerns the relative salience of the various roles attached to a specific status. That is, just as statuses are compared and ranked in importance, the roles associated with a single status also are compared and ranked. For example, the status of father competes with other statuses a man may hold (e.g., employee, husband, son, brother). Each of these statuses has a set of roles associated with it; fathers take on the role of provider, nurturer, companion, disciplinarian, and so on with reference to their children. Furthermore, just as a man may rank the status of father as more salient than that of brother, he also may rank provider more salient than nurturer or disciplinarian more important than companion. The way a man enacts the father roles provides insight into the meaning that he attaches to that role.

Commitment. The term *commitment* is an important concept in identity theory, but its use is confounded by multiple meanings. Writers apply different definitions to the concept, and it is not always clear to what they are applying that meaning. For example, Stryker and Serpe (1982) define commitment as

> the degree to which the person's relationships to specified sets of others depend on his or her being a particular kind of person, i.e., occupying a particular position in an organized structure of relationships and playing a particular role. . . . [The concept of commitment] provides a useful way of conceiving "society's" relevance for social behavior, doing so by pointing to social networks—the number of others to whom one relates by occupancy of a given position, the importance to one of those others, the multiplexity of linkages, and so on—as the relevant considerations. (p. 207)

This conceptualization views commitment as linked to a network of relationships, not to an identity per se. The theory developed here assesses a father's commitment in terms of two factors: (a) the number of, and extent to which, persons expect or require him to hold the status of father and enact father roles, and (b) the importance of these relationships to him.

Burke and Reitzes (1991) define commitment as "the sum of the forces that maintain congruity between one's identity and the implications for one's identity of the interactions and behaviors in the interactive setting" (p. 244). This means that when a father's perceptions of others' responses to his parental behaviors, attitudes, and enactment of parent roles are not aligned with his own perceptions of himself in those roles, the strength of his response to the misalignment is the degree of his commitment to that role. For example, if a father shrugs off negative comments about his failure to provide child support for his children, it can be interpreted that his conception of father-as-provider role is not important to his identity as father or that his status as father is low in salience. This definition indicates the commitment concept refers to a commitment to an identity.

However, commitment also has been defined as (a) "the willingness of social actors to give their energy and resources to a particular course of action" (Gecas, 1980, p. 1); (b) a promise, that is, "an obligation to remain in and maintain a relationship over time" (Tallman, Gray, & Leik, 1991, p. 17); and (c) as "consistent lines of behavior resulting from an actor's assessment of the balance of costs over rewards" (Becker, 1960, cited in Gecas, 1980, p. 2). According to these ideas, the concept of commitment refers to a commitment to people, objects, goals, or groups and not to an identity.

Herein lies a source of confusion. It is evident that an individual makes commitments to his or her *self* via adherence to a particular identity as well as commitments to *others* via promises and consistent lines of behavior. Because our theory defines father involvement as behaviors that promote interaction and reflect a commitment to a child, we are concerned with both types of commitment. Thus we are concerned with a man's commitment to (a) establishing, maintaining, or changing his identity and role-related behaviors as father and (b) actions taken to maintain a relationship with his child over time. To keep these two aspects of commitment distinct, in the following pages we differentiate between commitment to self and commitment to others when appropriate.

Although commitment has been defined and applied differently, the consequences of commitment are clear. "The greater the commitment to an identity, the more consequential it is for the individual's conduct" (Stryker, 1980, cited in Gecas, 1982, p. 14). Burke and Reitzes (1991) suggest that a consequence of commitment is the moderation of the relationship between an identity and role performance commitment (p. 244). This means that individuals use "their behavior to increase rewards and values received for having a particular identity" (p. 244). "High levels of commitment . . . result in involvement in activities, in organizations, and with role partners, all of which support the person's identity" (p. 245).

Commitment implies decision making and choice behavior.[4] Stryker and Serpe (1982) emphasized that role-related behavior involves making choices. Based on the work of these authors, we formulated the following proposition pertaining to father identity: To the extent a father is embedded in a social structure that provides options—with an opportunity for him to choose behaviors from those options—then the degree to which he chooses to enact specific roles associated with father status indicates its saliency vis-à-vis other statuses and roles. The way choices are manifested is illustrated with the earlier example concerning the decision to attend a child's music recital. Choices and decisions are expected to be based on salience of roles and the actions and reactions of significant others.

An identity theory principle states that people seek to create and maintain stable, coherent identities and that they prefer to evaluate their identities positively (Schwartz & Stryker, 1970). Also, people establish their aspiration levels (including identity aspirations) in a way that is designed to maximize self-esteem (Rosenberg, 1986). This propensity for both a positive evaluation of identities and an alignment between what people aspire to and their sense of self-worth means that the decisions and choices people make are likely to be based on an assessment of rewards and costs associated with choice alternatives (Becker, 1960). Regarding fatherhood, we propose that, all else being equal, fathers are more likely to make role choices perceived as relatively pleasant and entailing few barriers than to make role choices perceived as aversive and difficult to enact (Tallman & Gray, 1990). However, when all else is not equal, the degree of commitment to self and others is expected to affect behavioral choices. Therefore, when level of commitment to father identity (self) is high and level of commitment to the child (other) is high, father identity saliency also is expected to be high. A high degree of salience is expected to modify difficulties or unpleasant situations, and fathers are expected to pursue involvement with their children in spite of such difficulties.

Significant Others. Identity theory is an outgrowth of symbolic interaction theory (Burke & Tully, 1977; Gecas, 1981; Stryker & Serpe, 1982). Therein lies the importance of significant others to identity formation, to the salience hierarchy of identities, and to the behavioral choices that a person makes that reinforce or change identities. The importance of significant others follows from Mead's and Cooley's conceptualization of the development of the self. Stryker and Serpe (1982) summarize this idea:

> We come to know who and what we are through interaction with others. We become objects to ourselves by attaching to ourselves symbols that emerge

from our interaction with others, symbols having meanings growing out of that interaction. As any other symbols, self symbols have action implications: they tell us (as well as others) how we can be expected to behave in our ongoing activity. (p. 202)

Burke and Tully (1977) tie this notion of self to identity by stating that "the self as a whole is a collection of identities, each of which is experienced indirectly through interactions with others" (p. 883).

Finally, we emphasize that individuals enact specific role behaviors that are relatively congruent with their identity in a specific position (Burke & Reitzes, 1981; Burke & Tully, 1977; Stryker, 1968; Stryker & Serpe, 1982). Significant others are important to the formation, maintenance, or change in father identity insofar as they respond to a man's behavior and attitudes related to fatherhood. In addition, a father's perceptions of others' (re)actions define the degree and strength of his commitment to father identity.

Time. A theory that attempts to predict change in behavior must include a temporal element. To examine change in father identity, it is necessary to know the initial state of father identity before the predicted change takes place (i.e., the marital separation). Only then can we assess what, if any, change occurs in identity. Over time, fathers experience life events, such as their divorce or their own or their former spouses' remarriage. These events also will affect father identity and father role behavior over time. This view reflects Wells and Stryker's (1988) interpretation: "What is important to recognize is that neither stability nor change in self is a given, and that life-course processes help to account for both" (p. 209).

The time dimension necessitates a longitudinal examination of father identity and father involvement behaviors. The reciprocal effects of father-child interaction on father's subsequent identity and involvement behavior need to be considered because behavior has consequences that influence future behavior. (Re)actions of significant others, including the child, have an impact on the maintenance and change of father identity and role behavior. Thus we predict that father identity will change as relevant life events occur, as the set of the father's significant others changes, and as children adapt to the divorce and mature. The proposed theory of father involvement incorporates a longitudinal dimension to delineate the conditions under which men continue or discontinue parenting postdivorce and after remarriage.

A Theory of Father Involvement Postdivorce

Theoretical Assumptions

With the central concepts of the theory specified, our next step is to set forth the basic theoretical assumptions. Space limitations prohibit a complete explication of all the principles associated with identity theory that stem from the symbolic interaction framework. However, because the theory of father involvement proposed here is premised on these principles, the following statements are offered as general assumptions.

1. Most behavior is associated with the performance of some role or roles.
2. Roles are shared expectations or meanings attached to behavior.
3. The meaning of roles is understood through interaction.
4. Identity is the meaning a person attributes to the self as an object in a social situation (status) or social role.
5. Shared meanings are the essence of social identity.
6. Because an individual has many statuses and roles, an individual has many identities.
7. Therefore identity is self-meaning relative to various statuses held and roles performed and is developed, maintained, and changed through experience, interaction, and negotiation with others.

Our theory of father involvement conceptualizes fatherhood as a status with a variety of roles (e.g., provider, disciplinarian, companion) attached to that status. After divorce, fathers retain the status of father, but the roles associated with fatherhood are difficult to maintain if the father and child no longer live in the same household. Fathers become the nonresidential parent in about 90% of divorce cases (U.S. Bureau of the Census, 1986).

Holding the status of father and enacting the roles associated with fatherhood create a potentially salient identity for a man. As stated earlier, people are expected to enact specific role behaviors that are relatively congruent with their identity in a specific status (Burke & Reitzes, 1981; Burke & Tully, 1977; Stryker, 1968; Stryker & Serpe, 1982). Therefore fathers are expected to behave toward their children in ways that reflect (a) the value they place on fatherhood and (b) their interpretation of what a good father does and/or is. However, there is variation among men in what it means to be a father and what constitutes "good" fathering. For example, two men who give equal salience to their parent identity may enact the roles associated with fatherhood quite differently because of differences in the way they interpret what it means to be a good father. One father may work 14 hours a day, 6 days a week, to provide the material goods he thinks his child should have. He believes he is a wonderful parent. In this case, there is congruency between identity and role behavior. Another man may consistently skip work to go watch his son play soccer, and he also believes he is a wonderful parent. Here there is also congruency between identity and role behavior. Thus, when determining the salience of father status and roles, careful consideration must be given to an assessment of the perceived content by individual fathers.

When a father loses the daily, routinized, familiar opportunities to parent after divorce, his identity as a father is expected to be affected. Only in cases in which father identity salience is extremely high or extremely low is no change in role behavior expected. This expectation stems from the earlier discussion of commitment. Fathers at the extreme ends of the identity salience hierarchy (those who are extremely committed or extremely uncommitted to their parent identity) are less likely to perceive alternatives to that identity. They will have made more (or fewer) investments (side bets) in that identity (Becker, 1960). They will be more (or less) anchored in that identity through significant others' expectations for them to enact fathering roles effectively. Thus the extremes are expected to be stable over time. In most other instances, we hypothesize that father parenting role identity will gain or lose salience depending on events, specific circumstances, and the influence of significant others.

In summary, as a family reorganizes after marital separation, a man must choose (or is forced to choose) new patterns of involvement with his children. The level of this involvement will depend on several things: (a) the salience of his father identity vis-à-vis other identities, such as a lover, worker, friend, or new husband; (b) the salience hierarchy of the variety of father roles that might be enacted; (c) a commitment to his view of himself as a parent and the degree to which this view is aligned with his perceptions of significant others' responses to his parenting, which, in turn, depends on (d) the expectations significant others have for his behavior. We suggest that fathers reinforce, reconfirm, or change their father identity by choosing from various alternative behaviors based on feedback from significant others (Burke & Tully, 1977). The most likely significant others who are potential sources of influence on father identity and postdivorce involvement with children are the former spouse, parents, former in-laws, coworkers and/or colleagues, friends, lovers, a new spouse, stepchildren, and the children themselves.

Relationships Between Concepts

The concepts that are considered relevant to the development of father parenting role identity have been identified and discussed. We summarize the interrelationships among these concepts with the following theoretical propositions:

1. To the extent that father identity is enmeshed with other identities, father identity will have high salience and father roles are likely to be enacted.
2. The more a father is embedded in a network of relationships that are premised on his being a father and those relationships are important to him, the more he will be committed to the status and roles of fatherhood.
3. The greater the salience of father status, the greater the commitment to that status (commitment to self).
4. The greater the salience of father status, the greater the commitment to one's child (commitment to other).

Father Identity and Role Choices

We identified factors that establish, maintain, or change father parenting role identity for the purpose of explaining the rationale for using identity theory as the underlying framework for the theory. We now discuss father parenting role choices and show how these choices affect father involvement.

It was stated earlier that, just as statuses are compared and ranked in importance, so too the roles associated with a single status are compared and ranked. How a particular father ranks the many roles associated with his father status is the basis on which he invests his resources in children, other things being equal. The roles chosen to be enacted are closely tied to the interpretation a man makes concerning what it means to be a father. Choices associated with the expenditure of time, money, and energy are an indicator of the salience of roles associated with father identity. These ideas are summarized in the following propositions:

5. A father will make choices favoring enactment of father role behavior (as opposed to role behavior associated with a nonfather identity) when father status is more salient than other statuses.

6. A father will make choices favoring enactment of father role behavior (as opposed to role behavior associated with a nonfather identity) when the actions and reactions of significant others favor father involvement.
7. A father will enact parenting role behavior that is relatively congruent with his father identity.
8. All else being equal, a father will be more likely to make role choices that he perceives as relatively pleasant and entailing few barriers than to make role choices he perceives as aversive and difficult to enact.
9. The salience of father roles will affect the ways a father chooses to be involved with his child.

Test of the Relationship Between Father Parenting Role Identity and Father Involvement

A test of the initial relationship between father parenting role identity and father involvement was conducted to determine if further work on the theory was warranted. A mail survey was completed by nonresidential fathers with children ages 18 and younger, most of whom lived in central North Carolina. This was a convenience sample of 76 respondents solicited from church groups in the area.[5] Father parenting role identity was measured using McPhee, Benson, and Bullock's (1986) Self-Perceptions of the Parental Role Scale. This instrument measures parental role satisfaction, perceived competence, investment, and role salience. Father involvement was operationalized as father contact with child, measured as frequency of visits, writing letters, and paying child support. The correlation between father parenting role identity and father involvement was .34 ($p < .01$).

Further analysis provided evidence of a positive relationship between father parenting role identity and father involvement. This test measured father involvement by examining the degree to which fathers engaged in 11 activities with their children (responses asking for the degree of involvement ranged from *not at all* [1] to *very much* [5]). These activities included helping with schoolwork, celebrating holidays, and attending school- or church-related functions. The correlation was .39 ($p < .01$) between these summed items and father parenting role identity.

Although the causal direction of these relationships is unknown, we have some confidence that the two principal variables are associated positively. Thus, although these data are preliminary, they provide the impetus to continue the process of theory construction.

Father Parenting Role Identity and Father Involvement: Variables That Moderate the Relationship

In this section, we address the question: Which factors moderate (strengthen or weaken) the hypothesized relationship between father's parenting role identity and involvement with children? The identification of valid moderators enables us to understand more clearly why some fathers are more involved with their children following separation by explaining the mechanisms by which a specific component of identity becomes translated into a patterned set of behaviors. The moderators were selected because of their importance in the life of a divorced father.

Mother's Preferences and Beliefs. Research conducted by Ahrons (1983) has indicated that mothers serve as gatekeepers to the father-child relationship. More recent research supports these early findings (Arendell, 1992a; Dudley, 1991). The residential mother's preferences for father-child contact and her regard for his parenting abilities moderate the relationship between father parenting role behavior and father involvement. Her preferences for frequent contact and positive regard for father's parenting will strengthen the relationship, whereas contrary preferences and beliefs will weaken it.

Father's Perceptions of Mother's Parenting Skills. We hypothesize that a father's belief that the mother is a good parent will weaken the relationship between the father's parenting identity and his involvement. This belief has received little attention in the extant literature but was identified as a potential moderator by Babcock (1989). Some fathers report feeling less needed postseparation when their former wife is a "good mother."

Father's Emotional Stability. Past research indicates that a father's emotional stability affects how he reorganizes his parenting relationship postseparation. Fathers who are depressed, anxious, and suffering see their children less often than do fathers who are not in these emotional states (Grief, 1979; Hetherington et al., 1976; Kruk, 1991;

Wallerstein & Kelly, 1980b). Based on their findings that nonresidential fathers were more depressed and anxious than residential ones, Stewart, Schwebel, and Fine (1986) concluded that contact with children has a stabilizing effect on men postdivorce. Thus there is some evidence to suggest that a father's emotional stability will strengthen the relationship between father parenting role identity and father involvement.

Mother's Emotional Stability. Although no empirical evidence could be found to serve as a basis for formulating specific hypotheses regarding the moderating effects of a mother's emotional stability, identity theory suggests that a father's parenting identity will be heightened (increase in saliency) if he perceives that his children are poorly parented by their mother postseparation. This is particularly true if other significant persons in his life (parents, friends, lover) express expectations regarding what constitutes adequate parenting and if these expectations are at variance with the children's current situation. There is some evidence suggesting that women experience depression and anxiety postdivorce that is associated with less effective parenting (Hetherington, Cox, & Cox, 1982). Thus we expect that a mother's emotional instability will strengthen the relationship between father parenting role identity and father involvement as a father tries to compensate for a mother's poor parenting.

Sex of Child. Although some evidence suggests that sons see their fathers more often postseparation than do daughters (Bowman & Ahrons, 1985; Furstenberg, 1988a; Kelly & Wallerstein, 1977), findings from the National Health Interview Survey showed no gender differences (Seltzer & Bianchi, 1988). Given these conflicting findings, we hypothesize that the relationship between father parenting role identity and father involvement is stronger for boys than for girls because fathers and sons typically have more shared interests and activities (Barnett & Baruch, 1986b; Radin & Goldsmith, 1985) and because mothers may press for more father involvement with sons than with daughters. These two factors may make the translation process from identity into behavior easier with sons than with daughters.

Coparental Relationship—Competition and Cooperation. There is substantial evidence that certain dimensions of the quality of former spouse relations are related to the level of father involvement following separation in terms of both contact and financial support (Ahrons, 1983;

Hetherington et al., 1982; Issacs, 1988; Kelly & Wallerstein, 1977; Kurdek, 1986; Peterson, 1987; Tschann, Johnston, Kline, & Wallerstein, 1989). The most important dimensions are coparental competition and cooperation. Using social conflict theory to conceptualize the former spouse relationship, coparental conflict, competition, and cooperation are defined as distinct components (Buehler, Betz, Ryan, Legg, & Trotter, 1992; Trotter, 1989). Conflict is defined as disagreements about goals, issues, and scarce resources, whereas cooperation and competition are patterns of behaviors that people choose when faced with disagreements (Camara & Resnick, 1988; Deutsch, 1973; Sprey, 1979). Cooperation is defined as behaviors that allow for continued interaction in spite of differences and even fundamental disagreements (Horowitz, 1967). When parents cooperate, it implies that they are willing to place their children's needs above their own individual interests and negative emotions (e.g., revenge, dominance, jealousy). According to conflict theory, without cooperation the management of conflict remains primarily competitive. Competition is defined as a state of negative interdependence between family members such that gains for one member mean losses for others (Sprey, 1979). Two major types of coparental competition are possible: direct and indirect. Direct competition is represented by overt behaviors (e.g., yelling, screaming, attacking) that are expressions of a negative interdependence between spouses. Indirect competition is represented by passive-aggressive attempts to triangulate children in parental conflict (e.g., using them as spies and allies or denigrating the other parent in front of the children). An analysis of existing research using this conceptualization indicated that father involvement is related more to coparental competition than to conflict (Trotter, 1989). Thus we hypothesize that coparental competition (both direct and indirect) weakens the relationship between father parenting role behavior and father involvement by creating a negative and aversive environment in which important child-related issues are processed. Similarly, we hypothesize that cooperation between former spouses strengthens the relationship between these variables. We also hypothesize that coparental conflict in itself does not moderate this relationship, because it is how the conflict is handled that is important rather than the level of conflict per se.

Father Economic Well-Being and Employment Stability. The literature on father involvement postseparation points to two important economic factors: economic well-being and employment stability. Both factors are related positively to the payment of child support and to the amount of support paid (Furstenberg & Nord, 1985; U.S. Bureau of the Census, 1986; Weiss, 1984). Fathers define their parenting role post-separation primarily in terms of economic support (Babcock, 1989). Thus we hypothesize that higher levels of economic well-being and a stable employment history will strengthen the translation of father's identity into involvement.

Encouragement From Others. Because behavior is not selected and enacted in a social vacuum, and based on our earlier proposition about relationship networks, we hypothesize that father's translation of identity into involvement behavior will be influenced by the opinions of relevant others. Thus encouragement from important persons to continue paternal involvement will likely strengthen the translation process, whereas discouragement will weaken it.

Figure 4.2 presents the complete theoretical model, including life events that are inside and outside the control of the individual, variables hypothesized to have direct effects on father parenting role identity and father involvement, and effects that moderate the relationship between these variables. Moderating effects differ from direct effects. Variables exhibiting direct effects influence the level of a dependent variable, whereas a moderating variable changes either the strength or direction of a *relationship between variables* (James & Brett, 1984). For example, the question of whether or not boys are more aggressive than girls postdivorce involves testing the direct effect of sex of child on aggressive behavior. The question of whether or not the relationship between father involvement and child aggression is stronger for boys than for girls, however, involves testing the *moderating* effect of sex of child on the *relationship between* father involvement and child aggression. With few exceptions, we hypothesize that the moderators identified in Figure 4.2 change the strength of coefficients (strengthen or weaken them) rather than the direction of the relationship. Thus this component of the model represents our efforts to predict the effects of specific variables that strengthen or weaken the relationship between father parenting role identity and father involvement soon after separation.

Conclusion

This chapter developed a theory to explain why fathers absent themselves from their children's lives after separation and divorce. Because

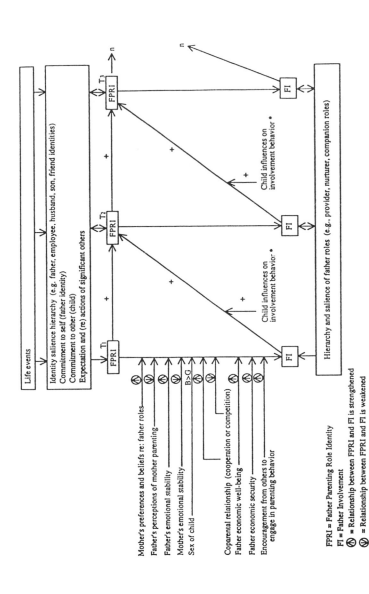

Life events

Identity salience hierarchy (e.g. father, employee, husband, son, friend identities)
Commitment to self (father identity)
Commitment to other (child)
Expectation and (re) actions of significant others

Mother's preferences and beliefs re: father roles
Father's perceptions of mother parenting
Father's emotional stability
Mother's emotional stability
Sex of child

Coparental relationship (cooperation or competition)
Father economic well-being
Father economic security
Encouragement from others to
engage in parenting behavior

Child influences on
involvement behavior *

Hierarchy and salience of father roles (e.g., provider, nurturer, companion roles)

FPRI = Father Parenting Role Identity
FI = Father Involvement
Ⓐ = Relationship between FPRI and FI is strengthened
Ⓦ = Relationship between FPRI and FI is weakened

* = The following aspects are included in this variable: child temperment, child's behavior in the father-child relationship, child's reactions to father's
    involvement behavior, child's evaluation of father as a person (father's personality attributes, child's respect and regard for father).

Figure 4.2. Theoretical Model of Father Involvement Postdivorce

separation and divorce are emotionally difficult life events, role identity salience will likely change after father-child coresidence ends. We hypothesize that the change in identity that accompanies the loss of daily interaction with a child is responsible for the extent to which an absent father stays involved (or becomes more or less involved) with his child. For some, the status of father may increase in salience, and these fathers will become more involved with children postdivorce. For others, even though father status may initially rank high in their identity hierarchy, new circumstances, situations, and significant others may discourage fathering behavior, and parenting role identity salience will decrease. As commitment to a given identity changes and commitment to others changes, father parenting role identity is expected to change. Furthermore, given any position that father identity holds in an identity hierarchy, the perceptions and beliefs of both parents, parents' emotional state, sex of the child, the coparental relationship, economic factors, and the degree of encouragement of friends and family members are expected to strengthen or weaken (moderate) the relationship between father parenting role identity and father involvement behavior. An initial test of the basic relationship between father parenting role identity and father involvement behavior provided support for the theory. Further efforts to validate this relationship and delineate the conditions under which the moderating variables operate will continue.

Notes

1. Because the concepts of status, position, and roles are differentially defined in the social psychological and sociological literatures, we want to offer the reader an explanation of how we use these concepts. *Position* and *status* are meant to be used interchangeably. *Status* is defined as an individual's place or position in a social structure, or network of social relationships. *Role* is defined as a set of expected behavior patterns, obligations, and privileges attached to a particular social status (Robertson, 1987).

2. Father involvement in this theory is defined as behavioral and economic involvement with the child. Involvement ranges from no involvement to high involvement (e.g., daily contact and adequate financial support). As conceptualized, involvement does not imply high-quality father-child interaction (e.g., warmth, authoritative discipline). Rather, we conceptualize *quality of fathering* as a variable that *moderates* the relationship between father involvement and child well-being. Specifically, based on research by Hetherington (1989), we hypothesize that the relationship between father involvement and child well-being is stronger for children who have fathers who exhibit good parenting skills (i.e., warm, noncoercive, inductive, consistent).

3. Cast (personal communication, August 1991) and White (personal communication, October 1991) called attention to the following point: One reason for this role ambiguity is that the identities of husband and father may be more intertwined for men than the identities of wife and mother are for women.

4. The distinction between choice and decision is offered by Tallman and Gray (1990). In their view, the term *choice* is best used when referring to the selection between routine options, such as which route to take to work. *Decision*, on the other hand, is best used when referring to "nonroutine situations under conditions of risk or uncertainty" (p. 423).

5. Because of the very high proportion of individuals who belong to churches in the South, the method of using church membership as a selection factor was viewed as less biased than it might be in other regions of the country.

5

Fathers' Diverse
Life Course Patterns and Roles

Theory and Social Interventions

WILLIAM MARSIGLIO

Men's life course patterns and paternal roles in the United States have become more diverse and dynamic in recent years because of changing childbearing, marriage, cohabitation, and divorce patterns (Ahlburg & De Vita, 1992; Bumpass, 1990). They have also been affected by shifting cultural images of fatherhood (Griswold, 1993). Consequently, the task of designing policies and programs that enhance the amount and quality of fathers' interpersonal involvement with their children, as well as fathers' financial commitment to them, has become increasingly complex. Now more than ever, these efforts must take into account the unique, varied, and dynamic aspects of contemporary fathers' life course experiences and roles.

My primary and modest objective in this chapter is to explore how a theoretical discussion of fatherhood is relevant to policymakers' and other social agents' efforts to foster constructive relationships between fathers and their children. I will cast most of my comments at a general level because detailed discussions about specific policy and program-

AUTHOR'S NOTE: This chapter is a revision of a presentation I gave at the National Science Foundation's conference "America's Fathers and Public Policy" in Washington, D.C., October 1993.

matic strategies appear elsewhere (Cutright, 1986; Fox & Blanton, 1995; Furstenberg, 1988b, 1989; Gerson, 1993; Griswold, 1993; Hanson & Bozett, 1987; Lamb & Sagi, 1983; Landers, 1990; Lerman & Ooms, 1993; Levine, Murphy, & Wilson, 1993; Marsiglio, 1995; Meyer, 1992; Pleck, 1993; Segal, 1990; Thompson, 1994). I discuss how social interventions designed to change the way fatherhood is perceived and practiced can be informed by drawing upon the scripting and life course perspectives, identity theory, and the complementary *univocal reciprocity* and *generativity* concepts described below. In the process, I underscore the value of studying the social psychological factors associated with fathers' involvement in their children's lives by discussing five interrelated objectives for altering the culture and conduct of fatherhood in the United States.

The two general areas I address include coresident fathers' interpersonal involvement with their biological or stepchildren, and paternal conduct (including child support) in the absence of, or after the termination of, men's coresident relationships with their children's mother. My discussion emphasizes aspects of life course events and specific role transitions associated with fatherhood, that is, becoming a biological or stepfather for the first time, experiencing a change in father's residential/custodial status with respect to his children, forming a joint household or relationship with another partner (and possibly her child[ren] in some cases), or temporarily relinquishing the breadwinner role because of a job loss.

Theoretical Issues and Fatherhood

Scripting and Life Course Perspectives

The scripting perspective (see Simon & Gagnon, 1986) can be used to conceptualize the relationship between different aspects of fatherhood. This approach proposes that there are essentially three distinct but interrelated levels of fatherhood activity. The most general level involves cultural and subcultural scenarios, or the stockpile of ideas related to the expression of fatherhood roles. These scenarios include the basic normative guidelines for how fathers should think, feel, and act. In their most general form, they would also include expectations about how others should think, feel, and act toward fathers. In addition to this normative emphasis, cultural scenarios can be viewed as including general knowledge, ideal images, and stereotypes about fatherhood (see LaRossa, 1988, for a discussion of the cultural scenarios of fatherhood).

Given that cultural scenarios exist at an abstract, collective level, individuals will tend to interpret the expectations associated with these scenarios and then use the scenarios as crude guidelines to construct and manage specific situations when they interact with others. An assumption of this *interpersonal scripting* process, the second level of the scripting perspective, is that various individuals, including partners and former partners, often play a significant role in shaping fathers' actual experiences and orientation toward their paternal roles. This interpersonal scripting process can also be restricted by circumstances largely beyond fathers' control (e.g., social structural factors related to the gender gap in hours and earnings, inflexible work schedules). Some fathers may therefore be unable to construct their lives according to their preferred ideals (Gerson, 1993).

The third level of this perspective, *intrapsychic scripting*, conveys the notion that fathers will at times privately construct images about how they want to present themselves as fathers. Men will to some extent develop their personal need states or expectations about being a father figure by reflecting upon prevailing cultural or subcultural scenarios germane to fatherhood. They will also use these scenarios to anticipate and seek specific interaction episodes that will enable them to confirm their self-images as fathers. In some instances, their thoughts about fatherhood will actually reflect their concerns about their role performances, and others' assessments of them, in their related roles as husband/partner and masculine male (Marsiglio, 1991a).

These three levels of activity associated with paternal conduct are embedded within a dynamic historical context that is characterized by interrelated demographic, cultural, and social structural changes. In demographic terms, fathers today are less likely than their recent counterparts to experience the orderly, traditional sequencing of family-related experiences (marriage, paternity, and serving as the primary breadwinner while coresiding with offspring during all of their childhood and adolescent years). It is now much more common than 50 years ago to observe various permutations of fatherhood, including wedlock and out-of-wedlock paternity; coresident and nonresident status; biological and stepfatherhood; being a father while married, remarried, or single; begetting unplanned children during adolescence or early adulthood, fathering both biological and stepchildren who may or may not live together, and fathering children with the aid of modern reproductive technologies (Bozett & Hanson, 1991; Gerson, 1993; Griswold, 1993; Marsiglio, in press). At a cultural level, Gerson (1993) has also observed that the "demise of cultural consensus on the meaning of manhood has left men in a no man's land, searching for new meanings and definitions of maturity" (p. 5). Likewise, fundamental changes in the postindustrial economy have led to a decline in the majority of men's real earnings and an increase in women's attachment to the labor force. These patterns have in turn contributed to the demise of fathers' primary breadwinner role.

Today, the roles associated with being a resident biological father who is either married or cohabiting with a partner continue to evolve because of the factors noted above. Fathers' experiences are also intriguing because the norms related to being a nonresident, step-, or single father are ambiguous; consequently, the expression of the relevant roles is quite variable and difficult at times (Cherlin, 1978; Cherlin & Furstenberg, 1994; Greif, 1985; Marsiglio, Chapter 11, this volume; Thompson, 1994; Wallerstein & Corbin, 1986). Growing numbers of fathers are thus taking the initiative to shape their own paternal roles in new ways. The interpersonal scripting processes involving fathers, as well as their partners and children, will probably become more complex as increasing numbers of persons attempt to adjust to parents' fluid roles and varied life course patterns.

In the light of these conditions, it would be misleading to present a simplistic, generic view of the culture of fatherhood in the United States (Griswold, 1993). In Griswold's (1993) words:

> fatherhood in recent decades has become a kaleidoscope of images and trends, a sure sign that it has lost cultural coherence. . . . Buffeted by powerful demographic, economic, and political changes, fatherhood in American culture is now fraught with ambiguity and confusion. Not surprisingly, so, too, are fathers themselves. (p. 244)

Fathers' experiences may portend the evolution of a variety of cultural scenarios that assign unique meanings to the different fatherhood statuses and associated roles (e.g., biological resident father, biological nonresident father, resident single father, resident stepfather, young unwed father). Cultural stereotypes and ideal images for these statuses may be differentiated further according to social class and race/ethnic themes.

Cultural imagery that already has achieved some currency within the popular culture is the "good dad-bad dad complex" often associated with nonresident fathers (Furstenberg, 1988b). On the positive side, cultural images of the highly involved, attentive father have evolved alongside a series of representations of the same in Hollywood and in TV productions. In recent years the negative side of this imagery has been crystallized even more clearly in the public's eye because expressions such as "deadbeat dad" have been popularized. This label enables individuals to convey their views of fathers in candid and succinct fashion. These cultural stereotypes and images are likely to arouse feelings and expectations, among both fathers and those associated with them. Likewise, as more narrow, status-specific fatherhood images evolve and become a part of the collective consciousness, they too may affect fathers' self-perceptions and others' perceptions of them.

It appears, for example, that cultural stereotypes have emerged in recent years that depict young unwed fathers, particularly African American and to a lesser extent Hispanic fathers residing in the inner city, as uninvolved and oblivious to traditional norms related to men's sense of procreative responsibility (Marsiglio, 1991a). These images became more pervasive during the 1980s as the general public and policymakers increased their awareness of young unwed fathers and the larger adolescent pregnancy issue (Lerman & Ooms, 1993). Generally speaking, negative images of young unwed fathers stem from a mainstream interpretation of the family life course that views paternity as being "off time" if it occurs prior to other life transitions such as completing school, securing a job, and getting married (Jencks, 1990). These negative images are reinforced because so few young African American fathers live with their children and marry their children's mother (Marsiglio, 1987). Recent qualitative analyses of young African American fathers have also revealed that it is not uncommon for young African American mothers and their families to denigrate specific young fathers as well as disadvantaged fathers more generally (Furstenberg, Chapter 7, this volume; Sullivan, 1990). For instance, Furstenberg reports that young African American mothers often used the term *daddies* to distinguish nonresident fathers who made genuine attempts to fulfill their social paternal roles from nonresident fathers who did not. As with any idea, the cultural diffusion of these fatherhood images will be accelerated to the extent folk terms emerge that enable individuals to convey easily the essence of these images to themselves and others.

Men become aware of the cultural and subcultural scenarios related to fatherhood through a variety of sources including their exposure to media images and involvement with interpersonal communication networks, such as adult family members, friends, coworkers, children, and present or previous partners (Bozett & Hanson, 1991; Knijn, in press; Marsiglio, Chapter 1, this volume). It is unclear though how important these larger cultural scenarios are for the way men construct their paternal images. As Daly's (Chapter 2, this volume) qualitative analysis of first-time biological fathers living with their young children shows, many fathers construct their image of fatherhood from a fragmented set of behaviors performed by various people. It is possible that similar analyses focusing on "nontraditional" fathers might reveal features unique to the way nonresident, step-, and single fathers develop their perceptions about the paternal roles associated with each of their respective statuses, especially those aspects related to their paternal commitments and obligations. Because these types of fathers will have different experiences from those of typical coresident, biological fathers who are involved in a coupled relationship, they may be more likely to pattern their behavior after a particular person who is in a similar situation or actively negotiate their unconventional roles with their partners and children.

Univocal Reciprocity and Generativity

Although permutations of cultural scenarios may emerge that uniquely represent the different fatherhood statuses, these scenarios will probably incorporate a few common dimensions. For instance, specific scenarios are all likely to include images of how the norm of *univocal reciprocity* relates to fathers. *Univocal reciprocity* represents a type of moral norm that encourages individuals to engage in social exchanges with others without expecting to receive direct or immediate reciprocation (Ekeh, 1974; Scanzoni & Marsiglio, 1993). Historically, the biological parent-child relationship has typified this form of exchange, with an emphasis on fathers' financial obligations (Cutright, 1986; Griswold, 1993), and was reinforced through the institution of marriage. Although this norm is still highly valued in the abstract, its expression has become more tenuous because of the rise in individualism as a lifestyle value, more modern gender role attitudes, the growing diversity of family life course patterns, and changes in the household economy. The manner in which men adopt, modify, or reject the norm of univocal reciprocity toward their biological or stepchildren is salient to a discussion of contemporary fatherhood. Research that focuses on why some fathers are more likely than others to develop this type of commitment to their children is invaluable. In a more general sense, the *generativity* concept that is central to the adult development perspective is also relevant to a discussion of fatherhood. It refers to a type of nurturing quality in which individuals have an interest in creating and guiding younger generations. This developmental phase is thought to be an essential part of healthy adult development wherein individuals learn to be less self-centered while developing the need to be needed by others (Erikson, 1982b; Hawkins, Christiansen, Sargent, & Hill, Chapter 3, this volume). One respondent in Gerson's (1993) study captured the essence of this notion by commenting:

> You feel like you're gifted by having a child, taking care of somebody and being responsible for their growth and development. It was just something I looked forward to . . . someone being dependent on me, someone to share life with, to take care of—that was my need, too. (pp. 176-177)

The Life Course Perspective and Identity Theory

As described above, the scripting perspective emphasizes a multilayered approach to theorizing about fatherhood. Fathers' personal and interpersonal activities revolve around the adoption, interpretation, modification, and performance of paternal roles. This perspective can be complemented by viewing fathers' lives from a restricted life course perspective (Cooney, Pedersen, Indelicato, & Palkovitz, 1993; Elder, 1985). Many life events involve the adoption of new statuses and roles and, in some cases, the elimination of others. This life course approach highlights the dynamic aspect of fathers' activities by examining fathers' short-term transitional experiences and adaptations to these key life events. The scripting perspective, in turn, can inform the life course approach. It does so by providing a framework for viewing fathers' adaptations within a larger social context wherein age-graded norms and social expectations about the rights and responsibilities associated with particular statuses and roles prevail. The value of studying fathers' responses is accentuated in a cultural climate in which many fathers are apt to undergo changes in their paternal statuses and roles.

Although the scripting and life course perspectives are both helpful in considering the dynamic aspects of paternal roles, it is also important to consider how fathers organize the "self," especially in regard to their paternal roles. This type of analysis focuses on the nature of how the "self" is organized and affected by social factors, how this "self" structure is in turn related to paternal conduct, and the process by which the organization of the self sometimes shifts over time as individuals adjust to life course events and engage in negotiations with others, particularly current and former partners and their children. Identity theory provides a viable approach for considering fathers' experiences in this manner because it highlights the notion that at any given point in time fathers will have multiple statuses and potentially conflicting role demands.

Several scholars have recently discussed how identity theory can be used to interpret fathers' conduct with their children (see Ihinger-Tallman, Pasley, & Buehler, Chapter 4, this volume; Marsiglio, 1991a, 1995, and Chapter 1, this volume). According to identity theory, the multiple role identities fathers possess can be ranked in a salience hierarchy that reflects the relative probability that one of these will be expressed in different situations and chosen when conflicts between identities occur. The paternal identity may be more or less salient than other identities. The paternal identity or status will also have numerous roles associated with it, such as breadwinner, playmate, nurturer, moral teacher, and disciplinarian, that may also be ranked in a hierarchial fashion.

From Stryker's (1980) theoretical point of view, fathers' commitment to their identity as fathers and the particular role relationships related to it is based on several factors. Two of these include the extent to which maintaining specific role relationships requires fathers to be a particular kind of father and the strength of their conviction to sustain these relationships. It is thus reasonable to assume that men who have become fathers in recent years, compared with their earlier counterparts, will be more likely to vacillate in their commitment to their paternal role identity and experience shifts in their salience hierarchy. This is likely to occur because the familial context within which contemporary fathers experience their paternal roles is more likely to change during their tenure as a father. As a consequence, their needs for self-confirmation as a father are also likely to change.

Fathers' level of commitment to their paternal identity will rest to some extent on their response to the real and imagined expectations they and others associate with their specific circumstances (e.g., biological or stepfather, coresident or nonresident father, single or coupled relationship) and roles (e.g., breadwinner, nurturer, companion). Perceptions about whether and how particular fathers should demonstrate univocal reciprocity toward their children are likely to be quite important in this regard. Moreover, perceptions about how univocal reciprocity can be demonstrated in practical terms may differ considerably depending upon fathers' resources and others' expectations. Some nonresident fathers will be faced with the dilemma of whether they feel comfortable maintaining a sense of univocal reciprocity toward their children when their former partner, and perhaps the children themselves, make it difficult for them to feel as though they are involved in their children's lives. Others will struggle with their sense of inadequacy if they feel they are unable to contribute significantly to their children's financial support. Stepfathers will be confronted with similar problems as they struggle either to adopt or to resist univocal exchanges with their "stepchildren" (see Marsiglio, Chapter 11, this volume). Thus it would be useful to consider how life course processes and family structure experiences affect the way nonresident biological fathers, resident single fathers, and stepfathers develop, sustain, and sometimes relinquish their sense of univocal reciprocity, generativity feelings, or perceptions of equitable parental responsibility.

These observations illustrate the dynamic and negotiated nature of the commitment concept and the notion that fathers' paternal role identity is likely to be affected by social factors and others' attitudes and actions. Consequently, fathers' degree and type of involvement in their children's lives are subject to change resulting from interpersonal negotiations and contextual factors. One of the key defining characteristics of fathers' relationship with their children is whether they coreside. As Ihinger-Tallman et al. (Chapter 4, this volume) note, fathers are more likely to experience a shift in their salience hierarchy once coresidency ends. Likewise, fathers' saliency hierarchy may undergo changes if they were to begin to live with their nonresident children or someone else's children. Ihinger and her colleagues also suggest a number of theoretically relevant factors that are likely to affect fathers' commitment to their parental identity postdivorce such as the perceptions and beliefs of both parents, parents' emotional states, the child's gender, quality of the coparental relationship, economic factors, and degree of encouragement from friends and family members. They theorize that these variables will moderate the relationship between fathers' parenting role identity and their involvement with their children. This relationship may also be influenced by factors such as the father's and former partner's new romantic relationships or a change in the geographic distance between the child's and father's residences. It is noteworthy that resident and nonresident fathers' (and stepfathers') level of commitment to their parenting identity, their willingness to adhere to the norm of univocal reciprocity, and their sense of closeness to their children are related to their type of involvement with their children's mother (see Arditti, 1991; Arditti & Kelly, 1994; Furstenberg, Chapter 7, this volume; Furstenberg & Cherlin, 1991; Ihinger-Tallman et al., Chapter 4, this volume; Marsiglio, Chapter 11, this volume). Generally speaking, fathers who have a more cooperative and stronger relationship with their partner or former partner tend to be more committed to their parental identity. The nature of this association is complicated though because fathers' feelings toward their partner and their orientation toward their children may mutually influence one another. Understanding fathers' family-related transitions, and conditional commitment to being a parent, will therefore require in many instances an analysis of fathers' relationship with the mother of their children and the power dynamics of these relationships. Compared with situations involving resident fathers, these dynamics are likely to involve unique features and have profound consequences for nonresident fathers because many will be negotiating with a disgruntled former partner, and in some cases dealing with a new partner as well. Single fathers and stepfathers will have additional issues to deal with given their special circumstances.

Ex-partners' power struggles and disputes will sometimes be heightened by men's and women's different perceptions about cultural scenarios or, more specifically, family reality, parenting expectations, and conflict resolution strategies. Former partners may tend to have very different perceptions about what constitutes an acceptable level and type of paternal involvement. Resident mothers often complain about nonresident fathers' lax child support compliance, whereas some nonresident fathers justify their behavior by observing that their former partner uses child support payments to fulfill her own personal needs rather than those of the child (Gerson, 1993). The power dynamics and negotiated aspects of the interpersonal scripting processes are likely to affect fathers' involvement with their children in these families.

Interpersonal scripting episodes are also critical for many stepfathers because they will tend to develop their roles within an ongoing context of negotiated exchanges with their partner (and her children). These exchanges will oftentimes be affected by individuals' competing views about a stepfather's rights and responsibilities. Compared with biological, coresident fathers, stepfathers' interpersonal exchanges with their partners and children may therefore be burdened with an additional layer of complexity because the cultural scenarios pertaining to stepfathers' roles may be more ambiguous.

Fatherhood: Theory, Social Policy, and Programs

Developing social policies and programs, or business initiatives, that enable "good dads" to be better and "bad dads" to behave at least respectably is a formidable undertaking, particularly for poor inner-city young men. The prevailing view of fatherhood suggests that the "good" label hinges on fathers' desire and ability to transfer financial and emotional resources to their children (Hochschild, in press). Unfortunately, social policies and programs are not typically well suited for facilitating fathers' interpersonal involvement with their children. Likewise, they have been largely ineffective to date in terms of fostering nonresident fathers' financial support. Policymakers have little latitude in the types of direct approaches they can use with respect to the former because a fundamental tenet of American democracy continues to be the need to minimize government's intervention in families' affairs (Fishkin, 1983). However, concerted efforts to influence nonresident fathers' financial support are likely to have much greater promise.

Cultural scenarios pertaining to fatherhood will need to be revised in a manner that accentuates fathers' interpersonal and financial commitment to their children irrespective of fathers' particular circumstances. Men will need to incorporate these images into their intrapsychic scripting for fundamental changes in paternal conduct to occur. Although it will be difficult to foster basic changes in fathers' attitudes and behaviors on a large scale, it seems reasonable to assume that some significant changes can be facilitated. The scope of these changes will depend not only on men's individual-level changes but on social structural changes as well. These patterns of paternal conduct will also require that women provide much of the impetus, especially white middle-class women, because of white men's privileged position in the larger social order (Goode, 1982).

Social interventions must stress different types of enabling strategies that promote fathers' responsibility for their children, interventions that will have to address directly some fathers' poor economic prospects. Thus different strategies will be needed depending upon whether fathers are poverty stricken and highly disadvantaged or members of either the working or the middle classes (Erickson & Gecas, 1991). They will also need to address the reality that the sharp rise in nonmarital births among both poor and affluent women has meant that large numbers of fathers never live with their children (Ahlburg & De Vita, 1992). Indeed, some fathers never attempt to develop any meaningful connection with their children, and many others are initially involved but do not sustain their involvement over time.

Unfortunately, the general policy objective to encourage fathers to be more active in their children's lives cannot be grounded on a preexisting body of social science evidence that clearly supports the notion that children will benefit simply from living with a father figure or from having an involved nonresident father—irrespective of the quality of the father-child relationship (see Griswold, 1993; Marsiglio, Chapter 1, this volume, for reviews of the mixed findings). Some commentators even suggest that it may be wise to

> temper our strong convictions about the social and economic desirability of maintaining men's responsibilities to their children with a recognition that, for some portion of the population, we may be only making more mischief for families whose fortunes we are seeking to improve. (Furstenberg, Chapter 7, this volume, p. 146)

This line of reasoning makes considerable sense when viewed within the context of the prevailing social conditions in the United States. I suspect, however, that an innovative and controversial social policy will need to be adopted before responsible fathering will occur on a large scale in the relatively near future. Such a policy will need to be based, in part, on a parental ideology that conditionally affirms fathers' and mothers' equal rights and obligations to associate with their children and to provide for them financially. This type of approach, though seemingly radical within a U.S. context, has been adopted in Sweden. A formal social policy is warranted because the slow evolution of gender role attitudes and behaviors seems insufficient in and of itself to usher in a dramatic shift in paternal ideology and behavior in the relatively near future. The interconnections between paternal rights and obligations must therefore be stated explicitly and reinforced through formal channels.

Objectives for Reshaping Fatherhood

Although it is difficult to alter many of the social and cultural factors that affect how fathers perceive and practice their paternal roles, the previous theoretical discussion alludes to several themes that can inform efforts to increase resident and nonresident fathers' positive involvement in their children's lives. I explicitly discuss five interrelated objectives that highlight the connection between theoretical and policy issues. This discussion complements Pleck, Lamb, and Levine's (1986) earlier efforts to identify several basic factors that affect levels of paternal involvement: motivation, skills, social supports, and institutional barriers.

Expanding Cultural Scenarios of Responsible Fatherhood. The bread-winner role has been the mainstay of conventional cultural scenarios dealing with the "good dad" image as evidenced by the fact that most men (and women) perceive fatherhood as being inextricably linked to the provider role. It is not surprising then that these scenarios have been the foundation for social policy. However, in recent years policymakers and the general public appear to have become more receptive to the notion that the breadwinner role should not be the sole defining characteristic of a man's worth as a father. This emergent pattern has important implications for nonresident and economically disadvantaged fathers, respectively. In practical terms, there is growing recognition that punitive efforts to solicit child support from disadvantaged fathers, or young fathers with limited education and work skills, can discourage some of these men from developing a commitment to their children. Young fathers' partners may in some instances facilitate this disengagement process (Furstenberg, Chapter 7, this volume).[1]

Policymakers have recently begun to consider the merits of promoting a broader definition of responsible fatherhood as they attempt to address young and poor fathers' dilemmas. Some policymakers have wanted for a number of years to revamp AFDC regulations so that the benefits a mother and her children receive are not adversely affected if the unemployed father resides with them. It is unclear at this point what effect this legislation will have on individuals' decisions to maintain the same household either through cohabitation or marriage (U.S. General Accounting Office, 1992). It will be useful to consider how specific interventions that enable more fathers to live with their children might affect fathers' willingness to adhere to the norm of univocal reciprocity toward their children or alter their sense of generativity. What is clear is that positive interventions designed to motivate a disadvantaged father to develop and maintain his commitment to his child need to receive broad support. Efforts to promote fathers' social psychological investment in their paternal identity are likely to be ineffective, though, unless they are accompanied by opportunities for disadvantaged fathers to contribute significantly to their children's well-being—opportunities that are linked to significant social structural changes.

Social structural factors also play an important role in the lives of middle-class, coresident fathers. Haas's (1993) work in Sweden documents that the gendered nature of the labor market (sex-segregated occupations and the earnings gap) continues to affect Swedish men's paternity leave patterns. Even though Sweden possesses the most progressive set of family ideologies and policies of any country in the world, the Swedish experience has shown that bringing about a fundamental change in coresident fathers' behavior is a slow, protracted process. Unfortunately, there is no reason to believe that promoting fathers' nonbreadwinner roles will have a dramatic impact on paternal involvement levels in the United States without also introducing social structural changes.

Facilitating Paternal Identity and Responsible Fatherhood in Transitional Periods. There are various critical transition periods during which fathers' level of commitment to their paternal identity may be weak, strained, or in a state of flux. It is critical, then, to develop strategies that will heighten fathers' commitment to their children from the outset and/or circumvent fathers' disengagement from their paternal roles when life course events threaten to disrupt their lives and identity salience hierarchy. Those fathers who establish a pattern of constructive paternal involvement from the outset are probably more likely to adopt responsible paternal values and maintain a long-term commitment to their children. Moreover, for those fathers who have already established constructive relationships with their children, social supports should be available to sustain these types of relationships when parents dissolve or redefine their romantic relationships.

Recent pilot programs have attempted to encourage young fathers' long-term paternal involvement by ensuring that they do not retreat from their fatherhood responsibilities because they are presently limited in their ability to contribute financially to their child's support (Furstenberg, Chapter 7, this volume; Johnson & Sum, 1987; Pirog-Good, 1993;

Savage, 1987). Some programs have sought to solicit young unemployed fathers' participation when their children are newborns by providing fathers with alternative avenues for demonstrating responsible behavior (e.g., diligent pursuit of their high school degree, participation in a jobs training program).

These programs have at least three important features. First, they attempt to reinforce an expanded social and legal definition of what a father might be able to do to maintain his paternal identity. By emphasizing the interpersonal aspects of fathering, as well as activities involving responsible school participation and/or work training, these programs attempt to deemphasize the immediate implications of not being able to assume the breadwinner role and in turn emphasize the potential long-term financial benefits to the child. Children may reap other nonmaterial benefits from their relationship with their fathers as well. Second, this type of strategy recognizes the importance of capitalizing on the emotional energy fathers tend to feel immediately prior to and after the birth of their child (see Resnick, cited in Edwards, 1994). During this transitional period, social service and hospital personnel can more easily establish paternity and facilitate young fathers' feelings of univocal reciprocity toward their children. Because young fathers are probably more likely to be self-indulgent than older fathers, it will be a challenge to develop strategies to sustain young fathers' commitment to their children over time and to foster their sense of generativity at such a young age. The National Urban League's "Male Responsibility Project" is noteworthy in this regard because it attempts to alter young inner-city men's views about the subcultural scenarios dealing with fatherhood and masculinity (National Urban League, 1987). Young inner-city men are encouraged to delay fatherhood and concentrate on their educational and work roles. If they do contribute to an unplanned pregnancy and birth, they are expected to place their father identity at the top of their identity salience hierarchy and assume responsibility for their children. The third feature involves the notion that it is more prudent both to establish official paternity at the time of the child's birth and to help fathers adjust to their new role transitions immediately and effectively than to postpone intervention, which will make it more difficult to both establish paternity and provide fathers with ample time to establish a pattern of paternal irresponsibility.

Older fathers of young children could also benefit from comparable programs if these programs reduce resident and nonresident fathers' tendency to distance themselves from their children in response to their struggles with being unemployed. It is important to recognize the potential consequences of this life event for children's well-being because a larger percentage of children will experience a parent who loses his or her job than will experience their parents' divorce (Ray & McLoyd, 1986). Generally speaking, losing a job tends to have more significant consequences for men's mental health status than women's (see Jones, 1991). Many men will perceive that their importance and status within the family decline when they are unemployed. Research also suggests that fathers' job loss tends to accentuate preexisting poor relationships between fathers and their children. These problems are thought to emanate more from the father's personality than from children's behavior. Jones (1991) suggests several strategies for reducing the potentially negative consequences associated with fathers losing their jobs, including the provision of parenting classes, day care, and psychosocial supports that address the individual and family-related problems that result from, or are exacerbated by, fathers' job loss.

Facilitating Fathers' Direct Attachment to Their Children. A fundamental task for social agents will be to enhance fathers' tendency to forge commitments to their children directly. Too many fathers currently develop indirect commitments to their children that are contingent upon their feelings toward their children's mother. Minimizing fathers' conditional commitments is extremely important given the high rate of divorce and nonmarital childbearing in the United States.

Efforts to reduce fathers' conditional commitments will depend upon whether a fundamental transformation occurs in the division of "moral labor." Can a significant proportion of fathers be persuaded (or forced) to increase their child care responsibilities (Gerson, 1993)? To do so, it may be necessary to convince fathers that they, as well as their children, will experience a greater sense of personal development and well-being if they are more involved with their children. Hawkins et al.'s (Chapter 3, this volume) theoretical discussion of the generativity theme could inform an approach that emphasizes the personal growth benefits that more involved fathers might experience. Although this strategy is most likely to resonate with employed, middle-class fathers (Griswold, 1993), less advantaged fathers may benefit as well.

Bringing about a significant societywide change in the way fathers view and treat their children is likely to require dramatic structural, cultural, and legislative changes. Interventions that address the latter will need to grapple with child support, visitation rights, and child custody issues. Although the general public is likely to feel that the movement toward a more standardized and mandatory withholding strategy for a nonresident parent's income has considerable merit, some scholars (Arditti, 1991; Thompson, 1994) voice their skepticism about this approach because it does nothing to facilitate nonresident fathers' interpersonal, fathering roles. It is possible though that the government's efforts to implement a standardized child support system that largely eliminates the interpersonal, negotiated aspects of nonresident parents' (typically fathers') monthly payments to the resident parent will encourage some fathers to take a greater interest in their children's welfare and to interact with them more regularly. The fact that some research has documented a positive correlation between visitation patterns and child support payments is also grounds for encouraging greater paternal involvement among nonresident fathers (Czapanskiy, 1989; Maccoby & Mnookin, 1992; Seltzer, Schaeffer, & Charng, 1989; Teachman, 1991).

It is also worth debating more controversial proposals that could take the form of incentives for increasing fathers' emotional commitment to their paternal identity, their interpersonal involvement with their children, and their willingness to pay child support. For instance, fathers' rights groups in the United States and Canada have lobbied for legislation to ensure that fathers' contributions go directly for children's needs and that their support be contingent on their visitation rights being honored (Bertoia & Drakich, Chapter 12, this volume; Coltrane & Hickman, 1992; Drakich, 1989). This legislation would enable nonresident fathers (especially those who share custody) to know more precisely, and perhaps have *some* say in, how child support payments are used for their children—*provided* fathers fulfill their financial obligations and are not abusive toward, or blatantly neglectful of, their children. It would at least document that fathers' resources are being used for their children and it would encourage more liberal and enforceable visitation schedules (Arditti, 1991). Financially stable, older fathers are likely to be affected most by such an approach, but it could be adapted to accommodate other fathers as well.

Strategies to expand paternal rights are politically volatile because of their perceived consequences for single mothers' autonomy. They have been vigorously challenged by those who feel that they are "problematic insofar as . . . [they] can be used to strengthen men's control over women and children, in a society where men are already dominant socially, economically and politically" (Segal, 1990, p. 51; see Griswold, 1993, for a cogent profeminist analysis of these complex issues). They also could prove to be cumbersome pragmatically because they would necessitate the adjudication of men's and women's separate realities, as discussed earlier. Furthermore, those opposed to financial accountability guidelines point to most fathers' limited involvement in child care during and after their romantic relationship as evidence that it would be inappropriate to expand fathers' rights.

Nevertheless, accountability measures should demonstrate to fathers (and mothers) more clearly that men's commitment to fatherhood is first and foremost to their children, not to their former partner. These strategies might even encourage some nonresident fathers to feel more at ease about their financial responsibilities to their children—with the attendant consequence of facilitating healthier coparenting and father-child relationships. To some extent, a policy that would enable fathers to know that their financial contributions were being used to meet their children's needs could yield outcomes similar to those produced by the government serving as the enforcement agent for mandatory withholding legislation.

Some commentators have suggested that nonresident fathers should have more liberal child visitation rights that are in some instances linked to their child support obligations (Thompson, 1994). This strategy, though contrary to the states' practice of keeping these issues separate, is consistent with Chambers's (1983) and Haskins's (1988) position that child support noncompliance could be improved to the extent that fathers' attachment to their children can be enhanced through quality interaction. A well-defined enforcement strategy for protecting fathers' visitation rights could be developed that supplements the ongoing efforts to standardize child support payments. At the very least, demonstration projects that experiment with provisions designed to balance fathers', mothers', and children's rights and obligations should be evaluated. Unfortunately, there is little political support for such an idea. One reason for this is that vigorous efforts to enforce visitation systematically may prove to be counterproductive in those instances where children are forced to spend time with fathers they don't want to see. The adversarial nature of many coparental relationships complicates this process, an issue I will address shortly.

Just as recent efforts have been made to revise child support policies, attempts have been made at judicial reform so that judges will not unjustly discriminate against fathers in child custody cases. Although many observers contend that judges still tend to favor mothers in such cases, joint legal custody is more frequently granted today than it has been in the past and a small percentage of fathers (typically middle-class fathers) are even awarded sole custody. Fathers with some form of custody are provided with the legal authority to make important decisions on behalf of their children. These fathers are more likely to feel satisfied with their status than noncustodial fathers, and those who are more satisfied with their arrangement tend to engage in more frequent contact with their children (D'Andrea, 1983; Grief, 1979). However, some observers caution against viewing joint legal custody arrangements as a panacea because of the potential coparental conflict they may foster (Griswold, 1993). It is equally important to recognize that most men who are no longer living with their children's mother are still reluctant to assume the daily responsibilities associated with providing the primary residence for their children.

Nonetheless, a growing subset of custodial fathers are single fathers who coreside with their child in addition to having some form of custody status over them. Compared with other types of fathers, these single fathers probably experience a more direct form of commitment to their children and a greater sense of univocal reciprocity given the amount of parental responsibility they have accepted. They are also likely to experience some degree of role ambiguity and role strain because they have not been adequately prepared for this type of status (Greif & DeMaris, 1990), although coresident, single fathers' ability to adapt to their unfamiliar roles may actually be quite high for this select category of fathers (Risman, 1986).[2]

Reconceptualizing Divorce and Coparental Relations. Despite some legal scholars' strong reservations about the feasibility of professional mediation for partners undergoing separation and divorce (Levy, 1993), it seems prudent to give serious consideration to public policies that would provide couples with easy access to mediation during their divorce negotiations as well as subsequently when they may need to address new family situations (Arditti, 1991; Arditti & Kelly, 1994; Lamb & Sagi, 1983; Thompson, 1994). Thompson (1994) argues that policymakers should move away from "clean break" perceptions about divorce and foster instead "a new, and different, postdivorce relationship between former spouses in the interests of their children." The mediation process should also include the negotiation of parenting plans by which former spouses make explicit agreements concerning each partner's long-term postdivorce commitment to the child's well-being. And it could also mean discouraging former spouses from making private agreements that enable them to terminate contact, such as when fathers pay no child support but make no visitation demands, or when mothers request no child support award to avoid obligations to the father. (p. 213)

Voluntary or perhaps mandatory mediation classes for parents who are applying for a divorce could enable parents to understand potential coparenting issues more fully. These sessions might even assist former partners to negotiate their vested interests in a less confrontational manner. Parents could also develop viable strategies for dealing with issues if they do arise. This type of strategy could minimize the extent to which fathers' involvement with their children is curtailed because of conflict between the parents. Mediation sessions could also help fathers understand the unique features of their particular circumstances as nonresident, single, and perhaps even stepfathers. It might also serve to reinforce for fathers the notion that the norm of univocal reciprocity should be linked directly to the father-child relationship and not be contingent on their coresident status. In general, it is essential that a concerted effort be made to ensure that fathers feel connected to their children and develop and maintain a feeling of obligation toward them— without relying exclusively on punitive strategies. Attempts to facilitate nonconfrontational interpersonal scripting episodes, especially during transitional periods from one paternal status to another, could prove beneficial to children as well as adults (Arditti & Kelly, 1994).

Promoting Men's Greater Sensitivity to Children. Although the previous four objectives have focused on issues pertaining to men who are already fathers, it is critical to develop broad-based, farsighted policies/ programs that foster males' greater sensitivity to children in general. Adolescent and adult males should be encouraged to associate with and take care of children in both the public and the private realms (see Levine et al., 1993). Linkages between the education and business communities could be very fruitful in this regard, perhaps in terms of community service requirements. Programs that increase males' exposure to children may facilitate their personal growth and chance for developing a more nurturing personality that is consistent with the generativity and univocal reciprocity themes. Such exposure will by no means guarantee that fathers will assume a more active and positive role in their children's lives. Many men are simply uninterested in spending quality time with their children and may not even feel obliged to provide for them financially. However, the level and quality of many fathers' involvement could be enhanced for those who learn to feel more comfortable with the practical and interpersonal skills associated with child care. Unfortunately, the magnitude of these changes is likely to be quite meager unless the value of male caregiving is institutionally rewarded in the public sphere.

Summary and Conclusions

Recent demographic trends reveal a growing diversity and complexity to fathers' life course patterns even though men may be playing a reduced role as father figures in children's lives in the United States (Eggebeen & Uhlenberg, 1985). As increasing numbers of men are becoming nonresident fathers, stepfathers, and single fathers, it is imperative to examine the relationship between these patterns and social policy. The quality of this type of analysis can be enhanced if it is informed by key theoretical issues salient to contemporary fathers' diverse life course patterns and roles.

I have argued that several theoretical frameworks can inform policymakers' attempts to frame the policy questions relevant to fathers and children. These frameworks can also be used to assess various institutional approaches designed to facilitate father-child relationships. Several concepts including identity salience, commitment, univocal reciprocity, and generativity provide key insights to these relationships. Taken together, they contribute to an understanding of how fathers' participation in the negotiated, interpersonal relationship processes are related to their perceptions of and involvement with their children. Given the diversity of fathers' statuses and roles today, many fathers will experience multiple transitions involving their paternal identities throughout their adult years. Moreover, fathers will sometimes reevaluate the relative importance and nature of their paternal identity in the course of these transitions, and express their commitment to it in various ways.

Researchers need to consider the underlying processes that lead fathers to change their views about the saliency of their paternal identity at different points in their lives. Likewise, the processes by which fathers develop or relinquish a sense of univocal reciprocity toward their children warrant attention. These efforts should ideally contribute to a body of knowledge that will enable policymakers and program developers to make more informed decisions that will enhance fathers' constructive relationships with their children. This research will be invaluable if it enables social agents to understand more fully the processes by which parents' new romantic relationships and fathers' investments in "stepparenting" activities affect fathers' relationships with their own biological children. Meanwhile, other research that focuses specifically on stepfathers could inform recent discussions about reconsidering "the doctrine that family is largely determined by 'blood' and to assign, rather, a higher importance to the emotional, social, and material resources that parents, biological and nonbiological, provide" (Cherlin & Furstenberg, 1994, p. 378).

Throughout this chapter, I emphasized the dynamic and negotiated nature of the culture and conduct of fatherhood, at both the individual and the macro levels. One of the potential consequences of the dynamic nature of fathers' experience is that coparental power issues may become more prominent and complex as individuals attempt to define and redefine, negotiate and renegotiate, their family rights and obligations. As noted earlier, interested parties differ somewhat on what constitutes responsible paternal behavior in specific instances, but most agree in principle that fathers (particularly biological fathers) should contribute to their children's financial maintenance and should probably assume some level of responsibility for child care. Unfortunately, this basic understanding does not alleviate the difficulty of trying to develop a cultural, social, and legal context that is both sensitive to a liberal feminist ideology and supportive of fathers' forming strong paternal identities that are not based on their relationship with their child's mother. From a profeminist perspective, this type of context would need to acknowledge many women's legitimate concerns about their previously abusive partners, be sensitive to the implications of increasing men's power in relation to women and children, and recognize gender differences in parental child care patterns.

During the 1980s, Congress in numerous ways sought to address fathers' declining willingness to meet their financial responsibilities to their children. Congress supported more rigorous paternity establishment procedures, instituted more consistent child support guidelines that minimized judicial discretion, and developed mandatory salary-withholding mechanisms that enlisted the government's intervention in ensuring compliance (Thompson, 1994; see also Garfinkel, Oellerich,

& Robins, 1991). Policymakers must also develop nonpunitive strategies if fundamental, positive changes in paternal conduct, particularly child support, are to be achieved (Furstenberg, 1988b; Thompson, 1994). Activists positioned on various sides of this debate will need to move beyond the rhetoric and rely on commonsense principles for this to occur.

Individual fathers presumably can learn to be more committed to both the interpersonal and the financial expectations associated with their father roles (see Risman, 1986; Silverstein, 1993). Unfortunately, the prospects for fathers collectively becoming more committed to their parenting identity anytime soon appear to be quite slim (Ehrenreich, 1983; Furstenberg, 1988b). This should come as no surprise given that the cultural scenarios of fatherhood are fairly well established, are reinforced by adverse social structural conditions, and are complicated by the growing diversity of fathers' life course patterns. It seems unwise though to dismiss at this time the possibility that innovative social interventions might eventually encourage fathers in general to demonstrate much stronger commitments to their children.

Toward this end, I discussed five objectives for creating social conditions that would be more conducive to different types of fathers developing and maintaining their commitments to their children. These interrelated objectives invite social agents to broaden public perceptions about the meaning of responsible fatherhood, provide fathers with opportunities to adjust to critical transition periods associated with life course events, develop avenues for fathers to forge more direct relationships with their children, create institutionalized strategies that will minimize the adversarial aspects of coparental relationships that often negatively affect fathers' interaction with their children, and provide men with incentives to develop a more nurturing demeanor toward children. It is impossible to predict to what extent these objectives will ever be achieved. Many of the social initiatives in these areas will not appreciably affect fathers' involvement in their children's lives, especially in the short run, but their long-term benefits could be quite substantial. Moreover, the public's and policymakers' heightened interest in fatherhood issues in the United States today provide an appealing set of circumstances for the introduction and evaluation of innovative initiatives that will strengthen fathers' genuine commitment to their children.

Notes

1. Some men, of course, will tend to distance themselves from all of their potential fatherhood roles and disregard the norm of univocal reciprocity irrespective of outsiders' efforts to emphasize the importance of financial support. Formal legal efforts intended to guarantee that fathers support their children are not likely to deter nonresident fathers' interest in their children if they have the means to pay child support.

2. The selectively of this group is primarily due to those men who voluntarily choose to become coresident, single fathers after a separation and/or divorce. Some single fathers may inherit their status by default if their partner dies or deserts her children.

6

Paternal Involvement and Perception Toward Fathers' Roles

A Comparison Between Japan and the United States

MASAKO ISHII-KUNTZ

In many societies, the man's primary family role is that of economic provider. Consequently, women assume responsibility for the day-to-day care and supervision of children and are more likely to provide children with emotional and physical comfort (e.g., Leslie, Anderson, & Branson, 1991). It is important, however, to acknowledge fathers' roles and paternal influences derived from their caretaking, teaching, playing, and one-on-one interaction with a child. Several American studies report that children benefit emotionally and mentally from interaction with their fathers (e.g., Lamb, Pleck, & Levine, 1985, 1987). Paternal involvement also increases marital satisfaction (Morgan, Lye, & Condran, 1988).

Although there is an increasing number of American studies focusing on paternal involvement, we know little about contemporary Japanese fathers and the interaction with their children. Further, a direct comparison of paternal involvement has rarely been made using cross-national

AUTHOR'S NOTE: This chapter previously appeared as an article, with the same title, in *Journal of Family Issues* (1994, Vol. 15, No. 1, 30-48).

data. When the media portrayals of fathers are compared, the level of paternal involvement seems quite different between the two countries. Americans' interest in fathers has been highlighted by popular and professional magazines that emphasize *the new fatherhood*. In this new conception of paternal roles, men are expected to be more actively involved in all aspects of parenting. In contrast, postwar Japanese families are often called "fatherless" (Doi, 1973), and the shallow involvement of Japanese fathers is frequently the subject of the media. For example, a popular television commercial portrays a father as most appreciated when he is healthy and out of the house.

Although these opposite media images of the father exist, a direct Japan-U.S. comparison on fatherhood using comparable data has rarely been made. In this chapter, we assess the extent of men's involvement with their children and father-child perceptions using a representative cross-national sample of fathers and adolescent children.

Paternal Involvement

Since the mid-1970s, an active participation of fathers in caring for and educating children has been valued in the culture of American fatherhood (LaRossa, 1988). It is, however, too hasty to conclude that American fathers are no longer concerned with their breadwinning role. Clearly, their provider role remains a key component of the paternal role in most segments of American society today (Hood, 1986; Pleck, 1983). LaRossa (1988) therefore argues that the idea that American fathers are now intimately involved in raising their children is over-stated. That is, American men are less active in child care than what the culture would have us believe. Thus there is an important gap between *culture* and *conduct* of fatherhood and what we hear about new father-hood may be more journalistic in nature. This, however, is a subject of debate because Pleck (1993) suggests that the level and rate of increase in men's family involvement are greater than others have suggested.

When we focus on the father's actual one-on-one interaction with the child (whether feeding, helping the child with homework, or playing catch), the American fathers with preschool children participate in, on average, about 26% of the total hours spent in direct child care activities (Ishii-Kuntz & Coltrane, 1992a). Other studies indicate that American fathers in two-parent families in which mothers are nonemployed spend about 20% to 25% as much time as mothers do in child care activities

(Lamb, Pleck, Charnov, & Levine, 1987). In two-parent families with employed mothers, the level of paternal engagement is substantially higher than in families with nonemployed mothers (Lamb, Pleck, Charnov, & Levine, 1987; Pleck, 1983). This, however, does not mean that fathers are doing more, but it may mean that mothers are doing less. Thus American fathers are proportionately more involved when mothers are employed, even though their level of involvement in absolute terms may not change significantly.

Other studies found that American fathers spend much more time in child care when there are younger children in the family (Pleck, 1983). American fathers are also more interested in and more involved with their sons than with their daughters (Harris & Morgan, 1991; Lamb, 1981), particularly when their children are school aged (Marsiglio, 1991b). In addition, fathers are more involved with daughters if they also have sons (Harris & Morgan, 1991). However, there are not consistent regional, ethnic, or religious variations in the amount of time that fathers spend with their children (Pleck, 1983). In a more recent study, it was also found that men's participation in housework encourages them to share child-rearing activities with their wives (Ishii-Kuntz & Coltrane, 1992a).

In summary, there have been increases over time in average degrees of paternal involvement in the United States (Robinson, 1975). However, mothers continue to spend more time and take responsibility for most of the day-to-day care of their children regardless of their employment status. Many working women therefore are engaged in a second shift of taking care of their families after returning from a day of paid work (Hochschild, 1989).

In addition to the popular portrayal of "fatherless" families, past studies found that the Japanese father exercises a weak secondary role in the home and that only his economic function has remained strong in the wake of postwar social change (Doi, 1973; Reischauer, 1981). Others, however, argued that the "shadowy" Japanese father may be an exaggerated picture (Ishii-Kuntz, 1992; Vogel, 1979). The father's strong psychological presence at home is evident in a national survey of Japanese adolescents and college students (Office of the Prime Minister, 1981). When asked about the images of mothers and fathers, most Japanese youth emphasized understanding as the ideal maternal disciplinary style and authority as the ideal paternal disciplinary style. The same youth described the behavior of their fathers and mothers as being quite similar to the ideal. In a qualitative study, Ishii-Kuntz

(1993) also found that fathers are psychologically present, which implies that, despite the frequent absence of fathers at home, Japanese children expect their fathers to be authoritarian figures and believe that they, in fact, are.

Although several studies found that Japanese fathers are psychologically present at home, the amount of time they spend with their children is still limited. A national survey, for example, found that fathers in single-earner households, on an average, spent 3 minutes per day on weekdays and 19 minutes per day on weekends on family work including feeding, bathing, helping, and playing with their children (Management and Coordination Agency, 1981). Ishii-Kuntz (1993) also found that more than 75% of fathers in her sample spent less than 1 hour a week with children whereas these fathers spent approximately 54 hours a week, on the average, at work. At a national level, the labor statistics show that approximately 40% of Japanese spend more than 48 hours a week at work (Ministry of Labor, 1989). Further, the same data indicate that only 7.4% of Japanese firms had instituted a 5-day workweek policy whereas the majority of firms still maintained a 6-day workweek policy in 1988 (Ministry of Labor, 1989).

The level of paternal involvement in Japan also varies depending on the age of the child. Takeuchi, Uehara, and Suzuki (1982) surveyed 123 fathers of preschoolers about relations with their children in the first 5 years of life. These Japanese fathers were more active in caretaking when their children were infants and toddlers but reported a significant decline in their involvement during the later preschool years. Sofue (1981) also found that, after the earliest years of childhood, care of Japanese children is given over completely to the mother.

As for social class variation, Isogai (1972) found that middle school students of white-collar "salarymen" had fewer complaints against their fathers than did children of farming or working-class men. However, contact with fathers was limited across occupational groups. That is, both white- and blue-collar workers are frequently absent from their homes on weeknights and weekends. Isogai (1972) also reported that, even in rural Japan, few sons work alongside their fathers.

These studies reveal that there are some parallels as well as differences between American and Japanese fathers. Fathers in both countries are much less involved with children compared with mothers and spend more time with their children when they are younger. However, American fathers seem to interact with their children more frequently than do their Japanese counterparts.

Although these similarities and differences are found in previous research, caution must be taken whenever such a comparison is attempted. This is primarily due to the fact that these comparisons are based on data that are collected using various methods and measurements. Therefore differences in paternal involvement in Japan and the United States have never been assessed using comparable data. This study fills a void by using the data that were simultaneously collected in Japan and the United States using similar sampling procedures and identical questionnaires.

Father's and Child's Perceptions

Another aspect that has not been extensively studied using cross-national data is the affective dimension of father-child relationships. An increasing number of American studies focus on fathers who either share in or take primary responsibility for child care (Lamb, Pleck, & Levine, 1985; Russell, 1986). These studies provide some remarkably consistent results with respect to preschool-aged children whose fathers are involved in a major part of child care. Children with highly involved fathers are characterized by increased cognitive competence, increased empathy, less gender-stereotyped beliefs, and a more internal locus of control (Radin, 1982; Radin & Sagi, 1982).

Japanese studies also suggest that fathers' involvement with their children is extremely important, and thus the lack of such interaction leads to numerous behavioral problems of children. For example, the refusal of children to attend school, increasing rates of juvenile delinquency, and children's mental health problems and suicide are frequently attributed to Japanese fathers' physical absence from home resulting from work-related demands (Kumagai, 1981; Shwalb, Imaizumi, & Nakazawa, 1987).

Several American scholars have attempted to explain why fathers' involvement has an important impact on children. M. E. Lamb (1987), for example, explains why fathers' involvement has such a positive impact on children. First, particularly in the area of cognitive competence, children with two highly involved parents are exposed to the diversity of stimulation that comes from interaction with different people. Second, high paternal involvement allows both parents to engage in what is important to them. For example, fathers have an opportunity to satisfy a desire to become close to their children. Mothers maintain closer relationships with their children while pursuing career and other goals. In other words, increased paternal involvement in the family is likely to make both parents feel satisfied with their lives.

The foregoing explanations suggest that, although the quantity of paternal involvement is crucial, the quality of such involvement may also have a significant effect on children and fathers. What is perhaps most important but largely unexplored in previous studies is the affective dimension of father-child relationships. Among the previous studies that reported the positive impact of paternal involvement on children, few explored how fathers and children evaluate their relationships and to what extent such an evaluation is related to the frequency of their interaction. It is usually assumed that increased paternal involvement facilitates closer and richer personal relationships with children. Highly involved fathers may feel closer and more intrinsically important to their children. Thus greater mutual affect may be strongly associated with more involved parenting.

These explanations raise a second question: If an increased paternal involvement is associated with more affective father-child relationships, does this hold cross-culturally?

Method

Sample

The data analyzed here came from the Fathers and Children Survey sponsored by the Japanese government's Management and Coordination Agency (1986). The Japanese survey was conducted by the New Information Center, and an English version of the identical survey was simultaneously conducted by Kane, Parsons & Associates, Inc., in the United States. Respondents in two countries were generated by multi-stage cluster sampling. In the first stage, four or five regions in each country were randomly selected. The second stage of sampling differed somewhat between the two countries. In Japan, Family Registrar was used to randomly generate households. In the United States, households were selected randomly in the neighborhoods when the particular communities were chosen. These procedures resulted in nationally representative samples in both countries. The final sample in each country consists of those meeting the study criteria—a father and his child who is between 10 and 15 years of age living at home. If there was more than one child in the household in this age category, a focal child was randomly selected for an interview. The final sample sizes were 1,149 Japanese and 1,000 American father-child pairs. Face-to-face interviews were conducted separately for fathers and children from October through December 1986.

The major demographic characteristics of the sample are presented in Table 6.1. Significant cross-national differences were found with respect to father's age, education, occupation, mother's employment status, and child's birth order. The majority of Japanese fathers (65%) are in their forties and about one in four Japanese fathers are in their late thirties. The ages of American fathers are more evenly distributed, with almost 30% of them in their late thirties and early forties. Overall, American fathers in this sample are younger than their Japanese counterparts. A majority of fathers in both countries have completed at least high school. Approximately 34% of American fathers have at least some college education whereas the comparable figure for Japanese fathers is 27%. Given Japan's emphasis on education, this proportion of sample fathers who had some college education appears low. However, this figure is comparable to Ministry of Education statistics, which reported that about 28% of Japanese men went to college in 1988 (Ministry of Education, 1991).

Concerning fathers' occupations, whereas almost one in five American fathers have professional jobs, only 6% of Japanese fathers are in the same category. Japanese fathers are more likely to have clerical jobs and are more likely to be engaged in farming and fishing. About 44% of American mothers in the sample were employed full time whereas the comparable proportion for Japanese women was 16%. In contrast, one in four Japanese women are self-employed whereas only 5% of American mothers reported being self-employed. Finally, there are more *only* children in the American sample (12%) compared with the Japanese sample (8%).

Measurement

Paternal Involvement. The extent of paternal involvement was measured using children's and fathers' responses. Children were asked, "How much time do you spend talking or playing with your father or having him help you with your homework on days when your father is (or is not) working?" For the purpose of data analysis at a multivariate level, paternal involvement was reclassified to include four categories

Table 6.1 Demographic Characteristics of the Sample

Characteristic	Japan (n = 1,149)		United States (n = 1,000)		χ^2
Father's age					221.8*
29 ≤	0		20	(2.0)	
30-34	13	(1.1)	138	(13.8)	
35-39	293	(25.5)	297	(29.7)	
40-44	431	(37.5)	293	(29.3)	
45-49	318	(27.7)	155	(15.5)	
50 ≥	94	(8.2)	96	(9.6)	
Father's education					26.4*
less than high school	296	(25.8)	176	(17.6)	
high school	531	(46.2)	471	(47.1)	
college or more	308	(26.8)	343	(34.3)	
Father's occupation					416.6*
professional	73	(6.4)	187	(18.7)	
managerial	124	(10.8)	112	(11.2)	
clerical	213	(18.5)	15	(1.5)	
sales	73	(6.4)	57	(5.7)	
service	25	(2.2)	56	(5.6)	
laborers	303	(26.4)	412	(41.2)	
others	314	(27.3)	95	(9.5)	
not employed	12	(1.0)	41	(4.1)	
Mother's employment status					291.4*
full time	184	(16.2)	421	(44.2)	
part time	264	(23.2)	195	(20.5)	
self-employed	290	(25.5)	52	(5.5)	
not employed	387	(34.1)	275	(28.9)	
Son's age					3.9
10-12	260	(22.6)	297	(29.7)	
13-15	305	(26.5)	276	(27.6)	
Daughter's age					2.2
10-12	254	(22.1)	206	(20.6)	
13-15	330	(28.7)	221	(22.1)	
Birth order					12.4*
only child	86	(7.5)	117	(11.7)	
oldest child	473	(41.2)	370	(37.0)	
younger child	586	(51.0)	503	(50.3)	

NOTE: Percentages are in parentheses.
*p ≤ .01.

(each with 25% of the sample) ranging from 1 = *not at all involved* to 4 = *very actively involved*. Fathers were also asked how often (1 = *never* to 6 = *every day*) they are engaged in activities with their children: eating breakfast (or dinner) together, talking to each other, helping the child with his or her homework, and having time together for sports, taking walks, and other recreational activities. In addition, fathers were asked, "Which of the activities do you most often do on weekends (or days when you are not working)?" They chose three from six activities including spending the day at home or outside with children, relaxing alone, pursuing hobbies at home or outside (e.g., fishing, sports), working in and around the house, and doing work-related activities.

Children's Perception. Two measures of child's perception of his or her father were used. Children responded with yes or no to the statements: "I think my father really understands me" and "I think my father is very reliable."

Fathers' Perception. Men's own perceptions toward the paternal role were measured using two items. Fathers responded with yes or no to the statements: "I feel my relationship with my child is distant" and "I feel I understand my child well."

Control Variables. We found earlier that American and Japanese fathers differ significantly with respect to several key demographic variables. Therefore we included control variables: father's age, education, occupation, mother's employment status, child's sex, and the birth order.

Analyses

Descriptive statistics will be presented to compare the extent of paternal involvement in Japan and the United States. To examine the relationship between paternal involvement and children's and fathers' perceptions at a multivariate level, logit models are used. Logit models are a subset of log-linear models, and they are developed to analyze dichotomous dependent variables (Hanushek & Jackson, 1977). Logit models assume that the log-odds ratio of the dependent variable is linearly related to the independent variables. Therefore parameters generated by these models are interpreted in terms of odds and odds ratios.

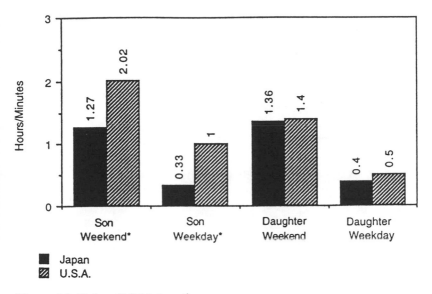

Figure 6.1. Father-Child Interaction
*$p \leq .001$.

Results

Children's reports on their fathers' involvement are presented in Figure 6.1. Although there is a significant cross-national difference in paternal involvement with sons, no such difference was found in father-daughter interaction. As shown in Figure 6.1, American boys, on the average, spend about 2 hours per day on a weekend and 1 hour on a weekday with their fathers. In contrast, Japanese boys spend only about half of that time with their fathers. American men interact with their adolescent sons much more frequently than with their daughters, which is consistent with the previous findings (Harris & Morgan, 1991; Morgan et al., 1988). Japanese fathers, on the other hand, spend slightly more time with their daughters than with sons.

Figure 6.2 shows the proportion of fathers who engage daily in various activities with their children. Although more Japanese fathers (54.6%) reported having breakfast with their children than their American counterparts (18.5%), more U.S. fathers reported playing sports, helping children with their homework, chatting, and eating dinner with

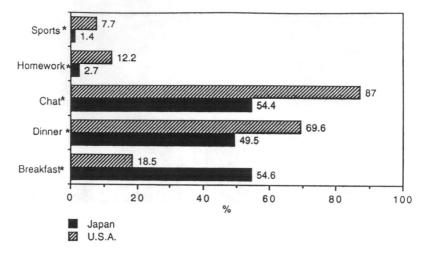

Figure 6.2. Fathers With "Everyday" Response
*p ≤ .001.

children as their daily routines. Many Japanese men either stay late at work or relax with their colleagues at bars after work, thus missing dinner and evening hours with their families (Ishii-Kuntz, 1993). Therefore Japanese men may consider breakfast time to be an opportunity to interact with their children.

In terms of various activities, approximately 87% of American fathers chat with their children every day compared with only 54% of Japanese fathers. Almost 70% of American (as opposed to 49% of Japanese) fathers eat dinner with their children daily. Fathers in both countries spend much less time engaging in sports and other recreational activities with children: 7.7% of American and 1.4% of Japanese fathers reported doing so daily. Finally, about 1 in 8 American fathers help children with their homework every day whereas the comparable ratio for Japanese fathers is 3 in 100.

Figure 6.3 shows how fathers in Japan and the United States spend their weekends. Whereas a majority of American men spend weekends with children (63.6%) and/or doing housework (72.6%), less than half (41%) of Japanese men interact with children, and only 7.3% of them are engaged in housework. Compared with their American counterparts, Japanese men are more likely to spend weekends alone or pursue their

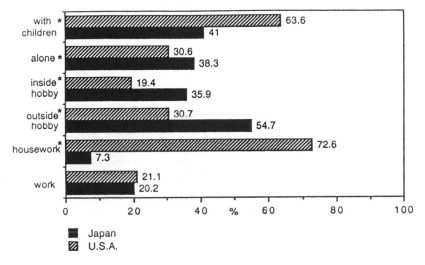

Figure 6.3. How Fathers Spend Weekends
*p ≤ .001.

own hobbies at home or outside. In her sample of Japanese fathers, Ishii-Kuntz (1993) found that more than 80% of men spend their weekends golfing, going to Pachinko (Japanese pinball machines) parlors or movies, or simply watching television. Of interest, similar proportions of Japanese and American men (20.2% and 21.1%, respectively) are engaged in work-related activities on weekends.

In summary, our data show that fathers in the United States spend considerably more time with their sons than do Japanese fathers. However, the amount of father-daughter interaction was similar between the two countries. American fathers also chat, have dinner, and play sports with their children, and help children with their homework, more frequently than Japanese fathers. Japanese men, on the other hand, are more likely to have breakfast with their children. Japanese men's limited interaction with their children is also evident in how they spend their weekends. Whereas more Japanese men spend weekends alone or pursuing their own hobbies, American men spend more time interacting with their children and sharing housework with their wives.

Table 6.2 shows the logit model parameters that are expressed in terms of odds. As shown, the increased paternal involvement is significantly associated with American children viewing their fathers as under-

Table 6.2 Logit Estimates for Paternal Involvement and Children's Perception[a]

| Variable[b] | Understanding | | | Reliable | | |
	Japan	United States	Difference	Japan	United States	Difference
Paternal involvement	1.30	1.63*	0.33	0.98	1.78**	0.80*
Chatting with children	1.59*	2.09***	0.50	1.35	1.89**	0.54
Dinner with children	1.22	1.99**	0.77*	1.13	1.75**	0.62*
Breakfast with children	1.62*	1.13	−0.49	1.45*	1.22	−0.23

a. The variables—father's age, education, and occupations; mother's employment status; child's sex; and the birth order—are controlled.
b. The baseline categories are *not at all involved* (paternal involvement), *never* (chatting, dinner, and breakfast), and *no* (understanding and reliable).
*$p \leq .05$, **$p \leq .01$, ***$p \leq .001$.

standing and reliable. In other words, children who frequently interact with their fathers are almost twice as likely to report that their fathers are understanding and reliable as children who have less interaction with their fathers. Of interest, no such relationships were found in the Japanese sample.[1] However, a significant cross-national difference was found only with respect to the impact of paternal involvement on children's rating of how reliable their fathers are (difference = .80).

Turning to various activities in which fathers are engaged, we found that American children who frequently chat and/or have dinner with their fathers are more likely to view their fathers as understanding and reliable. Japanese children who frequently chat with their fathers are also more likely to feel that their fathers are understanding. In addition, Japanese children who frequently have breakfast with their fathers indicated that their fathers are understanding and reliable. However, although the effects of having dinner with children are found to be much stronger for the American sample (differences of .77 for understanding and .62 for reliable), the effects of chatting with children and having breakfast are not significantly different between the two countries.

Table 6.3 presents the impact of paternal involvement on fathers' own evaluations. In both Japan and the United States, increased paternal involvement is related to positive self-image of fathers. That is, fathers whose children reported frequent father-child interaction are significantly more likely to view themselves as understanding and emotionally close parents. Both Japanese and American fathers who frequently chat

Table 6.3 Logit Estimates for Paternal Involvement and Fathers' Perception[a]

	Understanding			Emotionally Close		
Variable[b]	Japan	United States	Difference	Japan	United States	Difference
Paternal involvement	1.68*	1.53*	−0.15	1.48*	2.48***	1.00**
Chatting with children	1.77**	2.53***	0.76*	1.85**	2.34***	0.49
Dinner with children	1.89**	2.03***	0.14	1.67*	1.99**	0.32
Breakfast with children	2.04***	1.56*	−0.48	1.95**	1.83**	−0.12

a. The variables—father's age, education, and occupations; mother's employment status; child's sex; and the birth order—are controlled.
b. The baseline categories are *not at all involved* (paternal involvement), *never* (chatting, dinner, and breakfast), and *no* (understanding and emotionally close).
*$p \leq .05$, **$p \leq .01$, ***$p \leq .001$.

and have dinner and breakfast with children also have a positive evaluation about their paternal role. When the effects of these activities are compared between the two countries, American fathers who spend more time with their children feel significantly closer to their children than do their Japanese counterparts. Another difference was found concerning the impact of chatting with children on father's perception of how understanding they are: The impact was significantly stronger for American fathers.

Compared with the relationship between paternal involvement and children's perception, the amount of father-child interaction has a more profound and similar effect on fathers' own evaluations in both countries. This implies that the increased paternal involvement has a more direct effect on fathers than their offspring.

Discussion

This study compared the extent of paternal involvement and the child's and father's perception between Japan and the United States. We found that American fathers spend almost twice as much time with their sons than do their Japanese counterparts. However, no such cross-national difference was found with respect to the amount of father-daughter interaction.

Furthermore, Japanese fathers were found to spend slightly more time with their daughters than with their sons. In general, Japanese parents tend to be much more protective of their daughters than their sons from birth to adult years. A longer period of single daughters' cohabitation with parents and a lower propensity to live alone (Brinton, 1992) seem to support the above contention. To many Japanese fathers, their daughters' wedding day is the saddest time of life because they feel that their daughters have been "taken away" from them (Chiba, 1988). On the other hand, adult sons are much more likely to form extended family households. Because of these differences, it is speculated that Japanese fathers feel that they need to spend more time with their daughters than with their sons.

When we examined different activities, we found American fathers chat, have dinner, and play sports with their children more frequently than do Japanese men. American men also help with children's homework more often than their Japanese counterparts. Of interest, Japanese fathers have breakfast with their children more frequently than American fathers. This suggests that breakfast time is frequently used by Japanese fathers to make up their frequent absence resulting from work demands. These findings imply that, when we compare the extent of paternal involvement cross-nationally, it is necessary to examine different types of father-child activities rather than using aggregate time spent between fathers and children.

Another interesting set of findings from this study concerns the different pattern of associations for paternal involvement and children's perceptions toward their fathers in the two countries. Whereas the amount of father-child interaction is significantly associated with how children view their fathers in the United States, Japanese children's perceptions of their fathers are largely unaffected by the amount of time they spend with their fathers. Stated another way, American children who spend more time with their fathers are significantly more likely to view their fathers as understanding and reliable. This finding, however, does not mean that father-child interaction in Japan is largely ineffective. Indeed, children who have breakfast time with their fathers in Japan are more likely to have positive views toward their fathers.

In both countries, we found that the increased paternal involvement is associated with positive assessment of a father's own role. Fathers who have longer hours of interaction with their children, who chat, and who have dinner and breakfast more frequently with them see themselves as understanding and emotionally close. This supports our prediction that increased father-child interaction is associated with more affective assessment of fathers' roles. Most important, this association holds for both Japanese and American father-child pairs.

The history of fatherhood in Japan differs greatly from that of the United States. However, recent social and demographic changes suggest that Japanese men may be undergoing a transition toward being more "nurturant fathers" than "workaholic absent fathers" (Ginsberg, 1990). This is due to increasing health and family problems that working men face ranging from *Karoshi* (death by fatigue), which many middle-aged Japanese men have suffered, to children's *Toko kyohi* (refusal to attend school).

Another important factor related to paternal involvement is the decline in extended households in Japan. Tsuya (1992) found that coresidence with parents increases wives' full-time employment in the labor market, but at the same time, it reduces husbands' participation in housework and child care. Because multigenerational coresidence in Japan is predicted to decline (Martin & Tsuya, 1991), the availability of older female family members to ease burdens of household responsibilities may decrease in the future. This and increasing female labor force participation, in turn, place more demands on Japanese men to take an active role in parenting and household responsibilities.

Despite a lower level of fathers' involvement, many Japanese children seem to learn paternal authority. It is, therefore, important to acknowledge an important mediating role that Japanese mothers play in transmitting fathers' values to children. This aspect of mothers' role was described by Vogel (1963), who surveyed middle-class urban homes and found that Japanese mothers built up an artificial image of the absentee father as an authoritarian figure. We can argue that, because of Japanese mothers' somewhat exaggerated portrayal of fathers' authority and its impact on children, the amount of father-child interaction does not have a direct effect on how children view their fathers. Furthermore, it may be that mother-child (as opposed to father-child) interaction has a much more profound impact on how Japanese children see their fathers. We found that maternal employment is negatively related to children's perception of their fathers. This implies that, when Japanese mothers are not available as mediators to convey a positive image of fathers, children's views of their fathers become less positive regardless of the amount of father-child interaction. Finally, this study demonstrates that a direct cross-national comparison is useful to reevaluate some of the crucial assumptions we make when we examine father-child relationships.

Note

1. In a separate analysis, the interaction terms among countries, paternal involvement, and father's (understanding and emotional closeness) or child's (understanding and reliable) perception were included to examine whether the effects of paternal involvement on children's and fathers' perceptions vary between Japan and the United States. The results in Tables 6.2 and 6.3 are obtained from analyzing logit models separately for each country. These tables also include the difference in effects from the above pooled analyses.

7

Fathering in the Inner City

Paternal Participation and Public Policy

FRANK F. FURSTENBERG Jr.

High levels of marital instability and soaring rates of out-of-wedlock childbearing among couples who live together temporarily, if at all, have dramatically revised the social organization of parenthood in the United States (Ahlburg & De Vita, 1992; Bumpass, 1990). Households containing children and their biological parents, once the dominant form of the family in this country, have steadily receded during the last third of the twentieth century (Furstenberg & Cherlin, 1991). The nuclear family form is still far from obsolete, especially among middle-class whites. But parenting apart has become standard practice for African Americans, some Hispanic subgroups (most notably Puerto Ricans), and, to a growing extent, low-income whites as well (U.S. Bureau of the Census, 1992). Most African American children growing

AUTHOR'S NOTE: This chapter was prepared while the author was a Fellow at the Center for Advanced Study in the Behavioral Sciences. I am grateful for the financial support provided by John D. and Catherine T. MacArthur Foundation #8900078. The initial research was supported by grants from Manpower Demonstration Research Corporation and by the MacArthur Foundation Research Network on Successful Adolescent Development Among Youth in High-Risk Settings. I benefited from support and comments by Gordon Berlin and Kay Sherwood at MDRC and my colleagues in the MacArthur Research Network. I also gratefully acknowledge the assistance in collecting data of collaborators on the project including Jeanne Brooks-Gunn, Nadra Franklin, Jacqueline Hart, Spencer Middleton, and Barbara Sugland.

up today never reside with their biological fathers or reside with them only briefly; only a small minority live with them continuously throughout childhood (Bumpass & Sweet, 1989).

These demographic trends conceal a tremendous variety of experiences among black parents who do not adhere to the once (and probably still) widely cherished ideal of raising children in a nuclear family. Some nonresidential fathers play an active role in their children's lives; many do not or do so only for a time (Mott, 1990; Seltzer, 1994). This chapter tries to look at the reasons some fathers become involved and stay involved and the reasons others do not.

My intention is to build this understanding from the ground level, using data from case studies of young parents. This chapter makes no claims of testing theories of why men become involved fathers, whether explanations might be economic, sociological, or social psychological (Marsiglio, Chapter 1, this volume). I am attempting only to provide a good sense of how young mothers and fathers account for the way that men perform as parents.

Because some of the data that I draw upon were initially intended for policymakers, particularly those interested in designing services for young fathers, I conclude by addressing the question of how to build stronger alliances between men and their children. This is no easy task, and the reader should be forewarned that my observations do not readily translate into promising programs or policies.

Framing the Question

The research reported in this chapter was stimulated by work on fathering that I have done over the past decade or so. I have argued that two seemingly contradictory trends in men's involvement in the family are occurring at once: A growing number of fathers are retreating from the family at the very same time that others are becoming more involved parents (Furstenberg, 1988b). These divergent patterns are to some extent class linked and class located, but at all social levels, parents are reinterpreting their responsibilities, resulting from a breakdown in the gender-based division of labor.

The grim side of the picture emerges from a series of social and demographic surveys examining men's involvement with their children when they do not live with them. The evidence is quite compelling: The great majority of fathers who live apart from their children see them infrequently and support them irregularly (King, 1994; Seltzer & Bianchi, 1988).

Some researchers contend that this pattern of shadow fathering—a family role without much substance—in fact parallels relatively weak ties among fathers and their children who reside together (Morgan & Harris, 1991). Yet, over the same period of time that fathers have been retreating from the family, the segment of highly dedicated dads seems to be growing as well. More married fathers may be assuming a larger share of child-rearing responsibilities, and the number of custodial fathers and men sharing custody with the mothers of their children is growing. Higher paternal commitment can be traced to a growing cultural emphasis on fathering, increasing demands for child care assistance from women in the labor force, and increasing social constraints on nonresident fathers who attempt to escape their financial and emotional obligations (Griswold, 1993).

There is no reason to believe that these competing trends in men's involvement cannot coexist. As William J. Goode (1982) has perceptively pointed out, the power of men to resist cultural change that robs them of their traditional prerogatives should not be underestimated. Even when that resistance weakens, high levels of marital instability foster paternal disengagement because men may eschew responsibilities for children from a prior marriage even as they assume them in a new family. It is entirely possible, then, that more good dads and bad dads are being produced at the same time. What I have referred to elsewhere as the "good dads/bad dads complex" is best thought of as a set of conflicting cultural standards rather than as discrete packages of behaviors acquired by some men but not others.

Disadvantaged minorities represent a special case of the general transformation in parenthood that has occurred during the second half of the twentieth century. Quantitative differences in the level of family change create qualitatively distinctive kinship responses. All but a tiny minority of low-income blacks will have children before they marry, if they marry at all. And most who marry will not remain in stable unions. Thus parenting apart has become standard practice for most blacks, especially if they are poor when their families are formed.

The divergence between the family experiences of white and black Americans has attracted a tremendous amount of political attention and aroused enormous public concern, presumably because of the absence of male influence and support in the lives of black children. A continuous and contentious debate has been waged over the past several decades among researchers and public policy advocates about the sources and consequences of race differences in marriage patterns. Numerous explanations have been advanced to account for the distinctive features of family formation among black Americans ranging from practices rooted in Africa, the experience of slavery and exploitation, racial discrimination and social isolation, persistent poverty and inequality, and adaptation to policies designed or ill-designed to remedy racism and economic disadvantage (Cherlin, 1992; Farley & Allen, 1987; Gutman, 1977; Hill, 1993; Jencks & Petersen, 1991; Massey & Denton, 1993; Murray, 1984; Rainwater & Yancey, 1967; Ruggles, 1994; Valentine, 1968; Wilson, 1978, 1987).

I doubt that it is possible to step back completely from this highly charged discussion of the causes of African American family patterns. Still, it may be informative for those who want to understand possible points of intervention to know more about how family roles—especially the responsibilities of fathers—are defined by young people forming families today in inner-city communities. At the same time, it is important to keep in mind that the youths in this study represent only a small, albeit a highly visible, segment of African Americans. I do not intend my observations to apply to African Americans more generally, and, conversely, much of what I will report about fathering in the inner city is not confined to African American parents.

How the Data Were Collected

The objective of this chapter is deceptively simple: to discover how young parents construe paternal obligations and how they understand the barriers to fulfilling those obligations. Over the course of 5 years or so, I have had lengthy conversations with 20 young parents, several of whom had been couples at one time. Most of the young adults I interviewed were part of a sample of 250 children of teenage mothers whom I have been studying since the mid-1960s. (The others were their partners.) The young adults—now in their mid-twenties—were the offspring of women who initially had been featured in a study of adolescent parents in Baltimore (Furstenberg, 1976; Furstenberg, Brooks-Gunn, & Morgan, 1987). During the course of that study, the children were interviewed when they were preschoolers, again when they were in their mid-teens, and a third time in 1987 when most were in their early twenties. By that point, about a third of them had become parents. After the last of these interviews in 1987, Brooks-Gunn and I conducted a set of "delayed probe" interviews with 15 of the 250 young people whom we had surveyed, designed to remove some of the constraints imposed by the survey format.

I expanded my qualitative case studies of the Baltimore youth with a second series of interviews in 1991, when I was asked by the Manpower Demonstration Research Corporation (MDRC) to conduct a focus group of young mothers exploring the reasons men remain involved with their children or disengage from them (Furstenberg, Sherwood, & Sullivan, 1992). Following the focus group, I talked to some of these women and their partners individually. Unlike the interviews in 1987, these talks were primarily about parenthood.

Two years later, I reinterviewed half of the 20 young adults that I had talked to previously. This time I spoke to each two or three times over a period of several months and also interviewed a partner or parent to get a different perspective on what I was learning from the young adults. These interviews were supplemented by a dozen additional interviews conducted by students collaborating on the project. These most recent conversations dealt with parenthood issues extensively.

I make no claims that the participants I interviewed at length are representative of a larger population, even of the Baltimore study. They were selected catch-as-catch-can to provide a variety of experiences. But because I know a lot about them, I can locate them in a larger universe of youth who are often labeled as members of the "underclass." This social category usually conveys impressive homogeneity. However, considerable variation existed even within this cadre of second-generation teenage parents.

Daddies and Fathers: What Fatherhood Involves

Classifying fathers along a single dimension of caring is bound to oversimplify men's involvement with their children. Men have complex ways of expressing their commitments to children, and children have equally complex ways of admitting and honoring these commitments. Still, both parents and children readily distinguish between good and bad fathering. Both the individual interviews with men and women and the group discussion that I held with young mothers revealed a widely shared standard for what is involved in being a "good father." I detected little or no variation in this standard when my informants recalled experiences with their own fathers and when they discussed how men should behave in the families they were forming. Many referred to the standard as "doing for your children," which might be taken to mean "doing right" by them.

A distinction was often drawn between "fathers" and "daddies," that is, biological parents and sociological parents. Speaking of her father, who has been a drug addict for many years, Shawna Nelson told me, "If I take friends over there, I don't introduce him as my father. . . . I never did call him my daddy." Although the contrast between daddies and fathers was widely recognized, some don't even reserve the term *father* to mean the progenitor. Tyron Lewis, one of the men whom I spoke to several times, stated that the "man who bore him" wasn't his father: "A father is the person that is going to raise you and keep you on the right track and really put your mind in the right frame of mind." Most everyone in my study would agree with Tyron that "doing for your children" above all means that fathers are actively involved in their children's lives. If they are not, someone else may take their place as the child's daddy.

Amy Roberts, a 24-year-old mother, recalled what her boyfriend, Jordon, promised when she told him that she was pregnant: "Do whatever you want to do," he said. "I'll do what I have to." When I asked what he had meant, Amy explained:

> That he was going to take care of his daughter. He was going to be the father. Be the man he suppose to be and take care of his responsibilities by taking care of the child. . . . That he was going to be there for Nicole when Nicole needed him, and he was going to be there even when she didn't need him.

In a group discussion with young mothers, Amy's views about the role of fathers in their children's lives were echoed by a number of other women. Among other things, "doing for your child" means that fathers are there to "buy the Pampers," an oft-repeated phrase that represents "bringing home the bacon" in a much reduced form. As one mother in the group explained, "Sometimes when we can't do, they should be able to do."

Almost everyone present shared Amy's view that fatherhood in-volved more than just helping to support children financially. Concern that fathers remain emotionally involved in their children's lives ran high. Most had vivid memories of their fathers fading out of their lives or, like Shawna, were still dealing with fathers who aren't really there.

Perhaps it is not surprising, then, that "doing for your child" means maintaining a constant presence in the child's life. "Just a phone call before bedtime," one member of the group stated. Another went even further: "I wouldn't care if he didn't give him nothing, but if he was to spend more time with him. . . . I would have paid child support if he would just spend a little more time with the children."

This quote should not be taken literally or, at least, not understood to mean that most young mothers would actually forgo financial support if their children's fathers were more emotionally reliable. In part, many women are discounting the expectation that men will provide regular assistance. At least, they should expect—as several put it—that fathers provide some "quality time." Above all, these strongly articulated opinions testify that "being a daddy" involves more than material assistance.

I found no disagreement among any of the young men that I spoke to about the meaning of "doing for your children." Hal, a recent father, observed: "Some people are just not ready for that kind of responsibil-ity. It's a cop-out to leave. I wanted more for my son than just another cop-out. . . . I am going to make sure he has the best."

The absence of variation in men's and women's definitions of what being a good father meant contrasts starkly to men's performance as fathers. A number of the men that I spoke to were, by their own admission, finding it difficult to live up to their standards, much less to satisfy the demands of their former partners.

Jordon Jones, the father of Amy Roberts's child, would not have taken issue with her statement about what fathers should do for their children. His own ideas of being a good father were very close to what Amy had understood Jordon to mean when he promised to "do for his child." Jordon spoke disparagingly of his buddies who are just making kids and not taking care of them. Yet Jordon admits that he is pretty much like his friends. He sees Nicole only infrequently and doesn't really have the means to support her: "When she sees me she knows who I am. But she asks where I am." Jordon says that he tries to be a good father, but Amy makes demands on him that he can't satisfy. In fact, Jordon confessed to me that all he has accomplished in life "is making three babies" whom he can't really care for.

This theme of broken promises recurs among most of the young adults I talked to. Lionnel and Wanda, another couple I interviewed, told a story that closely resembles Amy and Jordon's respective accounts. Wanda now bitterly recalls Lionnel's promise when she first became pregnant 7 years ago: "He was going to do for him. Things his father didn't do for him. He turned out and did the same as far as his kids. He's not around for them." As it happened, I had talked to Lionnel back in 1987 shortly after his son was born. His interview confirms Wanda's recollection. Speaking of his son:

> I love him a lot. He will be with me one day. I'll see to that. I'm not gonna let him go through what I went through because I can see how much it does hurt. I want him to know that I am his father. . . . I'll do all I can for him.

Lionnel didn't mention that shortly after Wanda became pregnant he had disappeared for 6 months. But he admitted even then that he was having trouble living up to his own standards, much less satisfying Wanda's mother, who expects more from him than he can do right now. When I visited Lionnel again in 1993, he had a second child by Wanda but had seen neither of his children for the past 6 months. Wanda obtained a court order preventing him from visitation after Lionnel refused to return the children after a visit to his family. Lionnel explained that there was a family misunderstanding. Wanda said he tried to kidnap his son.

Lionnel is currently not paying child support. Unemployed and recovering from an illness, Lionnel seems resigned to losing contact with the children, although he says not seeing them "weighs on him." When I spoke to him, however, he seemed more concerned with the loss of his relationship to his most recent girlfriend.

Men like Lionnel and Jordon are common among the young fathers I studied. But I also spoke to other fathers who were managing to remain involved in their children's lives. Tyron Lewis worried a lot about being a good dad long before Tyron Jr. was born. I first met Tyron in 1987, and like many of his 20-year-old counterparts in my study, Tyron was struggling at the time to get a stable job and strike out on his own. At the time, Tyron was involved with "a beautiful young lady" but insisted that "right now I'm just not ready to become a father. . . . There is always time for children. I figure around 25 or 26, I'll think about having a child."

Six years later, things had not worked out for Tyron as he had planned. Unemployed for several months, he was staying at home with his 3-year-old and looking after the 10-year-old son of his partner. Tyron had been able to obtain de facto custody of his child when Tyron Jr.'s mother, an alcoholic, was neglecting him. Distracted by his own concerns about making a living and inexperienced in child care, Tyron was feeling the pressure that he had hoped to avoid.

Ricky Andrews, the father of Angie Tyler's child, had the easygoing and authoritative manner with his 4-year-old daughter that Tyron lacked. Ricky's appearance at the doorstep of Angie Tyler's house brought the six or so children in the household out to greet him, as well as a swarm of other kids who were playing on the block. I had met Ricky 2 years earlier, shortly after I had interviewed Angie. Here's what Angie told me about Ricky's performance as a father: "Ricky checks on us because my mother made him promise to make sure we OK."

"Why Ricky?" I asked Angie, who replied, "Because she always know he always been around and be a big part of our lives. . . . She know he would be the best person to look out for us."

"And so he's still quite involved with the kids and also your sister's kids?" I asked.

"They call him daddy. The oldest one [not Ricky's daughter], she call him daddy. I mean he basically the only steady male figure that's been there, you know."

In the Baltimore study there are unquestionably fewer Rickys and Tyrons than Jordons and Lionnels. Yet men who stay involved with their children are esteemed by everyone I spoke to, and those who do not are the object of much opprobrium. Many fathers who disappear from their children's lives feel shame and a sense of loss. My interviews were devoted in part to collecting information on how young adults explain the relatively limited production of good dads. Their accounts suggest that the development of paternal responsibility is an open-ended and uncertain process. What follows is my attempt to chart some of the central features of that process as seen through the eyes of the men and women who are living it. We will learn that the process is powerfully shaped by the acquisition of certain attitudes and habits in childhood. But the successful performance of the paternal role also requires men to negotiate a difficult series of adult transitions.

Before Men Become Fathers

Ideas of what it means to be a father are formed long before men become parents. Conceptions of what inner-city fatherhood involves are drawn from personal history, participation in a culture where biological fathers rarely reside with their children, and exposure to mainstream American culture where images of fatherhood are in flux.

Only a few of my informants grew up in households where a father was continuously present or even continuously involved in their up-bringing when absent from the household. Some, like Tyron Lewis, had loving, caring stepfathers, grandfathers, uncles, and older brothers who were daddies to them. But even in a culture where biological daddies are in short supply and other men often step in to fill the breach, children still speak longingly (and sometimes bitterly) about the fathering they missed out on. Wanda, commenting on Lionnel's desire to do more for his child than his father did for him, observed that she, too, shared his aspirations: "That's something I always wanted. If I ever had kids, I want my kids and their father to have a good relationship because I didn't have one with my father. My father wasn't there."

As African Americans, the men and women I talked to were acutely sensitive to living out certain cultural stereotypes. Duane, the father of three, described his own father in the following way:

> Like he act like a typical black father that doesn't live with the family. Like he'll get you and take you shopping and stuff like that. That's not being a father. . . . Everything I learn about I learned out on the street.

Possibly, my presence as a white man talking to them about family life contributed to that sensitivity, but I doubt it. I am more inclined to believe that the image of the missing black father is both generated internally from collective experience and also reflected and perhaps amplified by the way that African Americans are generally portrayed in the mass media.

African American males, especially those in the inner city, feel the weight of their personal histories, their culture, and the rising expectations for fathers that all men experience in American society as they approach fatherhood. Women share these high expectations and high apprehensions. These excessively high expectations appear to complicate the process of establishing and maintaining paternal commitments.

Most men enter parenthood feeling that they have much to overcome and conscious that, to succeed, they must somehow defy the odds.

Becoming a Father

Burdened with this heavy baggage of expectations, the men in this study typically entered parenthood without preparation or planning. With only a few exceptions, they did not decide to become fathers when they did. Parenthood is something that just happened to them. This observation is partially but not completely consistent with Elijah Anderson's (1989) perceptive account of gender interactions and parenthood among inner-city black youth in Philadelphia. Anderson argues that men routinely entice young women to have sex by promises of providing a conventional family life, what he calls the "fairy-tale prospect of living happily ever after" in a nuclear family. When pregnancy occurs, he argues that there is a "hit and run" ethic. Some men "own up" to their responsibilities and others deny them altogether.

Some cases in this study fit Anderson's scenario of deceptive dealings. The gender interactions, as Anderson suggests, indicate a high amount of misunderstanding, illusion, and uncertainty. Both the process leading up to pregnancy and the decision to have a child, once conception occurs, reflect a confusing mixture of motives and misinterpretations in the way young men and women communicate in their sexual liaisons.

Most men and women wanted to have sex, but they were often unprepared for the consequences. Sooner or later pregnancy happens and usually both men and women say they are surprised when it does. The question of whether unplanned pregnancies are also unwanted is extremely complicated. Bringing a child to term could be taken as evidence that the child was desired, but as far as I was able to tell, rarely did either the men or women feel unambiguous about having a child. Most felt some amount of pride and excitement about the prospect of parenthood, and most felt uncertain about whether they should have the child and how it would work out in the future. Whether to have a child or not is frequently viewed as a close call, depending on a volatile mixture of desires and interests between young women and men as well as their families, friends, and advisers.

Ricky Andrews told me what happened when Angie Tyler got pregnant:

Ricky: I didn't think it would happen 'cause she had birth control, anyway. . . . That's what she said.

FF: She said she had birth control?

Ricky: Yeah. I didn't really question. Maybe she didn't say. And then. . . . Maybe I was making the assumption that she had it. But it didn't bother me whether she got pregnant or not. I did remember asking her about a baby one time, about children. She had children. I said, "Well, I like children. I wouldn't mind having some." Not at this particular moment or this year, but eventually. But I want to get myself together so I can take care of the child.

When Angie discovered that she was pregnant, she had the child without ever informing Ricky.

At the same time, Ricky discovered that another woman he was dating had become pregnant. I asked Ricky how the decision about the second pregnancy was resolved.

Ricky: She decided. Like—I decided I don't need [it]. "Well, if you want to keep the child, that's fine with me. . . . Whatever you want to do. I don't want you to be held back just cause you doing it for me." She decided to abort the child.

In recollecting his conversations, Ricky was actually more explicit in stating his preferences than many men I interviewed, but he, like most, had conflicting motives to sort out—responsibility, pride of paternity, and interest in maintaining or not maintaining the relationship, among others. Women, too, were balancing similar concerns. Couples differed in the extent to which the partners shared a common perspective or believed that they did.

At one extreme were cases of "contested parenthood" in which men denied responsibility for the conception. Everyone I spoke to agreed that men are obliged only to support children they have fathered. Because relationships are sometimes casual and often impermanent, doubts about paternity are not unusual. Uncertainty about paternity sometimes resulted in protracted discussions that continued until the child was born.

In several cases, men were forced to acknowledge their children because of the appearance of the baby or, conversely, expressed doubts when the baby did not resemble them. Chelsea Terrell recalls that her baby's father initially doubted paternity. "He asked me would I get a blood test. So after I had the baby, we supposed to have got the blood test, but he saw that she looks just like him." Three or four other women mentioned that they had considered or actually had obtained blood tests as a means of convincing their partner that he was responsible for the pregnancy. Blood tests, however, represent a "last resort" among couples unable to reach agreement.

Contested parenthood is not nearly as common as negotiated parenthood. Most of the men and women that I spoke to described a short period of bargaining following pregnancy, ending in a resolution to make a go of it. Unlike Anderson (1989), I have the impression from both men's and women's reports that most prospective fathers sincerely want to "do for their children." Given the high level of uncertainty engendered by life experience and social practice, the pledge of paternal commitment is regarded conditionally by men and warily by women.

Behind the scenes, but in no way playing bit parts, are family members and friends who rally around the prospective parents (see Anderson, 1989; Furstenberg & Talvitie, 1979; Rains, 1971). With varying levels of enthusiasm, family members register their opinions, encouraging the couple either to terminate the pregnancy or to have the child. Families also voice their support or lack of confidence in the fledgling relationship. Many of the men I spoke to perceived their partners' family as unsympathetic and skeptical of their commitment. Jordon complained that Amy's mother was responsible for his eventual disengagement:

All I know is that I was trying. Her mother wouldn't let me. . . . Her mother wouldn't let me take her. "Well, you have to wait till Amy come home." So I left that day cause it happened to me twice. . . . I say, "Well, I'm her father."

Jordon acknowledged, however, that his own mother was hostile toward Amy, criticizing the way she was taking care of her child. Parents, feeling protective of their children and prospective grandchildren, commonly issue warnings to the young mother. This is one point in the process of parenthood where family history and community experience often conspire to create a conditional commitment to shared parenthood. In the worst circumstances, both family lines, as happened to Amy and Jordon, disapprove of the other parent. This disapproval undermines the shaky confidence of the young couple in collaborating. The mother's family, fearing that the young father will disappoint their daughter, can be quick to observe his failings. Expecting his eventual withdrawal, they jealously guard their prerogatives over their future grandchild. The father's family, in turn, especially if they have little acquaintance with the mother and her family, may also voice misgivings. Sometimes they insist on obtaining proof that he is responsible for the pregnancy, thus alienating the young mother and her family. Often, in the interest of protecting him, they remind him of the difficulty of meeting his responsibilities and the problems he will encounter as he attempts to live up to his end of the bargain.

It would be wrong to view the family's interests as invariably undercutting the father's legitimacy or interfering with the young couple's ability to form a durable relationship. As often as not, one or both families support their decision to have the child and back up their mutual obligation to raise the child. Parents may offer material and emotional support for a variety of reasons: because they approve of the father (or in the case of paternal kin, the mother), because they believe that it is in the child's best interest to know his father, or, among parents deeply imbued with religious or traditional family values, they may simply feel it is the right way to form a family.

In this small study, families weighed in on both sides, sometimes supporting and sometimes sabotaging the partnership. Even within families, kin do not always agree on the desirability of one course of action, and sometimes the sentiments of one or another family member shift over time. I have no way of knowing for sure, but I think that families now exert less pressure on men to remain involved than they once did. I found no instances, for example, of families urging their children to marry or even live together as was common when I was studying the parents of my informants in the mid-1960s (Furstenberg, 1976). The young mothers' kin, even while they continued to believe that fathers ought to do for their children, were resigned to their disengagement. In some cases, they felt their children were better off without the father's assistance. Mostly, however, they felt helpless to mobilize pressure to enlist his support.

Where families were more supportive, men tended to be more involved. (No doubt, the reverse is true as well.) And some men, regardless of their family's support or lack of it, were unconditionally committed to being involved. I hesitate to count with so few cases, but at least half the fathers (by their own or their partner's retrospective accounts) initially appeared to be strongly committed to raising their children. Despite the fact that the birth was usually viewed as ill-timed and greeted with much apprehension, commitment at the time of the birth generally ran high (see Mott, 1990). Many young men described their children's births as the most important moments in their lives.

Parenthood, for men as well as women, is frequently regarded as a transition to adulthood. At least for some men, fatherhood is seen as a source of attaining maturity in a world that provides few rapid and tangible routes to adult development. Men whose prospects of development were frequently frustrated by a sense of exclusion from schools, from the workplace, and, in a broader sense, from participation in society, saw family formation, however flawed the process, as a chance to redeem themselves. Deprived of many conventional expressions of success, fatherhood offered them a compelling opportunity to be a man (Marsiglio, 1993a).

In the larger sample from which these cases were drawn, nearly all of the young mothers (93%) reported in 1987 that the father of their child had acknowledged paternity. In more than half of these cases, fathers had a formal or informal agreement to pay child support. Over half saw their children at least weekly, including a fifth who were residing with their child. Half of the fathers living outside the household had taken their children overnight at least once during the past year. If the relatively high involvement of the men in this study at the time of their children's birth had been sustained, the course of fatherhood would be quite different than the pattern that typically evolves.

Eroding Commitments

I have already suggested that the commitment to paternity is fragile. Young inner-city men enter parenthood in a culture that is suspicious of their ability to honor their pledges, and they assume the paternal role possessing only meager means of overcoming these suspicions. What ordinarily follows, then, is a period of disillusionment and disengagement. Sometimes this process occurs swiftly and irretrievably; more often it is gradual and uneven.

The women I spoke to have no problems explaining why men opt out. Both in the group discussion and in their individual interviews, the women offered a number of reasons men often don't deliver on their promises to do for their children.

Beebee: That's how most of them are. I mean they get scared away.

Chelsea: (sarcastically) That's the responsibility of the father.

Beebee: Yeah. They got to grow up.

Chelsea: Even when they're older, some of them—not even the younger [fathers]—they scared.

("What are they scared of?" I asked the women in the group.)

Chelsea: I guess failing, maybe failing the child or not standing up to the mother's standards or something. It takes too much for them.

Amy: Not being able to—when the child come to you specifically and ask for something—they scared because they might not be able to get it to them at that particular time.

Angie: He wasn't scared. He just spoiled and he always had everything his way.

The discussion continued as women elaborated on these themes, describing why men are ill-prepared to assume the responsibilities of parenthood. Their explanations—fear, self-indulgence, and immaturity—are not so different as they might first appear. All have a common root in the socialization experiences of many young fathers in the inner city.

Most of the men, too, acknowledged that their family lives had not adequately equipped them to become parents. As I have already mentioned, nearly all spoke of being emotionally undernourished by their biological fathers, leaving some feeling inadequately trained in how to be a caring father.

I was also struck by how many of the men acknowledged explicitly or implicitly that they were ill-prepared to make sacrifices for their children. A few, agreeing with the women, admitted that they were used to being indulged or spoiled by their mothers. Jordon commented, "I was a spoiled brat. [My mom] used to buy me everything." Others merely indicated that it was difficult to subordinate their needs to the needs of their children or partners. "I do what I can," Lionnel told me, "but I've got to live too."

Training in child care differs markedly for women and men. To be sure, some teenage males had cared for their siblings, perhaps even more than several of the women I interviewed. Generally, however, many fewer men than women entered parenthood possessing caregiving skills. In this respect, I doubt whether the participants in this study are very different from young adults in the population at large.

I asked Lionnel whether he had ever changed his son's diapers. He told me that he had been afraid to pick up his child for fear "that I would squish him. And I ain't never changed him." Of course, most of the women admitted that they, too, felt unready to be parents. But as Wanda complained about Lionnel, "He can't say nobody ever taught him to do that because you can learn as you go by as I did. I had no idea what to do with a baby."

Learning on the job proved to be more difficult for men. Despite their resolutions to the contrary, most men felt more restricted than they had imagined by domestic routines. Women frequently complained that men were unreliable partners in child care because they were unwilling to give up street life for home life. From their perspective, men thought that they received too little credit for what they did.

This disparity in perception is also not unique to inner-city couples (Hochschild, 1989; Thompson, 1993). The difference in this population, however, is the centrality of street life. Most of the fathers I talked to had been accustomed to coming and going as they pleased. The absence of domestic routines, and sometimes the absence of work routines, makes it difficult for men and women to establish common and coordinated family schedules. Men, whose lives were centered outside the household, were not reliable partners in planning for child care. Showing up when they pleased, they quickly became auxiliary figures rather than coparents.

Contrasting perceptions of involvement in child care are heightened by the fact that women usually are living with their children and men usually are not. Women therefore compare men's performance against the standard of how much time they are spending with their children. By this standard, men almost always come up short. Men often apply a different yardstick: how much they are doing compared with what their friends do. By this standard, they feel that they deserve commendation.

Assessment of the generosity of child support provided produces similar perceptual differences by gender. Predictably, women feel they get too little, and men feel that more is expected of them than they are capable of providing. Child support has a symbolic meaning that goes beyond its considerable economic importance. For example, women resent what they perceive to be men's selfishness in withholding material support from their children. Amy complains that Jordon has made only one support payment even though they had an agreement. "It was suppose to be $22. He sent only $14." She says that as soon as the office of child support is informed that Jordon has a job, he quits. "How I see it, if it's your child, take care. . . . Do what you're suppose to do."

To Jordon, and men like him who feel chronically inadequate as providers, these demands for more assistance touch a raw nerve. The constant requests and complaints are a disturbing reminder that they are failing as fathers, repeating a pattern of inadequate fathering that they were determined to break. Fathers may begin to experience a sense of moral disengagement. Here is Jordon presenting his side of the story:

> I do what I can. . . . It was kind of hard for me to keep a job. . . . It was like Amy was always wanting money. . . . I give it to her but there were times I didn't give it to her because of the fact that she would spend it on her. Sometimes if I send money downtown, then the mother only (gets) $40 back or $20 back. So I just sometime give to them . . . or sometimes I send it downtown. Long as the government know that I'm taking care of my kids, I'm happy.

Jordon was explaining why he feels there is little connection between his efforts at work and his contribution to his children. He provided a number of "techniques of neutralization" for absolving himself from responsibility for child care: He doesn't have the money, the money isn't going to his child, and his child support payments (sending the money downtown) remove him from the process. These and other explanations that fathers provide for not paying child support are ways that men rationalize why they cannot or should not "do" for their children. (For more discussion of this subject, see Furstenberg et al., 1992.)

It is theoretically possible for men with limited means of providing material assistance to provide abundant emotional nurturance, but sharing and caring, in fact, are inextricably connected in the minds of most of my informants. Women who see men spend on themselves, their friends (new girlfriends in particular), and even other family members (including other children) resent the absence of support offered to them and their children. For their part, men are frequently in the position of having too few resources to spread around among legitimate claimants. Faced with this dilemma, men who often possess limited skills at managing competing demands resolve them impulsively by giving to whoever is closest at hand when they have resources to expend. For some, the closest at hand are themselves.

The differences in perceptions among men and women are sharpened by the instability of relationships. Relatively few of the young parents had formed durable partnerships. However, almost everyone—men and women alike—placed a high value on lasting relationships, and many hoped to marry someday. Few thought that time was close at hand or that the person who had fathered or borne their child was a suitable candidate for a marriagelike relationship. The instability of these unions appears to have two important implications for why fathers disengage.

First, the transitory nature of youthful relationships seriously impairs the parents' capacity to collaborate. In previous writings, I have observed that many men—and some women as well—think of marriage as a package deal (Furstenberg & Cherlin, 1991). A man's allegiance to his children is maintained in part by the bond established with his children's mother. When that bond dissolves, men sometimes have difficulty establishing a direct relationship with their children. And when they do, divorced women are threatened by the men's success at establishing an independent relationship, feeling as though they should serve as gatekeepers to their children. Obviously, couples vary in the extent to which they subscribe to the notion of marriage as a package deal, but these family constructions can be a serious impediment to managing parenthood successfully in the wake of divorce. By extension, the same sorts of constructions occur among young unmarried couples.

Jordon, who became involved with Amy 8 years ago, complained that she has lost interest in him. Her coolness toward him interferes with his relationship to his children. Amy, who is now in a serious relationship with another man, countered:

> Stop telling me that in order to do for your child, we got to be together. . . . When I was talking to him on the phone yesterday, it was the same thing. "You know I want you back. I've changed." I say, "Well, how can you prove to me that you've changed? You just last month told me you was gonna take her Easter shopping. She did not see you."

In other cases, a different sort of dilemma resulting from the shifting currents of failed relationships occurs. The weakness of the bond—not its strength—presents a problem in establishing a collaboration among young parents. Men's attachments to their children must be reinforced by women who barely know their children's fathers. The reciprocal is true for men, who may have children with women who are virtual strangers to them. The absence of a culturally defined arrangement for building emotional bonds between parents in these circumstances leaves it up to the young people to work it out for themselves. Even parents with good intentions, reasonable maturity, and strong interpersonal skills find this task challenging.

Building ties is complicated when men disappear during pregnancy, as Lionnel did, or shortly after their children are born, as did several other men whom I interviewed. Frightened by the responsibilities they are asked to assume, men are often unable to forge a secure alliance with their former sexual partners and hence with their children. In a certain sense, this situation is the mirror image of packaging marriage and parenthood together. Unmarried parents are frequently forced to construct a family configuration without much cultural support and too little emotional glue.

While they are trying to build these bonds, many are forming new partnerships. Of course, this happens to divorcing couples as well, but the rapidity of these transitions among young, unmarried parents is probably greater. These new relationships have somewhat different implications for men and women. In either case, young fathers are likely to reduce their involvement with their children.

Custodial parents, usually women, have some stake in advancing the idea that the biological father can be replaced by a surrogate parent in the household. It is simply emotionally and financially neater for mothers to incorporate their partners into the family. So young mothers often encourage their new partners to develop bonds with their children or to have children together as a means of strengthening their relationship. Occasionally young mothers actively discouraged fathers from maintaining ties with children from previous relationships. More than a few of the men I spoke to complained that they were subject to conflicting demands from current and previous partners. Ricky Andrews, who had a daughter with Angie Tyler before marrying the mother of his second child, recalled what happened when he told his wife:

> We'd already been together for like five or six months. She starts counting. It was hard holding that relationship together and try to keep a friendship with Angie. I want to see the child. Lead to an argument with her, with Angie, and so them two are arguing and, I'm playing referee.

So far, Ricky has managed to hold things together. Many fathers don't. New partners, in the eyes of many women, heighten the contrast between daddies who do and daddies who don't do for their children. Women sometimes even promote this idea—that their current partners are prepared to do more for their children than the biological father. Amy, who firmly asserts that Jordon should be caring for his child, reports that her current partner has stepped in to fill the breach: "After five years, he feel as though he has an obligation, and it is the responsible thing to do because of the fact this child is calling him 'daddy.' "

I asked Amy how she felt about that. She replied, "I say thank you for that. You are doing for your child that is not even yours." Jordon, in turn, complained that someone else has replaced him and said about Amy: "She's like—I don't care what you do." To the extent women are successful in helping to install a new man as daddy, their actions are part of what may become a self-fulfilling prophecy.

Fathers realize that their legitimacy is being called into question, often in large part because they are doing so little for their children. Occasionally, the realization that their place is being ceded to someone else leads men to invest more in their children—at least for a time. But more often, it produces a sense of resignation. Fathers like Jordon may be forced to admit that someone else is doing for their children more than they are and that someone else has become their children's daddy. Although the downward spiral of fathering occurs in all segments of American society (Furstenberg & Cherlin, 1991), conditions in the inner-city population make maintaining strong bonds between children and their nonresident fathers particularly problematic. The observation that most fathers' efforts appear meager from the perspective of the women and children obscures the fact that, at any given time, many fathers may be helping out some of their children or someone else's. It is not uncommon for young men to have fathered several children by different women as is the case for Jordon, Duane, Lionnel, and Ricky.

As fathers and daddies, men can accumulate enormous responsibilities at a young age, creating an unbearable overload of obligations. This places them in the situation of having to distribute resources either unevenly or meagerly. Usually, they do both, dissatisfying their former and present partners and their dependents. It was not unusual for a woman to complain that her children's father devoted more time and attention to his current partner and her children, whom he may not even have fathered, than he provided to his biological offspring. But I also heard complaints from women that their partners were devoting too much time to children outside the household or diverting resources away from them and their children.

Faced with competing obligations, some men manage by devoting more attention to some of their children—sometimes an older son, sometimes a child bearing the same name, or, more commonly, children in their current household—at the expense of others. "A serious juggling act" was the way one of my informants described it. I am not very sure of the rules guiding this selection process, if such rules exist. I am reasonably certain that selective attention is one mechanism men use for resolving the overload of obligations. Thus, at any given time, fathers may be doing for some children and not for others. They may be neglecting their biological children while being a daddy to someone's else child. Over time, they may relinquish previous commitments as they move from one relationship to the next.

Although both men and women strongly subscribe to the ideal that biological fathers should do for their children, as we have seen, "real daddies" are men who play a role in their children's lives. Relatively weak attachments to prior relationships often lead men to invest disproportionately in current families, relinquishing ties to children from earlier unions. This has the effect of reinforcing the notion that fatherhood is earned rather than granted or achieved rather than ascribed. I would argue that this principle has become an accepted standard within the African American community that I studied, and I would suggest that, as marriage weakens in American society, it is becoming a more widely accepted standard in our culture at large (Cherlin & Furstenberg, 1994; Woodhouse, 1993).

Sustaining Commitments

I have tried to explain why so many of the men I observed fall short of their own expectations to do for their children. If the majority of men disengage from some, if not all, of their children, how can we account for the fact that a distinct minority do not?

Vernon Wood is part of this minority. Vernon was going out with Tami McDonald for almost 5 years before she became pregnant. According to Vernon, the pregnancy was a "misplanned accident," but the timing of the birth didn't really make much difference to either of them. Both had been planning to live together. Having a child only "slowed down these plans" because they realized that they weren't ready to "jump out and go into an apartment." Both had debts and were forced to rely on their families until they were able to establish a separate household. Vernon has a steady job and Tami works at two jobs, and the young couple planned to marry the following year. They already have had to postpone the wedding once when Vernon realized he was going to have to use his savings to replace his car. Without a new car, he wouldn't have been able to keep his job.

In the meantime, Vernon sees his child almost every day. He pays the cost of child care and some of the routine expenses. Tami pays for much of the rest, although both their families provide a lot of assistance to the young parents. With their help, plus their two salaries, Tami and Vernon are able to provide very well for their child.

Like several other of the young couples who were planning to marry, Vernon and Tami feel that their relationship has been tested over time. Despite the ups and downs, Vernon feels pretty confident about their commitment to remain together. "Sometimes you get a little depressed but we still stay together. . . . I can say that anything bad that happened between us in the past has made us strong."

Where did this commitment to build a family with Tami come from? I asked Vernon. Immediately he pointed to his own family history. "I grew up in a beautiful family. I came from a very nice mother and father. They were always there for me." Vernon believes that he was taught a sense of responsibility, especially by his mother. He refers to himself as a mama's boy. "My mother was always there, you know. Do your work! Do your work! Most kids don't respect their parents."

Vernon complains that many of the guys he grew up with were indulged by their parents. "I mean their parents bought them anything. Need a pair of tennis shoes. Got a pair of tennis shoes. Need an outfit. Got the outfit." That kind of upbringing, he says, prepares you for the fast life. "As you get older, your mind is blank. You want to do, but you can't." From an early age, Vernon sought out friends who thought the way he did. Nearly all of his current friends are settling down with families. In this respect, Vernon is typical of the involved fathers I interviewed. They report associating with men like themselves who are strongly committed to caring for their children.

Vernon's ties with Tami's family and hers with his solidify their relationship and their mutual obligations to their daughter. "My mother treats Tami like my sister. I mean she loves her. I mean she's kind of into the relationship with us. Her parents love me. Her grandfather acts like I'm his little son."

Finally, it works to the advantage of the young couple that they have only one child and that neither has children from a previous relationship. Vernon experiences none of the cross-pressures that were so common among men who had fathered children with several partners. Taught the value of sacrifice, equipped with the skills for realizing those values, given the opportunity to exercise those skills in the labor market, Vernon was able to attract a partner with similar values, competencies, and economic resources. Add to that the support provided by both families and a network of friends, and you have a social formula for sustaining paternal involvement.

Because it is so clear, Vernon's case may oversimplify the explanation for why fathers stay involved. We might do well to consider Ricky Andrews, the father of Angie Tyler's youngest child. Ricky did not grow up in a stable family. He was raised by his brother after their mother died when Ricky was 12. Ricky was friendly with Angie before she had her child, but their sexual relationship was very brief. In fact, Angie never told Ricky that she was having his child. He learned about it from a friend after the child was born. "It was like bam! A ton of bricks. It was like, why didn't you tell me? That's all I could say. . . . I was messed up for a while after that."

Perhaps Angie didn't tell Ricky because he was already engaged to another woman who was expecting. Now married and the father of a second child, Ricky has insisted on supporting his daughter. As I reported earlier, he does so against the strenuous objection of his wife, who feels shortchanged by Ricky's sense of obligation to his oldest child.

Ricky is something of an anomaly among the involved fathers because he lacks so many of the supports that are common to this group. He works two jobs to provide support for both of his families. He lacks the family assistance that is typical of men who exhibit a preserving commitment to their children. He is able to maintain a high level of involvement with Angie's daughter against the wishes of his current wife. His relationship with Angie has been so difficult at times that Ricky feared he might be cut off from his child.

When I first spoke to Ricky in 1991, I asked him why he was such a dedicated dad in the face of obstacles that deterred many men from doing for their children. "I don't know. Maybe I believe in [it]. When the child started calling me daddy. God! Pretty special." I waited for Ricky to say more. When he didn't, I said that I had talked to fathers who got scared when their children started calling them daddy because it meant that they were responsible for their children.

That's true. You got to take responsibility. It's like anything else. Like if you owning a car, you are responsible for paying for it. If you living alone, you responsible for paying for it. If you work, you responsible for showing up and doing your job. So why can't you be responsible for taking care of your child?

Where did he get this sense of obligation? I probed.

I guess . . . Well . . . I can't tell you, man. When I lost my mother at the age of 12, I stayed with my brother ever since. He would work and he would just work and go home. And work and go home. Get to be where I don't want him to have to take care of me . . . as I got older. I guess being around a give type of person. A person who take care and was responsible set some kind of example for me.

The last time I spoke to Ricky was one afternoon in the summer of 1993 when he was visiting his daughter and Angie's other children, to whom Ricky tries to be a daddy as best he can. He spoke about the mounting burdens he was facing in meeting the growing obligations of two families. Ricky was taking courses at a local community college to learn how to operate a small business and was setting up a business with some of his friends. It was unclear how things were going to work out in this new venture, but I would be surprised, whatever happens, if Ricky retreats from his paternal responsibilities.

Even more than Vernon, Ricky sees himself as different from many of the men he grew up with and most of the young fathers who inhabit his community. Both men use this difference to their advantage, as a way of underscoring their commitments to their children. In this respect I was reminded of talking to children of addicts who themselves eschewed drugs and alcohol. They think of themselves as exemplifying a different code of behavior, and they seek out and associate with others who subscribe to their way of life.

These men, although strongly interested in economic success, seem to exhibit a much lower concern for their own material well-being. Ricky told me, "I don't really care for money. I only work because I have to." He went on to explain that he needs the money to support his kids. Taught by family, through involvement in the church and community, men like Ricky and Vernon place a lower value on possessions and a higher premium on sharing. They manifest less of the "selfishness" that many women complained their children's fathers displayed.

As important as men's values are for the way they perform as fathers, supportive structures are required for men to act successfully on their beliefs. Committed as Ricky is to caring for Angie's child, I doubt that he could do it if she refused to make a place for him in the family. Somehow Ricky was able to be a friend to her after their brief romantic relationship ended. Perhaps it is not surprising that Angie's mother took almost no part in caring for her children. Her low involvement left room for Ricky.

I have given less space in this chapter to young fathers like Vernon and Ricky not because they are unimportant to the view of fatherhood that I have been depicting. To the contrary, they illustrate the same points that I made at greater length earlier in the chapter. Perhaps they deserve more attention, but men like them were in short supply in my study. Vernon's case is predictable if unusual. His support for his son flows from a variety of structural and psychological conditions that happen to coincide. Ricky's case is more anomalous, but he, too, has solved many of the ordinary problems that many of his peers are unable to overcome.

Enhancing the Prospects of Young Fathers

I have identified a number of ingredients that contribute to sustaining or eroding paternal involvement among young families in the inner city. When ill-timed pregnancies occur in unstable partnerships to men who have few material resources for managing unplanned parenthood, they challenge, to say the least, the commitment of young fathers. Fatherhood occurs to men who often have a personal biography that poorly equips them to act on their intentions, even when their intentions to do for their children are strongly felt, and fatherhood takes place in a culture where the gap between good intentions and good performance is large and widely recognized.

The mix of these conditions, I believe, produces varying patterns of involvement by fathers. But an examination at one point in time is bound to produce a misleading picture, especially if that point is close to the entrance of fatherhood. Indeed, a principal purpose of this chapter was to explain how and why the process of fatherhood changes over time for men in the inner city.

The picture I have drawn from a small number of in-depth interviews is uncomfortably bleak. Unfortunately, the results of these case studies are entirely consistent with most data produced by surveys showing that disengagement of young fathers is common, especially among young parents in highly disadvantaged populations (Danziger & Radin, 1990; Marsiglio, 1987; Sullivan, 1989).

It is not easy, as I observed at the outset, to develop prescriptions for altering the circumstances. I can offer no easy recommendations for policymakers and practitioners who are attempting to serve the population I studied. I have tried to show that the problems young men face are nested in a cultural and structural matrix of conditions that cannot be treated one by one. Community campaigns, family life education in the schools, family planning services, mentoring programs, better educational and training programs, services for young fathers, counseling for young couples, and the like are all commendable interventions but, I fear, are likely to be ineffective and weak palliatives, especially if delivered separately. They may rescue some men and provide needed support for others, but none of these programs or even all of them in combination are strong enough medicine to correct the conditions described in this chapter.

I do not advocate abandoning efforts targeted at young fathers, believing that we should direct services instead primarily to children and their caretakers. To the contrary, I think we must be prepared to do more to devise ways of keeping fathers involved. Fathers are directly involved in producing children whom they often cannot care for even when they want to. Moreover, I believe they are sorely missed by both women and children when they are incapable of delivering on their promises.

This particular conclusion has implications for current efforts to improve the collection of child support, a topic that has been written about elsewhere (Furstenberg et al., 1992; Garfinkel, 1992). Like most people in this country, I endorse efforts to strengthen the legal and organizational mechanisms for ensuring that nonresidential parents (usually fathers) help pay for their children. However, these sentiments must be grounded in realistic expectations of the likely outcome of stronger enforcement efforts in low-income populations. The most prominent obstacle to effective enforcement is, of course, the availability of income possessed by low-income fathers. Men, as I noted earlier, are frequently compelled to allocate scarce resources among many needy claimants. Whatever prescriptions we devise to resolve these competing interests, we must recognize that stronger enforcement will probably do little to aid impoverished children when their fathers have little to contribute materially.

Under such circumstances, women will ordinarily not invest a great deal of time in aiding government efforts to collect child support. Perceiving only small gains for their efforts, they may feel that active collaboration will only antagonize their former partners. Beyond that, some will even resist efforts to cooperate, having very little interest in maintaining connections that only complicate their lives and—as they see it—their children's lives too. So we should probably temper our strong convictions about the social and economic desirability of maintaining men's responsibilities to their children with a recognition that, for some portion of the population, we may be only making more mischief for families whose fortunes we are seeking to improve.

Men can be brought back into the family only when they have more resources—material and emotional—to invest in their children. Only then will they be admitted into the family by women and their kin, and only then will they have confidence that they have a rightful claim. Currently, too many men discover a painful revelation after they become parents: They are in no better position to assume fatherhood than their fathers were when they became parents.

The disengagement of fathers is the outcome of cultural and economic processes that are inextricably fused together. Racial discrimination and economic exclusion are at the heart of a culture in which men are simultaneously indulged and disdained by women and where men in turn become outcasts, even in their own eyes. If we continue to maintain the stratification that creates and sustains this culture, there is no hope of eradicating it by public exhortation or condemnation.

Listen to Tyron Lewis, intermittently unemployed and struggling to support his son and maintain a new relationship with a woman who is carrying the economic load. As he described his situation, there was a tone of desperation and undertone of anger in his voice.

> You looking at a young man who really hasn't had a steady job in the last, two years. I had work but, it just don't seem, where I can get nothing that's . . . steady. If it's not that, it's at the time I was going through things with my son—far as his, mother. I would have to take off from work because he's my best interest. So in the process of jobs—laying me off with things getting slow [and] because of my personal problems too—here, it is now two years later and my son turned two. . . . I'm just starting to get my, life the way it's suppose, to be—step by step. That's where I gotta go. It's like a ladder.

How far are we prepared to go to assist Tyron up the ladder? Can we upgrade his inadequate education, providing him with marketable skills?

Are we willing to supplement low-income jobs so that Tyron makes more than $5.00 an hour, the wage he made at his last place of employment? Are we prepared to consider creating public works jobs for men like Tyron when employment in the private sector is not available? Just what are we prepared to do for him?

Will Americans spend tax dollars for black men, like Tyron, who are usually regarded as members of the undeserving poor? Can we afford to enable him, and others much less equipped than he, to enter the economic mainstream? Maybe the question is better put the other way around: How much longer can we afford not to help Tyron up the ladder?

8

Fathering Behavior and Child Outcomes

The Role of Race and Poverty

JANE MOSLEY
ELIZABETH THOMSON

Since the 1970s, researchers and policymakers have been looking for the "new father," one who takes an active role in child rearing and who may become an equal child-rearing partner when both parents are employed full time (Fein, 1978). Although children reared by such fathers continue to be in the minority, most scholars and policymakers view "new fatherhood" as a worthy and attainable goal.

The benefits of fathering for children are frequently taken for granted, in spite of the fact that most studies of parenting combine mothers' and fathers' behavior or ignore fathers' behaviors altogether. Some recent studies focus completely on fathering, but this approach misses the context of most fathering, which takes place in the context of mothers' behaviors. Only the rare father is a primary parent (Radin, 1982).

Fathering research has most often focused on white, middle-class families, where children have considerable alternative resources to a

AUTHORS' NOTE: This research was supported by grant HD26122 and Center Grant HD05876 from the Center for Population Research, National Institute of Child Health and Human Development. The National Survey of Families and Households was funded by NIH Grant HD21009.

highly involved father. Where fathers might make a bigger difference in children's lives—under the stress of poverty or minority group status—research on fathers is limited, and the focus is more often on nonresident fathers. In this chapter, we investigate effects of poverty and minority status on mothering and fathering in original two-parent families, that is, families in which children are either born to or adopted by both parents. Because single parenthood is strongly associated with poverty and race, this decision eliminates a considerable proportion of poor and/or black families from consideration. On the other hand, our choice redresses some of the imbalance in research on black and/or poor families, in which family disruption and single motherhood are so often featured. We consider how the stressors of poverty and minority status affect fathering and mothering behaviors, and to what extent fathering, in particular, mediates or buffers the effect of each stressor on children.

Fathers and Mothers

Empirical research makes clear that fathers have lower levels of involvement with children than mothers (e.g., Horna & Lupri, 1987; Nock & Kingston, 1988). Not only do fathers spend less time in child care or household work tasks associated with children, but they are also less involved than mothers in parent-child leisure or teaching activities. Some of the difference between fathers and mothers is, of course, due to the emphasis on economic providing as a central component of fathering and the fact that fathers spend more hours in paid work than mothers. Although fathers' paid employment hours do reduce time with children (Nock & Kingston, 1988; Thomson, 1993), the differences in fathers' and mothers' employment do not account for the lower involvement of fathers in their children's lives.

What do we know about the influence of "involved" fathers on children? Baumrind (1966), studying parents together, found that "competent" children (as measured by friendliness, independence, and assertiveness with peers) tended to have "authoritative" parents. Authoritative parenting consisted of an appropriate balance between support (warmth, communication) and control (maturity demands, discipline). This combination might be attained in many families by gendered parenting roles—mothers as nurturers and fathers as standard setters and disciplinarians. Radin (1982) found, however, that children with highly involved and *nurturant* fathers tended to be more cognitively competent and to better acquire skills leading to achievement motivation. In a recent study of family structure effects on children, Thomson, Hanson, and McLanahan (1994) reported that fathering activities with children, such as sharing meals and spending leisure time together, contributed to children's academic performance and emotional well-being, controlling for mothering activities.

Economic Stress and Fathering

Children in economically stressed families may be in even greater need of fathering than those in more comfortable circumstances. The large body of research on class differences in parenting has generally viewed both parents as a unit, even attributing mothers' parenting goals to fathers' occupational experiences (Kohn, 1977). Numerous studies find that socioeconomic status is inversely associated with an emphasis on obedience (versus autonomy) and with the use of physical punishment (e.g., Alwin, 1987; Gecas, 1979; Kohn, 1977).

McLoyd's (1990) review of links between income and parenting argues that economic deprivation adversely affects child development in part through its effect on parental behavior. Anxiety, depression, and irritability states are exacerbated by economic hardship, and this in turn increases the tendency of parents to be punitive, erratic, unilateral, and somewhat nonsupportive in relationships with children. She notes that much of the research on parenting differences by income focuses on mothers. One exception to this is research by Elder and his colleagues (Elder, Van Nguyen, & Caspi, 1985; Lempers, Clark-Lempers, & Simons, 1989; Whitbeck et al., 1991); their studies point in particular to fathers' behavior as the most important link between perceived economic stress and child outcomes (Elder, Conger, Foster, & Ardelt, 1992). The authors suggest that economic stress affects fathering behaviors more strongly than mothering behaviors because it challenges a central component of the fathering role, economic providing.

In a recent study, Sampson and Laub (1994) suggest that positive parenting provides a buffer for children living in poverty. They found that, in a sample of low-income families, living in low-income neighborhoods, parental involvement was inversely associated with boys' juvenile delinquency. Thus the problem for poor parents is to maintain high levels of parental support and control in the face of economic stress, given that their children are perhaps in greater need than children living with less disadvantaged parents.

Using national survey data, McLeod and Shanahan (1993) examined effects of current and persistent poverty on child outcomes and the extent to which mothering (but not fathering) behavior mediated those effects. Although maternal behavior did explain the effects of current poverty on child outcomes, they found no evidence that mothering mediated effects of persistent poverty on children.

Race Differences in Fathering

McAdoo (1986b) argues that most research on African American families ignores black fathers as socializers of their children in any economic or social context. Few studies focus on black families and those that do tend generally to focus on middle- to higher income fathers. Bowman (1993) found that, among middle-income families, black fathers were more involved in child rearing and had more nurturant interactions with children, compared with white fathers. Cazenave (1979) argues that the more economically secure black fathers are, the more involved they are in child rearing. While white fathers react to economic strain with harsh parenting, black fathers may simply withdraw.

As with much of the research on income and parenting, the unit of analysis is often parents; where a distinction between parents is made, the focus is usually on mothers. Thus it is sometimes difficult to determine the distinct contributions of fathering. There seems to be contradictory evidence of parenting styles among blacks (McLoyd, 1990). On one hand, studies suggest that black parents are more severe, punitive, and power assertive in the discipline of their children than white parents, even among those of similar socioeconomic status. Other studies suggest only that black parents expect earlier autonomy and exert firmer controls on children than white parents, while remaining highly supportive. One of the few studies to differentiate between mothers and fathers (Bartz & Levine, 1978) supported the latter view, with essentially the same results for both parents. Using a national sample, Alwin (1984) found that black parents placed relatively more emphasis on obedience than autonomy, in comparison with white parents, controlling for socioeconomic differences between blacks and whites. Alwin reported no overall differences between mothers' and fathers' values.

Baumrind (1972) reported that black parents were more likely to be classified as "authoritarian" than whites, at least in their relationships with daughters. She did not, however, find that black authoritarian parents were more likely to have withdrawn children, as is true for whites, and suggests that this parenting style has a different character across race. Among whites, the style may be associated with an "authoritarian personality," with parental behaviors viewed as punitive and unfair. Among blacks, however, parents' authoritarian controls may be designed to prepare children for a hostile world, in which they will face racism and greater economic stresses than white children (Peters & Massey, 1983). This explanation is consistent with Bronfenbrenner's (1986) hypothesis that parenting behaviors interact with the extrafamilial environment to produce particular child outcomes. Brody et al. (1994), examining two-parent black families, argue that parents' behavior with their children may be more important in situations where few other social supports exist.

Race and Income

When investigating effects of poverty and race on parenting and child well-being, one must keep in mind the extremely large income differential by race in the United States. For example, more than 40% of black children are currently poor, compared with 12.5% for whites (Children's Defense Fund, 1992). Blacks face a greater risk of unemployment than whites (Buss & Redburn, 1983), and black workers have been disproportionately affected by the structural changes in the economy. Because black families are much more likely to face economic difficulties than whites, it is difficult to disentangle influences of economic disadvantage from the stress of minority group status.

The experience of poverty is also different for blacks and whites. Duncan (1984) reports that black families spend longer periods of time in poverty than do their white counterparts. Ellwood (1989) studied children born in 1970 over the first 10 years of their life. During those years, 5% of white children and 22% of black children experienced short-term poverty spells, lasting from 4 to 6 years. Only 3% of white children were poor for 7 or more years, compared with 34% for black children.

Even at similar levels of socioeconomic status, black and white families often face quite different environments. Kessler and Neighbors

(1986) concluded that, holding social class constant, blacks are more distressed than whites. McLoyd (1990) asserts that the higher levels of punitiveness among black compared with white parents are due in part to these differentials. McLeod and Shanahan (1993) investigated race as well as poverty effects on children in their recent study. They found little difference, net of poverty, between black and white children, and no evidence that poverty and race interacted in their effects on children; that is, poverty effects were similar for black and white families.

In the remainder of this chapter, we investigate effects of poverty and minority status on parental behaviors and child outcomes, and the extent to which effects of these external stressors on children are mediated by parenting. We focus on the comparison of fathering and mothering behaviors, and the common couple construct, parental control. We also investigate the buffering hypothesis—that behaviors of black and/or poor parents buffer otherwise adverse effects of poverty and minority status on children.

Sample and Measures

We used data from the 1987-1988 National Survey of Families and Households (Sweet, Bumpass, & Call, 1988) to investigate effects of poverty and race on mothering, fathering, and child well-being. The NSFH is based on a nationally representative sample of the continental U.S. adult population, including oversamples of selected minority groups and family types ($N = 13,014$). A randomly selected "primary respondent" completed a personal interview about her- or himself and about other family and household members. Some information was collected with a self-administered questionnaire. In addition, spouses of married primary respondents ("secondary respondents") were asked to complete a self-administered questionnaire, including many of the same questions asked of the primary respondent. The overall response rate for the NSFH was 74.3%, and 83.1% of spouses completed the secondary respondent questionnaire.

We limited our analytic sample to married couples with children under 19 living in the household, with all of the children born to or adopted by the couple. Almost all of the children were born to the couple after marriage, a few were adopted, and a few couples married after their child was born. We excluded families in which the randomly selected "focal child" was under age 5, because few of the parenting or child well-being measures were the same for children under 5 and those 5-18. In this sample, the spouse participation rate was 82.2%. As noted further below, we used predicted values for some indicators to include as many of these families in our analysis as possible.

Information on the focal child's well-being was provided by the randomly selected primary respondent, who could be either the mother or the father. *Academic performance* was reported on two different scales, depending on the age of the focal child. For adolescents (age 12-18), the primary respondent reported the child's usual grades, from *mostly Fs* (0) to *mostly As* (4), with midpoint categories such as *mostly As or Bs* (3.5). For children 5-11, who frequently do not receive letter or numerical grades, the child's school performance was rated from *near the bottom of the class* (0) to *one of the best in the class* (4). *School behavior problems* were measured for both age groups by a dichotomous indicator, with a value of 1 if the child had dropped out of school or, in the past year, had been suspended or expelled or had experienced sufficient behavior problems that the parent was asked to meet with a teacher, and 0 otherwise.

Parents were also asked to rate the child on 12 behaviors, from *not at all true* (1) to *often true* (3) during the past year. Based on a confirmatory factor model in which these responses were treated as ordinal indicators (Muthén, 1988), we constructed normalized factor scores for four behavioral dimensions, each represented predominantly by responses to the descriptors listed below:[1]

> *Externalizing*: loses temper easily; bullies, is cruel or mean to others
> *Internalizing*: fearful and anxious; unhappy, sad, or depressed
> *Sociability*: gets along with other children; carries out responsibilities on her or his own; always does what you ask
> *Self-direction*: is willing to try new things; keeps self busy; is cheerful and happy

Three measures of parenting behavior were constructed, one for fathers, one for mothers, and one for the couple as a unit. *Mother* and *father activities* with children were elicited in self-administered questionnaires completed by each parent. Questions referred to "the children," not specifically to the randomly selected focal child. Parents reported weekly breakfasts, weekly dinners (0-7), frequency of three home activities (playing or working on a project, reading or helping with homework, having private talks), and frequency of outings with children (the last four items rated on a scale from 1 = *never* to 6 = *almost every day*). Because home activities might overlap considerably, we averaged those three responses and then averaged the mean response with individual indicators of breakfasts, dinners, and outings. Cronbach's alpha for the constructed scale was .71 for mothers and .74 for fathers.

A third measure, *parental control*, was constructed from responses to questions about rules for the focal child, obtained in the personal interview with the primary respondent. We computed an average score from three indicators. The first measures the child's supervision at home. Parents were asked: "Would (child) be allowed to be at home alone overnight, if you went on a trip? at night, if you were gone until midnight? in the afternoon after school, between 3:00 and 6:00 p.m.?" Responses (yes or sometimes, no) to these questions approximated a Guttman scale and were scored as follows: 1 = *allowed home alone overnight*; 2 = *at night, not overnight*; 3 = *in afternoon, not at night or overnight*; 4 = *none of these times*. The second indicator is a measure of television restrictions, based on two questions: "Do you restrict the amount of television that (child) watches? types of programs?" Responses (no or try, but not successful, versus yes) were scored as follows: 1 = *no (successful) restriction*; 2.5 = *restrict amount or programs*; 4 = *restrict amount and programs*. This scoring creates the same distance between the most and least restrictive parents as for the supervision indicator. Third, parents were asked: "When (child) is away from home, is (he/she) supposed to let you know where (he/she) is . . . hardly ever, sometimes, most of the time, or all the time?" Because more than 80% of parents reported "all the time," we dichotomized this response (1 = *all the time*, 0 *otherwise*). The parental control summary scale, which averages these three indicators, therefore gives a much smaller weight to the "inform whereabouts" response than to the more variable supervision and television restriction measures. The scale's reliability was estimated at .56, which is on the margin of acceptability for a three-item scale. Extensive analyses of other potential combinations of parental responses and a few additional questions asked only for children of selected ages produced no more reliable measures. Correlations of this scale with measures of mother and father activities were .36 and .28, respectively.

Poverty was measured by dividing household annual income by the poverty line for households of the same composition. We classify as "poor" two-parent families living in households with annual incomes less than 25% more than the poverty income for that household. We chose this level to provide sufficient numbers of poor families to test hypotheses about differential effects of parenting under economic stress and because reports for a single year might underestimate the experience of poverty, particularly for black families.[2] Race was measured at the couple level, coded as white or black if both parents reported the same race or if only the primary respondent participated in the survey and reported her or his own race. Among the couples for whom both spouses' race was known, only three white primary respondents had a black spouse, and only four black primary respondents had a white spouse.

All models control for the parents' education, categorized as no high school diploma, high school graduate, some postsecondary schooling, or bachelor's degree. We used the maximum education reported for either parent, or the education of the primary respondent when the spouse did not participate in the survey.

In spite of double sampling and the lower socioeconomic status of black families, the number of poor, black, two-parent families is relatively small for the types of analyses we conducted. Nonresponse on any of the variables in our analysis therefore poses more serious problems than in larger samples of black families. Most of the nonresponse was due to nonparticipation of spouses. In addition, significant proportions of responding parents did not answer questions on income and/or the self-administered questions on parent activities; only a few primary respondents did not provide valid responses for child well-being or parental control. We included cases with nonresponse on parent activities by substituting values for mother and father activities, predicted from race, poverty, parent education, and child's age and sex, and including dummy variables in the model for cases with substituted values. We also included cases with nonresponse on income by adding a third income category (don't know whether poor or not). Scores were predicted for father activities in 17.5% of white families, 24.0% of black families; for mother activities, in 7.4% of white families and 17.9% of black families. Because most of the nonresponse was due to nonparticipation of secondary respondents, virtually no families had predicted scores for both parents' activities. As shown in Tables 8.2 and 8.3, approximately 11% of white and black families did not report income and were included in the "don't know" category of poverty.

Table 8.1 Poverty Status by Race

	Percent Poor[a]	
	Black	White
All families	15.5	6.7
focal child male	12.7	6.2
focal child female	18.5	7.2
Number of families	204	1,024

SOURCE: 1988 National Survey of Families and Households; original two-parent families, focal child age 5-18.
a. "Poor" is defined as household income less than 1.25 times the poverty income for households of similar composition. Number of cases is unweighted; percentage poor is weighted.

Analysis and Results

Table 8.1 presents weighted distributions and unweighted number of families by race and poverty status. It is no surprise that black families are more likely to be classified as poor than white families. Because our analysis focuses on two-parent families, and black two-parent families are more selective on socioeconomic status than white two-parent families, the differences are not as extreme as would be the case for all types of families.

We found several statistically significant interactions of race, poverty, or parenting and child's sex, and so present all of our findings separately for boys and girls. Tables 8.2 and 8.3 show results from baseline models of parenting behavior and child outcomes. Mean scores are adjusted for effects of child's age, parent education, and race (for poverty effects) or poverty (for race effects).[3] For boys, poverty had no statistically significant effects. Among girls, on the other hand, poverty significantly reduced grade point averages and initiative and increased school behavior problems.

Parental behaviors were not significantly affected by poverty for either boys or girls—or for the sample as a whole. Observed differences in parent activities are, in fact, in the direction opposite to that hypothesized, with higher scores for poor parents.

Race differences in outcomes were very similar for boys and girls, with *lower* externalizing or internalizing problems and *higher* sociability scores among black families, compared with white families. That is,

Table 8.2 Outcomes and Parent Behaviors by Poverty Status and Race, Boys

	Poor	DK Poor	Nonpoor	Black	White
School performance (5-11)	2.86	3.12	2.99	3.05	2.98
Grade point average (12-18)	2.85	2.92	2.83	2.95	2.82
School behavior problems	.16	.20	.16	.18	.16
Normalized temperament scores					
externalizing problems	.02	−.14	−.03	**−.24**	**.00***
internalizing problems	−.02	−.11	−.03	**−.10**	**−.03***
sociability	−.02	.13	.03	**.16**	**.02***
initiative	.03	.08	.04	.08	.03
Father activities	3.91	3.75	3.77	3.68	3.80
Parental control	2.18	2.13	2.05	**2.23**	**2.04***
Mother activities	4.73	4.33	4.42	**4.07**	**4.50***
Number[a]	51	70	575	117	579

SOURCE: 1988 National Survey of Families and Households; original two-parent families, focal child age 5-18.

NOTE: Entries are mean scores, adjusted for linear effects of child's age and categorical effects of education and race (for poverty differences) or poverty (for race differences).

a. Number of families with valid information on parent education, poverty status, and race ($n = 696$). Valid cases for each variable range from 670 to 685.

*Net poverty or race difference (entries in bold) statistically significant; $p < .05$

among original two-parent families, black children were reported to have better temperament or emotional outcomes than white children, net of parent education, poverty, and child's age.

Parental behaviors also differed by race, and again in a similar way for boys and girls. Although the observed scores for black fathers were also lower than for white fathers, the differences were not statistically significant. Black mothers reported *less* frequent activities than white mothers, and parental control scores were higher for black families.

We also tested interactions between effects of race and poverty on each outcome and each parental behavior, separately for boys and girls. Only two significant interactions were found. The negative effects of poverty were slightly larger for black girls than for white girls. For boys, the race difference in mother activities was found only for nonpoor families, not among poor families. Both interactions depend, however, on very small numbers of families (under 15) and do not alter conclusions drawn from additive models of poverty and race effects.

Our second set of analyses focused on the extent to which differences in parenting behavior mediated or suppressed race and poverty effects

Table 8.3 Outcomes and Parent Behaviors by Poverty Status and Race, Girls

	Poor	DK Poor	Nonpoor	Black	White
School performance (5-11)	3.06	3.03	3.24	3.07	3.23
Grade point average (12-18)	**2.82**	**2.89**	**3.16***	3.17	3.09
School behavior problems	**.13**	**.02**	**.06***	.09	.05
Normalized temperament scores					
externalizing problems	.00	−.06	−.05	**−.16**	**−.03***
internalizing problems	.03	−.03	−.04	**−.08**	**−.02***
sociability	−.05	.05	.10	**.17**	**.06***
initiative	**−.04**	**.02**	**.05***	.05	.04
Father activities	3.84	3.60	3.65	3.59	3.67
Parental control	2.09	2.17	2.17	**2.31**	**2.13***
Mother activities	4.74	4.44	4.43	**4.21**	**4.50***
Number[a]	60	75	542	111	566

SOURCE: 1988 National Survey of Families and Households; original two-parent families, focal child age 5-18.
NOTE: Entries are mean scores, adjusted for linear effects of child's age and categorical effects of education and race (for poverty differences) or poverty (for race differences).
a. Number of families with valid information on parent education, poverty status, and race ($n = 677$). Valid cases for each variable range from 665 to 667.
*Net poverty or race difference (entries in bold) statistically significant; $p < .05$

on children. We found virtually *no change* in the direct effects of poverty or race, controlling for father activities, parental control, and mother activities. That is, parental behavior, when measured by either fathers' or mothers' behaviors, did not mediate any effects of race or poverty on children. This finding is shown in Tables 8.4 and 8.5 (for boys and girls, respectively), in that the regression coefficients for black families and poor families are approximately equal to the difference in adjusted means presented in Tables 8.2 and 8.3. For example, in Table 8.2, for school performance, the difference between poor and nonpoor children is roughly −.13. Turning to Table 8.4, the poverty coefficient for school performance is −.11. The slight difference between these two figures is due to the fact that Tables 8.4 and 8.5 also controlled for parental control.

This does not mean that parental behaviors are irrelevant for child well-being, however. As shown in Table 8.4, father activities improve child well-being, net of the effects of mother activities. Mother activities have statistically significant positive effects on most boys' outcomes (negative coefficients for problems, positive coefficients otherwise).

Table 8.4 Parenting Effects on Boys' Outcomes

Parental Behavior	School Performance (age 5-11)	Grade Point Average (age 12-18)	School Behavior Problems	Normalized Temperament Scores			
				Externalizing	Internalizing	Sociability	Initiative
Poor families	-.11 (.19)	-.04 (.19)	.010 (.056)	.053 (.070)	.017 (.043)	-.072 (.068)	-.019 (.041)
Black families	-.10 (.14)	.16 (.12)	.015 (.040)	-.269** (.048)	-.095** (.030)	.184** (.047)	.075** (.028)
Father activities	.09* (.05)	.04 (.04)	-.035** (.014)	-.042** (.017)	-.020* (.011)	.031* (.017)	.021** (.010)
Parental control	-.09 (.13)	-.08 (.09)	.044 (.030)	.085** (.037)	.042* (.023)	-.082** (.036)	-.041* (.022)
Mother activities	-.04 (.05)	.10** (.04)	.001 (.014)	-.031* (.016)	-.026** (.010)	.065** (.016)	.035** (.010)
R^2	.134**	.116**	.034**	.088**	.046**	.069**	.061**
Valid cases	336	345	670	685	685	685	685

SOURCE: 1988 National Survey of Families and Households; original two-parent families, focal child age 5-18.
NOTE: Entries are unstandardized OLS regression coefficients, with standard errors in parentheses. Each model includes controls for child's age in years, parent education categories, and a dummy variable for poverty status missing.
*$p < .05$, one-tailed; **$p < .05$, two-tailed.

Table 8.5 Parenting Effects on Girls' Outcomes

Parental Behavior	School Performance (age 5-11)	Grade Point Average (age 12-18)	School Behavior Problems	Normalized Temperament Scores			
				Externalizing	Internalizing	Sociability	Initiative
Poor families	-.22	-.36**	.075**	.072	.073*	-.167**	-.097**
	(.16)	(.16)	(.032)	(.065)	(.041)	(.062)	(.037)
Black families	-.10	.10	.027	-.141**	-.063**	.108**	.010
	(.12)	(.12)	(.025)	(.049)	(.031)	(.047)	(.028)
Father activities	-.02	.01	-.002	-.041**	-.014	.035**	.014
	(.04)	(.04)	(.008)	(.016)	(.010)	(.015)	(.009)
Parental control	-.09	-.04	.015	-.060	-.022	.036	.005
	(.13)	(.09)	(.021)	(.041)	(.026)	(.039)	(.023)
Mother activities	.10**	.05	-.026*	-.041*	-.014	.032**	.010
	(.04)	(.04)	(.008)	(.016)	(.010)	(.015)	(.009)
R^2	.081**	.083**	.030*	.056**	.031**	.063**	.042**
Valid cases	341	326	665	667	667	667	667

SOURCE: 1988 National Survey of Families and Households; original two-parent families, focal child age 5-18.
NOTE: Entries are unstandardized OLS regression coefficients, with standard errors in parentheses. Each model includes controls for child's age in years, parent education categories, and a dummy variable for poverty status missing.
*$p < .05$, one-tailed; **$p < .05$, two-tailed.

Overall, differences in the coefficients for mother and father effects are not great. We also estimated models using only fathering activities and parental control and excluding mother activities. However, the results were very similar to models in Table 8.4 and Table 8.5. The largest change took place in the outcome of sociability, where the fathering coefficient was reduced by almost one third when mother activities was added to the equation. High levels of parental control appear to have detrimental effects on boys' temperament, rather than positive effects. This may result from association of authoritarian parental personalities with the highest levels of control but might also reflect a reverse causal explanation, with boys' problem behaviors eliciting control attempts. We return to this issue in our discussion of interactions, below.

For girls, parenting behaviors have less consistent effects. Father activities affect only externalizing and sociability, while mother activities appear to influence school performance, school behavior problems, externalizing, and sociability. Parental control has no significant effects on any outcomes for girls.

Explained variance for all of these models is quite low, and estimated regression slopes appear quite modest. What do these figures mean in terms of fathering and mothering behaviors? Fathering and mothering activities range on a scale from 0 to 7. A unit increase in father (or mother) activities is equivalent to increasing weekly meals with children by four or moving two places up on the frequency of home and leisure activities. Such differences are associated with approximately a 4% decrease in externalizing behavior or a difference of one tenth of a grade point for boys. By contrast, differences between black and white families, or between poor and nonpoor families, even when adjusted for effects of parents' education, are quite a bit larger than a one-unit increase for father or mother behavior.

We also tested theoretically derived hypotheses about different effects of parental behavior on children in poor versus nonpoor, black versus white families. We considered statistically significant increments in explained variance as well as significant regression coefficients for single interaction terms as evidence of potential interactions. A few robust interactions emerged, consistent with the buffering hypothesis, and primarily for poverty effects. Table 8.6 illustrates some of the most pronounced differences we found in effects of parental behavior by poverty and race.

Father's activities with children produced only one instance that supported the buffering hypothesis: Girls in poor families with more

Table 8.6 Parenting Interactions With Poverty

	Poor	Nonpoor
Boys:		
School behavior problems		
low parental control	.33	.11
high parental control	.07	.20
Externalizing		
low mother activities	.20	−.03
high mother activities	−.11	−.04
Girls:		
School performance		
low father activities	2.91	3.38
high father activities	3.13	3.14
School behavior problems		
low mother activities	.18	.07
high mother activities	.10	.04

SOURCE: 1988 National Survey of Families and Households; original two-parent families, focal child age 5-18.
NOTE: Entries are mean scores, adjusted for linear effects of child's age and categorical effects of parent education and race. Linear effects of the other two parental variables are also controlled in each estimate. All entries represent statistically significant incremental effects of the linear interaction between poverty and the specified parental behavior but are presented here as categorical effects.

active fathers were reported to be doing better in school, but father activities produces no differences in nonpoor families. More evidence was seen in examining mother activities. Mother activities were negatively associated with boys' externalizing behaviors only in poor families, and the negative association with girls' school behavior problems was stronger in poor than in nonpoor families. The association of parental control with boys' school behavior problems was also much stronger among the poor than the nonpoor.

Discussions and Conclusions

In our sample of two-parent families, girls living in poor families were experiencing more difficulties than those in nonpoor families, but poverty appeared not to affect the well-being of boys. Parenting did not account for poverty effects on girls' outcomes, in part because we found no significant effects of poverty on parental behaviors. On the other hand, we found some evidence for the buffering hypothesis, in that parenting behaviors had stronger positive effects for poor children than for other children.

Among those living in two-parent families, black children appeared to be doing better than white children, at least in terms of temperament. The lower levels of mother activities and higher levels of parental control found in black families do not account for these differences. We did not find that parenting effects were particularly different in black compared with white families.

One of the lessons we draw from these analyses is that two-parent black and white families may be much the same and that it is a mistake to overemphasize "cultural" differences in parenting behavior or family relationships. Such differences are frequently assumed, particularly for fathers' behavior. When subjected to rigorous statistical tests, however, presumed differences may turn out, as in our analysis, to be more assumed than real. Poverty is more likely to adversely affect children's lives, to require extra effort on the part of parents to buffer children from economic stress, and our attention should be turned to the links between poverty and race rather than focused on race differences in family behaviors.

This book is about fathers, and we argued earlier that fathering should be viewed in the context of, or at least in parallel with, mothering. First, we note that fathers' activities with children were significantly lower, as we would expect based on prior research, than mothers' activities. Our analyses reveal significant positive effects, particularly for boys, of father activities with children, net of positive effects for mother activities. This rosy picture may be tempered somewhat, if we consider the adverse effects of parental control on boys' temperaments. One explanation for these effects is that problem boys elicit parental control attempts. But why would we expect parents to exert stricter controls on boys who *internalize* as well as externalize, or on boys who are less sociable and show less initiative? A more parsimonious explanation for these findings is that the most restrictive parenting, net of supportive activities with children, leads to negative outcomes for boys. To the extent fathers are responsible for and/or enforce strict rules for children, the positive effects of their "engagement" with children may be canceled out, at least for sons.

Race differences were found only for mothers, and not for fathers, similar to studies showing much less variation in the fathering than the mothering role. Thus, in two-parent families at least, black fathers are no more "marginal" (Stier & Tienda, 1993) to children than white fathers.

Our central question in this chapter was how father activities, particularly those of poor and black fathers, are associated with their children's outcomes. We have attempted to construct the best possible measure of father and mother activities using the NSFH data. We did not, however, include measures of the quality of father-child or mother-child relationships. Although some indicators of relationship quality are in the NSFH data, they are quite skewed toward positive relationships, suggesting social desirability bias. Additionally, they are more likely to be the result of children's problem behaviors than are the types of indicators used to measure mother and father activities. Nevertheless, it may be that fathers' affective responses or their symbolic role as family provider/caretaker are what makes a difference to children, and we have not captured these components of the father role in our measures.

The role of fathers in child well-being is more theorized than studied. As noted in our review, much of the empirical research on fathers is based on small, select samples; it excludes the mothering context within which most fathering behavior occurs, or combines information on mothers' and fathers' behaviors so that the particular contributions of each parent are obscured. We hope this analysis provides further stimulus to the increasing body of research on fathers and their children, while at the same time encouraging the joint study of fathering and mothering behavior.

Notes

1. These analyses and other measurement analyses reported here were conducted with reports from parents in all family types, not just original two-parent families (Thomson et al., 1994).

2. It should be noted that poverty as measured is only current poverty and this may have quite different effects than persistent poverty. McLeod and Shanahan (1993), in examining similar issues, found different results when current poverty versus persistent poverty was used.

3. Unadjusted means were very similar to those presented in Table 8.2.

9

What Fathers Say
About Involvement With
Children After Separation

JUDITH A. SELTZER
YVONNE BRANDRETH

Divorce, like marriage, comes in two varieties—his and hers (Bernard, 1972/1978). Even more than within marriage, where they share their children and financial resources, men's and women's experiences of separation and divorce differ. Children are more likely to live with their mothers than their fathers after marital disruption (Maccoby, Depner,

AUTHORS' NOTE: This chapter is a slightly edited version of an article, with the same title, in *Journal of Family Issues* (1994, Vol. 15, No. 1, 49-77). This research was supported by grants from the National Institute of Child Health and Human Development (NICHD) (HD-24571), the Office of the Assistant Secretary for Planning and Evaluation, the U.S. Department of Health and Human Services (91ASPE236A), and the University of Wisconsin Graduate School. Computing support came from the Center for Demography and Ecology, which receives core support from the Center for Population Research of the NICHD (HD-5876). The National Survey of Families and Households was also funded by the Center for Population Research, NICHD (HD-21009). We are grateful to Carol Roan, Kay Tuschen, and Leslie McCall for research assistance; to Vaughn Call for help with the education and marriage history data; to Elizabeth Uhr for editorial advice; to Barbara Corry for word processing assistance; and to Terry Arendell, Larry Bumpass, Mary Faltynski, Robert Mare, William Marsiglio, R. Kelly Raley, Carol Roan, Nora Cate Schaeffer, Robert Schoeni, and an anonymous reviewer for helpful comments. The opinions expressed in this chapter are our own and do not necessarily reflect those of the sponsoring agencies. A previous version of this chapter was presented at the 1993 meeting of the Population Association of America, Cincinnati, Ohio.

& Mnookin, 1988; Seltzer, 1990; Sweet & Bumpass, 1987). In part because their children do not live with them, fathers fare better economically than mothers (Garfinkel & McLanahan, 1986). Despite the clear differences in fathers' and mothers' experiences of divorce, most knowledge of parenting and children's welfare after separation comes from resident mothers' reports. This is particularly troublesome for policymakers who try to improve children's economic welfare by reforming the child support system (e.g., Furstenberg, Sherwood, & Sullivan, 1992; Haskins, 1988). Reforms attempt to alter the behavior of nonresident parents, usually fathers. Without information about the financial resources and beliefs of these major actors, policy changes may not be effective.

Resident mothers and nonresident fathers differ in their economic interests in matters of child support, and the few studies that are able to compare parents' reports show that nonresident fathers report paying more child support than mothers report receiving (Braver, Fitzpatrick, & Bay, 1991; Schaeffer, Seltzer, & Klawitter, 1991; Sonenstein & Calhoun, 1990). Differences in parents' reports result, in part, from higher rates of survey participation for resident mothers than nonresident fathers (Cherlin, Griffith, & McCarthy, 1983; Schaeffer et al., 1991). Although nonresident fathers may report higher child support payments because of the social desirability of paying child support, they may also include in their reports financial transfers of which mothers are ignorant, such as visitation expenses and direct payments to children or to a third party on the children's behalf (e.g., paying a physician or dentist for a child's checkup). Similarly, our knowledge of what happens during nonresident fathers' visits with their children comes from mothers, who are unlikely to be present to observe what goes on (Furstenberg & Nord, 1985). Fathers are also more appropriate respondents to questions about their problems in arranging visits, although both parents' reports would be preferable (e.g., Braver, Wolchik, Sandler, Fogas, & Zvetina, 1991). Nonresident fathers certainly are better sources of information about their own attitudes toward the children and their paternal responsibilities.

This chapter uses data from the 1987-1988 National Survey of Families and Households (NSFH) to describe nonresident fathers' involvement with children in the fathers' own words. This chapter has three goals. First, it describes nonresident fathers using data from the NSFH, a recent nationally representative sample of adults. Based on unmatched samples of parents, the description focuses on the degree to which the sample of nonresident fathers resembles a comparable sample of resident mothers on social, economic, and demographic characteristics. Second, it examines levels of paternal involvement, including financial transfers to children, child support, and frequency of visits, and compares nonresident fathers' reports with those of resident mothers. We ask whether nonresident fathers and mothers describe paternal involvement in the same way after differences in the rates of survey participation are taken into account. The third goal is to describe nonresident fathers' attitudes about their role as a parent.

Nonresident Fathers and the Paternal Role

When Do Men Act Like Fathers?

Marriage and parenthood are becoming increasingly separate institutions in the United States (Cherlin, 1988b). Today, nearly a quarter of births occur to unmarried parents, and a third of children born to married parents experience the breakup of their parents' marriage (Bumpass & Sweet, 1989; National Center for Health Statistics, 1990, Table 1-31). Many of these children acquire social parents through their biological parents' remarriage and nonmarital cohabitation (Bumpass & Sweet, 1989), although the process of acquisition is often complex (Mott, 1990). Because children in single-parent households usually live with their mothers, the father role is in considerable flux, both for men who live apart from their biological children and for those who live with the biological children of another man (e.g., Furstenberg, 1988b; Marsiglio, Chapter 11, this volume; Seltzer, 1991). Men's rights and responsibilities to children may be codified in custody and child support laws, but the role of father for separated and divorced men is largely voluntary. Evidence of voluntarism comes from surveys showing low rates of child support awards and payments and limited social contact with children after separation (Furstenberg, Nord, Peterson, & Zill, 1983; Seltzer & Bianchi, 1988; U.S. Bureau of the Census, 1991, Table C) despite federal and state efforts to improve child support enforcement and mothers' claims that they prefer fathers to be involved after separation (Furstenberg, 1988b). Certainly some men show strong commitment to their paternal responsibilities despite the difficulty of negotiating their involvement with the children's mother, a (sometimes uncooperative) former spouse or lover. Understanding the role of nonresident fathers requires more information about how fathers view their responsibilities to children and how they view the costs and benefits of their relationships with children. To date, social research offers little insight into the factors or individual characteristics that encourage some men to continue acting like fathers even when they no longer live with their children. Fathers' involvement with children before a separation may explain some nonresident fathers' greater investment in child rearing, but the evidence on this is mixed (Lowery, 1986; Wallerstein & Huntington, 1983; Wallerstein & Kelly, 1980a). Although few men anticipate divorce and becoming a nonresident father (Lund, 1987), the attitudes toward family responsibilities and fatherhood developed during marriage may be important determinants of continued involvement after disruption.

Nonresident Fathers' Attitudes Toward Parenthood

Attitudes and Survey Participation. Nonresident fathers may express attitudes toward the role of father in a way that makes it particularly difficult to study such men. They may express their feelings about paternity by denying that they have children who live elsewhere. Men may feel no emotional ties to children whom they see infrequently, if at all (Furstenberg, 1988b), and some men may not know that they are biological fathers. Survey coverage of nonresident fathers is poor, both for national surveys, such as the Current Population Survey (Cherlin et al., 1983), and for surveys of child support populations (Schaeffer et al., 1991). Thus any study of men's attitudes toward the role of nonresident father must confront the question of how nonresponse affects the degree to which the findings characterize all men who might have biological children living elsewhere. Because it is important to know fathers' views of the separation process and their attitudes toward continued involvement with children, we attempt to identify a sample of nonresident fathers for which bias from nonparticipation is less severe. Our strategy is to restrict attention to a smaller, well-defined subsample of fathers using a demographic characteristic of the families prior to separation to define the sample. This approach differs from previous strategies by identifying samples based on an independent variable that may predict paternal involvement. Previous strategies either compare resident and nonresident parents without attention to differences in survey participation rates (e.g., Stephen, 1989) or identify resident and nonresident parents who report similar levels of involvement, thereby selecting the sample on the basis of the dependent variable (e.g., Peterson & Nord, 1987). Sampling on the dependent variable biases parameter estimates from the conventional statistical models that researchers generally use to examine fathers' contact with children after separation.

Sources of Variation in Fathers' Attitudes. Nonresident fathers' attitudes toward parenthood depend on their (a) current family arrangements, (b) relationships with their former spouses and children, (c) social background, including education and other aspects of fathers' social placement, and (d) involvement with nonresident children. Current family arrangements include whether the nonresident father is remarried or living in a nonmarital union, whether he lives with other children, and the characteristics of these children (e.g., biological or stepchildren). Women mediate men's relationships with children by supervising and delegating child-rearing tasks to fathers when both parents live with their children (Backett, 1987). However, little is known about how second wives or cohabiting partners affect nonresident fathers' activities and attitudes about caring for children who live with their mother. When nonresident fathers remarry, they decrease their involvement with children from a previous relationship, perhaps because the new relationship competes with earlier ones for the father's time and attention (Furstenberg et al., 1983; Seltzer, 1991; Seltzer & Bianchi, 1988). Some fathers who remarry, however, may do so because they hold strong family values that lead to their continued commitment to paternal responsibilities to children after divorce. If their new wives share these family values, they may facilitate nonresident fathers' involvement with children.

The number, sex, and biological/step composition of children with whom men live may also affect their attitudes about being a parent. The more children for whom fathers are responsible, the more complicated and unmanageable it may be to look after them. On the other hand, having more children may also make the tasks of child rearing more interesting and sociable. Fathers are more involved in child rearing when they have sons (Marsiglio, 1991b; Morgan, Lye, & Condran, 1988), but their greater involvement may increase the strains of being a parent. Whether the children are biological or stepchildren also affects fathers' attitudes about child rearing. Men who live with stepchildren adopt many of the tasks of child rearing, but they are less engaged socially and emotionally with their stepchildren than are resident biological fathers (Thomson, McLanahan, & Curtin, 1992). Stepfamily relationships are more complex than those in original families and require that relative strangers become intimates in a short period of time (Beer, 1988). When men live with both biological and stepchildren, they are more likely to see themselves as fatherlike in their stepfather role than when they live with stepchildren only (Marsiglio, Chapter 11, this volume). Thus men who live with both biological and stepchildren may perceive greater benefits of paternity, but they may also view the task of balancing the competing demands of biological and stepchildren as complicated.

Nonresident fathers' attitudes about parenting also depend on the characteristics of the ex-wife/partner and of their nonresident children. Resident mothers may be gatekeepers who limit fathers' contacts with children or the conditions under which contact may occur (e.g., Wallerstein & Kelly, 1980b), thus continuing women's management of the father-child relationship even after separation. Resident mothers' remarriage may decrease paternal involvement after separation, perhaps because remarriage increases the complexity and strains of balancing old and new family relationships (e.g., Furstenberg et al., 1983; Seltzer & Bianchi, 1988). Resident mothers' education may also affect nonresident fathers' attitudes about child rearing. Resident mothers with more education may be better able to support themselves and therefore have greater independence from their children's nonresident fathers than mothers with less education. Mothers' education also affects how they structure their own and their children's time (Medrich, Roizen, Rubin, & Buckley, 1983). Highly educated mothers may exercise more control over children's schedules, limiting nonresident fathers' own responsibility for coordinating children's time commitments. The number and sex of nonresident children may also affect fathers' attitudes toward parenthood in much the same way that children's characteristics affect fathers' attitudes when they share the same household. However, evidence on nonresident fathers' greater involvement with sons than daughters after divorce is mixed (Furstenberg et al., 1983; Hess & Camara, 1979; Hetherington, Cox, & Cox, 1982; Mott, 1993; Seltzer, 1991; Seltzer & Bianchi, 1988).

Fathers' social background, particularly education, is another source of variation in their attitudes about being a parent. A father's education affects his attitudes about having children (Hoffman & Manis, 1979), the values he thinks are important for children to learn (Alwin, 1984), and his attitudes about how women and men should divide family responsibilities (Mason & Lu, 1988). Fathers with higher education may be more involved in child rearing, in the light of the positive association between education and egalitarian gender role attitudes. When fathers are more involved, they are likely to view child rearing as more social. Nonresident fathers with higher educations may be more critical of their own and of resident mothers' performances as parents. Highly educated fathers may also see the tasks of child rearing as complicated if they have had greater exposure to theories of child development and child-rearing manuals.

Finally, fathers who maintain close ties with their children who live elsewhere may derive greater benefits of parenthood. They are likely to see the activities of child rearing as more sociable and interesting. Nonresident fathers who see their children frequently and who pay child support are more likely to think that they are doing a good job of being a father, compared with those who do not keep ties to children. Alternatively, fathers who find the tasks of parenting especially onerous or painful may respond by disengaging from their nonresident children and limiting their participation in child rearing after divorce (Hetherington, Cox, & Cox, 1978; Lund, 1987).

Method

Sample

Ideal data for a problem of this type would include a sample in which both parents reported about child rearing after separation. In the best of all possible worlds, these reports would be supplemented by data from an external criterion that could be used to validate mothers' and fathers' reports about the same outcome (joint legal custody, paying child support, and so on). These data requirements cannot be met by large, national surveys; yet data from national surveys are essential for describing the family and living arrangements of U.S. children. This chapter uses data from independent (unmatched), cross-sectional samples of nonresident fathers and resident mothers in the 1987-1988 National Survey of Families and Households (NSFH). The NSFH is a probability sample of adults living in households, with oversamples of African Americans, Puerto Ricans, Mexican Americans, single parents, stepparents, cohabiting couples, and recently married persons. We use sample weights to take account of unequal probabilities of sample selection (Sweet, Bumpass, & Call, 1988).

We use data from primary respondents. The first stage of the analysis uses data from approximately 1,500 mothers who live with children under 18 whose father is living in another household, and approximately 480 fathers who report that they have children under 18 living in another household with their mother. Both samples include parents whose children were born in and outside of marriages. The unit of analysis in each subsample is the family defined by the parent's report. The overall response rate for the survey was 74%, but response rates were lower for never-married, separated, and divorced men (Sweet & Bumpass, 1989).

The second stage of the analysis uses data from those divorced nonresident fathers who responded to the self-administered questionnaire items about attitudes toward parenthood ($n = 184$). Nonresident fathers for whom the attitude items are missing were less likely to live with other minor children, to pay any child support, or to visit their nonresident children. This suggests that men for whom paternal responsibilities are less salient are underrepresented in the section of the analysis dealing with role attitudes.

Procedures and Measures

The NSFH questionnaire was designed to obtain the same information about the nonresident parents' involvement with children from both resident and nonresident parents. Questions about nonresident parents' contact with children asked about contact with a randomly selected child identified at the beginning of the sequence about nonresident parents' involvement. The sequence also included measures of conflict between parents on six aspects of postseparation child rearing and a small number of items asking the respondent to describe the other parent's characteristics, such as whether the parent had remarried and had children since the breakup of the previous relationship. In addition, the questionnaire includes detailed education, marriage, and fertility histories that we use to determine respondents' education at marriage, parents' marital status when the random child was born, and time separated. For ever-married respondents, the data include information about the characteristics of the respondent's first spouse at the time of marriage. The first part of this chapter uses data from personal interviews with resident mothers and with nonresident fathers.

The second part combines the personal interview data with information from a self-administered questionnaire completed at the time of the survey to describe nonresident fathers' attitudes. Respondents were asked how they evaluated their experience as parents on six dimensions, measured as semantic differentials. The question begins with the instruction: "If you do not have any children under age 19, skip to . . ." The introduction to the semantic differentials asks: "How would you describe the things you do as a parent? Would you say that they were . . ." The items refer to all parenting activities without specifying that respondents should think only about the children who live with (or apart) from them and without referencing a specific child. The semantic differentials have values ranging from 1 to 7 and include these pairs of contrasts: boring versus interesting, unappreciated versus appreciated, lonely versus sociable, poorly done versus well done, complicated versus simple, and overwhelming versus manageable.[1] We discuss these attitude items in detail below.

We consider four groups of independent variables in the analysis of role attitudes: father's current family arrangements, characteristics of the ex-wife and children from that relationship, the father's social background, and father's involvement with nonresident children. Current family arrangements are indicated by a dichotomous variable coded 1 if the father is remarried or living with a female partner and 0 if he is single, and by four dichotomous variables describing the children who live in the father's household. Of these, three indicate the step- and biological relationship between the father and children in the household: only stepchildren, step- and biological children, and only biological children. The omitted category is no children. We also identify cases in which the father lives with at least one boy, regardless of whether the child is a biological or stepson. Characteristics of the previous relationship include the number of children in the divorced family, the ex-wife's education at marriage (years completed), and a dummy variable indicating that the ex-wife has remarried (versus not remarried or the father does not know her marital status). Father's background is measured by his education in years of schooling completed. Nonresident father's involvement with children is measured by number of times the nonresident father and child visited each other in the previous year, annual amount of child support paid, and number of extended visits (i.e., visits lasting longer than a weekend). For cases with missing data on child support payments and number of extended visits, we substitute the mean value for nonmissing cases and include dummy variables to identify cases with imputed values on these variables. The analysis also controls for the length of time that the nonresident father and children have been separated, distance between the nonresident father's household and where his children live, and whether the father is white (versus non-white).

Analysis Strategy

First, we compare the sample of nonresident fathers with the sample of resident mothers to evaluate the degree to which the former suffers from lower response rates. This stage of the analysis defines a subsample of nonresident fathers that is comparable to a similarly defined subsample of resident mothers. We evaluate comparability based on demographic characteristics of the samples, such as whether the parents were married when the child was born, race, and parents' education. Information about demographic characteristics comes from self-reports as well as proxy reports, that is, resident mothers' reports about the children's nonresident father and fathers' reports about the children's mother. We compare the distributions of these key variables across the two samples. Once we identify samples with similar distributions, we compare reports about paternal involvement for the restricted, similarly defined subsamples of nonresident fathers and resident mothers. We use logistic and ordinary least squares (OLS) regression to predict various aspects of involvement, controlling for family background and whether the respondent is the mother or father. These models include interactions of the independent variables by sex of respondent to determine whether conclusions about the factors that predict involvement depend on who the respondent is.

In the second stage of the analysis, we use the restricted subsample of nonresident fathers to describe their view of the father role and to examine the association between family characteristics, including current level of involvement with children, and fathers' role evaluations. This stage has descriptive goals in the light of the severe limitations of using cross-sectional data to examine causal relationships between attitudes and behavior. We estimate two models for each of the role evaluations. The first estimates the association between family characteristics and role attitudes without taking into account nonresident fathers' contact with children and child support. The second includes nonresident fathers' involvement. We enter the involvement variables as a separate step because these variables define the context in which fathers conduct the activities of parenthood for children who live apart from them. Although the causal association between these activities and fathers' attitudes is ambiguous, the measures of child support and contact do describe behavior in the year prior to the survey in which the fathers report their attitudes. Despite the obvious qualifications required when using cross-sectional data to predict attitudes, we include this part of the analysis because the NSFH data provide unique insight into attitudes about paternal responsibilities to children. Our analysis of this large, representative sample complements work on nonresident fathers that uses small, selective samples with in-depth interviews (e.g., Arendell, 1992a; Furstenberg et al., 1992; Haskins, 1988). Both approaches further understanding of why some fathers participate in child rearing after separation and others do not.

Results

Nonresident Fathers and Survey Participation

Who Are the Nonresident Fathers? Table 9.1 shows selected characteristics of the parents and families represented by the two unmatched samples of mothers and fathers. Mothers are those who report that they have a biological child under age 18 whose father is alive but living in another household (*n* = 1,503). Fathers are those who report that they have a biological or adopted child under 18 who is living with his or her mother in another household (*n* = 482). As noted above, the child referent is randomly selected when more than one of the respondent's children lives apart from the other parent. The dramatic difference in unweighted numbers of cases occurs, in part, because the NSFH double-sampled single parents and those in stepfamily households. These conditions increase the number of resident mothers in the sample because they are, by definition, living as single parents or, if remarried, living with a stepfather to the random child. When the data are weighted to take account of unequal probabilities of sample selection resulting from oversampling, the numbers of cases are closer, but resident mothers still outnumber nonresident fathers by nearly two to one, suggesting severe underrepresentation of nonresident fathers. Table 9.1 includes weighted statistics.[2] Sample sizes vary somewhat across horizontal panels of the table because of missing data on the characteristics of interest.

Other evidence in Table 9.1 is also consistent with underrepresentation of nonresident fathers in the NSFH sample. The first row shows that 52% of the resident mothers have randomly selected children who were born within marriage, compared with 62% for nonresident fathers. The second row in Table 9.1 shows that, among respondents who reported about a child born in a marriage, approximately equal percentages had that child in a first marriage.[3] That the sample of nonresident fathers includes a much higher percentage of men who report that the random child was born in a marriage is consistent with a number of other differences between the samples of mothers and fathers shown in Table 9.1. For instance, compared with whites, African Americans have higher rates of nonmarital childbearing, and the racial composition of the nonresident-father sample includes a lower percentage of African Americans compared with the mother sample. Differential representation of nonmarital relationships in the two samples is also consistent with the higher percentage of fathers who say that they have a legal agreement governing their separation from the child's mother.

Table 9.1 also shows proxy and self-reports about each parent's current marital status and whether they have had additional children since the relationship with the child's other parent ended. Fathers are more likely to report that they and the child's mother are remarried, whereas mothers are slightly more likely to report that both parents had additional children. The table also shows sample differences on reports about legal aspects of the parents' separation and their relationship after the separation.

The bottom part of the table shows that nonresident fathers report much more frequent contact with children than do mothers. Fathers are more likely to say they saw the random child last year, that they had extended visits lasting longer than a weekend, and that they paid child support. However, among those who report paying or receiving any child support, the difference in amounts of support paid/received is small ($34 a month more based on fathers' reports) and is not statistically significant. Greater similarity between fathers' and mothers' reports conditional on having a legal agreement or paying support is consistent with Peterson and Nord's (1987) findings from the Survey of Income and Program Participation.

Table 9.1 shows that the samples of resident mothers and nonresident fathers in the NSFH are not comparable, in part because of differential rates of survey participation. To compare mothers' and fathers' experiences of separation and divorce requires samples with reasonably comparable response rates. We therefore examine a subset of parents for

Table 9.1 Selected Characteristics of All Resident Mothers and Nonresident Fathers

| | Respondent | | | |
Characteristics	Resident Mother		Nonresident Father	Statistical Significance
Relationship				
Child born in marriage	52.0%	(1,474)	62.0% (446)	**
Child born in first marriage, for marital births	87.6%	(781)	86.0% (276)	n.s.
Race: African American	30.4%		22.7%	*
White	59.0		66.1	
Other	10.6		11.2	
	100	(1,503)	100 (482)	
Mother is (re)married	22.7%	(1,503)	32.4% (426)	***
Father is (re)married	33.1%	(1,293)	40.9% (482)	*
Mother had more children	29.5%	(1,503)	22.6% (430)	*
Father had more children	28.2%	(1,269)	25.5% (482)	n.s.
Child				
Mean age (years)	8.7	(1,503)	9.8 (482)	**
Child is a boy	51.2%	(1,481)	53.8% (481)	n.s.
Legal aspects of separation				
Legal agreement exists	55.4%	(1,498)	71.3% (462)	***
Child support award, for those with a legal agreement	91.6%	(844)	90.6% (320)	n.s.
Parents have joint legal custody, for those with a legal agreement	19.1%	(810)	29.6% (309)	**

(Continued)

whom response rates are likely to be more comparable than for the undifferentiated samples described in Table 9.1. We use information from Table 9.1 about parents' marital status when the referent child was born to identify more similar samples.

Table 9.2 reports the characteristics of resident mothers and nonresident fathers who reported about a random child who was born in the respondent's first marriage. Table 9.2 includes more characteristics than Table 9.1 because, for families of children born in marriage, the marriage and fertility histories provide information about time since separation, sibship size, and each spouse's education at first marriage.

Table 9.1 Continued

	Respondent		
Characteristics	Resident Mother	Nonresident Father	Statistical Significance
Relationship after separation			
Frequency of father's visits with child:			
not at all	29.1%	19.7%	**
once a year	11.2	8.0	
several times a year	17.6	18.3	
1 to 3 times a month	15.6	21.6	
once a week	12.1	16.7	
several times a week	14.4	15.8	
	100 (1,492)	100 (468)	
Father has extended visits, for those with any visits	28.6% (921)	43.4% (343)	***
Any child support paid/ received in past year	45.8% (1,420)	77.4% (425)	***
Mean monthly payment, if any	$187 (610)	$221 (288)	n.s.
Parents have conflict about the children	47.9% (1,485)	57.4% (460)	**

SOURCE: National Survey of Families and Households, Wave 1, 1987-1988.
NOTE: Statistics use weighted data. Unweighted numbers of cases in parentheses. Tests of statistical significance use weighted data to take account of double sampling for specific subgroups. Column totals may not equal 100% because of rounding error.
*$p \leq .05$, **$p \leq .01$, ***$p \leq .001$.

Table 9.2 shows much greater similarity between the samples of resident mothers and nonresident fathers when we restrict attention to parents of children born in the respondent's first marriage. Mothers and fathers each report that they have been separated about 7 years (81.4 and 89.2 months, respectively). The racial composition of the samples and the family size (whether each parent had more children and number of children in the divorced family) are also very similar for the two samples. However, the percentage of fathers who report that their former wife is remarried is slightly greater than the percentage of resident mothers who are remarried (40.4% versus 31.5%, respectively).

The data show substantial similarity between proxy and self-reports about how much education the parent had completed at the time of the first marriage. The only difference between resident mothers' reports about their schooling and nonresident fathers' reports about their ex-

Table 9.2 Characteristics of Resident Mothers and Nonresident Fathers of Random Children Born in First Marriages

Characteristics	Resident Mother		Nonresident Father		Statistical Significance
			Respondent		
Relationship					
Separated < 12 months	8.4%		5.9%		n.s.
Mean duration of separation (months)	81.4	(681)	89.2	(232)	n.s.
Individual parent					
Race: African American	13.3%		10.4%		n.s.
White	78.8		79.0		
Other	7.9		10.6		
	100	(681)	100	(232)	
Mother is remarried	31.5%	(681)	40.4%	(210)	*
Father is remarried	39.4%	(625)	46.3%	(232)	n.s.
Mother had more children	23.0%	(681)	21.7%	(214)	n.s.
Father had more children	26.0%	(614)	23.8%	(232)	n.s.
Mother's education at first marriage (years)					
< 12	31.6%		24.3%		n.s.
12	43.8		56.4		
13-15	15.6		12.5		
16+	9.0		6.8		
	100	(568)	100	(227)	
Father's education at first marriage (years)					
< 12	28.3%		30.9%		n.s.
12	47.5		45.9		
13-15	16.1		13.4		
16+	8.1		9.9		
	100	(656)	100	(176)	
Child					
Mean age (years)	10.6	(681)	11.2	(232)	n.s.
Child is a boy	49.6%	(673)	55.3%	(232)	n.s.
Mean number of minor children	1.6	(681)	1.6	(232)	n.s.

(Continued)

wife's schooling is that a slightly higher percentage of mothers report that they had not finished high school when they married. However, differences between the two samples in mothers' and fathers' education

Table 9.2 Continued

Characteristics	Respondent				Statistical Significance
	Resident Mother		Nonresident Father		
Legal aspects of separation					
Legal agreement exists	80.6%	(679)	87.1%	(221)	n.s.
Child support award, for those with a legal agreement	93.2%	(545)	91.0%	(186)	n.s.
Parents have joint legal custody, for those with a legal agreement	20.2%	(521)	32.6%	(180)	**
Relationship after separation					
Mean distance apart (miles)	409	(632)	524	(225)	n.s.
Respondent does not know location of former spouse	7.8%	(678)	0.7%	(226)	***
Frequency of father's visits with child:					
not at all	18.7%		17.4%		n.s.
once a year	12.8		7.7		
several times a year	21.7		18.4		
1 to 3 times a month	22.7		24.0		
once a week	12.8		16.8		
several times a week	11.2		15.6		
	100	(677)	100	(222)	
Father has extended visits, for those with any visits	36.3%	(476)	52.6%	(171)	**
Number of extended visits, if any:					
1	32.1%		18.9%		n.s.
2	25.1		19.6		
3+	42.9		61.6		
	100	(167)	100	(88)	
Any child support paid/ received in past year	63.8%	(636)	85.8%	(200)	***
Mean monthly payment, if any	$222	(396)	$265	(168)	n.s.
Parents have conflict about the children	57.0%	(674)	60.2%	(219)	n.s.
Mean number of topics of disagreement (0-6)	1.3	(674)	1.8	(219)	**

SOURCE: National Survey of Families and Households, Wave 1, 1987-1988.
NOTE: Statistics use weighted data. Unweighted numbers of cases in parentheses. Tests of statistical significance use weighted data to take account of double sampling for specific subgroups. Column totals may not equal 100% because of rounding error.
$*p \leq .05, **p \leq .01, ***p \leq .001$.

are not statistically significant. Parents' reports about how much education the child's father had when the parents were married are also similar for this subsample.

Resident mothers and nonresident fathers both report approximately equal distances between the child's household and that of the nonresident father. However, a much higher percentage of mothers say that they do not know where the other parent lives (7.8% versus 0.7%, respectively). Nonresident fathers may keep track of where their children live even when they do not maintain contact with that child. Without paternal involvement, mothers lose track of where the father lives. Alternatively, this pattern may reflect a difference between the samples rather than a reporting difference between mothers and fathers.

Table 9.2 also shows that, for parents of children born in a first marriage, resident mothers and nonresident fathers report very similar levels of involvement. Nearly 81% of mothers and 87% of fathers say that they have a legal agreement about child support, visiting, or custody. Among those with a legal agreement, just over 90% of parents in both samples say that their agreement covers child support. Nonresident fathers are still more likely than mothers to report that they have joint legal custody of their children. Without a criterion, such as actual court documents describing the custody arrangement, it is impossible to determine whether this is a reporting difference that occurs because joint legal custody may be more salient to nonresident fathers who see it as an indication of their commitment to children or a difference resulting from sample selection (i.e., greater survey participation of involved fathers). Fathers' and mothers' reports about how frequently visits occur are similar, but about half of fathers say that their visits are extended stays compared with just over 36% of mothers. This pattern is mirrored in reports about child support. Nonresident fathers still are more likely to report that they paid child support than mothers are to say that they received child support (85.8% versus 63.8%). Fathers may pay child support to a third party, such as the welfare agency or for health insurance, which might explain some of the difference in parents' reports.[4] Among those who receive any payments, fathers report paying slightly more than mothers receive, but as in the previous table the difference is not statistically significant at conventional levels. Finally, fathers report somewhat more areas of disagreement about postdivorce child rearing than do mothers.

The patterns in Table 9.2 and the contrast with the previous table suggest that restricting the sample to parents of children born in the first marriage reduces nonparticipation bias in estimates of levels of involvement based on nonresident fathers' reports. Although differences between resident and nonresident parents' reports persist even in the restricted sample, many of the differences are consistent with the different knowledge and points of view held by resident mothers and nonresident fathers. Additional analyses not shown indicate that comparisons between parents of children born in any marriage, not just a first marriage, lead to conclusions that are generally similar to those based on Table 9.2. In the remainder of this chapter, we restrict the analysis to children born in parents' first marriages, instead of children born in any marriage, because the NSFH data include information about first spouses' education. This enables us to incorporate both parents' education into analyses of fathers' involvement after separation and their attitudes about being a parent. Education is an important predictor of fathers' ability to pay child support (Seltzer, Schaeffer, & Charng, 1989) and of parents' attitudes about child rearing (Alwin, 1984).

Does It Matter Whether Fathers or Mothers Report? We ask two questions about differences between resident mothers' and nonresident fathers' reports. First, do conclusions about the level of involvement depend on the reporter? Second, do data from resident mothers and nonresident fathers suggest different conclusions about the factors that predict involvement after divorce? On the first question, Table 9.2 suggests that, even for explicitly defined subsamples for which problems of nonparticipation bias are reduced, nonresident fathers report greater involvement on some aspects of postdivorce child rearing than do resident mothers. To address the second question, we estimated models predicting (a) whether the father paid any child support, (b) amount of support paid in the year, (c) whether he visited the child, (d) number of visits in the year, and (e) whether there were any extended visits lasting longer than a weekend. Dichotomous outcomes were examined in logistic regressions, and amount of support and number of visits were examined in OLS regressions. Independent variables included those commonly used to predict paternal involvement after separation, including time separated, race, each parent's marital status and education, family size, whether the father had additional children, legal arrangements, and, for the contact outcomes, the random child's age and sex. We estimated fully pooled models, including an indicator of whether the respondent was the mother or father and the interaction of this variable with all other independent variables. Estimating the interactions did not significantly improve the fit of any of the models. However, mean differences between fathers and mothers persisted on all of these outcomes, except whether the father had any visits, when we controlled for main effects but excluded interactions.[5] We do not report the details of these analyses because of our null findings about sex differences in predictors of involvement and because the net mean differences generally replicate the zero-order associations reported in Table 9.2. We conclude that for the restricted sample of divorced parents whose children were born in the respondent's first marriage the factors that predict variation in paternal involvement are the same whether mothers or fathers report about them.[6] However, resident mothers and nonresident fathers do differ in their reports of mean levels of important aspects of paternal involvement, even when other factors are taken into account.

What Do Nonresident Fathers Say About Being a Parent?

This stage of the analysis uses the sample of nonresident fathers of a random child born in the parents' first marriage to describe how fathers feel about their role. As noted above, respondents completed a self-administered questionnaire including responses to six semantic differentials characterizing their attitudes about parenting tasks. Table 9.3 shows the means and standard deviations of each item for this sample. The items have been recoded so that positive evaluations have higher scores. Note that Table 9.3 shows the role evaluations only for nonresident fathers for whom all of the parental role evaluations were completed in the self-administered questionnaire. This restriction reduces the initial sample size of 232 by 48 cases. Of these, most fathers either indicated that they were not parents or left all of these items blank but answered questions about other roles in the same series. To shed light on this missing data problem, we used information from another questionnaire sequence in which men were asked how much they agreed or disagreed with the statement: "I often wish I could be free from the responsibility of being a parent." Nonresident fathers who did not complete the semantic differentials were more likely to want to be free of parental responsibilities. Thus the role attitudes examined here describe the beliefs of nonresident fathers for whom the paternal role is more salient and, perhaps, more desirable.

Table 9.3 shows that nonresident fathers in this sample generally view their parenting activities as interesting, appreciated, sociable, and

Table 9.3 Means and Standard Deviations for Nonresident Fathers'
Evaluation of Their Parent Role

| | | Father Lives With Other Minor Children | |
Aspect of Role	All	Yes	No
Interesting	5.79	5.83	5.75
	(1.21)	(1.15)	(1.27)
Appreciated	5.62	5.61	5.63
	(1.39)	(1.42)	(1.37)
Sociable	5.64	5.94*	5.35*
	(1.50)	(1.26)	(1.65)
Well done	5.71	5.79	5.64
	(1.15)	(.98)	(1.29)
Simple	4.45	4.47	4.42
	(1.61)	(1.67)	(1.56)
Manageable	5.03	4.80	5.27
	(1.68)	(1.78)	(1.54)

SOURCE: National Survey of Families and Households, Wave 1, 1987-1988. Sample is nonresident fathers
of a random child born in father's first marriage. Fathers must have completed the self-administered
questionnaire and all role-related items.
NOTE: Scores on role evaluations range from 1 to 7. Statistics and tests of statistical significance use
weighted data. Unweighted number of cases is 184: 85 with other minor children and 99 without other
minor children in the household.
*$p \leq .05$.

well done. Mean scores are somewhat lower for evaluations of how
manageable and simple the activities are. As might be expected, nonresident fathers who also have biological and/or stepchildren in their
household see parenting as more sociable than do fathers without
children at home. Other differences by whether there are children in the
household are small. Although the items are somewhat skewed toward
the positive ends of the 1 to 7 scales, each variable includes a sufficient
number of cases across values of the scale to use OLS regression for
descriptive purposes.

To determine whether the individual role evaluations described a
single underlying construct, we conducted a series of exploratory factor
analyses using principal components analysis and varimax rotation. The
procedure suggests that the items produce two factors. The first factor
reflected the degree to which fathers evaluated their parenting tasks as

rewarding. The items interesting, appreciated, sociable, and well done had the highest loadings on this factor. The second factor was quite weak. As a result, we constructed a summary index of the potential benefits of parenthood by summing responses to the four items that defined the first factor.[7] The index ranges in value from 10 to 28 with a mean of 22.8 and a standard deviation of 4.2 for the sample used in the attitudes analysis below. The alpha for this index is .81. This compares favorably with the reliability for a six-item index, .68. We treat the remaining items, evaluations of how simple and how manageable the parenting activities are, as single items.[8]

Table 9.4 reports OLS estimates for the associations between family characteristics and the summative index for the benefits of parenthood and the individual scales for how simple and how manageable parenting activities are. The analysis examines four groups of independent variables: current family arrangements, characteristics of nonresident children and their mother, father's social background, and father's involvement with children from the previous marriage. The table shows two models for each dependent variable—one with and one without the measures of nonresident fathers' involvement with children after divorce. The factors included in our models explain only a small proportion of the variation in nonresident fathers' role evaluations. Nevertheless, our data show intriguing patterns. We evaluate statistical significance using a two-tailed test because the implications of previous research, in general, do not suggest directional hypotheses. Because of the small number of cases in the sample, we also draw attention to associations that are statistically significant at $p \leq .10$. We discuss Model 1 first.

Fathers who are remarried or cohabiting report that being a parent is less manageable than do fathers who are single. Fathers' remarriage is not associated with reports about the benefits of paternity or about how simple the tasks of parenthood are, although the sign for the latter coefficient is negative. Compared to not living with children, living with stepchildren only and living with both step- and biological children increase fathers' reports of how manageable parenting is, perhaps because the father's new partner or wife takes more responsibility for the children when some are hers from a previous relationship. Fathers who live with biological children only also report greater benefits of being a parent than do those without children in their household. Including the three variables describing the step-/biological composition of children explains a statistically significant proportion of variation in the benefits index and in the manageable item ($F = 2.96$, $p \leq .05$, and $F =$

Table 9.4 Selected Variables From OLS Estimates of Effects of Family Characteristics on Nonresident Fathers' Evaluation of Their Parent Role

	Benefits Index		Simple		Manageable	
	1	*2*	*1*	*2*	*1*	*2*
Current family arrangements						
Father remarried or cohabiting	−.019	.080	−.125	−.136	−1.46*	−1.50*
	(.913)	(.936)	(.325)	(.338)	(.325)	(.341)
Only stepchildren in household[a]	.574	.598	.486	.499	1.16*	1.20*
	(1.36)	(1.35)	(.482)	(.489)	(.483)	(.493)
Step- and biological children[a]	2.53	2.24	−.631	−.667	2.95*	3.01*
	(1.83)	(1.84)	(.650)	(.666)	(.651)	(.671)
Only biological children	2.95*	3.08*	.381	.389	.677	.689
in household[a]	(1.21)	(1.21)	(.432)	(.436)	(.432)	(.440)
At least one boy in household	−2.53*	−2.35*	−.441	−.435	−.926*	.964*
	(1.06)	(1.08)	(.378)	(.390)	(.379)	(.393)
Nonresident children and ex-wife						
Number of children in	.096	.044	.131	.189	−.100	−.074
divorced family	(.392)	(.410)	(.140)	(.148)	(.140)	(.149)
Ex-wife's education (years)[b]	−.375†	−.299	.132†	.156†	−.188*	−.178*
	(.224)	(.232)	(.080)	(.084)	(.080)	(.084)
Ex-wife remarried	−.035	−.063	.042	.029	−.419	−.403
	(.772)	(.783)	(.275)	(.283)	(.275)	(.285)
Father's background						
Father's education (years)	.015	−.021	−.122*	−.122*	.002	−.002
	(.140)	(.144)	(.050)	(.052)	(.050)	(.053)
Involvement with nonresident children						
Number of visits in past year	—	.767	—	.044	—	−.016
(÷ by 100)		(.678)		(.245)		(.247)
Annual child support paid	—	.021	—	−.005	—	−.001
(÷ by 100)		(.018)		(.006)		(.006)
Number of long visits in	—	.072	—	−.005	—	−.014
past year		(.076)		(.027)		(.028)
Constant	27.8*	26.5*	4.65*	4.52*	8.18*	8.19*
	(2.58)	(2.62)	(.919)	(.947)	(.920)	(.955)
R^2	.123	.167	.120	.138	.227	.231
S.E.E.	4.30	4.26	1.53	1.54	1.53	1.55

SOURCE: National Survey of Families and Households, Wave 1, 1987-1988, nonresident fathers of random child born in father's first marriage.
NOTE: Data are unweighted, $N = 174$. Benefits index is described in the text. Standard errors are in parentheses. All models control for months separated, distance to children of divorce, and whether the father is white. Models with involvement variables include dummy variables to indicate missing data on child support payments and number of long visits.
a. Omitted category is no children in the household.
b. Ex-wife's education is years of completed schooling at marriage, based on father's proxy report.
†$p \leq .10$, *$p \leq .05$.

7.23, $p \leq .01$, respectively) but not for the simple item ($F = 1.56$).[9] Fathers who live with either a step- or biological son report fewer benefits of being a father and also find being a father less manageable, but the presence of a son is not associated with reports of how simple the tasks of parenthood are. In analyses not shown, we also find that the presence of preschool-age children in the household is not associated with nonresident fathers' role evaluations.

Characteristics of nonresident children and their mother and the father's ex-wife are also associated with fathers' role evaluations. Ex-wife's education has a significant, negative association with benefits that nonresident fathers perceive in the parent role. Mothers with more schooling may be more critical of men's performance as fathers or rely less on men during and after marriage. As a result, nonresident fathers whose ex-wives are highly educated may not evaluate their performance as fathers favorably either.[10] Compared with fathers whose ex-wives have less education, those whose ex-wives have more education see parenting activities as simpler but less manageable. Perhaps when fathers have less opportunity to supervise their children or to organize their children's schedules, their activities as fathers are simple but difficult to manage psychologically because of the lack of control. Neither the number of children in the divorced family nor the age and sex of the random child referred to in the fathers' reports about visits affect his role evaluations. (Tables for age and sex of child not shown.)

A father's own education is negatively associated with how simple he thinks parenting is but not with the perceived benefits of these activities or with how manageable they are. Compared with those with less education, fathers with more education may think that child rearing is complicated because they are influenced by theories of child development and the advice of child-rearing experts. The finding that father's education does not affect reports about how manageable parenting is may occur because educated fathers are better equipped to manage the responsibilities of being a parent than less educated fathers, but those with more education may face greater demands for balancing paid work and family obligations.

With a minor exception, none of the coefficients for the variables described above changes appreciably when the nonresident father's child support and visits with children are entered into the analysis (see Model 2). Only the coefficient for the effect of ex-wife's education on the benefits index declines in magnitude and loses statistical significance. The results show that taking account of fathers' involvement with nonresident children does not affect fathers' evaluations of the benefits of parenting activities or how simple or manageable these activities are. The absence of association between any of the measures of paternal involvement and nonresident father's attitudes may result from respondents interpreting the items as asking questions about tasks they do for children who live with them rather than for their nonresident children. We also examined the association between fathers' attitudes and conflict with the resident mother. Conflict is not associated with perceptions of the benefits of being a parent or how manageable parenting tasks are. However, when conflict is higher, fathers are less likely to think that parenthood is simple (not shown).

Summary and Discussion

Our findings show that the NSFH, an important national study of U.S. adults, underrepresents nonresident fathers. This is consistent with findings from other large national data sources. Difficulties of locating and interviewing nonresident fathers lead to high nonresponse rates for this important population. Recent efforts to reform the child support system are informed by social research that relies on resident mothers' reports and highly selected samples of nonresident fathers. To develop more effective policies and to address the concerns of all nonresident fathers and their children requires information about the characteristics of more representative samples. We compare nonresident fathers' and resident mothers' reports about their relationship, demographic characteristics, and fathers' involvement with children after separation to identify a subsample of fathers for which nonparticipation biases are smaller.

We find that when we restrict attention to nonresident fathers and resident mothers who report about fathers' contact with a child who was born in the respondent's first marriage, parents describe their own and the other parents' characteristics much more similarly. A few differences persist, but most are not statistically significant at conventional levels. However, nonresident fathers still report somewhat higher levels of involvement with children after divorce than do mothers. This may occur because fathers have greater knowledge about how much child support they pay or because the time they spend visiting children is more salient to them than it is to resident mothers. Nevertheless, for some aspects of paternal involvement, nonresident fathers' and resident mothers' reports are quite similar. Also, the family and individual characteristics that predict fathers' involvement are the same whether they are based on mothers' or fathers' reports. This suggests that other national samples that also underrepresent nonresident fathers may still be useful for studying paternal involvement in child rearing after separation if analyses are restricted to samples of families separated by divorce.

We used the restricted subsample of fathers to examine attitudes about being a parent. Even in this sample of men who identified themselves as nonresident fathers, a significant minority did not respond to questions about being a parent. Nonresident fathers who skipped these items were more likely to report that they felt burdened by the responsibilities of parenthood. Among men who completed the role evaluations, most described their parenting activities positively. Characteristics of the children with whom the nonresident father lives have important effects on attitudes about being a parent. Living with other biological children increases fathers' perceptions of the benefits of paternity, and those who live with at least one stepchild report that parenting is more manageable, perhaps because there are clearer rules about fathers' responsibilities for children who live with them than for nonresident children. Our findings about the greater importance of coresident children than nonresident children for fathers' attitudes about parenthood support views of contemporary fatherhood that emphasize its sequential nature (Furstenberg, 1988b; Seltzer & Bianchi, 1988).

Our results also reinforce the view that women orchestrate men's relationships with children. We find that nonresident fathers' remarriage or cohabitation decreases fathers' reports about how manageable it is to be a parent. The ex-wives' (resident mothers') education also affects nonresident fathers' attitudes about being a parent. When mothers are more highly educated, fathers report that being a parent is simpler, but mothers' education has a negative effect on reports about the benefits of paternity. The resident mother's education and having a new partner are more important predictors of the nonresident father's role evaluations than his contributions to child support and the time he spends with his divorced children, neither of which was associated with the attitudes examined here.

The finding that mothers and stepmothers are important for understanding men's experience with the father role is paradoxical, given our emphasis in this chapter on identifying a reasonably representative sample of nonresident fathers who can speak for themselves about parenthood. When parents live together, mothers have power to direct men's interactions with their children (Backett, 1987). Women's control over children is much more pronounced when fathers and children live apart. Mothers control younger children's schedules and construct guidelines within which nonresident fathers may spend time with the children. Nonresident fathers have some autonomy when they are actually with their children, and those without a new wife or new partner gain experience in child rearing without a female moderator. Experience may enhance fathers' ability to pursue an independent relationship with children, but these efforts may be circumscribed by mothers who prefer to avoid their former spouse or who are busy juggling the demands of paid employment and family responsibilities. Understanding how separated parents negotiate child rearing and learning what arrangements are better for children are critical tasks for future research. Our findings point to the importance of examining these issues with data from well-defined samples of both mothers and fathers and to the difficulty of pursuing these questions when some nonresident fathers manage child rearing by disengagement.

Notes

1. We treat all of these items as bipolar. Assuming that the items are bipolar is reasonable for such items as poorly done versus well done, but to some respondents the contrast between other end points on the semantic differentials (e.g., overwhelming versus manageable) may not represent direct opposites. Differences in the degree to which each semantic differential is bipolar may explain discrepancies between results for items that one might otherwise expect to reflect a similar underlying construct (e.g., manageable and simple).

2. Tests of group differences use weighted data and the weighted number of cases for evaluating statistical significance. Weighted sample sizes are 690 and 393 for resident mothers and nonresident fathers, respectively.

3. The designation of parents' marital status at the random child's birth reflects the respondent's report about his or her own marriage and fertility. We cannot take into account whether the child was born in the first marriage of both parents because the data are not from matched parents in the same family.

4. Nonresident parents have been required since 1975 to pay child support to state welfare agencies when their children receive AFDC (Garfinkel, 1992).

5. The net difference between mothers and fathers on whether the father had any visits extending longer than a weekend was in the expected direction but only marginally significant ($t = 1.82, p \leq .10$).

6. We also estimated interaction models predicting these five aspects of paternal involvement for the unrestricted sample of all resident and nonresident parents (as shown

in Table 9.1). These models include fewer independent variables than are available for parents of children born in first marriages. For the dichotomous outcome of whether or not the father visits the child, we find that the factors predicting involvement depend on the sex of the respondent. For other aspects of involvement, inclusion of the interaction terms does not significantly improve the fit of the model.

7. The correlation between this equal-weights index and one that uses factor weights is .99.

8. We investigated whether to combine these items as a second summative index, but the low reliability of the index, .18, precluded this strategy. Results of the exploratory factor analyses are similar for weighted and unweighted data and for varying definitions of the sample of nonresident fathers.

9. Taking into account whether the father lives with at least one child from a previous relationship (i.e., whether he has physical custody of a child) does not improve the fit of the model for any of the three dependent variables (results not shown).

10. Ihinger-Tallman, Pasley, and Buehler (Chapter 4, this volume) point to the importance of former and current wives as significant others who influence fathers' identity after divorce.

10

Single Fathers With Custody

Do They Change Over Time?

GEOFFREY L. GREIF
ALFRED DeMARIS

With the number of fathers raising children alone following separation and divorce continuing to rise, such parenting arrangements are becoming institutionalized. Between 1970 and 1992, these fathers increased more than 300% to over 1.25 million while the number of single mothers during that same time period increased by 250% to slightly over 7 million (U.S. Bureau of the Census, 1993).

The systematic study of single fathers in the United States is only about 20 years old and began with a handful of small surveys undertaken in the mid-1970s. The research quickly established that, at least among those studied, fathers were capable of raising children satisfactorily and felt comfortable as the primary nurturers. As the research expanded to using standardized measures with larger surveys of more representative populations, it has tended to use cross-sectional data. With one exception (Greif, 1987), no longitudinal data targeting this population have been gathered.

Longitudinal research serves the purpose of establishing patterns of change as well as the direction of change (Menard, 1991). Learning how a particular group of fathers progresses over time offers researchers, policymakers, and clinicians the opportunity to further assess the potential viability of these families. It also offers the chance to refine interventions for those who may be experiencing difficulties that are not detectable through one-shot research approaches. This chapter reports on a 2-year (21-month) follow-up of a 1987-1988 survey of 117 single fathers with custody who participated in a larger survey. The focus in this analysis is on whether single fathers, many of whom have been raising children alone for a number of years, report changes related to their parenting role between Time 1 and Time 2. We also focus on the manner in which characteristics of fathers measured at Time 1 predict parenting outcomes 21 months later. These outcomes include several measures of the fathers' adjustment to single parenting. Because adjustment at Time 2 is heavily dependent upon the degree of adjustment already evinced at Time 1, Time 1 outcome measures are controlled in a multivariate analysis of Time 2 outcomes. In this manner, we are able to ask: Controlling for fathers' parenting adjustment at Time 1, what other characteristics of fathers are predictive of adjustment at Time 2? Implications for clinical practice with this population are offered based on the analysis.

Literature Review

How Do Divorced Fathers Adjust Over Time and What Factors Are Related to Their Adjustment?

It is well established that separation and divorce is usually a time of great stress and signals a difficult transition for most participants (Coleman & Ganong, 1990). Feelings of anger, frustration, and denial are common (Johnston & Campbell, 1988). Sadness and mourning for the loss of the relationship are typical reactions. Physical and mental health problems have been noted to be higher among the divorced when compared with married and single respondents as divorce remains, over time, a "nagging stressor" (Kitson & Morgan, 1990).

In a 4-year panel investigation comparing pre- and postdivorce psychological well-being of Chicago residents, significant depression was found in the newly divorced where it had not appeared previously (Menaghan & Lieberman, 1986). A subanalysis of those who were divorced at the time of the first interview found that their depression increased. It is suggested that certain conditions, including economic viability, may deteriorate over time as friends who initially rallied subsequently withdrew support as it was assumed the divorce crisis had abated. Gender was not a major predictor (Menaghan & Lieberman, 1986).

Interviews with 40 men (68% of whom were fathers) maritally separated between one and 6 months and then reinterviewed 3 to 4 months later were conducted to explore the impact of marital disruption (White & Bloom, 1981). At the time of the first interview, the majority felt they were adjusting better than they had anticipated. Loneliness was the most difficult problem confronting the men. Factors related to poor adjustment were attendance in psychotherapy, increased religious activity, social isolation, and decreased job performance. Almost every man in the study reported having moderate to severe difficulty in at least one area of adjustment. Four fifths of the fathers in the group noted that the presence of children increased their own difficulties. Approximately two thirds of those reinterviewed felt they had adjusted to their situation, while almost one third seemed worse off, with a handful reporting no change.

In a study of 123 divorced men (54% of whom were fathers), change was noted during follow-up interviews conducted 6 months and 1 year postdivorce (Mitchell-Flynn & Hutchinson, 1993). For example, feelings of loneliness, and concerns about finances and the reactions of coworkers, diminished while worries about children's adaptation grew. Men who were without children naturally did not have this last concern.

As alluded to above, when parenthood is factored in, new stresses exist. Divorced parents are coping not only with the loss of the marriage but also with the extra stress of raising children during this time of transition. The parent may be feeling guilty about subjecting a child to a single-parent experience with the ongoing emotional, financial, and physical strains that so commonly accompany it. The parent may also be upset about diminished contact with the child and, if contested, with dragging the child through an acrimonious court process.

Wallerstein and Kelly (1980b) found in their study of 60 divorcing families over a 5-year period that time seemed to help most parents. At the 5-year mark, two thirds of the men and more than half of the women reported that getting divorced had enhanced their lives, with those reporting sound adjustment initially seeming to stabilize the most. One third of men and women seemed to be functioning adequately initially. By the 5-year mark, this figure rose to as high as 57% of the women and 50% of the men. A few parents who were having problems initially were having even more problems with time. Fathers displayed less improvement than mothers. Having a history of problems initially was a predictor of problems at follow-up.

Tschann, Johnston, and Wallerstein (1989) also found a link between preseparation functioning and functioning 2 years later among an initial sample of 184 divorcing families. Women who had conflict with their ex-spouses or a great deal of either positive or negative attachment fared worse. For men, lower socioeconomic status, a conflictual relationship, and attachment also predicted problematic adjustment.

Divorced fathers reportedly experience more parental role strain than married fathers. In a comparison of 155 divorced fathers with 812 married fathers, Umberson and Williams (1993) uncovered higher levels of psychological distress and alcohol consumption among the former. They also found that the number of years the fathers were divorced was positively correlated with strain. The researchers hypothesize that this could be due to role strain increasing with time or that those with high levels of role strain remain unmarried.

Closely aligned with how a single parent may adapt over time is the question of the children's adjustment. Children whose parents divorce are clearly at greater risk for a wealth of problems, from the academic to the emotional, than children whose parents are married (Amato, 1993). Amato (1993) hypothesizes this may be due in part to children being subjected to parental conflict. A responsive or sensitive parent, sensing distress in his child, could potentially suffer along with the child. The children in Wallerstein and Kelly's (1980b) sample fluctuated over time, with many showing some improvement at 18 months and then a decline at 5 years. Specifically, over one third were depressed and one third were unhappy with their relationships with one or both parents at the 5-year mark. Overall, the majority of the sample had an initially acute period of distress followed by stabilization, with one third faring well over time, one third having difficulties, and the remainder falling between the two extremes.

What Is Known About Single Fathers With Custody and How They Adjust Over Time?

Perhaps contrary to popular belief, research has consistently established that single-father-headed families are viable (Greif, 1995). The literature reports that these fathers are satisfied with their role and fulfill it at least as well as single mothers. With a few exceptions, the literature tends to focus on middle-class white fathers whose income is usually between that of single mothers and married fathers (Meyer & Garasky, 1993). Fathers who experience a change in income after assuming custody appear to fare worse than those whose income is initially lower but does not vary (Greif, 1990).

Fathers gain custody for reasons ranging from the mother's mental incompetence or not wanting the children (Rosenthal & Keshet, 1981) to the children choosing the father and his having more financial resources (Chang & Deinard, 1982; Greif, 1985). Court decisions involving disputed custody are infrequent. Most are decided by mutual agreement (Bartz & Witcher, 1978; Rosenthal & Keshet, 1981). For example, the Greif and DeMaris (1989) survey of 1,132 fathers reports that 60% had the court rubber-stamp a prearrangement, 9% won custody after a brief battle, and 11% won custody after an extended one, with 13% not going to court at all.

Fathers who choose to have custody, a group Mendes (1976) calls seekers, tend to adapt more easily to the demands of parenting than those who have custody thrust upon them (assenters). Greif and DeMaris (1990) found that comfort with single parenting was greater for men who (a) had been in that role for a number of years, (b) were not affiliated with a religion, (c) had a satisfactory social life, (d) had a good relationship with the children, (e) had a higher income, (f) rated themselves highly as a parent, and (g) reported that visitation between the child and the mother was handled amicably or that there was no visitation (Greif & DeMaris, 1990). Fathers who contested custody in court and won held more positive attitudes toward their children than those who gained custody without a court battle (Greif & DeMaris, 1989).

Balancing work and child care appears to be one problematic area. Fathers often feel that a primary allegiance is to their work and that they are defined by their success in their career. When they feel pulled between the work and home world, they experience difficulties (Chang & Deinard, 1982; Gasser & Taylor, 1976; Greif, 1985). Those with cooperative work situations and supportive networks adapted more smoothly to these pulls (Greif, DeMaris, & Hood, 1993).

Dating also proved to be a problematic area. In two different studies, nearly 50% of the fathers reported troubles adjusting to socializing after being married (Chang & Deinard, 1982; Gasser & Taylor, 1976). Perhaps closely related to this is their relationships with their ex-wives. When this relationship goes well, father, children, and ex-wife may benefit (Greif, 1990), but when there are problems, or ongoing acrimony, adaptation may suffer. DeFrain and Eirick (1981), for example, report that one third of the fathers in their study inappropriately pulled the children into parental conflicts by enlisting their support against the children's mothers.

Finally, one study examined single fathers over time. Greif (1987) followed 28 fathers who remained single 3 years after being respondents in a 1982 cross-sectional survey (33 other fathers who were single at the time of the first survey were recontacted and 22 had remarried while 11 fell into other categories, including no longer having custody; only 5 of the 61 no longer had custody). The average length of time with custody at Time 2 was 6.8 years. Single fathers' satisfaction with social life, difficulty dealing with loneliness, comfort being single, satisfaction with child care, satisfaction with the relationship with the children and with the children's adjustment, and rating of the ex-wife as a parent did not change significantly from Time 1 to Time 2. The ex-wives' involvement with the children had increased and the ratings the fathers gave themselves as a parent decreased (Greif, 1987, p. 256). Clearly, the limited data on fathers suggest that, although adjustment does not generally become more problematic over time, it does not appear to become noticeably smoother either. We hypothesize that one of the reasons single parenting may *not* become easier is that the longer the father has custody, the more likely he is to be raising teenagers, a period of development that poses problems for a parent that are qualitatively different from those posed by younger children.

Methodology

To explore the issue of fathers' adaptation over time with a larger sample, fathers who had participated in a 1987-1988 survey were recontacted approximately 2 years after initial contact. The purpose was to explore issues facing fathers who were raising children alone. The 1987-1988 survey was conducted by placing a four-page questionnaire in *The Single Parent*, the membership magazine of Parents Without Partners (PWP), the largest self-help organization for single parents in the United States. Its membership numbered over 160,000 at the time. Fathers who had sole custody of children 18 years old and younger were asked to complete a 104-question instrument and return it in a postage-guaranteed mailer to the authors. Only fathers with sole custody at least 5 nights a week were included as it was believed that those with less custody were actually in a joint custody situation. Returns were accepted during a 4-month period following the initial publication of the questionnaire. After inappropriate or incomplete questionnaires were discarded, a sample of 933 was amassed. The return rate is difficult to determine as the exact number of fathers with sole custody of children 18 years old and younger is unknown by PWP. In addition, estimates as to the number of those who would qualify but do not read most of each issue of the magazine that contained the questionnaire are unavailable. Using a method used for a previous survey (Greif, 1985), the return rate is placed at roughly 20%.

A second sample was gathered contemporaneously by graduate students who sought the names of custodial fathers from court records in the Baltimore, Washington, and Philadelphia areas. Fathers were mailed a letter and the same questionnaire. The purpose of this approach was to gain a more heterogeneous sample than that provided by PWP. A total of 199 responses were received, approximately an 8% return rate. Following a statistical comparison of the two samples, it was determined they were sufficiently similar to be combined into a total sample of 1,132. The typical father's income was $33,400 with a modal income of $30,000. By way of comparison, white male householders (96% of the fathers in the study were white) with no wife present earned an average of $26,247 in 1986 (U.S. Bureau of the Census, 1987). Allowing for inflation 2 years later, the surveyed fathers were earning a few thousand dollars more on average than the typical U.S. father. (For further information on the demographic characteristics of the sample, see Greif & DeMaris, 1990.)

Approximately 2 years after the initial survey, graduate students reached by telephone 158 single fathers with custody who participated in the initial research. The fathers were randomly selected from the respondents who had agreed on the written questionnaire to be telephoned. An additional 16 fathers who were contacted had either remarried or were still single and no longer had sole custody. Approximately 25 other fathers' telephone numbers were no longer valid. With one exception, all the single fathers agreed to complete the same questionnaire and return mail it. Fathers who did not return the questionnaire were telephoned one more time and, occasionally, were sent a new questionnaire. This yielded a final sample of 123 (with missing data, it was reduced to 117) fathers, a 74% return rate. It is this group that provides the longitudinal data for this chapter.

Measures

Predictors of Subsequent Parenting Adjustment. The original survey measured several characteristics of fathers that would be of interest as predictors of subsequent parenting adjustment. These were father's age, education, and annual income, the number of years he had been married prior to the separation or divorce, the number of years he had sole custody, the method of obtaining custody (contested in court versus not contested in court), whether the ex-wife was ordered by the court to pay any child support, the number of nights the children typically spent per month with their mother, and the number of changes in his work routine the father had to make to accommodate having custody of his children.

Additionally, the survey asked, "Which parent was most involved in spending time with the children in the year before the breakup?" The possible responses were "father," "mother," or "it was shared." This variable was included as a dichotomous variable contrasting the first response with the other two. Support for custody on the part of significant others was assessed by asking fathers to rate how supportive each of the following had been of his having custody: parents, in-laws, friends, coworkers, boss, neighbors, children's teachers, clergymen, ex-wife, and dates. Possible ratings were "very supportive," "somewhat supportive," "not at all supportive," and "does not apply" (the last was coded as missing). The mean response across all 10 items was used as a scale of social support (reliability = .82). Finally, the survey asked, "Did you want sole custody when you first knew the marriage was ending?" Possible responses were "wanted it very much," "wanted it somewhat," "wanted joint custody," and "did not want custody." This was also made into a dichotomous variable contrasting the first response with all others.

Other Characteristics. The quality of fathers' social lives was tapped with items assessing their frequency of dating and having sex (each measured on a scale from 1, *never*, to 4, *once a week or more*), and their expressed satisfaction with their social life (ranging from 1, *very unsatisfied*, to 5, *very satisfied*). Their relationships with their ex-wives were assessed by a single item asking, "How much conflict exists now between you and your ex-wife?" This item ranged from 1, *none*, to 4, *a great deal*. The frequency of communication between the ex-wives and their children were assessed by asking fathers how often the ex-wives telephoned the children, ranging from 1, *never*, to 6, *once a week or more.* Additionally, fathers whose ex-wives were court-ordered to pay child support (a total of 34 at the 2-year follow-up) were also asked to state the amount that the ex-wives were supposed to pay per week.

Parenting Adjustment. Five variables were used to assess the extent of adjustment to single fatherhood evinced by custodial fathers at the 2-year follow-up. The quality of the father's relationship with his children was measured using the Index of Parental Attitudes (IPA), one of nine short-form scales that, taken together, constitute the Clinical Measurement Package (Hudson, 1982). The scales in this package were all designed to measure the severity of problems that people have in different areas. The IPA, in particular, measures the severity of problems in parent-child relationships, as perceived by the parent. The instrument consists of 25 statements such as the following: "My child gets on my nerves." "I get along well with my child." "I feel that I can really trust my child." Respondents indicate how frequently they experience these feelings toward a referent child or children, with responses ranging from "rarely or none of the time" to "most or all of the time." In this study, fathers were asked to complete this scale in reference to "the children living with you."

Scores on the IPA range from a low of zero to a high of 100, with higher scores signifying more problematic relationships with children. The scale has a clinical cutting score of 30. That is, those scoring 30 or higher are considered to have a clinically significant problem in their relationships with their children. The IPA has been shown to have strong internal-consistency reliability and to discriminate well among groups of clients in therapy who were judged by therapists to have problems with their children in varying degrees of severity. The IPA has also been found to possess good convergent, discriminant, and construct validity (Hudson, 1982). For the current sample, the alpha reliability for the IPA at both Time 1 and Time 2 was .89, suggesting strong internal consistency.

Four other single-item measures were used to assess various aspects of the fathers' parenting experience at follow-up. Fathers were asked to report their satisfaction with the "children's progress in most areas" (1 = *very unsatisfied* to 5 = *very satisfied*). Fathers were also asked to rate themselves as a parent (1 = *poor* to 4 = *excellent*) and to report how comfortable they were as single parents (1 = *very uncomfortable* to 5 = *very comfortable*). Finally, fathers were asked, "How difficult has the combination of working and raising your children been for you?"

Possible responses were "very difficult," "somewhat difficult," and "not at all difficult." This variable was dichotomized, contrasting the last response with the first two.

Data Analysis

The primary data analysis of interest in this study was an examination of which factors predicted more versus less successful parenting adjustment over time. Each of the five measures of parenting adjustment was therefore regressed on the predictors of subsequent parenting adjustment enumerated above using either OLS regression (IPA, satisfaction with children's progress, rating of self as a single parent, comfort as a single parent) or logistic regression (difficulty in combining work and child care). Because of substantial correlations between Time 1 and 2 measures for most of the dependent variables in the study, all equations additionally controlled for the Time 1 measure of the dependent variable. In this manner, for each dependent variable, we were able to ask: Given the level of adjustment evinced at Time 1, what other factors at Time 1 influence fathers' adjustment to parenting at a later time? In each case we also estimated a second model in which the sex and age distribution of the custodial children at Time 1 were added to the basic model, to see if these family structure variables (DeMaris & Greif, 1992) had any impact on parental adjustment once other factors were controlled. In no case were these family structure variables significant predictors of parenting adjustment net of other factors. Hence these analyses are not shown.

Results and Discussion

We began by performing a series of paired *t*-tests (approximately interval variables) or McNemar's tests (nominal variables) to assess whether there was a significant change from Time 1 to Time 2 in the following characteristics of fathers: IPA, satisfaction with children's progress, rating of self as a single parent, comfort as a single parent, difficulty in combining work and child care, frequency of dating, frequency of sex, satisfaction with social life, extent of conflict with ex-wife, support for having custody from significant others, nights per month children spend with ex-wife, frequency with which ex-wife telephones the children, whether ex-wife is under court order to pay

GEOFFREY L. GREIF and ALFRED DeMARIS   203

child support, weekly amounts ex-wives pay who are under such an order, and fathers' yearly income. These results were, with one exception, all nonsignificant, so they are omitted here. The exception was whether the wife was under court order to pay child support. The percentage of fathers whose wives were under such an order increased slightly over time, from 24.8% to 29% ($p = .048$). It appears, then, that there is little change over time in fathers' relationships with their children and their ex-wives, support they received from significant others for having custody, and financial circumstances, at least over a 2-year period. This supports earlier research (Greif, 1987).

Although there were very few changes in most characteristics of fathers over the 21-month follow-up period of this study, we nonetheless expected to find that some characteristics of fathers at Time 1 would be predictive of higher or lower quality parenting adjustment at Time 2. This question is different than asking whether there was any change in adjustment over time. Rather, in this second analysis, we were interested in which fathers, as differentiated by characteristics measured at Time 1, were better adjusted as single parents at Time 2. Because adjustment at Time 1 would naturally be related to adjustment at Time 2, for each regression involving a Time 2 measure of parenting adjustment, we controlled for the analogous measure at Time 1. This is very much like controlling for a "pretest" score in experimental research, when analyzing group differences in a posttest measure. This technique automatically adjusts for the dependence in outcome scores across time periods, thus providing more accurate tests for the other factors.

The results of regressing indexes of parental adjustment on the predictor set of interest are shown in Table 10.1. Each column of the table lists unstandardized coefficients for the regression of the dependent variable named at the top of the column on the predictor set. Although not shown in the table, R^2 values range from a low of about .13 for the difficulty of combining work and child care responsibilities (JOB) to a high of .61 for the index of parental attitudes (IPA2). These are not particularly interesting statistics, however, because they are inflated by the substantial correlation that exists for most of the dependent variables between Time 1 and Time 2 measures.

Only a few predictors appear to have consistent effects on measures of parenting adjustment. Of interest, those who fought for custody in court appear to have higher average scores on the IPA at follow-up, controlling for initial IPA scores, than those who did not experience a

Table 10.1 Results for the Regression of Parental Attitudes at Time 2
on Characteristics of Fathers at Time 1

Time 1 Predictors	IPA2	Dependent Variable PROGRESS	RATING	COMFORT	JOB[a]
Time 1 measure	.735**	.399**	.587**	−.129	−.856
Age	.030	−.002	.004	.025	−.029
Number of years married	.007	−.005	−.006	−.027	.100
Number of years sole custody	.194	−.006	−.001	−.017	.092
Achieved custody through the court	3.252*	.244	−.023	−.461*	−.120
Education	.318	.031	.017	.010	−.071
Income (in thousands)	−.029	.006	.000	.011	.017
Wife ordered to pay support	−1.252	−.090	−.035	.477*	.493
Nights per month children spend with ex	−.298	.029	.011	−.077*	−.013
Number of job changes	.020	.006	.056*	−.068	.064
Wanted custody very much	−2.057	.143	.212**	−.190	1.286*
Father most involved in child care	2.455*	.100	−.002	−.111	−.863
Support for custody	.996	−.203	.061	−.253	−1.027

NOTE: Minimum N for any analysis is 117. IPA2 = index of parental attitudes at Time 2; PROGRESS = satisfaction with children's progress; RATING = rating of self as a single parent; COMFORT = comfort as a single parent; JOB = combination of working and raising children has not been difficult.
a. Results for a logistic regression.
*p < .05, **p < .01.

court battle for custody. This suggests that contesting custody is associated with more problematic relationships with one's custodial children over time. In a previous article, Greif and DeMaris (1989), however, reported that contested custody was associated with fewer problematic relationships with children at the time of the initial survey. We discuss these contradictory, yet intriguing, findings below. Contested custody is also negatively related to comfort as a single parent, suggesting, again, that those who won custody through the courts are less comfortable as single parents after some time has elapsed. Fathers who were the primary parent in child care before their marital separations emerge as having more problematic relationships with their children at follow-up, controlling for their IPA scores at Time 1. This counterintuitive finding, like that for contested custody, will be explored in greater detail below.

Satisfaction with the children's progress since taking over custody appears to be predicted only by prior satisfaction with same at Time 1.

Controlling for that, no other variables exert significant effects on this variable. Fathers' ratings of themselves as single parents, on the other hand, are affected not only by their ratings of themselves at Time 1 but also by the number of changes they have made at work to accommodate to single parenting and by whether they initially wanted custody "very much." Apparently, fathers who have made more changes in their work routines and those who initially wanted custody very much are those who tend to rate themselves higher as parents at Time 2. This makes considerable sense. Those who have made more changes at work have clearly "sacrificed" more to become good parents. Having done this, they should then appraise their efforts at parenting more highly. Those who initially were very intent on having custody have, in all likelihood, also worked more than others at being good parents. Hence their higher self-ratings as parents are intuitively reasonable.

Of interest, neither comfort as a single parent nor the perception that combining work and child care is "not difficult" is related to earlier measures of the same variable. With respect to comfort as a single parent, it has already been mentioned that those who contested custody are less comfortable than others. In addition, the table shows that fathers are more comfortable in this role when the ex-wife has been ordered to pay child support and when children spend fewer nights per month with her. Perhaps, when ex-wives are court ordered to pay child support, such action adds legal reinforcement to the father's right to custody. This, in turn, may psychologically buttress the father's sense that he is properly the primary parent. The fewer nights the children spend with the mother, the greater the likelihood that the father will be able to parent without interference. For the father who feels comfortable in his parenting role, this would be beneficial. Finally, the only significant predictor of the perception that combining work and child care has not been difficult is the initial desire for custody. Fathers who initially wanted custody very much are more likely than others to believe that juggling work and child care demands has not been difficult. It appears that a strong motivation to be the custodial parent at the outset is sufficient to offset some of the potential stress created by having to change one's work schedule to accommodate this role.

The regression analyses in Table 10.1 revealed that fathers who contested custody and who were the primary parent prior to the separation appeared to have more troublesome relationships with their children at follow-up. Because these results were somewhat counterintuitive, we engaged in a closer examination of the relationships between these

206   Single Fathers With Custody Over Time

Table 10.2 Means Over Time on the Index of Parental Attitudes, by Father's Involvement in Child Care Before the Divorce and Method of Obtaining Custody

| | | Index of Parental Attitudes | | |
	N	Time 1	Time 2	Row Means
Method of obtaining custody				
no court contest	96	13.17	12.95	13.06
court contest	21	11.06	14.90	12.98
Parent most involved in child care before the divorce				
mother or both	64	14.89	14.05	14.47
father	53	10.25	12.39	11.32
column means	117	12.79	13.30	

variables and scores over time on the IPA. Means on the IPA at Times 1 and 2 (initial survey and follow-up survey) are shown in Table 10.2, by whether fathers achieved custody through a court contest and by whether the father was the primary child caretaker before the divorce. A repeated measures ANOVA (not shown) revealed that the following differences between means in the table are significant: the row mean for "Mother or Both" versus the row mean for "Father," with respect to which parent was most involved in child care; the column means; and the interaction between method of obtaining custody and time in their impact on the IPA score. The significance of this last effect means that the change in IPA score over time is not the same for those who won custody through a court contest as it is for those who did not.

The pattern of means in the table is quite informative. First, the IPA scores generally increased between the initial and follow-up surveys (12.79 versus 13.30). Thus over time there has been a slight trend toward more problematic relationships with children for this population of fathers. (The reason this change is significant in the repeated measures ANOVA but not using the paired *t*-test is that the ANOVA controls for additional sources of variance in the IPA, and hence produces a more sensitive test.) Second, the row means for which parent was most involved in child care before the breakup reveal that, ignoring the time effect, IPA scores are lower, on average, for fathers who were the primary parents before the breakup. This is, of course, what one would expect. On the other hand, when the time factor is taken into consideration, it appears that these same fathers have experienced an increase in IPA scores between surveys, while those in the "Mother or Both" category have, if anything, experienced a slight decrease. This interaction is not significant by a formal test, but it suggests that the trend in relationships with one's children is "moving in opposite directions" for these two groups of fathers. The increase in IPA scores over time for the "Father" group, but not for the "Mother or Both" group, is apparently responsible for the significant effect of this variable on IPA in Table 10.1. Table 10.2 therefore clarifies this result by showing that, while fathers who were primary caretakers of children before the divorce increased in IPA score more than others over time, they are still lower in IPA overall (have less problematic relationships) than those who were not the primary caretakers.

A similar trend is observable in the means on the IPA for groups distinguished by whether or not custody was achieved through a court contest. In this case, the interaction effect revealed by these mean differences across time is significant. In particular, those who contested custody experience an increase in problematic relationships over time, while those who obtained custody without a court battle experience a slight reduction in problematic relationships over time. Moreover, those who contested custody start out with lower IPA scores than other fathers but end up (in the follow-up survey) having higher ones.

Overall, differences between means in Table 10.2 are relatively small, yet, we would argue, meaningful. Although the IPA has a theoretical range of 0 to 100, the empirical range observed in our sample across both time periods was 0 to 42. Moreover, the standard deviation at both times was approximately 9 points. Hence, in observing that fathers who were primarily responsible for child care prior to separation from their wives were 4.64 (14.89 − 10.25) points lower on the IPA at Time 1, compared with other fathers, we are finding a one-half standard deviation (.43 standard deviations, to be exact) increase in the IPA score. In our view, these are not dramatic differences. Nevertheless, such differences in attitudes toward one's children should not be regarded as trivial.

The trends in Table 10.2 may be accounted for by the differences between different groups of fathers in the extent to which they are "invested" in parenthood. Fathers who fight for custody in court and fathers who were the primary caretakers before the divorce have each invested more time, effort, and emotional energy into the parenting process and may have been more "sensitive" fathers from the beginning. Perhaps their expectations are therefore higher regarding the rewards that parenting will bring, compared with others. They may consequently be more at risk for subsequent disappointment at a later date when their children push for their own independence, misbehave, or otherwise give the appearance of not being grateful for the efforts that their fathers have expended on their behalf. The fathers may also be more attuned to the pain their children are experiencing from the divorce.

Implications and Conclusions

The findings lend further credence to the viability of the single-father family. With few exceptions, the answer to the guiding question is that a father's situation appears to remain stable over time. Of note for the therapist is the potential for problematic relationships to emerge over time for fathers who have been involved in parenting prior to the divorce and then contest custody. In addition, fathers feel more comfort as a parent if they receive child support and the children spend fewer overnights with the mother. It may be, as mentioned, that these more involved and "contesting" fathers have close relationships with their children that may stem from their predivorce involvement. They may be more sensitive to the modulations in their own and their children's emotions and thus may be more apt to experience problems. These fathers may also be the ones that are most apt to seek therapeutic assistance. Two foci of clinical intervention in these situations can be boundary making and teaching about appropriate developmental expectations.

Minuchin (1974) writes that "the boundaries of a subsystem are the rules defining who participates, and how. . . . The function of boundaries is to protect the differentiation of the system" (p. 53). For the single father who fought for and won custody of the child (sometimes at great personal and financial cost), that child may begin to take on too central a role to the father's well-being and self-identity. The child's ups and downs rebound into the parental subsystem to a greater degree than they should. The relationship between father and child then may objectively be more problematic or may be perceived that way by the father. For the father who has had to prove his parental competence in court, drawing boundaries and assuming a more distant role could be especially difficult. This father, fearing relitigation, may believe that active and involved parenting is expected of him when, depending upon the age of the child, more emotional distance between parent and child would be appropriate. The father may continue an overactive parenting role to ensure that, upon investigation, he will have fulfilled every potential requirement of involved parenting.

The role of the therapist is to help the father in this situation to walk a difficult path between staying involved so that he feels he is parenting effectively and assuming a position of distance so that he can help the child toward age- and culture-appropriate separation and individuation.

Teaching about age-appropriate developmental expectations may help here. The father's expectations of the child may be frozen at the age at which he fought for the child. Having defended his own parenting skills before a judge at one point in time, he may be loathe to shift from those parenting behaviors in the future. Educating the father about what to expect at new ages may help him to modify his behavior.

Receiving child support from the mother not only legally validates the father's right to be a sole parent, it may also provide him additional resources in terms of child care and living arrangements. Such support can add to his sense of competence. The therapist can assist the father in this area by validating his right to receive child support. If the child is spending a number of nights with the mother, this may keep the father off balance in establishing his own sense of self as a single parent. The therapist can work with the father and nonresident mother (when appropriate) concerning roles for both parents. If the well-being of the child is their target, as it should be, clarifying for the parents who should fulfill which parenting functions can comfort a father who is feeling shaky about his own role. A second related issue is that problematic relationships may arise for fathers whose children are visited frequently by the mother if that visitation is inconsistent. Having to explain to the child why visitation has not been kept or promised gifts have not arrived can stress the child and thus the father-child relationship. It is common in single-parent families that the custodial parent bears the brunt of anger that is felt toward the noncustodial parent.

The therapist should discuss possible options with the family members by asking them how they see this arrangement working, how they would like it to work, and what the conditions are under which expectations for involvement in specific parenting tasks should change. By describing what some of the pitfalls are for families, the therapist can normalize their situations for them.

Future research needs to focus on representative samples with a special eye toward their change over time. As the number of single fathers continues to grow, the importance of gaining such knowledge cannot be overestimated, both in learning about fathering as well as in learning about the development of children of divorce.

11

Stepfathers With
Minor Children Living at Home

Parenting Perceptions and Relationship Quality

WILLIAM MARSIGLIO

In recent years, a growing proportion of men have been playing either formal or informal stepfather roles in the United States. This trend has evolved because of (a) the rising proportion of births to unmarried women and the associated increase in postbirth marriages among these women, (b) rising rates of divorce and remarriages (or cohabitation) of women with children, and (c) maternal child custody patterns (Ahlburg & De Vita, 1992; Da Vanzo & Rahman, 1993; Hernandez, 1988; Miller & Moorman, 1989). Although it is difficult to generate precise estimates because of the growth in cohabitation, estimates using the 1987-1988 National Survey of Families and Households suggest that almost 4 million stepfathers live with stepchildren under 19 years of age (Larson, 1992). This figure will probably increase slowly in the foreseeable future because of the demographic patterns noted above and the fact that the emerging shift away from child custody dispensation policies that favor mothers has yet to be accompanied by a pronounced change in divorced parents' preferences for the maternal residence pattern

AUTHOR'S NOTE: This chapter is a revised version of my article, with the same title, in *Journal of Family Issues* (1992, Vol. 13, No. 2, 195-214).

(Maccoby, Depner, & Mnookin, 1988). The social significance of the relationship between nonbiological, coresiding father figures and "their children" is accentuated today because contemporary nonresident biological fathers, on average, have limited contact with their nonresident children (Furstenberg, 1988b; Furstenberg & Harris, 1992; see also Mott, 1990; Seltzer, 1991).

Scholars from various disciplines have underscored stepfathers' potential importance as role models and/or substitute parents to their partner's children (e.g., Coleman & Ganong, 1990). Most observers agree that stepfathers, particularly in stepfamily households, can have a significant influence (positive or negative) on their stepchildren's emotional, social, intellectual, and financial well-being (Bray, 1988; Chapman, 1977; Coleman & Ganong, 1990; Hetherington, 1987; Oshman & Manosevitz, 1976) and that this influence may vary depending on a child's age and gender (see Bray, 1988, for a series of references). However, there is less certainty as to what specific type of relationship (e.g., parent, friend, or some combination of the two) and parenting strategies stepfathers should generally adopt to benefit their stepchildren the most. According to Hetherington (1987), successful stepfathers tend to be supportive of their partner's parenting style and avoid trying to take over the family system—especially during the initial stages of the relationship (see also Visher & Visher, 1978).

It is well understood that cultural norms regarding appropriate stepfather behavior are less precise than norms pertaining to biological and adoptive fathers. The implication of this pattern is that stepfamily members' interaction is likely to be affected irrespective of stepfathers' particular parenting style. Indeed, some researchers contend that this ambiguity increases adjustment problems for various stepfamily members (Cherlin, 1978; Giles-Sims, 1984; Kurdek & Sinclair, 1986; Schwebel, Fine, & Renner, 1991).

Although a number of researchers have considered various aspects of stepfathers' attitudes and interactions with their stepchildren, most of this research is based on small, nonrepresentative samples (Coleman & Ganong, 1990). This study uses national cross-sectional data for a recent cohort of married and cohabiting stepfathers to examine stepfathers' perceptions about various aspects of the stepfather role and the quality of their relationship with the oldest stepchild.

Stepfathers as Social Parents

Social Parenting and the Stepfather Role Identity

As noted above, norms regarding stepparenting are ambiguous in Western societies, but the importance of *biological* connections between parents and children continues to be reinforced through popular culture and legal proceedings. A key aspect of cultural definitions of biological parenting is the notion that exchanges between parents and children tend to be (and should be) based on univocal reciprocity, a theme that has been a central part of both scientific and traditional definitions of *family* (Scanzoni & Marsiglio, 1993; see Flinn, 1988, for a sociobiological interpretation of the emotional and motivational differences between step- and genetic parents). A univocal interdependency implies that individuals engaged in a social exchange relationship do not expect immediate or direct reciprocation—exchanges tend to occur out of a sense of duty or obligation and are often generalized (Ekeh, 1974).

A blood relationship, although an important source for this type of interdependency, is not the only source of univocality (Gerstel & Gross, 1987; Stack, 1974). Stepfathers, for example, can experience varying levels of univocal reciprocity toward their blood children as well as toward their stepchildren. Thus stepfathers' level of univocal reciprocity may depend, in part, on their self-perceptions about their father status, which will in turn be influenced by significant others' reactions to them.

Structural symbolic interactionists' views are instructive here because they argue that an individual's self comprises a variety of role identities (Stryker, 1980). These role identities represent the "internalized positional designations" a person develops and maintains through his or her interactions with others. Being a stepfather is one type of role identity, an identity males are capable of experiencing in different ways. Males who perceive and treat their stepchildren as if they are their own biological offspring will probably feel a greater sense of commitment (and univocal reciprocity) to their stepchildren than will stepfathers who feel they have developed some other form of relationship with their stepchildren.

Stepfathers' Perceptions and
Quality of Stepfather-Stepchild Relationship

Consistent with Clingempeel, Brand, and Segal's (1987) claim that variables from at least three levels of analysis (stepfamily household, extrahousehold network, and social institutional) influence the "quality of family relationships and child outcomes in stepfamilies" (p. 66), a diverse set of factors probably shapes stepfathers' perceptions about their stepfathering role and the quality of their relationship with their stepchildren. This study, given the measures available in the data set used, focuses on a series of variables associated with the stepfamily household level including family structure, demographic and attitudinal characteristics of family members, and intrahousehold relationship variables.

Researchers have studied extensively how the structural profile of stepfamilies affects interaction dynamics and child outcomes (see Cherlin & Furstenberg, 1994; Coleman & Ganong, 1990; Ganong & Coleman, 1987). The present research differentiates between stepfather family households in which only minor stepchildren reside from those in which both step- and biological (including adopted) children live. Previous research with biological fathers and stepfathers found that, compared with fathers living only with stepchildren, fathers coresiding only with their biological children reported higher levels of involvement in project/playing activities and private talks with their children (Marsiglio, 1991b). This study also suggested that fathers coresiding with both biological *and* stepchildren were slightly more likely to engage in play activities with their children than were fathers living only with stepchildren. Similarly, stepfathers who coreside with both biological and stepchildren, compared with their counterparts who coreside only with stepchildren, may be more inclined to assume a father role for all children living at home irrespective of their biological relationship to them. Being a biological parent to children living elsewhere also could influence the quality of the relationship between the stepfather and stepchild within the household. Some of these fathers may be reluctant to see themselves as a father figure to coresiding stepchildren because they feel guilty and experience a form of cognitive dissonance (Visher & Visher, 1978).

In addition to the family structure variables, two demographic variables, stepchildren's age at the time their stepfamily unit was formed and their gender, may be related to both stepfathers' perceptions about parenting and the quality of their relationship with their stepchildren. It is likely that stepfathers will feel more "fatherlike" and have a better relationship with their stepchildren if they assume fathering responsibilities when their stepchildren are young (Pasley & Healow, 1987). The role that stepchildren's gender plays as an independent variable, on the other hand, seems more complicated (Hetherington, 1987). Although some research has indicated that stepfathers tend to have better relationships with their stepsons than with stepdaughters (Hetherington, Cox, & Cox, 1986; Santrock, Warshak, Lindberg, & Meadows, 1982), the significance of stepchildren's gender may be apparent only after other factors are taken into account.

Stepfathers may demonstrate a preference for male stepchildren because they are more likely to share similar interests with them. This pattern could be reinforced if boys' biological fathers do not play a prominent role in their lives; some research has shown that stepchildren have a difficult time maintaining emotional attachments to both step- and biological fathers at the same time (White, Brinkerhoff, & Booth, 1985; see also Pasley, 1985). In addition, if boys tend to have a more troubled relationship with their single mother than do girls, boys may welcome a stepfather figure into the household (Brand, Clingempeel, & Bowen-Woodward, 1988; Hetherington, 1987). Alternatively, boys may be more protective of their mothers than girls are, and they may feel a greater sense of loyalty to their biological father—especially if the natural father retains an active interest in them. Thus some stepfathers may have a more difficult time forging a high-quality relationship with their male stepchildren when they experience particular circumstances. Finally, the length of time that a woman lives as a single mother prior to the current marriage/cohabitation relationship and the length of time that a stepfather is involved with his partner and her children are two additional variables that may interact with the child's age and gender to affect stepfathers' perceptions (these variables may also be directly related to perceptions).

A few intrahousehold relationship variables are also relevant to the present study and include the quality of a wife's/partner's relationship to her children and the father's relationship with his wife/partner. These variables are salient because mothers tend to play a "gatekeeper" role with respect to their children (Haas, 1988). An extremely positive mother-child relationship could minimize the extent to which males have the opportunity to establish a fatherlike relationship with their stepchildren; however, a strong mother-child relationship could also act as a catalyst for stepfathers to play a more central role in family interactions involving stepchildren. Meanwhile, a stepfather who has a very satisfying relationship with his wife/partner will probably be given (and/or pursue) greater opportunities to develop a fatherlike status in the household and establish a positive relationship with the mother's children (see Brand et al., 1988, for an alternative hypothesis). Finally, individuals who formalize the stepfather-mother relationship through marriage, compared with cohabiting parental figures, are likely to expand all family members' perceptions about stepfathers' parenting responsibilities.

Stepfathers' socialization values for their children, in particular the conformity theme identified by Kohn (1959, 1976, 1977), represent the final variable I consider here. Stepfathers who have extremely high expectations for their children to follow rules and be obedient may have a more difficult time establishing a high-quality relationship with their stepchildren than will stepfathers who have more moderate (and perhaps low) expectations for their children. This pattern may be accentuated if stepchildren are unaccustomed to the type of expectations their stepfathers have of them. At the same time, stepfathers who are extremely lenient with their children may also have a more difficult time forming a high-quality relationship with them compared with stepfathers with more moderate expectations.

Methods

Sample

Data for this study are from the National Survey of Families and Households (NSFH) conducted in 1987-1988 by the Center for Demography and Ecology, University of Wisconsin—Madison (see Sweet, Bumpass, & Call, 1988). This cross-sectional survey included face-to-face interviews and a self-administered questionnaire with a national probability sample of 13,017 U.S. adults aged 19 and older (with an oversampling of several population subgroups). One adult per household was randomly selected to serve as the primary respondent. A secondary respondent questionnaire was administered to the legal or nonlegal partner of the primary respondent in those instances where the couple was coresiding. The oversampled subgroups for the primary respondents can be weighted to represent a national sample. Statistics and analyses reported here are based on weighted data, and sample sizes represent unweighted frequency counts (statistical tests are based on reproportioned unweighted frequencies).

The analysis sample consisted of 195 males (primary respondents) who (a) were coresiding with at least one stepchild 18 years of age or younger who lived at least half time in the household (respondents represented a subset of those persons who had at least one biological, step-, adopted, or foster child aged 5 to 18 living in the household and were consequently asked a series of questions related to parenting)[1]; (b) were coresiding with their wife or nonlegal partner; (c) were not currently enlisted in the armed forces; and (d) provided an assessment of their relationship with their oldest stepchild (I focused on the eldest stepchild to simplify analyses). I combined husbands and male cohabitors because I assume that the "sexually bonded primary relationship" is a more valid, general approach for conceptualizing contemporary families and primary relationships (see Scanzoni, Polonko, Teachman, & Thompson, 1989). Husbands and male cohabitors were generally similar in terms of their responses to analysis variables. However, compared with male cohabitors, husbands tended to be 5 years older and had been with their partner for 2 more years.

Based on weighted percentages, about 14% of the overall sample was black and stepfathers were on average 37 years of age; 89% were married, and 55% had no biological children living with them. The mean duration of stepfathers' marital or cohabiting relationship was about 4½ years. The oldest minor stepchild was on average almost 8 years of age when the couple first married or cohabited and 12 years old at the time of the survey.

Measures

Stepfathering Perceptions. Respondents evaluated the accuracy of seven statements regarding specific aspects of the stepparenting experience as they pertained to their current family (1-5, *definitely false* to *definitely true*; see Table 11.1 for a complete list of items). An additional item determined respondents' perception about the relative difficulty of stepparenting versus parenting. Respondents *read* the following statement prior to answering the individual items: "Here are some statements about families with stepchildren. How true is each of these statements FOR YOUR FAMILY?" Note that, although the questions are worded at a general level, respondents were instructed to respond

Table 11.1 Percentage of Distribution for Stepfathers' Perceptions of Aspects of the Stepparenting Experience in Their Families

Stepfathering Perceptions[a]	Definitely False	Somewhat False	Neither True nor False	Somewhat True	Definitely True
a. It is harder to love stepchildren than it is to love your own children.	37.6	14.2	21.3	17.9	9.0
b. A stepparent is more like a friend than a parent to stepchildren.	32.8	17.7	16.4	29.3	3.7
c. It is just as easy to discipline stepchildren as it is your own children.	10.9	19.9	11.2	26.5	31.5
d. It's hard to get relatives to treat stepchildren the same as your own children.	29.3	20.3	19.2	21.6	9.7
e. Raising stepchildren is hard because they are used to different rules.	29.5	19.8	17.3	26.6	6.8
f. Stepparents don't have the full responsibility of being a parent.	52.3	15.7	14.0	15.2	2.8
g. Having stepchildren is just as satisfying as having your own children.	9.2	19.6	16.1	17.2	37.8

NOTE: Sample sizes vary from 185 to 187 depending on the individual item (weighted percentages).
a. Respondents read the following statement prior to answering the individual items: "Here are some statements about families with stepchildren. How true is each of these statements FOR YOUR FAMILY?"

in terms of "YOUR FAMILY." It is impossible to determine how well respondents followed these instructions.

A principal components factor analysis with the initial seven items, using the varimax rotation option, produced a two-factor solution. Subsequent multivariate analyses focused primarily on the five-item index identified by Factor 1, which includes items a, b, c, f, and g. Factor loadings for these five items were .66, .75, −.56, .57, and −.71, respectively. Items a, b, and f were subsequently reverse coded so that higher values for the summative index would correspond with a more intense fatherlike orientation, and the mean value was substituted for missing data in seven cases (range 4-40, alpha = .72, $\overline{X}$ = 18.06, SD = 3.69). In general, then, this index represents the degree to which stepfathers perceive their role identity and role performance as being desirable and fatherlike in nature.

Father-Child Relationship Quality. Respondents reported the quality of their relationship with every child living at home (1-7, *very poor* to *excellent*; $\overline{X}$ = 5.86, SD = 1.03). A measure for stepfathers' perceptions of their relationship with their eldest minor stepchild was created from these reports.

Other Independent Measures. Stepfathers' race, age, and level of completed education were included primarily as control variables. A dummy variable was created to differentiate stepfathers coresiding with only stepchildren 18 years of age or younger from those who lived with at least one biological (including adopted children) and one minor stepchild. Another dummy variable identified stepfathers who had a biological child living outside the household. A four-item index (range 4-28) was used to assess the extent to which stepfathers held socialization values for their stepchildren emphasizing traits indicative of conformity to external authority and obedience (Kohn, 1959, 1976, 1977). This subscale (alpha = .81 for this sample) was developed previously through factor analytic methods (Seccombe, Marsiglio, & Lee, 1991). Individual items measured the degree of importance (1-7, *not at all important* to *extremely important*) stepfathers placed on their children's following family rules, being kind and considerate, controlling their tempers, and obeying stepfathers' requests.

Additional variables assessed the duration of stepfathers' marriage or relationship with the wife/partner (months), length of time between the wife's/partner's last marriage/cohabitation and the current relationship (months), and the stepchild's age (at the time of his or her parents' marriage/cohabitation) and gender. The intrahousehold relationship variables included stepfathers' marital status, the quality of stepfathers' relationship with the wife/partner (1-7, *very unhappy* to *very happy*), and the wife's/partner's relationship with the child (1-7, *very poor* to *excellent*). Unfortunately, data limitations (large amount of missing data) reduced the reliability of assessing two theoretically meaningful variables: the frequency of contact that nonresident biological fathers had with their child as assessed by the child's mother (1-6, *not at all* to *more than once a week*) and the amount of time a wife/partner spent as a single mother prior to her current relationship (months).

Analysis Strategy

Using nationally representative data, I first tabulate stepfathers' perceptions of seven different aspects of the stepfather role. I then use multivariate techniques to determine the extent to which family structure, individual characteristics, and intrarelationship factors predict stepfathers' tendency to perceive that their role identity and role performance are fatherlike in nature, controlling for their race, age, and educational level. In a subsequent model, I examine whether these factors—stepfathers' role identity perceptions and socialization values emphasizing conformity, and a maternal measure of the mother-child relationship—are related to the quality of stepfathers' relationship with the eldest stepchild. Variables for marital status and relationship duration were included in preliminary models, but they were not significant and are therefore deleted from the final models. Additional exploratory models are estimated that test possible interaction terms combining children's age and gender with selected variables.

The independent measures for the two multivariate models are very similar, and both models include controls for stepfathers' race, age, and educational attainment. Note that in the first model a general measure of sibling gender composition is used because stepfathers reported their perceptions about stepparenting in general rather than in reference to a specific child. Meanwhile, the gender variable in the second model identifies the gender of the oldest stepchild because the quality of relationship item refers to a specific child. Finally, although the previous theoretical discussion highlighted the importance of two variables—the child's relationship with his or her biological father living elsewhere and the duration between the wife's/partner's previous marital/cohabitation relationship and the current one—the poor quality of the NSFH data for these variables precluded including them in the final models. A few tentative observations related to these measures based on exploratory analyses with restricted subsamples are noted below.

Results

Stepfathers' Perceptions

How do stepfathers perceive and experience their stepfather role as it relates to their stepchildren? A partial answer to this question can be gleaned by examining stepfathers' responses to the seven items displayed in Table 11.1. These data reveal that stepfathers have diverse perceptions about the various aspects of stepfathering tapped by the individual items. Not a surprise, Table 11.1 indicates quite clearly that a significant proportion of stepfathers' reports can be interpreted to mean that they perceive themselves as having a positive fatherlike role identity, although many also believe their identity as a father is tenuous. Almost 52% of stepfathers disagreed at least somewhat with the idea that it is harder to love stepchildren than your own children, and 52% firmly disagreed with the statement suggesting that they did *not* have full responsibility as a parent (only 17% agreed at least somewhat with this latter statement). On the other hand, 33% said that it was at least "somewhat true" that they were more like a friend than a parent to their stepchildren. Finally, 19% and 31% of stepfathers reported that it was either "much harder" or "a little harder" to be a stepparent than a natural parent, respectively (results for this item are not reported here).

Having documented stepfathers' varied perceptions about their stepparenting role in general, the next analysis considers how family structure, individual-level characteristics, and intrahousehold relationship variables are related to a specific set of stepfathers' views. This simultaneous, multiple regression model is restricted to the five-item index discussed earlier that measures stepfathers' perceptions about having a fatherlike status in relation to their stepchildren (see Table 11.2).[2]

Although the family structure, personal characteristics, and intrahousehold relationships items tended to explain only a small amount of the total variance in this model ($R^2 = .10$), several notable findings can be observed. First, stepfathers coresiding in households in which only stepchildren were present, controlling for whether these stepfathers also had a biological child living outside the home, were less likely than fathers living with both step- and biological children to have perceptions consistent with a fatherlike role identity.[3] In addition, stepfathers whose children were younger when the parents married or began to

Table 11.2 Multiple Regression Model for Stepfathers' Perceptions About Having a Positive Fatherlike Role Identity/Role Performance

Predictors	b	Beta	r	$\overline{X}$	SD
Control variables					
race (black = 1, other = 0)	1.28 (1.01)	−.10	.16**	.14	.28
stepfather's age (years)	−.04 (.04)	−.08	−.11	36.59	7.10
completed years of education (years)	.10 (.12)	.06	.03	12.66	2.28
Family structural and demographic/personal characteristics					
coresiding only with stepchildren (yes = 1, other = 0)	−1.70** (.74)	−.19	−.22**	.55	.41
age of oldest stepchild at the time of parents' marriage/cohabitation (years)	−.22** (.09)	−.20	−.28*	7.84	3.32
coresiding only with male stepchildren (yes = 1, other = 0)	−.43 (.69)	−.05	−.02	.58	.40
stepfather with biological child living elsewhere (yes = 1)	1.30 (.73)	.13	.09	.30	.38
Intrarelationship variables					
marital status (1 = married, other = 0)[a]	— (.30)	—	−.02	.89	.26
stepfather's relationship satisfaction with wife/ partner (1-7, *very unhappy* to *very happy*)	.59* (.30)	.14	.09	6.00	.95
length of relationship (months)[a]	—	—	.16**	55.85	38.21
Intercept	17.30				
Adjusted R^2	.10				
N	174				

NOTE: Analyses are based on listwise deletion of cases. Standard errors shown in parentheses. Weighted data with significance tests based on unweighted sample size.
a. Preliminary models included marital status and length of relationship variables, but final models do not include them because they were not significant.
*p < .10, **p < .05.

cohabit were more likely to have fatherlike perceptions. Meanwhile, the gender of stepfathers' eldest stepchild was *not* significantly related to stepfathers' perceptions. As expected, stepfathers were more likely to report "fatherlike" perceptions if they were happier with their relationship with the marital/cohabiting partner.

Six alternative models were also estimated to test for possible interactions between the gender and age variables for the oldest child and (a) frequency of contact between the biological father and child, (b) the amount of time between the wife's/partner's last marriage/cohabitation relationship, and (c) the duration of the stepfather's relationship with his wife/partner. Only tentative conclusions should be drawn from the analyses using variables a and b because they are based on much smaller analysis samples ($n = 132, 128$) because of high rates of missing values on these variables.[4] None of these interactions was significant at the $p <$ .10 level. However, the interaction terms combining child's gender and the measure for biological father-child contact were significant at the $p < .10$ level. This exploratory finding suggests that more extensive contact between a child and his or her biological father may be more detrimental to stepfathers developing a fatherlike role identity when the oldest stepchild is a boy.

Relationship Quality Among Stepfathers and Stepchildren

The final analysis examines the extent to which stepfathers' perceptions about stepfathering, and other factors, are related to their self-reports on the quality of their relationship with the eldest stepchild. In a bivariate context, stepfathers who were black, had less education, lived with stepchildren and biological children, had a younger stepchild, and were happier with their marital/cohabitation relationship tended to report having a better relationship with their stepchildren. However, none of these variables was a significant predictor in the simultaneous, multiple regression model (see Table 11.3) at the conventional level of significance (i.e., $p < .05$). Thus these data did not confirm the hypotheses predicting that family structure (living only with stepchildren) or demographic characteristics of children (age and gender) would be significant predictors of stepfather-stepchild relationship quality in a multivariate context.

Several variables, including the index for stepfathers' perceptions about their fatherlike role identity, were significantly related to relationship quality. Stepfathers who had more fatherlike perceptions, so-

Table 11.3 Multiple Regression Model for Stepfathers' Quality of Relationship With the Oldest Minor Stepchild Living at Home

Predictors	b	Beta	r
Control variables			
race (black = 1, other = 0)	.12	.03	.16**
	(.25)		
stepfather's age (years)	.00	.03	−.05
	(.01)		
completed years of education (years)	−.06*	−.13	−.19***
	(.03)		
Family structural and demographic/personal characteristics			
coresiding only with stepchildren (yes = 1, other = 0)	−.00	−.00	−.14**
	(.19)		
age of oldest stepchild at the time of parents' marriage/cohabitation (years)	−.01	−.04	−.21**
	(.02)		
gender of stepchild (male = 1, female = 0)	−.12	.05	−.06
	(.16)		
stepfather with biological child living elsewhere (yes = 1, other = 0)	−.07	−.03	.01
	(.18)		
stepfather's socialization values emphasizing conformity (4-28)	.08***	.24	.32***
	(.02)		
stepfather's fatherlike perceptions	.10***	.36	.40***
	(.02)		
Intrarelationship variables			
marital status (1 = married, other = 0)[a]	—	—	−.00
stepfather's relationship satisfaction with wife/partner (1-7, *very unhappy* to *very happy*)	.04	.04	.14*
	(.08)		
length of stepfather's relationship with wife/partner (months)[a]	—	—	.01
wife/partner's quality of relationship with stepchild (1-7, *very poor* to *excellent*)	.32***	.22	.36***
	(.10)		
Intercept	.93		
Adjusted R^2	.30		
N	176		

NOTE: Analyses are based on listwise deletion of cases. Standard errors shown in parentheses. Weighted data with significance tests based on unweighted sample size.
a. Preliminary models included marital status and length of relationship variables, but final models do not include them because they were not significant.
*p < .10, **p < .05, ***p < .01.

cialization values that emphasized conformity to external authority and obedience (plotting procedures revealed no evidence for a curvilinear relationship in a bivariate context), and a wife/partner who had a positive relationship with her eldest child tended to report having a more positive relationship with their stepchildren. Although each of these variables had a sizable influence on relationship quality, the standardized estimates reveal that the index for stepfathering perceptions was clearly the strongest predictor. Although it is clear that wives'/partners' relationship with their children is related to stepfathers' own reports of relationship quality, the causal direction of this relationship cannot be determined precisely using these cross-sectional data. It is possible, for instance, that a stepfathers' relationship with his children is enhanced by his wife's/partner's relationship with her children and the stepfather-stepchild relationship in turn affects the mother-child relationship.

Additional exploratory models were estimated to test the hypotheses positing that stepfathers' relationship with their stepchildren might be influenced by a number of interactions. The individual interaction terms tested in the previous models for stepfathers' perceptions were included alternatively in this set of models. None of the interaction terms was significant.

Discussion

As discussed earlier, several prevailing demographic patterns have increased the extent to which males are assuming some type of stepfather role toward coresiding minor children in the United States. Using a contemporary national sample of stepfathers living with minor stepchildren that includes *both* married and cohabiting males, this study showed how stepfathers perceive their stepfathering role and evaluated the quality of their relationship with their stepchildren. This research also documented that stepfathers' perceptions and the quality of their relationship with the oldest stepchild were not related to their racial background, educational level, or age in a multivariate context.

The descriptive analyses revealed that stepfathers have diverse perceptions about their current stepfathering experiences and the multivariate analyses suggested that family structure variables, individual-level characteristics, and intrarelationship factors were generally poor predictors of stepfathers' belief that they had a fatherlike role identity or opportunity to perform a father role. The multivariate results did indicate, however, that stepfathers who lived with stepchildren and biological children in the same household, compared with their counterparts who coresided only with stepchildren, were more likely to report perceptions consistent with a positive fatherlike role identity. One interpretation of this finding is that the responsibilities and feelings associated with having biological children *present in the household* may have a spillover effect on the way stepfathers experience their stepfather role. Furthermore, this study confirmed the hypotheses that, when fathers initiate their stepfather role earlier in a child's life, and when stepfathers evaluate their relationship with their wives/partners more positively, they will be more likely to perceive that they are a "father" to their partners' children. One surprise was that stepfathers who had formalized their relationship with their partner through marriage did *not* perceive their stepfathering role differently than did cohabiting stepfathers. This finding suggests that getting married (or being involved with a partner for a longer period of time) does not tend to strengthen stepfathers' sense of having a positive fatherlike role identity above and beyond any changes that may have resulted from making a commitment to coreside. Thus this study supports the strategy of incorporating cohabiting males who coreside with children into future research on stepfathers.

The final question this research addressed involves the quality of stepfathers' relationship with their stepchildren based on stepfathers' accounts. It is important to bear in mind when interpreting these findings that the NSFH data do not provide separate assessments from stepchildren or wives/partners of the stepfather-stepchild relationship. Despite this shortcoming, much can be learned from studying a national sample of stepfathers' self-reported perceptions. For example, contrary to previous studies using smaller, nonrepresentative samples (Bray, 1988; Hetherington, 1987; Hobart, 1987), no evidence was found to support the hypothesis that stepchildren's gender would be associated with the quality of stepfathers' relationship with their stepchildren. Separate interaction terms combining child's gender and age with measures for the relationship duration of stepfather-partner and the amount of time that lapsed between the wife's/partner's previous relationship and the current one also were not significant. In addition, no support was found, using these cross-sectional data, for the notion that stepfathers will tend to improve their relationship with their stepchildren as the duration of their relationship with the child's mother increases.

Results did suggest, however, that stepfathers' beliefs about the quality of their relationship with their stepchildren were related to stepfathers' perceptions about their role identity, their socialization values, and their wife's/partner's relationship with the respective children. One of this study's more important findings was that having stronger fatherlike perceptions was positively related to stepfathers' views about the quality of their relationship with their stepchildren after controlling for factors such as children's age, stepfather-partner relationship duration, and stepfather's marital status. Although it is *not* possible to make a direct comparison, this finding is relevant to Hetherington's (1987) suggestion that stepfathers should avoid becoming too involved in their fathering role, especially during the earlier months/years of the relationship. In this sample, fathers who felt more fatherlike reported having *better* relationships with their stepchildren. Stepfathers' perceptions, of course, may or may not be consistent with stepchildren's perceptions or other measures of family members' well-being, and they do not assess the extent to which stepfathers attempt to take over the family system. Furthermore, these analyses do not rule out the possibility that a recursive relationship exists between fathers' perceptions and the quality of their relationship with their stepchildren. In other words, fathers who have better relationships may develop a stronger role identity as a father.

In a related context, and contrary to expectations, those stepfathers who were more likely to expect their children to conform to external authority and be obedient actually reported having better relationships with their oldest stepchild. This is surprising because it seems reasonable to expect that fathers who have extremely high expectations for their stepchildren to adhere to family rules (sometimes new rules for the stepchildren) will be more likely to have a tension-riddled relationship with them than will stepfathers with more moderate views. Perhaps stepfathers with these types of socialization values are primarily concerned with maintaining order within the household and simply have lower expectations (compared with their counterparts who hold less rigid views) for their relationships with their stepchildren. If stepfathers who emphasize conformity values do have lower standards for evaluating relationship quality, they may also be more likely to assess favorably the quality of their relationship with their stepchildren. It also is possible that this relationship is to some extent an artifact of measurement error. More specifically, the conformity socialization value items were measured using a rating rather than ranking scale, which means that stepfathers who wished to portray themselves as competent, involved fathers may have had a tendency to report that all of these values were of considerable importance to them (Seccombe et al., 1991). The same type of response bias may also be a part of the relationship quality item, and therefore some of the common variance shared by these two measures may actually be due to correlated error terms. Thus, in the absence of more sophisticated statistical modeling, caution is warranted when interpreting this finding.

The third significant predictor of stepfather-stepchild relationship quality in this model, mother-child relationship quality, does not support the notion that close mother-child bonds will restrict stepfathers' ability to develop a strong relationship with their stepchildren. On the contrary, this finding suggests that strong mother-child relationships may facilitate similar relationships between stepfathers and their stepchildren. However, these analyses cannot determine the underlying processes responsible for this statistical relationship, so it is unclear how mothers' attitudes and parenting style or children's personality characteristics affect this pattern.

Although the NSFH provides a unique opportunity to use a contemporary, national sample to test important hypotheses about how stepfathers perceive their role and relationship toward their stepchildren, these data do not address a variety of key issues. For example, although this study included measures of duration of time spent as a single mother, mother-child relationship quality, and stepfather-wife/partner relationship quality, the NSFH data did not directly assess mothers' normative expectations for how their partner should be involved with their children. The global measure of relationship quality between mother and child also does not capture the many subtle relationship dynamics that may account more directly for the type of relationship that stepfathers have with their stepchildren. For instance, it is important to identify the respective types of parenting styles that the mother and stepfather employ in interacting with their children. Stepfathers who adopt what Hetherington (1987) has labeled a "permissive parenting style" and are involved with a wife/partner using a more authoritative approach may be viewed more positively by stepchildren than if the stepfather or mother used a different parenting style. Future data collection efforts should also gather more information about the quality of children's relationship with their biological father, especially from the child's perspective. In sum, this study underscores the clear need for researchers concerned with a range of interrelated issues pertaining to families, primary relationships, children, and gender to focus more systematic attention on the experiences of stepfathers in contemporary U.S. society.

Notes

1. The survey instrument's various skip patterns mean that only stepfathers who have a biological, adopted, or foster child between the ages of 5 and 18 have the opportunity to report on stepchildren younger than age 5.

2. Similar models were estimated for the summative two-item index (range 2-10, $r = .39$) identified by the second factor (items d and e). Stepfathers with younger stepchildren and those who had been in their marital/cohabiting relationship for a shorter period of time were more likely to score high on this index. Moreover, those who perceived greater resistance from relatives and felt that preexisting family rules minimized their parental authority were less satisfied with their relationship with the oldest stepchild ($p < .01$).

3. For the restricted subsample of respondents whose wife/partner reported on the frequency of contact between their children and the noncustodial biological father ($n = 140$), a higher level of contact was associated with a lower fatherlike orientation among stepfathers at the bivariate level ($r = -.20$; $p < .05$), and this relationship approached a conventional level of significance in a preliminary multivariate model ($p < .07$).

4. A comparison of analysis variables for those respondents answering item a with those who did not revealed only two differences: Respondents with missing data on this item were, on average, 3 years older and had completed 1 less year of education ($p < .05$).

12

The Fathers' Rights Movement

Contradictions in Rhetoric and Practice

CARL E. BERTOIA
JANICE DRAKICH

Fathers' rights groups in Canada[1] have exercised considerable pressure on the restructuring of divorce and child custody practices and law (Crean, 1988; Dawson, 1988; Drakich, 1988, 1989; L. Lamb, 1987; Maynard, 1988; Rauhala, 1988). The strength underlying this pressure is in its appeal to the use of concepts currently held in reverence in North American culture. These concepts, such as coparenting and continuing parent-child relationships, are couched in the deeply held principles of "equality" and "rights." The most visible indication of the centrality of these latter concepts to fathers' rights groups is in the names they use for their groups. Human Equality Action Resource Team (HEART), Fathers for Justice, and In Search of Justice are but a few examples of names of Canadian fathers' rights groups. Fathers' rightists and the groups that represent them use equality concepts to promulgate the

AUTHORS' NOTE: This chapter previsouly appeared as an article, with the same title, in *Journal of Family Issues* (1993, Vol. 14, No. 4, 592-615). This research was funded by the University of Windsor Research Board—Grant No. 8889. We want to thank Mary Lou Dietz at the University of Windsor for her helpful comments and suggestions on this chapter. We also want to extend our appreciation and thanks to the editor, William Marsiglio, and the reviewers of the *Journal of Family Issues* for their helpful, thoughtful, and comprehensive comments.

notion that fathers are being treated unfairly by the legal system governing divorce, child custody, child access, property distribution, and support payments. They use this rhetoric to legitimate their lobbying efforts on behalf of increasing the power and control available to fathers after divorce. A substantial body of popular literature documents fathers' alleged divorce injustices (Conine, 1989; Peacock, 1982; Roman & Haddad, 1978), which have been given life by Hollywood depictions of the downtrodden divorced father (see Drakich, 1988). The fathers' rights discourse currently reverberating in the academic and popular literature and the media is seductive. It supports cherished principles and appeals to idealized notions of postdivorce families. However, the seduction of equality obscures the contradictory and statistically supported realities of the divorce, child custody, and parenting experiences of divorced mothers and fathers (see Arendell, 1986; Chambers, 1979; Furstenberg, Nord, Peterson, & Zill, 1983; Weitzman, 1985). The recent work of Martha Fineman (1991) and S. Boyd (1993) examines the rhetoric of fathers' rights groups and underscores the inconsistencies between the "facts" underlying this rhetoric and relevant scholarly evidence in the area of family and divorce.

This chapter examines a different level of contradiction, the contradiction between the fathers' rights movement's public rhetoric on family law issues and the private, self-interest posturing and framing of the experience of its members. The subjective, individualized accounts of members of fathers' rights groups contrast with the fathers' rights public rhetoric to delineate these contradictions. Twenty-eight fathers and four women from four fathers' rights groups were interviewed about their reasons for joining the group, their conceptualization of fatherhood, and their opinions on joint custody, child access, divorce mediation, and support payment enforcement programs. In addition, some 100 members were observed in group meetings over a period of 18 months. The interviews and observations provide the private "masculinist discourse of divorce" (Arendell, 1992a, 1992b) and permit an examination of its relationship to the collective, social movement level of fathers' rights' public rhetoric by contrasting the two.

Sample and Methodology

Data were collected through in-depth, open-ended interviews with 32 members and observation of two fathers' rights groups in Ontario.[2] Not all of the group members were fathers with young children. Occasionally, women joined groups, as did one man who was experiencing problems with support payments to an ex-spouse. The intensive interviews lasted from 1½ to 3 hours and were conducted primarily in 1989. All interviews were tape-recorded and transcribed. Data were analyzed using the constant comparative method (Glaser & Strauss, 1967; Strauss, 1988). The sample was a snowball sample. However, care was taken to interview members at various levels of activity and responsibility within the groups (i.e., executive, active members and casual members), and because approximately 15% of the membership in some of these organizations is composed of women (i.e., second wives, dating partners, and mothers without custody), four women members were interviewed. Observations of group meetings were conducted on two groups: One group's regular monthly meetings were observed for 18 months and a second group's meetings were observed for 4 months. Notes were kept recording such data as how many people attended the meetings, the gender composition of the meetings, and topics discussed. The observation period began in 1988 and concluded in 1990.

The fathers interviewed ranged in age from 25 to 47; all but one were employed and represented occupations from laborer to medical doctor. Professionals, white-collar workers, and blue-collar workers each represented approximately one third of the sample. Altogether, the fathers had 52 children ranging in age from 2.5 to 19 years with various forms of child custody arrangements. Fifteen fathers had access to their children, three did not have access, five had sole custody of all or some of their children, and four fathers had joint custody of their children. One man, who was involved because of current spousal support problems, had adult children from a previous marriage. Of the four women interviewed, three were current spouses of the male members and one had joint custody of her children. The women ranged in age from 35 to 45 years and were full-time employees in primarily white-collar and professional occupations. The members interviewed were at different stages in the termination of their relationships or varied in time elapsed from divorce. Excluding the women-spousal members, 66% of the 29 members had been divorced for a period ranging from 2 years to 10 years. The remaining 34% had been separated for a period ranging from 6 months to 1½ years.

To obtain fathers' rights groups' public accounts, we reviewed newspapers, magazines, television programs, radio interviews, proceedings in the House of Commons and the Legislative Assembly of Ontario, and fathers' rights groups' newsletters, brochures, campaign literature, and self-help manuals; we attended public events, such as the Fathers' Day March, an annual general meeting of a national umbrella organization representing fathers' rights and other pro-family groups, and public forums on family law issues.

Initial Involvements

Fathers' rights groups in Ontario formed in the mid-1980s in response to family law reforms and initiatives such as the revision of the Divorce Act, equalization of family assets, a presumption of joint custody, mandatory mediation, access enforcement, and the establishment of the Ontario Support and Custody Enforcement Branch. They lobbied most vigorously, although unsuccessfully, in support of mandatory joint custody (see Drakich, 1988) and access enforcement, and in opposition to the Ontario Support and Custody Enforcement Branch. Fathers' rights groups begin with the assumption that fathers are discriminated against in the divorce process. The groups have constructed a public rhetoric based on equality and gender-neutral models to underscore their rights and to influence law reform. To win public support and reach potential members, fathers' rights groups advertise and promote the concept of equality in their brochures, in mission statements, and through media exposure. The literature of the groups involved in this study mirrors their public representation of equality and fathers' rights on television and radio. One group's brochure states the following goals:

> To assist non-custodial parents to obtain equitable access with their children in cases where shared parenting is not possible. To give moral support to members through difficult court battles, access denial, unfair maintenance, etc. To promote equality!

Other groups emphasize the rights of fathers and the rights of children:

> "Fathers Demand Rights"[3] can and does provide . . . information concerning your rights and the rights of your children.

The public rhetoric of equality and rights established fathers' rights groups as advocates for fathers postdivorce. Examination of data reveals that the majority of men involved in the fathers' rights movement are drawn to these groups because they are experiencing personal troubles (Mills, 1959) with child custody, child access, or child support. Most of these men are angry[4] with the divorce process and are shocked by what has happened to them. The president of a fathers' rights group described the members this way:

> Some of these poor people have never had to deal with this type of thing. They don't know how to defend themselves. They just sit in the courtroom with their mouths open saying this can't be going on. And yes, they feel unjustly treated.

A father of one child reflected:

> We all think that it won't happen to us. And I didn't think that it would happen to me either, until it did. I never thought about it. It was sort of distant. So you're talking about a guy who is really shocked. It's not so much what really happened. It is the shock, I think, that really shakes guys the most.

There are two exceptions to the above characteristics of fathers in our study. In both cases, the men had settled their divorces several years prior to their involvement in the groups and had amicable relationships with their former spouses. One father joined the group to promote the idea of coparenting, and the other father joined to find support for primary parenting.

There is very little indication in discussions or interviews with fathers that they joined the group because of their commitment to a general principle of equality for fathers and mothers. As one executive member put it, the men were there because they had problems:

> Now the men that you hear in our meetings are men that are at the extreme. They've been abused in the system.

Another indicated that access to children was a primary reason for involvement, saying:

> Ninety-five percent of the guys at "Fathers Demand Rights" were there because they had problems not getting access to their kids. It was all pretty much child oriented. The problems were basically with access.

Most of the fathers, however, did invoke the rhetoric of rights to explain their membership in the group: their right to access to their children; their right to a decent standard of living, which has been denied them because of exorbitant child support payments; and their right to control the activities of their former wives and children. A father denied access to his two children remarked on his right to access:

> Nobody should have the right to deprive you of your family under any circumstances. No judge can say I can't see my kids.

Another expression of rights was made by a father who had access to his two children and was awaiting the custody settlement. He voiced anxiety about his inability to control the movement of his former spouse and children:

> The other one of my concerns is her mobility. That is, one of my fears is that she is waiting for the court, if she gets sole custody, there are very little restrictions on her.

Although fathers attended meetings to gain emotional support from the group and to find ways of solving their financial, custodial, and access problems, the following father suggests that fathers' concerns were more directly addressed by group members than by lawyers:

> I liked what I heard and went with them because, basically, the lawyers that I had previous, as far as I'm concerned, were incompetent.

The feeling that the group dealt with the rights of fathers was echoed in the interviews. One father explained that when he separated from his wife he looked toward the fathers' rights group to explain and help him understand his situation:

> How I got involved? I split up. I had some problems knowing what my rights were, what I could do and what I couldn't do. You don't know the legal system, so you're wondering how does everything work as far as separation, divorce, and custody.

Or, as this father, who has a restraining order on him as a consequence of assaulting his wife, put it, fathers' rights groups were the only source of support in getting what he wanted:

> I realized what condition I was in, in terms of not being able to get what I wanted, which was what was left of my family deal . . . they [fathers' rights groups] were pretty well the only voice in the wilderness that [was] saying there was a chance.

Overall, the men involved in the fathers' rights movement are angry men: angry about paying out what they consider to be huge sums of money in child support, angry that they have limited access to their children, and angry with the whole divorce and child custody process. They join fathers' rights groups for personal reasons and for personal gain. Our data do not support the public image of fathers' rights groups as groups motivated by concerns of equality to transform the divorce process and postdivorce coparenting. Rather, what we have found is that fathers privilege their private troubles over fathers' rights groups' equality posturing. One executive woman member, in discussing problems of conducting group meetings, points to the privileging of personal troubles.

> Most of the men are very aggressive. And they are. They really are. A lot are angry. Our executive tries to get them to stop going on about how much child support they pay, and "she" [ex-spouse] is a bitch, and all that.

One father with sole custody, who joined the group for support in his everyday child care responsibilities, exposed this private/public contradiction when he was asked about the members' expressed custody preferences:

> I can kill a conversation with one of these groups if I asked, "Would you be willing to take sole custody?" And many of these men have not seriously entertained this question or thought about it.

Thus initial involvements in fathers' rights groups are motivated by self-serving interests rather than a desire for equality—whether we interpret equality as equal opportunity to obtain sole custody or equal responsibility for children. The mission statements of fathers' rights groups inaccurately portray what actually happens within these groups and how the groups are used. The following section compares the public platforms of fathers' rights groups with respect to the alleged injustices and discrimination and the private positions of its members. The multilayered and interconnected discourse of "rights" is difficult to separate out and present in mutually exclusive categories. Our approach in what follows is to focus on the issues that fathers' rightists identify as major sites of discrimination: maternal preference in awarding custody, maternal control of the children, and maternal financial privilege.

Maternal Preference in Custody

The argument made by fathers' rights groups is that there is gender bias in Canadian child custody law and in the application of the law, despite the formal gender neutrality of "the best interest of the child" doctrine introduced in the 1970s. Accordingly, fathers are discriminated against by an apparent maternal preference in awarding custody, a vestige of the "tender years doctrine." Fathers' rightists support this assertion with the statistic that mothers get sole custody of their children in 86% of the cases. Yet they fail to acknowledge that this statistic represents the mutual decision of both parents to award sole custody to the mother (Boyd, 1989, 1993; McKie, Prentice, & Reed, 1983). Moreover, they fail to concede that when men are the petitioners they are more likely to be awarded custody. Available Canadian data indicate that the award of custody, in father petition cases, is either almost equally distributed to mothers and fathers (McKie et al., 1983; Richardson, 1988) or, as reported in another study of one jurisdiction, the majority of father petitioners were granted custody—74% in Provincial Court and 91% in Supreme Court[5] (McClure & Kennedy-Richardson, 1987). Data from some U.S. researchers also support the almost equal distribution of custody awards in contested cases (Polikoff, 1983; Weitzman, 1985). However, the recent work of Maccoby and Mnookin (1992) does strongly challenge the findings of Polikoff (1983) and Weitzman (1985) on equal distribution. Nevertheless, the statistical reality of sole maternal custody in undisputed cases is the foundation of fathers' rights groups' claim of discrimination. Their platform for justice for fathers involves two arguments. First, they appeal to gender equality in parenting skills and in parenting roles by arguing that the role of fatherhood has changed. They would contend that the father of the 1980s and 1990s is one who nurtures and is involved in all activities of the family with his children. As one father of two children with access argues:

> More and more, men in particular are becoming more aware of parenting roles. I think that in society, the businessman is not just interested in business

any more. He is more interested in the family, and that is what is happening as we change in that attitude. There is also a change in the women's role. The women's role is now one of woman in the work force. The majority of them now. [In] marriages, both parents are working. It changes the role of the woman who would stay at home, bake the pies, and wash the clothes. And now they are not doing this.

The belief that men are sharing in domestic and child care responsibilities is further revealed in the following account:

I think gone are the days of . . . they are recognizing that men want to be involved. We are no longer just cash receipt machines or breadwinners. We are playing an active role. With the wife out working, it is necessary that men are willing to take over and help. We are no longer back when our parents, or our parents' parents, where the man went out to work, came home to read his papers and smoke his pipe. And the wife did everything else. That's history.

Second, they appeal to their rights to affirmative action in the family division of labor. They argue that men have recognized women's rights in the workforce, and yet women deny fathers the right to equality in the family:

If we're going to talk about equal opportunity for women in the job place then we got to talk about equal opportunity for men in domestic matters.

Underlying statements such as the one above is the belief that, because of prejudice on the part of women and the state, equality in the family is not being allowed to emerge; thus fathers' rightists argue that they are being victimized by reverse discrimination. They perceive women as making social and economic strides outside of the home in the male-dominated sphere. However, in the female-dominated family sphere, these men feel that they are not being afforded equal opportunity to parent and share household responsibilities. As a consequence, they believe that they are discriminated against in custody arrangements because they are fathers. One father without access to his children points to the prejudice against fathers:

I am concerned that the women want equality in the workplace but they do not want equality in the home. . . . The attitudes that seemed to be portrayed is that men and women are not equal when it comes to child rearing. . . . But, in spite of that, we are.

Another describes discrimination:

It says in the Family Law Act that each parent has equal rights to apply for custody. But we know that we still got a bunch of old farts on the bench and society has been trained to think that women should have the children. And it is just basic cut and dry like that.

There are two levels of contradiction in the arguments that fathers bring forward to assert their rights as postdivorce fathers. The first contradiction is in the rhetoric for equality in sole-custody determinations. Despite the public claim that fathers want custody of their children, the majority of fathers interviewed did not embrace the idea of seeking sole custody. Fathers have not thought about sole custody, or they think that they cannot obtain custody, or they simply do not want it. One executive member supports the ambivalence of fathers' desire for sole custody in the following statement:

What happens at "Fathers Demand Rights" is that the guys are told to go for custody. They do have this much right to their children. But a lot of them don't think that. If a lot of them stopped and thought about—are they really that interested? A lot of them do want it. But I admire that guy that I was working with who came and sat down and said, "I don't want custody. What am I going to do with three kids?"

What was commonly expressed by fathers was that they did not want custody but did want liberal access to their children:

All I want is good access so that I am not a visitor. I want to have the freedom to phone them, and I want the freedom for them to phone me. I want to be able to see them when I want to without asking for permission all the time.

The second contradiction is in their perception of their participation in child care and domestic responsibilities. This is evident in one father's statement. He says that fathers are "willing to take over and help." The notion of helping resonated in the fathers' interviews. Not one of them realized that to speak of "helping" was to delegate the task of child care to mothers. That mothers are expected to assume primary responsibility for children is not surprising. The empirical evidence unequivocally supports the fact that mothers continue to be the parent responsible for all aspects of care of the child (Drakich, 1989; Hochschild, 1989). That fathers take for granted mothers' primary responsibility in child care is evident in their discussion of joint custody.[6]

Joint Custody Rhetoric

The question we are left with is this: What do fathers want in terms of child custody if they do not want sole custody but want equality? When fathers are asked what the fathers' rights movement is fighting for, invariably the first and foremost answer is to retain their rights to be a father to their children after divorce. The way that they see this being accomplished outside of marriage is through joint custody. Appeals to traditional and contemporary discourses on the family are incorporated into the appeal for joint custody by fathers' rightists. The nearly singular focus on joint custody as a remedy for father discrimination demonstrates the contradictory nature of fathers' claims. The voices of the fathers interviewed identify and help us understand the multifaceted and contradictory meanings that the concept of joint custody has for fathers' rightists. Because there are no statutory definitions of joint custody or statutory distinctions between joint legal and joint physical custody in Canadian law, untangling the meaning of joint custody for these fathers is important in understanding their version of coparenting after divorce.

Fathers' rightists argue that joint custody would allow them to accomplish their goal of participatory fatherhood by coupling the argument with the equality and rights discourse. One father, an executive member who has sole custody of his children, emotionally summarizes the cases of members' fight for joint custody:

> What we are dealing with is parents that are trying to save what little is left of their lives with their children. . . . No, they are not fighting for [sole] custody, they are fighting for shared parenting. Fighting for a share, to remain a human being, to remain a parent to their child. Sole [maternal] custody deprives them [fathers] of that. They have no rights.

This father's remarks echo the fathers' rightists' public discourse, which focuses on the coparenting aspect of joint custody in terms of equal sharing of responsibility and primary care (Henderson, 1988;

Roman & Haddad, 1978). Although some fathers talked about the joys of being with their children, not one father talked about wanting to have the responsibility of the everyday care of his children:

> On the one hand I want to fight for custody of the kids. I would like to have them with me full-time instead of with her. On the other hand to do it on my own would be more than I would want to do right now. 'Cause even having them with me for the weeks that I had them I wasn't used to it. I just wasn't set up for it. It was an aggravation running here and there and stuff.

It is interesting to note that this father, as much as the other fathers, at least has the ability to decide whether or not he wants to spend more time with his children—a luxury that most mothers do not have.

What we heard from many fathers was a view of sharing and coparenting that did not involve shared everyday care and responsibility but the continuation of their parenting role prior to divorce. One of the founders of a fathers' rights group responded to the interviewer as follows:

Interviewer: So you are looking at equal, shared, continuation of parenting?

Father: No. Because parenting is never equal. Continuing parenting, whatever that means to you as to your family unit. That will change according to your needs. According to the children's needs. According to their age, their sex.

Interviewer: What you want to do is replicate your role when you were married outside of a marriage relationship. You want to continue that same sort of role.

Father: Yes.

Thus, to him, joint custody does not necessarily mean equality in physical custody and everyday care but the right to exercise the level of parenting that went on prior to the divorce. For many of the other fathers, joint custody did not entail the equal division of child care between mothers and fathers:

> Joint custody doesn't have to be fifty-fifty. You can have a joint custody arrangement where you only see the child ten, fifteen, twenty percent. But at least you have an input into the child's life.

Another father went so as far as to say that 1% of the child care responsibilities was shared parenting:

> You can have ten percent, ninety percent and it's still shared parenting. Sharing one percent with the father and ninety-nine percent with the mother is shared parenting. Coparenting implies that it is not one person cut off. There is a sharing going on.

We can see from the preceding statements that the meaning of joint custody does not denote equal physical and primary child care responsibilities between spouses. What we see is men who either have not thought about what equality means in practice or have developed a vocabulary of motives that is more socially palatable than personal-troubles discourse. One woman executive member discusses the absence of fathers' realistic expectations in their fight for custody:

> I see a lot of them and these guys are fighting for these kids so hard and I say to them, "You know they are lovely when they are cute kids but what are you going to do when they reach this rotten age? How are you going to cope with it? Do you really want all that?"

That fathers have unrealistic expectations for child care is not surprising in the light of this executive member's observation from counseling fathers in two of the groups:

> Most people who come to me don't even talk about their kids. They are totally wound up with their own problems. And rightly so.

Joint custody for fathers' rightists is the vehicle to preserve their fatherhood role postdivorce. It is the legal recognition of their fatherhood that they argue is denied them in sole-maternal-custody arrangements. However, the postdivorce fatherhood role for many fathers means a continuation of their predivorce role and not a reconceptualized role of the equal parenting dad typified in the fathers' rights public rhetoric.

Maternal Control of Children

One common, strongly held belief is that mothers have all the power to control their children after divorce. Mothers decide what schools children go to; what events they participate in; which doctors, extended family, and friends they see; and when they see their fathers. The fathers interviewed felt that they had lost their position of power in the postdivorce family and, as a consequence, had lost control over their children:

> I mean, I hate to see my relationship with my child defined in terms of power. But my ex has all the power. She has all the marbles and I'm constantly kowtowing. And I don't like it.

The fathers sensed this loss of control most deeply in their access ("visitation" in the United States) to their children. Frustrated by restricted or inflexible access, one father said:

> You don't get any extra time. They shut you down. You get totally shut down when you are a noncustodial parent. They will make your life miserable. In my case anyways, is that I was shut down. No Christmas extra time. Just my regular couple of days. Christmas break. Easter break. Spring break. I got no extra time. I got just shut down in there.

A popular discourse used by fathers' rightists to appeal for joint custody as a remedy for limited access is "the best interest of the child" doctrine.[7] This discourse maintains that the child needs and has a right to have both parents in his or her life in the event of a divorce. This specific discourse appeals to the monolithic, conservative, and sexist biases that are inherent in the beliefs about the family (Eichler, 1988). The monolithic bias treats families as having universal experiences and structures and maintains that "there is a natural differentiation of functions within families on the basis of sex" (Eichler, 1988, p. 2). Moreover, it maintains that detrimental sociopsychological effects could occur if a parent, namely, the father, is denied influence over his child(ren). A lay developmental psychology is used by fathers to suggest that negative consequences could occur if a father is not present in his child's life. Although the following father uses the gender-neutral term of *parent*, he is speaking about fathers as he is a father who has been denied access to his children:

> Think of the effect on the children when one parent is cut out. In some places, that is good and I won't deny that. But in the majority of cases that is unhealthy for the child. So any focus that puts stress on the relationship and says to one party or the other that you are not a fit parent, or I doubt your

parenting abilities, or [that] gives me power to keep you away and thereby alter your personality or later your drive, and defeat you and keep you away from that child affects the child.

The role of the father in child development is explained by another father:

> In the developmental phases of the children, there comes a point where a father figure is necessary and which the mother figure is necessary. As the child develops, the need for a mother or father varies. So that they have higher needs under age 5 for the maternal care, and it is 50-50 from age 5 to 10. And I would think further on, there is a greater need for the paternal figure to be present. . . . One of the major things [joint custody] does is to provide a father figure which the child has some contact with . . . and to which to develop his own personality and develop his own identity.

Access to children is not the only area that fathers contend that mothers control. The majority of fathers believe that mothers control information about their children and decisions affecting their children's lives. Even though Ontario's Children's Law Reform Act 20(5) states that the parent with access has the right to make inquiries and receive information about the health, education, and welfare of the child(ren), many men assert that they are unable to get such information because they are not legally recognized as a parent when they divorce. As such, they insist that they cannot exercise their rights as fathers in the decision-making process because their wives have the legal power to deny them this information as a result of their noncustodial status. This father's experience was one of continued exclusion from his ex-wife's decisions involving his son. He recounts his feelings of being "shut down":

> I never knew what sports camp he was supposed to go to in the summer time. I had to find out on my own. His school—she can do whatever she wants. She can send him to any school. She can do whatever she wants. Or he [ex-wife's current partner] can. Whoever's got the custodial parenthood at the time can do whatever they want. They have so much power. They shut you down. She decided to send him to another school. Didn't say a word to me. The hell with you. If they really want to say nothing to you . . . you can't do anything in the world. You cannot. And you get frustrated and wonder what am I going to do. It took me a month to find out what school he's going to. I'm going to have an appointment with one of his teachers.

Although this father had problems with obtaining information from his former wife, he was able to procure the necessary information from other sources or, eventually, from his wife. Most fathers felt that having joint custody would give them more power and control in maintaining access to information about their children than they would have as noncustodial parents:

> What I did learn is that joint custody is extremely beneficial to maintaining certain access rights to information. Information about the child and access rights to the child. Without joint custody I had a lot of things that I could not do.

This father's description of joint custody reflects fathers' rightists' claim that, if fathers were granted legal status as a parent (i.e., had joint custody), this status would empower them to correct the perceived discrimination they face in accessing information on their children. Moreover, as the following father states, fathers will be able to exert paternal rights over their children:

> Once one person has sole custody, the other person doesn't have any right to interfere with education, their religion, or any of the upbringing, medical care, or anything of the children. With joint custody arrangements, the parent has a say.

Our interviews suggest that fathers are more concerned with being excluded from the decision-making process than with being denied information. Fathers' appeal to their right to information about their children masks the underlying issues of power and control. In fact, fathers' rightists deny that they are interested in power and control. The following father rejects the accusation that he is interested in power and control, but in his rejection he reveals that he wants to monitor his child's life and, he also implies, his ex-wife's parenting:

> This is what women bring up all the time. All fathers want [joint] custody to control their wives. They want access to information to control their wives. Screw off lady. I want access to information so that I can keep tabs on my child's life. I don't give a shit what you do. But you do have the responsibility of raising that child.

Maternal Financial Privilege

These fathers not only feel that mothers have been privileged with care and control of their children but also that their former spouses have been unjustly awarded outrageous child support payments. Indeed, the topic of support payments was the central issue, during the observation period, at the majority of meetings, across all the groups. The group discussions of support payments were most often focused on individual fathers' personal troubles with support payments. Usually, these fathers brought their problems to the group looking for advice, direction, and sympathy. Support payment concerns can be divided into three types: (a) concern about the amount that is being paid, (b) concern that support is paid but access is denied or limited, and (c) concern that the money cannot be monitored. Excluding the women-spousal members and the sole-custody fathers, 65% of the fathers interviewed had support payment concerns. The negative emotional response to support payments is charged by fathers' conviction that discrimination occurs in awarding custody and child support. One father alludes to the inherent discrimination of "mommy gets the kids and daddy gets the bills" when he says:

> So the whole concept that the children belong to the mother and that the husband has to pay support to the mother and children because she can't earn as much money in the workplace, I find a problem with that.

Another father puts it even more strongly:

> The men that come have been or are being denied access and at the same time being robbed of their whole paycheck.

Most men state that they are paying too much in child support and cannot live on what is left. They feel that the financial burden placed on fathers penalizes their lifestyles, as the following father states:

> I know men out there that have three jobs to maintain a standard of living for themselves and their children just so that they could see their kids.

Moreover, this statement suggests that mothers would deny access to fathers who do not comply with the financial support agreement—again, portraying women as having power and control over the lives of fathers and their children. Other fathers used the metaphor of rape to describe the consequences of mothers' power and control after divorce:

> After being jerked around all over the place. Like we had four remands or what you call adjournments. Then when I got into court and the master [judge] awarded [my ex-spouse] fourteen hundred dollars a month support, which

was two thirds of my income, and I was not allowed to see my daughter until I had a psychological assessment. . . . And it was such a major loss. I went into shock. . . . So that is how I got involved in "Fathers Demand Rights" because I felt like I was being royally raped.

This father, who was "jerked around," did not have access to his children and saw the rape in terms of control over his paycheck and access to his children. A father with access also uses the metaphor of rape but focuses the metaphor on the former spouse's control of his identity and relationship to his children as a father as well as of his income and skills:

> Can I say anything about my wife to my children? No. She did a bad thing. She committed rape of a father and the love between him and his children. That is what she did. . . . It was not only a rape of my children; it is also a rape of my resources. I was the one that went through university. I worked hard for where I am right now. She didn't. She got her job and she is working, but it is not as much as I'm getting.

These fathers' accounts focus on their victimization in the process of awarding support and access. However, underlying these accounts is the fathers' perception of the threat to their power and control. These pivotal factors, obscured by the rhetoric of rights, justice, and victim-ization, become more visible when fathers talk about their concern for where the support money is going:

> I feel insulted that the court is going to say that you have to pay so much support because the wife is going to put the money away and make it available for them to go on for postsecondary education. And I say, well you trust her and not me. I mean I can do it. You don't have to give it to her to give to them. How do I know that it is even going to go to them? In my court case, I'm going to pursue this.

Of the fathers, 40% want to maintain control of the support money—who spends it and how it is spent. The others would like to see some form of accountability for the funds, either because they feel that the payments are too high or that the money is being spent improperly. One father suggests that the acrimony of divorce arises in the settlement of child support when fathers question the disbursement of "their" money:

> So when you get down to child support, although it is needed for the child, the problem comes in: What level of monetary support and is the money going

to be used for child support? There it becomes the question number two. If you are going to order money for child support, what guarantee is there that it is used for child support?

The main reason articulated by the fathers interviewed and observed, for their concern about mothers' control of money, is that mothers will spend the money on themselves. According to one father, child support is just a form of alimony to the former wife:

> When it comes to child support, of course, the problem has occurred during the transition between getting away from the alimony standard and having a purely child support standard. Over the long term we see child support being used as alimony. Where you see large child support agreements coming around—because you know darn well that that money isn't being all used for the child—that money is being used to maintain a certain lifestyle for one of the parents. The parent who has gotten custody.

Another father, who did not have access to his children and who defaulted on his child support payments, monitored his ex-spouse's spending:

Father: She's usually out to 1:30 in the morning. Spending 150 bucks a week on bingo. Without my paying any money or support—she's spending money on bingo.

Interviewer: How did you find out?

Father: Well, I have friends at bingo monitoring her activities.

Most fathers ardently believe that mothers seek sole custody to maintain a high standard of living or to avoid paid work:

> I know why she's doing what she's doing to me to get sole custody and have child support is because she wants to have six hundred dollars a month. It's that money. Six hundred dollars free a month that they get clear to control a child to do whatever they want. Go anywhere they want. And she can sit back and literally retire and have money coming in.

Fathers' desire to control the spending of support payments is revealed in their demands for accountability. Here is a request from one father:

So I would like to see more standardization. In child support I would like to see more accountability where we could go to the courts in the future and say this is the acceptable standard for raising this many children.

Another father suggests that the courts order accountability:

It would be interesting if the courts would order the custodial parent to document every dollar spent. And that way that person who is paying his money, which is supposed to be going towards the children's upbringing, would have their mind at ease. But that is not the way it is. I think that the support is there for the children and it should be used for that.

All fathers' rightists recognize the difficulty in maintaining financial control, and many noncustodial fathers look to joint custody as a legal solution to their monetary concerns. They believe that joint custody will relieve them of their financial responsibility to the postdivorce family unit, or decrease their support payments, and/or allow them to maintain power over and control of their funds:

This is why when you talk joint custody, I think it's beautiful because of the fact that both parents wouldn't have to pay anything. So we are eliminating one factor, which is what one is going to be looking for in the other is that of money. Keeping that money—greediness—out, what do you have next? Nothing. . . . I'm not saying that I would agree to a shared joint custody. I'm not pushing that. I'm just saying the definition in law of joint custody where "father" can have Wednesdays and every other weekend, they call that joint custody. That's not a joint custody. You know why? Why is the father paying six hundred dollars a month? If it is shared joint custody as per law one should not pay the other. If you are talking equal share, an equal split. . . . True joint custody, the essence of joint custody, is shared equally.

Once again, joint custody is couched within the discourse of social equality. As this father suggests, it is unfair to expect fathers to pay child support if they do not have joint physical custody, but at the same time it is not necessary to pay child support if fathers do have joint physical custody. Although he does not want joint physical custody, he is unwilling, or at least resentful, to pay what he believes to be disproportionate child support.

The conceptualization of equality for fathers with support payment personal troubles privileges their money over their children's care. These fathers did not discuss the value of the nonmonetary contribution of the mother to the upbringing of the children in their considerations of equality. Because mothers' care of children is taken for granted, it is easy to discount or ignore in the fathers' equality equation. Moreover, fathers seem not to imagine the lifestyle consequences for their children in the absence of child support payments. Their posturing on child support challenges their caring father image and their alleged concern for the best interests of the child. The fathers in this study seem not to connect the withdrawal of their support to a reversal of the children's predivorce material conditions. A substantial body of literature now documents women's financial troubles after divorce. Several U.S. researchers (Albrecht, 1980; Duncan & Hoffman, 1985; Wallerstein & Blakeslee, 1989; Weitzman, 1985), comparing divorced men and women, report on mothers' socioeconomic downward mobility and fathers' upward mobility postdivorce. Canadian research also supports this trend of differential economic consequences for men and women after divorce (Richardson, 1988).

Related Research

The results of this research support the work of Arendell (1992a, 1992b) and Coltrane and Hickman (1992). The contrasting of private and public rhetoric in this chapter allows for a comparison with Arendell's study of men's masculinist discourse of divorce and Coltrane and Hickman's examination of fathers' rights public moral discourse. Arendell (1992a, 1992b) found that men believed that the system inherently discriminates against men in divorce and that men who represent a diversity of educational and professional backgrounds, and a diversity of separation and divorce experiences, share a masculinist discourse of divorce. The accounts from the men in Arendell's study are very similar to the accounts of the fathers presented here. The sites of discrimination and the explanations offered by the fathers' rightists resonate in the accounts provided by Arendell (1992a, 1992b) and Coltrane and Hickman (1992). Thus it would appear that personal troubles discourse for non-custodial fathers and the common themes of discrimination in access, support payments, and custody are consequences of institutionalized gender arrangements that privilege men. It is not surprising, then, that we hear fathers employ an equality discourse that is premised on gendered relations to children and (ex-)spouses. The similarity in the use of a masculinist discourse, a rhetoric of equality, and a rhetoric of rights for men in two countries with different laws and divorce processes—but no apparent differences in the gender organization of their societies—highlights the gendered nature of their discourse. These common findings on personal discourses suggest that fathers' rights groups on both sides of the border should share similarities in their public rhetoric. Coltrane and Hickman (1992) profile the discourse of fathers' rights groups as a language of entitlement. They indicate that fathers' rights groups employ a rhetoric of equal rights to lobby for gender neutrality in custody statutes and equal rights to their children. Moreover, fathers' rights groups assert that joint custody is the only reasonable solution to child custody. Coltrane and Hickman (1992) also found that fathers' rights organizations' perpetuation of patriarchal family relations, embedded in their agenda, was "veiled by a rhetoric of children's rights and gender neutrality" (p. 413). Fathers' rights groups were also found to use rhetoric to establish the existence of injustice to fathers. The four groups in this study offered statistics and horror stories to the media to the same end as the organizations studied by Coltrane and Hickman (1992, p. 406). Another interesting similarity is that the claims makers in the Coltrane and Hickman (1992) study did "not always distinguish between private troubles and public issues" (p. 416). Similarly, the private troubles of the fathers in our study formed the basis for the groups' custody and divorce reforms. Finally, fathers' rights groups in our study also used rhetorical strategies that "assumed a societal consensus about what was in the best interest of the children" (Coltrane & Hickman, 1992, p. 417). Research in Australia (Graycar, 1989) examining the debate on child custody indicates that fathers' rights groups in Australia share similar rhetorical strategies and also employ equality rhetoric. The similarities across countries invites more in-depth comparative research.

Conclusions

During the divorce process, fathers come to some realization that they have lost power and control over parts of their lives—usually their fatherhood or their standard of living—and the lives of their former spouses and children. Not only do these men feel that they have been stripped of their father role by the court, they also feel they have been abused by the court and treated unfairly. Although most fathers experience these losses and may feel discriminated against because they are

252 The Fathers' Rights Movement

fathers, it is fathers' rightists who have politicized these events. Fathers' rights groups have taken fathers' personal troubles and recast them as issues of equality and rights. Although fathers' rightists portray themselves as caring, loving fathers who have been denied their rights to equal custody and access to their children, they are more concerned about the equality of their legal status than their equality in everyday parenting. The voices of the fathers we have heard from in this chapter have been telling. Their self-disclosures point to the essentially economic and hegemonic underpinnings of their discourse. Although equality is the organizing principle of their rhetoric, a closer examination exposes a notion of equality that conforms to the gendered familial division of labor. The fathers' rightists are not lobbying for joint, equal responsibility and care of children after divorce; they want equal access to their children, to information, and to decision making. The individual, self-disclosed accounts reported here unveil a masculinist construction of equality that obfuscates the gendered differences and experiences of mothers and fathers. Fathers' rightists have co-opted the language of equality but not the spirit of equality. The fathers' own words, reported here, tell us that they do not want sole responsibility for children, nor do they want an equal division of child care and responsibility. What they want, they tell us, is to have equal status as legal parents, which would give them equal access opportunities to their children and to information. The rhetoric of fathers' rights gives the illusion of equality, but, in essence, the demands are to continue the practice of inequality in postdivorce parenting but now with legal sanction.

The rhetoric of equality premised on sameness obscures the differential material conditions and experiences of mothers and fathers. Most mothers are caregivers to children. Most fathers are not. Most mothers are economically disadvantaged by divorce. Most fathers are not. Most women (mothers) relative to most men (fathers) are paid less in the workforce (Armstrong & Armstrong, 1984; Ornstein, 1983; Statistics Canada, 1993), live below the level of poverty (Arendell, 1986), and maintain more contact with their children postdivorce if they are non-custodial parents (see Furstenberg & Nord, 1985; Gross, 1988, for women's visitation patterns; see Ambrose, Harper, & Pemberton, 1983; Furstenberg et al., 1983; Hetherington, Cox, & Cox, 1976; Loewen, 1988, for men's).

The discourse of equality has potent symbolic imagery for the structure and relationships of the postdivorce family and appeals to the popular gender-neutral ideals of contemporary society. The rhetoric of joint custody operationalizes this symbolic imagery and sustains its appeal by conforming to gender neutrality. The discourse of fathers' rights, and its companion rhetoric of joint custody, has entrenched the masculinist discourse of divorce in the public imagination and, as a consequence, has provided a collective voice for divorced fathers and a legitimizing context for their complaints and anger. Moreover, the discourse of fathers' rights establishes a vocabulary of motives for fathers that conceals or obviates fathers' accounts of their prior fathering practices.

The rich ethnographic data, here provided by fathers' rightists, reflect their perspectives on the fatherhood role after divorce. This role, as typified by these fathers, is one that contradicts the fathers' rightists' public depiction of fathers as participatory dads and coparents to their children. Indeed, fathers want to play a role in their children's lives, but for most, that role is merely a continuation of their predivorce role of the traditional father who exercises his power and control.

Notes

1. Although this chapter focuses on fathers' rights groups in Canada, these groups have had strikingly similar effects in other countries. See Graycar (1989), Holtrust, Sevenhuijsen, and Verbraken (1989), and Sevenhuijsen (1986) for a discussion of fathers' rights discourse in Australia and the Netherlands, respectively. See Coltrane and Hickman (1992) and Fineman (1991) for a discussion of fathers' rights groups in the United States.

2. Both the interview and the observational data were collected by Carl Bertoia, who had full and liberal access to the membership and meetings of three groups. In the fourth group, he had access to members and was allowed to observe introductory meetings. However, he was not allowed to attend general meetings because he did not have an active complaint. Of the three groups permitting liberal access, two were observed. The third was not observed because of the distance involved to attend meetings.

3. The name of the fathers' rights group appearing in the quotations is a pseudonym to protect the anonymity of the participants. Whenever a fathers' rights group is mentioned in a quotation used in this chapter, we will substitute the name "Fathers Demand Rights."

4. Research indicates that anger postdivorce is a fairly common response to marriage dissolution and suggests that anger is not unique to men belonging to fathers' rights groups (see Arendell 1992a, 1992b; Ambrose, Harper, & Pemberton, 1983; Hetherington, Cox, & Cox, 1976).

5. This study was based on 899 cases active from July 1, 1985, to June 30, 1986, in Kitchener, Ontario. There were 169 custody applications from fathers.

6. It is important to note that *joint custody* is a term used loosely to refer to either joint legal or joint physical custody. In the majority of instances, when fathers' rightists use *joint custody*, they mean joint legal custody of children. The Canadian Divorce Act 1985

identifies joint custody as an option for divorcing parents. There are no statutory definitions of joint custody at either the federal or the provincial levels. However, there are various interpretations of joint custody—legal and physical—found in case law. The legal principle underlying custody awards is the best interest of the child. There is no presumption of joint custody in Canada.

7. The "best interest of the child doctrine" is loosely defined in statutory law as the needs and circumstances of the child including emotional ties, child preferences, stable environment, and proposed plans for care and upbringing. The definition has been influenced by judges and courts through case law. However, it has been appropriated by a variety of other parties to a divorce. Psychologists, social workers, fathers' rightists, and lawyers have shaped the meaning of the "best interest of the child" to fit their self-interest, or societal values such as continuing, ongoing parent-child relationships postdivorce, or their professional interpretations. The resulting equivocal construct of "the best interest of the child" has privileged the apparent advocates of children's best interest at the expense of the children.

13

The Future of Fatherhood

Social, Demographic, and Economic
Influences on Men's Family Involvements

SCOTT COLTRANE

What will fatherhood look like in the twenty-first century? Can we expect American fathers to be aloof breadwinners like family men of the 1950s, or will they resemble the idealized "new" fathers seen cuddling babies and changing diapers in popular films and on the pages of women's magazines? When couples get divorced in the coming decades, will men ignore their children and become the "deadbeat dads" we've been hearing about in newspapers, or will they fight for custody like the characters played by Dustin Hoffman in *Kramer vs. Kramer* or Robin Williams in *Mrs. Doubtfire*? In short, will men be more or less involved in family life than traditional stereotypes and media imagery imply?

To answer these questions, we need to understand past and present patterns of family life and link different styles of fathering to various social, demographic, and economic conditions. This task is difficult because of the popular misconception that men's and women's family roles are separate and unchanging. Social scientists, like others, have

AUTHOR'S NOTE: This chapter is based on studies described more fully in *Family Man: Fatherhood, Housework, and Gender Equity* (in press, Oxford University Press, New York).

assumed that fathers should be breadwinners and that mothers should be responsible for home and children. As a consequence, family studies before the mid-1970s tended to ignore men's participation in child care and housework, and little information exists for making detailed comparisons with the past. More recently, researchers have begun to pay attention to what fathers do—and don't do—in and for families (Coltrane, in press; Gerson, 1993; Griswold, 1993; Marsiglio, 1993b; Parke, 1981). As the earlier chapters in this book demonstrate, we are beginning to develop systematic knowledge about men's family involvements, but we still have a long way to go. Drawing on recent interview studies, national surveys, and sociological theories, this chapter reviews the current state of knowledge about men in families. In contrast to recent political rhetoric about absent fathers and melodramatic hand-wringing over a supposed decline in "family values," I offer some surprisingly optimistic assessments about the future of fatherhood in America.

Pressures for Change in Men's Family Roles

The most important trend affecting American families in the latter part of the twentieth century has been women's increasing employment. In 1970 only about half of U.S. mothers with school-aged children were in the paid labor force, but by 1990 three quarters were employed, most in full-time jobs. Changes were most pronounced for those with the youngest children. In 1976, when the Census Bureau first began collecting labor force statistics on women with infants, 31% of mothers with children under 1 year old were in the paid labor force, but by 1990 over half were employed (U.S. Bureau of the Census, 1992).

In response to women's increased labor force participation in the 1970s, researchers, journalists, and other trend watchers began predicting that American men would begin assuming more of the parenting and domestic duties. According to many family scholars, a new fatherhood ideal emerged about this time (Fein, 1978; Furstenberg, 1988b; LaRossa, 1988; Parke & Tinsley, 1984). Starting in the 1970s, films like *Kramer vs. Kramer, Mr. Mom, Three Men and a Baby,* and *Mrs. Doubtfire* began celebrating men's love for children, even if the men were initially shown as comically inept. Similarly, television comedies like *Full House* and *Who's the Boss* began to show men as loving parents and relatively competent housekeepers. By the 1980s there were more fathers than mothers in television commercials, with more men than ever shown cuddling babies and pushing strollers (Coltrane & Allan,

1994). These images provided first-time parents with new models for father-child relationships, though some scholars argued that the new fatherhood images had little to do with reality (LaRossa, 1988).

Whether called the "new" father, the "modern" father, or the "androgynous" father, studies in the 1980s began to describe men who were nurturant, caring, and emotionally attuned to their children (e.g., Coltrane, 1989; Pruett, 1987; Radin, 1982; Risman, 1986; Russell, 1983). Survey research using large representative samples also reported small, but significant, increases in the average amount of time contemporary American fathers spent with their children (Goldscheider & Waite, 1991; O'Connell, 1993; Pleck, 1983). Some reviewers suggested that most of men's increased time with children was spent in direct interaction rather than in being routinely available to their children or assuming responsibility for their care and welfare (M. E. Lamb, 1987; Marsiglio, 1991b; Pleck, 1987). Many researchers reported that American husbands and fathers continued to do little housework, and some suggested that men were more eager than ever to avoid family responsibilities (Ehrenreich, 1983; Hochschild, 1989; Thompson & Walker, 1989).

Furstenberg (1988b) calls attention to the disparity between images of "good dads"—those increasingly involved with their kids—and "bad dads"—those who are physically, emotionally, and financially absent from their families. Both involved and absent fathering have proliferated over the past decades, and increases in both appear to result from similar social trends. These trends include women's rising labor force participation, the increasingly optional character of contemporary marriage, and the demise of the "good provider role" (Bernard, 1981; Hood, 1986). Fathers in the United States are simultaneously more present and more absent than they were in the 1950s, because there are almost as many "deadbeat dads" as there are "new fathers." In this chapter, however, I focus on the majority of men who continue to reside with wives, children, and stepchildren.

What would happen if large numbers of fathers participated more actively in daily family life? One outcome is that the gender balance of power in married couples would become more equal. When husbands share family work, employed wives escape total responsibility for the "second shift" (Hochschild, 1989). When fathers assume responsibility for children, the men develop sensitivities that have been assumed to come with being a mother. In addition, children with involved fathers thrive intellectually and emotionally, and develop more balanced gender stereotypes and expectations (Biller, 1993; Chodorow, 1978; Radin,

1991). Sharing domestic labor is also associated with less discrimination against women and more gender equality in the society at large (Chafetz, 1990; Coltrane, 1988, in press). Thus even small shifts in men's family work could have profound influences on the future shape of society.

The Division of Family Work

When men talk about what they do for families beyond breadwinning, they usually focus on direct child care: watching the kids, playing with them, disciplining them, teaching them skills, or promoting specific values. Usually left in the background are the indirect domestic tasks associated with running a household and physically maintaining the children. Mundane and repetitive tasks like cooking children's meals, washing children's clothes, and cleaning up after them are as much a part of child care as more direct activities, but they are less important to most men and are likely to be ignored. I include these routine tasks in considering men's changing family involvements because they provide an indicator of changes in the balance of family power.

Studies conducted in the United States during the 1970s and early 1980s showed that women did about three quarters of the total family work but 80% to 90% of baby care and indoor housework. Men tended to focus their at-home family labor on outside chores or playing with older children. According to random sample surveys and time use studies, husbands barely increased their hourly contributions to the inside domestic chores of cooking, cleaning, and laundry in the 1970s. Studies did find that employed women began putting in fewer hours themselves, so that men's proportionate contributions to family work rose slightly (Fenstermaker-Berk, 1985; Pleck, 1983; Thompson & Walker, 1989).

What difference does it make that women do most of the everyday family work? One consistent finding has been that psychological distress is greatest among wives with husbands who contribute little (Kessler & McRae, 1982; Ross, Mirowsky, & Huber, 1983). Family work can be fulfilling, but most women have been responsible for virtually all of the most time-consuming and less pleasant tasks such as cooking, cleaning, and washing. Because much of this work has been seen as obligatory, relentless, and lonely, American housewives were at risk for high levels of depression from the 1950s through the 1970s (Collins & Coltrane, 1995). Men's household chores, in contrast to women's, have tended to be infrequent or optional, and early studies showed that doing more of them did not lead to depression in men. Men have tended to concentrate their efforts on relatively fun activities like playing with the children or barbecuing on weekends, and when they perform inside chores, they often receive help from others (Barnett & Baruch, 1986a; Fenstermaker-Berk, 1985; Robinson, 1988; Thompson & Walker, 1989).

Because responsibility for child care is difficult to measure with simple survey questions, household labor studies have tended to reduce parenting to the number of hours spent directly feeding, bathing, dressing, instructing, or putting children to bed. Studies have consistently found that mothers spend double or triple the time fathers do in these activities, although men did increase their time with children slightly during the 1970s, especially in conventional gender-typed activities like physical play (Barnett & Baruch, 1986a; Lamb, 1981; Parke & Tinsley, 1984). But effective parents also provide encouragement to their children, meet their emotional needs, anticipate their problems, facilitate social interaction, challenge them intellectually, set limits, and enforce discipline. Few time use or survey studies have explored these sorts of parenting issues, but in-depth family studies show that mothers are primarily responsible for these activities as well (Coltrane, in press; Marsiglio, Chapter 1, this volume).

Most women have considered unbalanced divisions of family labor to be "fair." According to survey research conducted in the 1970s and 1980s, the majority of wives had extremely low expectations for help with housework and the maintenance aspects of child care. Although many women expressed a desire for husbands to spend more time with children, it was usually framed in terms of benefiting the children rather than substituting for their own labor. Women rarely sought help with behind-the-scenes attentive and coordinative family work, such as overseeing child care, managing emotions and tension, sustaining conversations, or maintaining contact with kin. Women have felt less entitled to domestic services than men and typically viewed husbands' domestic help as a gift that required an expression of appreciation. It is not surprising that women who try to share domestic tasks report that it sometimes threatens the harmony of the family relationships that they feel responsible for maintaining (DeVault, 1987; Hochschild, 1989; Hood, 1983; Pyke, 1994; Thompson, 1991).

Recent Changes in the Division of Family Work

Researchers studying families since the mid-1980s report some modest changes in the division of housework and child care. Compared with figures from the early 1970s, men's average hourly contributions to inside housework have almost doubled, whereas women's contributions have gone down by about a third. In the earlier period, men in dual-earner households were doing only about 10% of the inside chores, but by the late 1980s, they were averaging about 20%-25%. Although most husbands still did far less than their wives, the trend was toward more sharing of more tasks, especially if wives were employed.

The family work that husbands began doing more of included direct child care, shopping, and meal preparation. The most recent studies of dual-earner couples using representative samples indicate that men contribute an average of almost one third of the time spent on these tasks. Meal cleanup and housecleaning continue to lag behind, with men averaging about one quarter. Men doing laundry is still relatively rare, but dual-earner husbands contribute about 15% of the hours spent in clothes care, compared with the 2%-5% they contributed before 1970 (Coltrane, in press; Ferree, 1991; Gershuny & Robinson, 1988; Shelton, 1992). Although men are putting in more hours on family work, responsibility for noticing when tasks should be performed or setting standards for their performance are still most often assumed by wives. In the majority of families, husbands notice less about what needs to be done, wait to be asked to do various chores, and require explicit directions if they are to complete the tasks successfully. Most couples therefore continue to characterize husbands' contributions to housework or child care as "helping" their wives (Coltrane, 1989; Fenstermaker-Berk, 1985; Thompson & Walker, 1989).

Most studies have concluded that, even if couples share household labor before they have children, they shift toward more conventional gender-based allocations of family work when they become parents (Cowan & Cowan, 1992). Having children has thus tended to increase women's family work, whereas men's domestic responsibilities have remained more stable across the transition to parenthood. Men and women also tend to adjust their paid work time differently when children are involved. Having a child means working about 3 more hours on the job per week for men, but for women it is associated with spending about an hour less in the paid labor force each week. As

Shelton (1992) puts it: "The gender gap is present even with no children, but it is exacerbated by the presence of children in the household" (p. 69). In spite of the fact that the presence of children tends to increase women's family work more than men's, direct child care by fathers is the area marked by the most apparent change in the allocation of family work. Recent studies show that men are now contributing close to a third of the child care hours in dual-earner couples (Goldscheider & Waite, 1991; Pleck, 1987). Women still put in more hours supervising children and typically act as overseers when others watch them, but parents are increasingly likely to work different shifts and to alternate child care between them (Hoffman, 1989; Presser, 1988). Between the mid-1980s and the mid-1990s, fathers became the most common substitute caretakers for preschoolers when their mothers were working. In a third of U.S. two-parent households with a nonday shift worker, the father provides primary care for the preschool children while the mother works, and one in four preschool children with an employed mother are watched by the father (O'Connell, 1993). Will there be even more father involvement in the future? To answer that question, we can extrapolate recent trends in a straight-line fashion, but we should also pay attention to the reasons that the trends exist in the first place. For that, we must turn to sociological theories about the division of labor.

Explaining the Division of Family Work

Various theories have been advanced to explain how and why housework and child care are divided. Many explanations are based on in-depth studies of American couples and some originate from more macro theories, but few have been uniformly supported in scientific tests using national data. In part this is because the types of questions one can address in survey research tend to be relatively superficial and in part it is because there is so much variation between couples that unidimensional theories fail to capture the complexity of most people's lives. In the following sections, some leading theories of household labor are briefly reviewed and various social, demographic, and economic conditions associated with men's family work are summarized. I will return to this information to make some predictions about the future of fatherhood at the close of the chapter.

Culture and Socialization

Citing ethnographic and historical evidence, researchers report enormous variation in gender-linked divisions of labor across cultures and eras. Most scholars conclude that divisions of family labor are socially constructed within specific cultural and economic contexts rather than being ordained by god or fixed by biology (e.g., Chafetz, 1990; Thorne & Yalom, 1992). Anthropological explorations into patterns of kinship and family structure highlight the importance of culturally specific rituals, customs, and myths in perpetuating divisions of labor based on gender (Rosaldo, 1980). Historical analyses suggest that the Victorian ideal of separate spheres for men and women played a major role in shaping contemporary patterns of housework and child care in the United States (Bose, 1987; Coontz, 1992).

Overlapping with the above theories, psychological and socialization theories suggest that children and adults acquire beliefs about appropriate gender roles, and that people fashion their own family behaviors according to internalized factors (e.g., gender schemata and psychodynamic structures) and social prescriptions (e.g., gender scripts and stereotypes; Bem, 1981; Chodorow, 1978; Deaux & Kite, 1987; Gilligan, 1982). The basic idea in most cultural and socialization theories is that internalized values and gender ideals shape people's motivations and cause them to perform work appropriate to their gender and to avoid work inappropriate to their gender. Empirical tests of hypotheses derived from cultural and socialization theories using contemporary U.S. populations usually rely on attitude measures and yield mixed results. Some researchers conclude that abstract beliefs about what men and women "ought" to do are relatively inconsequential for actual behavior (Thompson & Walker, 1989), whereas others conclude that there is a consistent, though sometimes small, increase in sharing when men and women believe that family work should be shared (Pleck, 1983). According to a recent national survey, sharing child care is most common when husbands' attitudes favor it, and sharing housework is most common when wives' attitudes support it (Ishii-Kuntz & Coltrane, 1992a).

Economics and Practicality

Theories that consider the division of labor by gender to be a practical response to economic conditions are diverse and plentiful. New home economics theories suggest that women do the housework and child care because labor specialization maximizes the efficiency of the entire family unit. Women are assumed to have "tastes" for doing housework, and their (purportedly biological) commitments to child rearing are seen as limiting their movement into the marketplace (Becker, 1981). Resource theories similarly assume that spouses make cost/benefit calculations about housework using external indicators like education and income. Family work is treated as something to be avoided, and women end up doing more of it because their time is worth less on the economic market and because they have less marital power because of lower earnings and education (Geerken & Gove, 1983; Spitze, 1986). Researchers typically use income, education, or occupation to approximate individual resources and attempt to correlate these with reported divisions of family work.

In most studies, educational differences between spouses are rarely associated with divisions of labor, and men with more education often report doing more housework, rather than less, as resource theories predict. Similarly, total family earnings have been found to have little effect on how much housework men do, though middle-class men appear to talk more about the importance of sharing family tasks than working-class men. There may be more actual sharing among working-class couples, however, in part because men's and women's incomes are closer to each other than in middle-class families, and everyone must contribute just to get by. Although job loss or cutbacks for men are not automatically associated with their assumption of more responsibility for housework and child care (Marsiglio, 1991b), some studies of egalitarian couples reveal that underemployment or unemployment is central to the process of husbands adopting tasks previously performed by wives (Hood, 1983; Radin, 1982).

Most recent studies show that spouses with more equal incomes share more household labor, although women still do more than men when they hold similar jobs. Thus relative earning power is important, but there does not appear to be a simple trade-off of wages for family work (Coltrane & Ishii-Kuntz, 1992; Gerson, 1993; Hochschild, 1989; Thompson & Walker, 1989). Most studies find that the number of hours that people spend on the job is more important to the division of family work than simple earnings or occupational prestige. Early studies found that husbands of employed wives did no more family work than husbands of nonemployed wives, but as studies have become more sophisticated, they have discovered a fairly strong and consistent negative relationship between hours spent on the job and hours spent on family work. In other words, women still do more family work than men, but when they are employed more hours, they do less at home. This occurs when women have careers and identify strongly with their paid work but also when they put in long hours at relatively menial working-class jobs. Men are especially likely to share family work if their spouses are defined as full coproviders (Coltrane & Valdez, 1993; Hood, 1983). Conversely, when men spend fewer hours on the job, they perform more family work, and men married to wives who work the longest hours are likely to share the most. Fathers also share more child care when spouses work complementary shifts, when they can adjust their work schedules, and when other government or workplace programs promote sharing (Coltrane, in press; Haas, 1992; O'Connell, 1993; Pleck, 1985). In general, then, we can conclude that time demands and time availability—labeled practical considerations, demand-response capability, or situational constraints—enter into most people's decisions about the allocation of family work (e.g., England & Farkas, 1986; Peterson & Gerson, 1992; Spitze, 1988).

Gender Inequality

Other theories about family work also focus on power and practicality, but they put more emphasis on conflict and gender inequality. Most feminist scholars suggest that women are compelled to perform household labor because of systemic and pervasive discrimination in the larger society (Ferree, 1991; Haas, 1992; Peterson & Gerson, 1992; Thompson & Walker, 1989). Some researchers focus on economic market inequities that keep women's wages below those of men, effectively forcing women to be men's domestic servants (Blumberg, 1984; Hartmann, 1981). Unlike the new home economics, these theories do not assume a unity of husband's and wife's interests, and unlike many resource theories, they do not posit all individuals as utility maximizers with equal chances in a hypothetical free market. Different versions of theories in this tradition suggest that institutions like marriage, the legal system, the media, the educational system, and the economy also help to perpetuate an unequal division of labor in which women are compelled to perform domestic labor even if they also hold paying jobs (Chafetz, 1990).

Hochschild (1989) suggests that we can understand women's obligation to perform the second shift by paying attention to "gender strategies"—plans of action shaped by cultural notions of gender that are invoked in solving everyday problems. Other researchers use similar concepts to explain how the performance of family work serves to (re)construct the meaning of gender in everyday interaction, demarcate men from women, and reinforce men's privileged status (Coltrane, 1989; Fenstermaker-Berk, 1985; Thompson, 1991; West & Fenstermaker, 1993). Studies relying on inequality theories find that more domestic work is shared when wives negotiate for change, delegate responsibility for various chores, and relinquish control over managing home and children (Coltrane, 1989, 1990; Ferree, 1991; Pyke, 1994; Thompson & Walker, 1989).

Social, Demographic, and Life Course Predictors

Additional social, demographic, and life course factors have also been found to be associated with the sharing of family work, but they do not fit neatly into the theories discussed above. For example, men tend to do more family work when couples move away from their neighborhood of origin, have less frequent contact with parents, and have few substitute women caretakers nearby (Coltrane, in press). Parents who delay the transition to parenthood until their late twenties or thirties also tend to share more family work, even after controlling for the social and economic factors mentioned above, such as ideology, relative income, and job hours (Coltrane, 1990; Coltrane & Ishii-Kuntz, 1992; Daniels & Weingarten, 1982). Tentative findings also suggest that fathers who participate in the birth process and get involved in routine infant care are more likely than others to follow through with continued family work (Coltrane, 1989). Individuals who have divorced and remarried, especially those giving birth to a child in a second marriage, are also especially likely to share family work (Demo & Acock, 1993; Ishii-Kuntz & Coltrane, 1992b). Those parents who have fewer, older, or male children appear to share more than others (Ishii-Kuntz & Coltrane, 1992a; Marsiglio, 1991b). Finally, more domestic labor sharing occurs when employers offer leaves, benefits, and other "family-friendly" programs (Haas, 1992; Pleck, 1993).

Predicting the Future

Although the social theories and empirical findings reviewed above suggest a few conflicting predictions about the sharing of family labor, there is substantial agreement among them. In general, more sharing of parenting and housework is predicted when wives are employed more hours, make more money, and are willing to negotiate for change; when husbands are employed fewer hours, believe in gender equity, and get involved in infant care; and when couples delay getting married and having children, or if they are remarried or have fewer and older children. In addition, more family work tends to be shared by men when there are few other child care options and when workplace programs promote father participation. To see whether these conditions might become more common in the future, we need to consider some of the larger economic, social, and demographic trends that will affect us (see Coltrane, in press).

Economic Trends

Changes in the labor market are the driving force behind most of the family changes noted above, and recent labor market trends are expected to continue. Whereas husband-as-sole-breadwinner families used to out-number two-earner families by two-to-one, there are now twice as many two-earner families as any other type. Because of global restructuring of the economy and growth in the service sector, the demand for lower wage jobs will continue, and most of the new jobs will be filled by women. In the near term, the gender wage gap will shrink, and the labor market will continue to become less segregated by gender. With continuing cutbacks in the manufacturing sector, we can also expect more job loss or reduced employment among men than women. Women's employment will seem less optional in the future, mothers will tend to remain in the labor force continuously, and more women will move into management and professional positions. In general, women's earnings will approach those of men, and more wives will come to be seen as co-economic providers. These changes will put increasing pressure on men to do more with the children and around the house.

It is unlikely that business or government will substantially increase subsidies for child care, so more wives will bargain for help from husbands and others. If scheduling flexibility, nonday shifts, and part-time work among men increase as predicted, we can expect even more sharing of domestic labor. In an increasing number of couples, men will exercise significant responsibility for a few tasks previously considered "women's work," especially direct child care. Increased participation of men in shopping, cooking, and meal cleanup is also expected, in part because more men will be spending more time at home with children.

Social Trends

Along with economic changes, shifts in attitudes are moving us toward more sharing of family work. Most Americans, especially if they are younger, already say they subscribe to the ideal of equality of opportunity for men and women, and growing numbers will endorse such concepts in the future (Thornton, 1989). As two-earner families become even more common and most children spend some time in the care of others, fewer people will publicly proclaim that working mothers are negligent or that their children will suffer because their mothers have jobs. Although most people will continue to assume that women are better equipped for parenting than men, a growing proportion will subscribe to the idea that (at least some) men can nurture as well as women. In addition, the tendency for Americans to value personal well-being and individual achievement will continue to be strong, so women and men will not remain in relationships that are considered harmful or extremely limiting.

Within marriages, the expectations, bargaining strategies, and fairness perceptions of both spouses will undergo change as gender attitudes become less rigid. Men and women will define fewer activities as solely the province of one spouse or the other. This does not mean that changes in attitudes or behaviors will be swift or uniform. Men's attitudes about gender will remain more conservative than those of women, and many will continue to maintain their privileged position by not noticing when household tasks need doing or by remaining incompetent at emotional or family labor (see Goode, 1992; Segal, 1990). Nevertheless, some household tasks, like shopping and meals, will become less tied to gender identity in the future.

Changes in attitudes about men's role in child care will continue to lead the way, as two-parent families are likely to become even more convinced that children need frequent contact with their fathers. Many new fathers will be motivated to compensate for a perceived lack of emotional connection with their own fathers and an increasing number will seek personal growth and fulfillment from fathering activities (Cohen, 1993; Hawkins, Christiansen, Sargent, & Hill, Chapter 3, this volume; Marsiglio, Chapter 5, this volume). Although many men will interact with their children, and especially their sons, in relatively conventional "masculine" activities like games, sports, and physical play, a growing number will also develop capacities for a less directive and more attentive type of care. Expectant fathers will continue to participate in birth preparation classes and most will attend their children's births. With higher rates of employment among women with infants, more fathers will perform child care early in their child's life. More solo time spent in baby care will lead to greater attachment to the father role and more involvement in later child care. For a growing minority of fathers, participation in direct child care will also lead to the performance of related support activities and housework.

Demographic Trends

Changing attitudes toward gender and family life are tied to changing economic circumstances, and both shape demographic trends in marriage, divorce, and fertility. For example, continuing employment trends and emphasis on individual self-fulfillment are likely to sustain high levels of geographic mobility, educational attainment, cohabitation, and divorce. At the same time, the high value placed on romantic and family relationships, coupled with increasing dependence on two incomes, will keep marriage and remarriage rates relatively high. There will be more remarried couples in the future, with their more complicated forms of parenting and family labor sharing. Individualism and career commitments will cause more people to postpone marriage and childbearing, but the increasing emotional value of children will ensure that most couples will eventually have children. All of these demographic factors are linked to more sharing of family work between husbands and wives.

With more divorce, remarriage, and two-earner families, the bargaining position of wives and husbands will slowly change. Historically strict normative sanctions against cohabitation and out-of-wedlock birth will weaken, but not disappear. Women will remain more economically dependent on marriage than men, but men's economic incentives for marriage will increase as two incomes become almost essential. Women's obligatory performance of domestic chores used to be part of the marriage bargain, just as men's financial providing once was. Now, however, because most women will be coproviders, expectations for men to assume a share of the child care and housework should rise. People will spend more time single, divorced, and remarried, and the increasingly contingent nature of marriage will put additional pressure on men to make greater domestic contributions and on women to make greater financial contributions. Both men and women will be more likely to evaluate and select marriage partners on the basis of their potential for being both a provider and a homemaker.

Reflections on the Future of Fatherhood

The preceding analysis suggests that many American fathers will become more involved in their children's upbringing and begin to share more of the housework. Not all couples will move toward gender equality, however, and the changes noted above will often work at cross-purposes. Some couples will continue to follow conventional gender-segregated divisions of labor, while others will opt for virtual role reversal. Most, however, will fall somewhere in between, sharing some tasks and dividing others on the basis of conventional gender expectations. Some families will lament the changes and fight them at every turn. Others will accept and applaud them, attempting to divide tasks evenly and to move away from conventional gendered manager/ helper dynamics (for examples, see Coltrane, in press; Gerson, 1993; Hochschild, 1989). We can predict, however, that the general direction of change will be toward more acceptance of sharing between men and women and more sharing of family work in actual practice.

Even though gender equity will increase within many families, over-all economic conditions suggest that inequality between families will continue to rise. For this reason, the growing equity between wives and husbands might better be characterized as shared limitations rather than shared opportunities. As we move into the twenty-first century, two-earner couples will enjoy even greater relative economic advantage over single-earner families, one-parent families, and other households. Family type as defined by the number of people and the number of earners will become the most important basis of class standing in the United States. Outside of a small privileged elite, it will take two secure, well-paying jobs to ensure that a family stays in the middle class. Even many families with two earners will hover around the poverty level as more jobs become low paying and sporadic. Women and minorities will be disproportionately affected by problems of low pay, underemployment, and limited resources. Tragically, more American children will live in poverty.

How will families respond? Out of necessity, single parents and adults in lower income households will share substantial child care and housework with older children, kin, and others. When husbands are present in limited-income households, they will also share in more domestic tasks than they have in the past. New opportunities will be available to some women, and wives at all class levels and in all race/ethnic groups will continue to narrow the gap between their own and their husbands' earnings. Within the new patterns of increasing stratification, then, we can expect to see some movement toward more gender equality at many levels.

Among relatively privileged dual-earner couples, there will also be enormous variation. In the middle class, those without children will enjoy relative economic advantage and will devote more time and energy to their careers. Couples with children, at all economic levels, will be forced to make some career sacrifices, and because of continuing gender inequality in the job market, more of these sacrifices will be made by women than by men. Still, we will see more men tailoring their employment to fit their family needs. More fathers will select jobs on the basis of compatibility with child care arrangements, more will elect to work flexible or nonday shifts, and fewer men will unquestioningly assume that they owe their employers overtime or take-home work. Men's experiences of work-family conflicts will thus begin to look more like those of women.

Even though more men will opt for a "daddy track," changes in work culture will probably come slowly. Although normative sanctions are expected to weaken, men who choose to spend time with their children instead of working will continue to be thought of as less serious and risk being passed over for promotions. Still, as more men treat employment as women have tended to in the past, we can expect a slight weakening of gender discrimination on the job. As women work more hours and earn more money, they will become accepted as necessary providers, even if most will still not be considered fully equal providers. These small changes are apt to generate a snowball effect, building upon themselves and gaining momentum as incremental ideological and economic transformations accumulate.

Women's employment and men's assumption of family work are not temporary fads that will soon fade. Many men and women will continue to resist by harking back to halcyon images of separate spheres, but this backlash will not stem the flow of these historic changes. Even if we witness a revival of fundamentalist morality like we had in the early

1980s, there will be continuing pressures on women to work for wages and men to do more family work. In fact, a public renewal of appreciation for family and children would only serve to hasten some of the changes that are already under way. This is because new government income support programs that might reduce women's incentives for employment are extremely unlikely, as are government subsidies for child care that might reduce pressure on men to do more. The conservative trend toward limiting government and privatizing services thus reaches into families as much as any liberal social welfare program, and men will be expected to pick up at least some of the slack at home. As the analysis presented above indicates, most of the pressures for sharing family work are related to underlying demographic, economic, and social trends that have been building for many decades. Although not impervious to change, these trends will not abruptly reverse themselves.

As men begin to assume more responsibility for child care and housework, we can expect mixed reactions within families. More women will be relieved of full responsibility for domestic affairs, which, if desired, will have positive impacts on their mental health, marital satisfaction, and career development. For most women, sharing the physical burden of housework is an enormous relief, and for many others, sharing the emotional burden of worrying about the children can be liberating. On the other hand, trying to share with a husband who is a lousy housekeeper or an inattentive parent can raise a wife's anxiety to unacceptable levels. If women do not want more help and do not want to give up control over home and children, being forced to share can have negative impacts on their mental health and marital satisfaction. Some women continue to feel that asking their husbands to do housework demeans their masculinity or represents failure on their own part. For these women, increased sharing is experienced as troublesome and, whenever possible, they try to get back to gender-segregated patterns of household labor. Nevertheless, because people's consciousness tends to be shaped by their routine activities, even reluctant sharing, if moderately successful, can have the effect of diluting the influence of gender on future patterns of family labor allocation.

At least in the short run, conflicts between husbands and wives, and between fathers and children, will probably increase as more men begin taking some responsibility for the stressful day-to-day operations of households. Although this will provide opportunities for fathers to develop closer relationships with their children, it will also afford them more opportunities to have negative interactions. Proportionately more fathers than mothers physically and sexually abuse children, so the effects of more participation by fathers cannot automatically be assumed to have positive effects on children or their families. Many fathers pay more attention to sons than daughters and maintain more rigid gender stereotypes than mothers. Bringing such men into more active contact with children could therefore reinforce gender differences rather than working toward their demise. On the other hand, fathers who take sole or equal responsibility for children depart from the patterns exhibited by more conventional fathers. Although it is unclear what causes what, highly participant fathers adopt a more gender-neutral style of parenting that resembles mothers' styles more than traditional fathers'. Children of highly participant fathers tend to perceive them as more punitive than children with less involved fathers, a pattern that reflects the involvement of fathers in routine limit setting. In general, fathers who share parenting must give up the privileged status of outsider and hence tend to develop less romanticized and more realistic relationships with their children. Mothers often consider this to be a positive development, but fathers tend to be more ambivalent about it.

Fathers who take on responsibility for child care often report that the experience makes them more complete people. That is, fathering provides them opportunities to develop the more caring and emotional sides of themselves. To survive the daily trials and tribulations of child care, many parents find they must develop clarity about what is most important, patience with the uneven pace of children's development, and sensitivity to subtle differences in feelings and actions. What's more, good parenting strikes a balance between guidance and service. Aloof, authoritarian, and judgmental styles of interaction do not work well in early child care and tend to create more problems than they solve. Because men cannot rely on no-nonsense, directive, "masculine" styles of interaction, they are forced to develop more gentle and expressive ways of relating. Child care thus provides men a relatively safe opportunity to explore new ways of relating and to break down gender dichotomies. Caring for young children has a quality different from interactions with other adult men, which tend to be restricted to set patterns of concern for work, sports, and "things" (tools, cars, equipment, adventure, and so on). For most men, child care is also qualitatively different from their relationships with women, which are often marked by ambivalence about intimacy. With their children, in contrast, men can enthusiastically enter into a relationship predicated on unconditional love, emotional vulnerability, and innocence. This is a profound experience for many men, and although it sometimes makes their wives jealous because the men cannot give the same type of love to them, it tends to change the men (Coltrane, 1989; Ehrensaft, 1987). In their own words, it begins to "open them up" to various expressive possibilities, including sadness and loss surrounding their relationships with their own fathers.

Perhaps even more important, children with involved fathers tend to enjoy a number of social, emotional, and intellectual advantages. It is not entirely clear that this is because of the fathers' unique contributions or simply because the children enjoy the benefits of having two adults give them the kind of love, care, attention, and resources that promote optimum development. As fathers assume more of the tasks we associate with mothering, then, the potential for longer term change in gender relations will increase. Because most mothers and fathers will still act differently from each other, we will not abandon the old gender categories. Nevertheless, as more men perform family work, our concepts about what is appropriate behavior for men and women will be altered. We can already see this for a few activities. Men used to get embarrassed if they were seen pushing a baby carriage in public, but now fathers show off their snugglies and strollers as if they were status symbols. Cooking and washing dishes are other family tasks slowly coming to be seen as activities appropriately shared by husbands. Whether doing the laundry, vacuuming the floors, and cleaning the toilets will also move into the shared category remains to be seen. The simple fact that a few more routine family tasks will be performed by men carries the potential to alter our definitions of what it means to be a man. This does not guarantee that gender relations will become equal, only that the content of gender will be transformed in the process.

I see the erosion of separate gender spheres within the family as potentially contributing to a fundamental reordering of relationships between men and women throughout society. If men take on more responsibility for housework and child care, it will feed back into the distribution of resources and the changing nature of employment. Most women now work for wages, but they have not been fully accepted as providers. As more men take on household duties, the distinctions between men's work and women's work will weaken. Men and women workers who are parents will share the same sorts of limitations from employment obligations, but as more men take their family obligations seriously, employers will feel more pressure to change the structure of work. As women's wages and employment hours increase, men will be less able to define providing as their sole and primary duty, and they will be under more pressure to share domestic duties. Thus changes in housework and market work are reciprocal, and we can expect further change in both as men begin to shoulder more family work.

The changes that I see on the horizon are neither revolutionary nor inevitable. They will depend on many individual people making countless piecemeal decisions as they go about living their daily lives. Nevertheless, at least for those men who are married or remarried, the general direction of change is moving toward more sharing of family labor. This will not come easily, as most men and women will resist as much as they embrace the changes. Men will eagerly take on some tasks but bitterly resist the imposition of others. Women will eagerly delegate responsibilities for some forms of family work but at the same time will ferociously guard others. The shifts we will witness will be both painful and fulfilling. Both men and women will be ambivalent about many of the these changes and countless contradictions will emerge. Nevertheless, the general trend will be toward more sharing of family work and most men and women will find rewards in the changing patterns of labor allocation. Ultimately, these changes will propel us toward more equality between men and women. The big question is just how close we can come to true gender equity.

References

Adams, P. L., Milner, J. R., & Schrepf, N. A. (1984). *Fatherless children*. New York: Wiley.

Ahlburg, D. A., & De Vita, C. J. (1992). New realities of the American family. *Population Bulletin, 47*(2), 1-44. (Washington, DC: Population Reference Bureau, Inc.)

Ahrons, C. R. (1983). Predictors of paternal involvement postdivorce: Mothers' and fathers' perceptions. *Journal of Divorce, 6*, 55-69.

Albrecht, S. (1980). Reactions and adjustments to divorce: Differences in the experiences of males and females. *Family Relations, 29*, 59-68.

Allport, G. (1942). *The use of personal documents in psychological sciences*. New York: Social Science Research Council.

Alwin, D. (1984). Trends in parental socialization values: Detroit, 1958-1983. *American Journal of Sociology, 90*, 359-382.

Alwin, D. (1987). Social stratification, conditions of work and socialization. In N. Eisenberg, J. Reykowski, & E. Staub (Eds.), *Social and moral values: Individual and societal perspectives* (pp. 327-346). New York: Lawrence Erlbaum.

Amato, P. R. (1993). Children's adjustment to divorce: Theories, hypotheses, and empirical support. *Journal of Marriage and the Family, 55*, 23-38.

Ambrose, P., Harper, J., & Pemberton, R. (1983). *Surviving divorce: Men beyond marriage*. Brighton, UK: Wheatsheaf.

Anderson, E. (1989). Sex codes and family life among poor inner city youths. *Annals of the American Academy of Political and Social Science, 501*, 59-78.

Antonucci, T. C., & Mikus, K. (1988). The power of parenthood: Personality and attitudinal changes during the transition to parenthood. In G. Y. Michaels & W. A. Goldberg (Eds.), *The transition to parenthood: Current theory and research* (pp. 62-84). New York: Cambridge University Press.

275

276   References

Arditti, J. A. (1990). Noncustodial fathers: An overview of policy and resources. *Family Relations, 39,* 460-465.

Arditti, J. A. (1991). Child support noncompliance and divorced fathers: Rethinking the role of paternal involvement. *Journal of Divorce and Remarriage, 14,* 107-119.

Arditti, J. A., & Kelly, M. (1994). Fathers' perspectives of their co-parental relationships postdivorce. *Family Relations, 43,* 61-67.

Arendell, T. (1986). *Mothers and divorce: Legal, economic, and social dilemmas.* Berkeley: University of California Press.

Arendell, T. (1992a). After divorce: Investigations into father absence. *Gender and Society, 6*(4), 562-586.

Arendell, T. (1992b). The social self as gendered: A masculinist discourse of divorce. *Symbolic Interaction, 15*(2), 151-181.

Armstrong, P., & Armstrong, H. (1984). *The double ghetto: Canadian women and their segregated work* (rev. ed.). Toronto: McClelland & Stewart.

Babcock, G. (1989). *Fathers on the outside: Legal and social psychological aspects of postdivorce parenting.* Unpublished master's thesis, Washington State University, Pullman.

Backett, K. (1987). The negotiation of fatherhood. In C. Lewis & M. O'Brien (Eds.), *Reassessing fatherhood: New observations on fathers and the modern family* (pp. 74-90). London: Sage.

Bandura, A. (1977). *Social learning theory.* Englewood Cliffs, NJ: Prentice Hall.

Barnett, R. C., & Baruch, G. K. (1986a). Consequences of fathers' participation in family work. *Journal of Personality and Social Psychology, 51,* 983-992.

Barnett, R. C., & Baruch, G. K. (1986b). *Determinants of fathers' participation in family work* (Working Paper No. 136). Wellesley, MA: Wellesley College Center for Research on Women.

Barnett, R. C., & Baruch, G. K. (1988). Correlates of fathers' participation in family work. In P. Bronstein & C. P. Cowan (Eds.), *Fatherhood today: Men's changing role in the family* (pp. 66-78). New York: Wiley.

Bartz, K., & Levine, E. S. (1978). Childrearing by black parents: A description and comparison to Anglo and Chicano parents. *Journal of Marriage and the Family, 40,* 709-719.

Bartz, K. W., & Witcher, W. C. (1978). When father gets custody. *Children Today, 7*(5), 2-6, 35.

Baruch, G. K., & Barnett, R. C. (1986). Consequences of fathers' participation in family work: Parents' role strain and well-being. *Journal of Personality and Social Psychology, 51,* 983-992.

Baumrind, D. (1966). Effects of authoritative parental control on child behavior. *Child Development, 37,* 887-907.

Baumrind, D. (1972). An exploratory study of socialization effects on black children: Some black-white comparisons. *Child Development, 43,* 261-267.

Becker, G. S. (1981). *A treatise on the family.* Cambridge, MA: Harvard University Press.

Becker, H. S. (1960). Notes on the concept of commitment. *American Journal of Sociology, 66,* 32-40.

Becker, H. S. (1964). Personal change in adult life. *Sociometry, 27,* 40-53.

Beer, W. R. (Ed.). (1988). *Relative strangers: Studies of stepfamily processes.* Totowa, NJ: Rowman & Littlefield.

Belsky, J., Youngblade, L., Rovine, M., & Volling, B. (1991). Patterns of marital change and parent-child interaction. *Journal of Marriage and the Family, 53,* 487-498.

Bem, S. L. (1981). Gender schema theory: A cognitive account of sex typing. *Psychological Review, 88,* 354-364.

Benin, M. H., & Agnostinelli, J. (1988). Husbands' and wives' satisfaction with the division of labor. *Journal of Marriage and the Family, 50,* 349-361.

Berger, P. L., & Luckmann, T. (1966). *The social construction of reality.* New York: Doubleday.

Berk, S. F. (1985). *The gender factory: The apportionment of work in American households.* New York: Plenum.

Berman, P. W., & Pedersen, F. A. (1987). Research on men's transitions to parenthood: An integrative discussion. In P. W. Berman & F. A. Pedersen (Eds.), *Men's transitions to parenthood: Longitudinal studies of early family experience* (pp. 217-242). Hillsdale, NJ: Lawrence Erlbaum.

Bernard, J. (1978). *The future of marriage.* New York: Bantam. (Original work published 1972)

Bernard, J. (1981). The rise and fall of the good provider role. *American Psychologist, 36,* 1-12.

Bernard, J. (1983). The good provider role: Its rise and fall. In A. Skolnick & J. Skolnick (Eds.), *Family in transition* (pp. 125-144). Boston: Little, Brown.

Berry, V. T. (1992). From *Good Times* to *The Cosby Show:* Perceptions of changing televised images among black fathers and sons. In S. Craig (Ed.), *Men, masculinity, and the media* (pp. 111-123). Newbury Park, CA: Sage.

Beutler, I. F., Burr, W. R., Bahr, K. S., & Herrin, D. A. (1989). The family realm. *Journal of Marriage and the Family, 51,* 805-816.

Biller, H. B. (1993). *Fathers and families.* Westport, CT: Auburn House.

Blair, S. L., & Lichter, D. T. (1991). Measuring the division of household labor: Gender segregation of housework among American couples. *Journal of Family Issues, 12,* 91-113.

Blakely, M. K. (1983, August). Executive mothers: A cautionary tale. *Working Mother,* pp. 70-73.

Blumberg, R. L. (1984). A general theory of gender stratification. In R. Collins (Ed.), *Sociological theory 1984* (pp. 23-101). San Francisco: Jossey-Bass.

Bly, R. (1990). *Iron John: A book about men.* New York: Vintage.

Bolton, F. G. (1986). Today's father and the social services delivery system: A false promise. In M. E. Lamb (Ed.), *The father's role: Applied perspectives* (pp. 429-441). New York: Wiley.

Bose, C. E. (1987). Dual spheres. In B. Hess & M. Ferree (Eds.), *Analyzing gender* (pp. 267-285). Newbury Park, CA: Sage.

Bowman, M., & Ahrons, C. R. (1985). Impact of legal custody status on fathers' parenting postdivorce. *Journal of Marriage and the Family, 47,* 481-488.

Bowman, P. (1993). The impact of economic marginality on African-American husbands and fathers. In H. McAdoo (Ed.), *Family ethnicity* (pp. 120-137). Newbury Park, CA: Sage.

Boyd, S. (1989). Child custody law and invisibility of women's work. *Queen's Quarterly, 96*(4), 831-858.

Boyd, S. (1993). Investigating gender bias in Canadian child custody law: Reflections on questions and methods. In J. Brockman & D. Chunn (Eds.), *Investigating gender bias: Laws, courts, and the legal profession* (pp. 169-190). Toronto: Thompson Educational Publishing.

Bozett, F. W., & Hanson, S. M. H. (1991). *Fatherhood and families in cultural context*. New York: Springer.

Brand, E., Clingempeel, W. G., & Bowen-Woodward, K. (1988). Family relationships and children's psychological adjustment in stepmother and stepfather families. In E. M. Hetherington & J. D. Arasteh (Eds.), *Impact of divorce, single parenting, and stepparenting on children* (pp. 299-324). Hillsdale, NJ: Lawrence Erlbaum.

Braver, S. H. [L.], Wolchik, S. A., Sandler, I. N., Fogas, B. S., & Zvetina, D. (1991). Frequency of visitation by divorced fathers: Differences in reports by fathers and mothers. *American Journal of Orthopsychiatry, 61*, 448-454.

Braver, S. L., Fitzpatrick, P. J., & Bay, R. C. (1991). Noncustodial parent's report of child support payments. *Family Relations, 40*, 180-185.

Bray, J. (1988). Children's development during early remarriage. In E. M. Hetherington & J. D. Arasteh (Eds.), *Impact of divorce, single parenting, and stepparenting on children* (pp. 279-298). Hillsdale, NJ: Lawrence Erlbaum.

Brinton, M. C. (1992). Christmas cakes and wedding cakes: The social organization of Japanese women's life course. In T. S. Lebra (Ed.), *Japanese social organization* (pp. 79-107). Honolulu: University of Hawaii Press.

Brod, H. (1987). Introduction: Themes and theses of men's studies. In H. Brod (Ed.), *The making of masculinities: The new men's studies* (pp. 1-11). Boston: Allen & Unwin.

Brod, H., & Kaufman, M. (1994). Introduction. In H. Brod & M. Kaufman (Eds.), *Theorizing masculinities* (pp. 1-10). Thousand Oaks, CA: Sage.

Broderick, C. (1992, November). *A revisionist view of the contributions of Talcott Parsons and Reuben Hill*. Paper presented at the 22nd Annual Conference of the National Council for Family Relations, Orlando, FL.

Brody, G. H., Stoneman, Z., Flor, D., McCrary, C., Hastins, L., & Conyers, O. (1994). Financial resources, parent psychological functioning, parent co-caregiving, and early adolescent competence in rural two-parent African-American families. *Child Development, 65*, 590-605.

Bronfenbrenner, U. (1979). *The ecology of human development: Experiments by nature and design*. Cambridge, MA: Harvard University Press.

Bronfenbrenner, U. (1986). Ecology of the family as a context for human development: Research perspectives. *Developmental Psychology, 22*, 723-742.

Buehler, C., Betz, P., Ryan, C. M., Legg, B. H., & Trotter, B. B. (1992). Description and evaluation of the orientation for divorcing parents: Implications for postdivorce prevention programs. *Family Relations, 2*, 154-162.

Bumpass, L. L. (1990). What's happening to the family? Interactions between demographic and institutional change. *Demography, 27*, 483-498.

Bumpass, L. L., & Sweet, J. A. (1989). Children's experience in single-parent families: Implications of cohabitation and marital transitions. *Family Planning Perspectives, 21*(6), 256-260.

Burke, P. J., & Reitzes, D. (1981). The link between identity and role performance. *Social Psychology Quarterly, 44*, 83-92.

Burke, P. J., & Reitzes, D. (1991). An identity theory approach to commitment. *Social Psychology Quarterly, 54*, 239-251.

Burke, P. J., & Tully, J. C. (1977). The measurement of role identity. *Social Forces, 55*, 881-897.

Buss, T. F., & Redburn, F. S. (1983). *Mass unemployment: Plant closings and community mental health*. Beverly Hills, CA: Sage.

Camara, K. A., & Resnick, G. (1988). Interparental conflict & cooperation: Factors moderating children's postdivorce adjustment. In E. M. Hetherington & J. D. Arasteh (Eds.), *Impact of divorce, single parenting, and stepparenting on children* (pp. 169-195). Hillsdale, NJ: Lawrence Erlbaum.

Cazenave, N. (1979). Middle income black fathers: An analysis of the provider role. *Family Provider, 28*, 583-591.

Chafetz, J. (1990). *Gender equity.* Newbury Park, CA: Sage.

Chambers, D. (1979). *Making fathers pay: The enforcement of child support.* Chicago: University of Chicago Press.

Chambers, D. (1983). Child support in the twenty-first century. In J. Cassetty (Ed.), *The parental child-support obligation* (pp. 283-298). Lexington, MA: Lexington.

Chang, P., & Deinard, A. S. (1982). Single-father caretakers: Demographic characteristics and adjustment processes. *American Journal of Orthopsychiatry, 52*, 236-242.

Chapman, M. (1977). Father absence, stepfathers, and the cognitive performance of college students. *Child Development, 48*, 1155-1158.

Cheal, D. (1991). *Family and the state of theory.* Toronto: University of Toronto Press.

Cheal, D. (1992, November). *It's now or never: Modernity, postmodernity and the politics of periodization in family studies.* Paper presented at the Theory Construction and Research Methodology Workshop at the annual conference of the National Council for Family Relations, Orlando, FL.

Cherlin, A. J. (1978). Remarriage as an incomplete institution. *American Journal of Sociology, 86*, 634-650.

Cherlin, A. J. (1988a). *The changing American family and public policy.* Washington, DC: Urban Institute.

Cherlin, A. J. (1988b). The weakening link between marriage and the care of children. *Family Planning Perspectives, 20*, 302-306.

Cherlin, A. J. (1992). *Marriage, divorce, remarriage* (rev., enlarged ed.). Cambridge, MA: Harvard University Press.

Cherlin, A. J., & Furstenberg, F. F., Jr. (1994). Stepfamilies in the United States: A reconsideration. *American Review of Sociology, 20*, 359-381.

Cherlin, A., Griffith, J., & McCarthy, J. (1983). A note on maritally-disrupted men's reports of child support in the June 1980 Current Population Survey. *Demography, 20*, 385-389.

Chiba, A. (1988). *Chotto okashiizo, Nihonjin* [Something strange about the Japanese]. Tokyo: Shincho Bunko.

Children's Defense Fund. (1992). *Comparative nationwide and state data for 1990 and 1980 census.* Washington, DC: Author.

Chodorow, N. (1978). *The reproduction of mothering: Psychoanalysis and the sociology of gender.* Berkeley: University of California Press.

Cicourel, A. (1967). Fertility, family planning and the social methodological issues. *Journal of Social Issues, 23*, 57-81.

Clingempeel, W. G., Brand, E., & Segal, S. (1987). A multilevel-multivariable developmental perspective for future research on stepfamilies. In K. Pasley & M. Ihinger-Tallman (Eds.), *Remarriage and stepparenting: Current research and theory* (pp. 65-93). New York: Guilford.

Cohen, T. F. (1987). Remaking men: Men's experiences becoming and being husbands and fathers and their implication for reconceptualizing men's lives. *Journal of Family Issues, 8*, 57-77.

Cohen, T. (1989). Becoming and being husbands and fathers: Work and family conflict. In B. J. Risman & P. Schwartz (Eds.), *Gender in intimate relationships: A microstructural approach* (pp. 220-234). Belmont, CA: Wadsworth.

Cohen, T. (1993). What do fathers provide? In J. Hood (Ed.), *Men, work, and family* (pp. 1-22). Newbury Park, CA: Sage.

Coleman, M., & Ganong, L. (1990). Remarriage and stepfamily research in the 1980s: Increased interest in an old family form. *Journal of Marriage and the Family, 52,* 925-940.

Collins, R., & Coltrane, S. (1995). *Sociology of marriage and the family: Gender, love, and property* (4th ed.). Chicago: Nelson Hall.

Coltrane, S. (1988). Father-child relationships and the status of women. *American Journal of Sociology, 93,* 1060-1095.

Coltrane, S. (1989). Household labor and the routine production of gender. *Social Problems, 36,* 473-490.

Coltrane, S. (1990). Birth timing and the division of labor in dual-earner families. *Journal of Family Issues, 11,* 157-181.

Coltrane, S. (in press). *Family man: Fatherhood, housework, and gender equity.* New York: Oxford University Press.

Coltrane, S., & Allan, K. (1994). "New" fathers and old stereotypes: Representations of masculinity in 1980s television advertising. *Masculinities, 2,* 1-25.

Coltrane, S., & Hickman, N. (1992). The rhetoric of rights and needs: Moral discourse in the reform of child custody and child support laws. *Social Problems, 39*(4), 401-420.

Coltrane, S., & Ishii-Kuntz, M. (1992). Men's housework: A life course perspective. *Journal of Marriage and the Family, 54,* 43-57.

Coltrane, S., & Valdez, E. (1993). Reluctant compliance: Work-family role allocation in dual-earner Chicano families. In J. Hood (Ed.), *Men, work, and family* (pp. 151-174). Newbury Park, CA: Sage.

Conine, J. (1989). *Fathers' rights.* New York: Walker.

Cooney, T. M., Pedersen, F. A., Indelicato, S., & Palkovitz, R. (1993). Timing of fatherhood: Is "on-time" optimal? *Journal of Marriage and the Family, 55,* 205-215.

Coontz, S. (1992). *The way we never were.* New York: Basic Books.

Coverman, S. (1985). Explaining husbands' participation in domestic labor. *Sociological Quarterly, 26,* 81-97.

Cowan, C. P., & Cowan, P. A. (1987). Men's involvement in parenthood: Identifying the antecedents and understanding the barriers. In P. W. Berman & F. A. Pedersen (Eds.), *Men's transitions to parenthood: Longitudinal studies of early family experience* (pp. 145-174). Hillsdale, NJ: Lawrence Erlbaum.

Cowan, C. P., & Cowan, P. A. (1992). *When partners become parents: The big life change for couples.* New York: Basic Books.

Cowan, C. P., Cowan, P. A., Heming, G., Garrett, E., Coysh, W. S., Curtis-Boles, H., & Boles, A. J., III. (1985). Transition to parenthood: His, hers, and theirs. *Journal of Family Issues, 6,* 451-481.

Cowan, P. A. (1988). Becoming a father: A time of change, an opportunity for development. In P. Bronstein & C. P. Cowan (Eds.), *Fatherhood today: Men's changing role in the family* (pp. 13-35). New York: Wiley.

Cowan, P. A. (1991). Individual and family life transitions: A proposal for a new definition. In P. A. Cowan & M. Hetherington (Eds.), *Family transitions* (pp. 3-30). Hillsdale, NJ: Lawrence Erlbaum.

Cowan, P. A., & Cowan, C. P. (1988). Changes in marriage during the transition to parenthood: Must we blame the baby? In G. Y. Michaels & W. A. Goldberg (Eds.), *The transition to parenthood: Current theory and research* (pp. 114-154). Cambridge: Cambridge University Press.

Crean, S. (1988). *In the name of the fathers: The story behind child custody.* Toronto: Amanita.

Crockett, L. J., Eggebeen, D. J., & Hawkins, A. J. (1993). Fathers' presence and young children's behavioral and cognitive adjustment. *Journal of Family Issues, 14,* 355-377.

Crouter, A. C., Perry-Jenkins, M., Huston, T. L., & McHale, S. M. (1987). Processes underlying father involvement in dual- and single-earner families. *Developmental Psychology, 23,* 431-440.

Crowell, N. A., & Leeper, E. M. (1994). *America's fathers and public policy: Report of a workshop.* Washington, DC: National Academy Press.

Cutright, P. (1986). Child support and responsible male behavior. *Sociological Focus, 19,* 27-45.

Czapanskiy, K. (1989). Child support and visitation: Rethinking the connections. *Rutgers Law Journal, 20,* 619-665.

Daly, K. J. (1992). The fit between qualitative research and the characteristics of families. In J. Gilgun, K. Daly, & G. Handel (Eds.), *Qualitative methods in family research* (pp. 3-11). Newbury Park, CA: Sage.

Daly, K. (1993). Through the eyes of others: Reconstructing the meaning of fatherhood. In T. Haddad (Ed.), *Men and masculinity: A critical anthology* (pp. 203-221). Toronto: Canadian Scholars' Press.

D'Andrea, A. (1983). Joint custody as related to paternal involvement and paternal self-esteem. *Conciliation Court Review, 21,* 81-87.

Daniels, P., & Weingarten, K. (1982). *Sooner or later: The timing of parenthood in adult lives.* New York: Norton.

Danziger, S. K., & Radin, N. (1990). Absent does not equal uninvolved: Predictors of fathering in teen mother families. *Journal of Marriage and the Family, 52*(3), 636-642.

Da Vanzo, J., & Rahman, M. O. (1993). American families: Trends and correlates. *Population Index, 59*(3), 350-386.

Dawson, B. (1988). Fathers' rights groups: When rights wrong women. *Broadside, 9*(8), 6-7.

Deaux, K., & Kite, M. E. (1987). Thinking about gender. In B. Hess & M. Ferree (Eds.), *Analyzing gender* (pp. 92-117). Newbury Park, CA: Sage.

DeFrain, J., & Eirick, R. (1981). Coping as divorced single parents: A comparative study of fathers and mothers. *Family Relations, 30,* 265-273.

DeMaris, A., & Greif, G. L. (1992). The relationship between family structure and parent-child relationship problems in single father households. *Journal of Divorce and Remarrriage, 18,* 55-78.

Demo, D., & Acock, A. (1993). Family diversity and the division of domestic labor. *Family Relations, 42,* 323-331.

Demos, J. (1982). The changing faces of fatherhood: A new exploration in American family history. In S. H. Cath, A. R. Gurwitt, & J. M. Ross (Eds.), *Father and child: Developmental and clinical perspectives* (pp. 425-445). Boston: Little, Brown.

Deutsch, M. (1973). *The resolution of conflict.* New Haven, CT: Yale University Press.

DeVault, M. (1987). Doing housework: Feeding and family life. In N. Gerstel & H. E. Gross (Eds.), *Families and work* (pp. 178-191). Philadelphia: Temple University Press.

282   References

Dickie, J. R. (1987). Interrelationships within the mother-father-infant triad. In P. W. Berman & F. A. Pedersen (Eds.), *Men's transitions to parenthood: Longitudinal studies of early family experience* (pp. 113-143). Hillsdale, NJ: Lawrence Erlbaum.

Dinnerstein, D. (1976). *The mermaid and the minotaur.* New York: Harper & Row.

Doherty, W. J. (1986). Quanta, quarks and families: Implications of quantum physics for family research. *Family Process, 25,* 249-264.

Doherty, W. J. (1991). Beyond reactivity and deficit model of manhood: A commentary on articles by Napier, Pittman, and Gottman. *Journal of Marital and Family Therapy, 17,* 29-32.

Doi, T. (1973). *The anatomy of dependence.* San Francisco: Chandler.

Downey, D. B. (1994). The school performance of children from single-mother and single-father families: Economic or interpersonal deprivation? *Journal of Family Issues, 15,* 129-147.

Downey, D. B., & Powell, B. (1993). Do children in single-parent households fare better living with same-sex parents? *Journal of Marriage and the Family, 55,* 55-71.

Drakich, J. (1988). In whose best interest? The politics of joint custody. In B. Fox (Ed.), *Family bonds and gender divisions* (pp. 477-496). Toronto: Canadian Scholars' Press. (Reprinted in B. Fox, Ed., 1993, *Family patterns: Gender relations,* pp. 331-341, Toronto: Oxford University Press)

Drakich, J. (1989). In search of the better parent: The social construction of ideologies of fatherhood. *Canadian Journal of Women and the Law, 3*(1), 69-87.

Dudley, J. R. (1991). Increasing our understanding of divorced fathers who have infrequent contact with their children. *Family Relations, 4,* 279-285.

Duncan, G. (1984). *Years of poverty, years of plenty.* Ann Arbor, MI: Institute for Social Research.

Duncan, G. J., & Hoffman, S. D. (1985). A reconsideration of the economic consequences of marital dissolution. *Demography, 22*(4), 485-497.

Edwards, S. R. (1994). The role of men in contraceptive decision-making: Current knowledge and future implications. *Family Planning Perspectives, 26,* 77-82.

Eggebeen, D. J., & Uhlenberg, P. (1985). Changes in the organization of men's lives. *Family Relations, 34,* 251-257.

Ehrenreich, B. (1983). *The hearts of men: American dreams and the flight from commitment.* New York: Anchor.

Ehrensaft, D. (1987). *Parenting together.* New York: Free Press.

Eichler, M. (1988). *Families in Canada today* (2nd ed.). Toronto: Gage.

Ekeh, P. (1974). *Social exchange theory.* Cambridge, MA: Harvard University Press.

Elder, G. H. (1985). Perspectives on the life course. In G. H. Elder (Ed.), *Life course dynamics: Trajectories and transitions, 1968-1980* (pp. 23-49). Ithaca, NY: Cornell University Press.

Elder, G., Conger, R., Foster, M., & Ardelt, M. (1992). Families under economic pressure. *Journal of Family Issues, 13,* 5-37.

Elder, G. H., Jr., Van Nguyen, T., & Caspi, A. (1985). Linking family hardship to children's lives. *Child Development, 56,* 361-375.

Ellwood, D. (1989). *Poverty through the eyes of children.* Unpublished manuscript, Harvard University, John F. Kennedy School of Government.

England, P., & Farkas, G. (1986). *Households, employment and gender.* New York: Aldine.

Entwisle, D. R., & Doering, S. (1988). The emergent father role. *Sex Roles, 18,* 119-141.

FATHERHOOD 283

Erickson, R. J., & Gecas, V. (1991). Social class and fatherhood. In F. W. Bozett & S. M. H. Hanson (Eds.), *Fatherhood and families in cultural context* (pp. 114-137). New York: Springer.

Erikson, E. (1963). *Childhood and society*. Toronto: Norton.

Erikson, E. (1982a). *Identity and the life cycle*. New York: Norton.

Erikson, E. (1982b). *The life cycle completed: A review*. New York: Norton.

Farley, R., & Allen, W. R. (1987). *The color line and the quality of life in America*. New York: Russell Sage.

Farrell, M. D., & Rosenberg, S. D. (1981). *Men at midlife*. Boston: Auburn House.

Fein, R. (1978). Research on fathering. *Journal of Social Issues, 34*(1), 122-135.

Fenstermaker-Berk, S. (1985). *The gender factory*. New York: Plenum.

Ferree, M. M. (1988, November). *Negotiating household roles and responsibilities: Resistance, conflict, and change*. Paper presented at the National Council on Family Relations annual meeting, Philadelphia.

Ferree, M. (1990). Beyond separate spheres: Feminism and family research. *Journal of Marriage and the Family, 52*, 866-884.

Ferree, M. (1991). The gender division of labor in two-earner marriages: Dimensions of variability and change. *Journal of Family Issues, 12*, 158-180.

Fineman, M. (1991). *The illusion of equality: The rhetoric and reality of divorce reform*. Chicago: University of Chicago Press.

Fishkin, J. S. (1983). *Justice, equal opportunity, and the family*. New Haven, CT: Yale University Press.

Flinn, M. (1988). Step- and genetic parent/offspring relationships in a Caribbean village. *Ethology and Sociobiology, 9*, 335-369.

Fox, G. L., & Blanton, P. W. (1995). Noncustodial fathers following divorce. *Marriage and Family Review, 20*(1/2), 257-282.

Franz, C., McClelland, D., & Weinberger, J. (1991). Childhood antecedents of conventional social accomplishment in midlife adults: A 36-year prospective study. *Developmental Psychology, 60*, 586-595.

Furstenberg, F. F., Jr. (1976). *Unplanned parenthood: The social consequences of teenage childbearing*. New York: Free Press.

Furstenberg, F. F., Jr. (1988a). Child care after divorce and remarriage. In E. M. Hetherington & J. D. Arasteh (Eds.), *Impact of divorce, single-parenting and stepparenting on children* (pp. 245-261). Hillsdale, NJ: Lawrence Erlbaum.

Furstenberg, F. F., Jr. (1988b). Good dads—bad dads: Two faces of fatherhood. In A. J. Cherlin (Ed.), *The changing American family and public policy* (pp. 193-218). Washington, DC: Urban Institute.

Furstenberg, F. F., Jr. (1989, November). *Supporting fathers: Implications of the Family Support Act for men*. Paper presented at the Forum on the Family Support Act, National Academy of Sciences, Washington, DC.

Furstenberg, F. F., Jr., Brooks-Gunn, J., & Morgan, S. P. (1987). *Adolescent mothers in later life*. New York: Cambridge University Press.

Furstenberg, F. F., Jr., & Cherlin, A. J. (1991). *Divided families: What happens to children when parents part*. Cambridge, MA: Harvard University Press.

Furstenberg, F. F., Jr., & Harris, K. (1992). The disappearing American father? Divorce and the waning significance of biological parenthood. In S. S. South & S. E. Tolnay (Eds.), *The changing American family: Sociological and demographic perspectives* (pp. 197-223). Boulder, CO: Westview.

284   References

Furstenberg, F. F., Jr., & Harris, K. (1993). When and why fathers matter: Impacts of father involvement on the children of adolescent mothers. In R. Lerman & T. Ooms (Eds.), *Young unwed fathers: Changing roles and emerging policies* (pp. 117-138). Philadelphia: Temple University Press.

Furstenberg, F. F., Jr., Morgan, S. P., & Allison, P. D. (1987). Paternal participation and children's well-being after marital dissolution. *American Sociological Review, 52,* 695-701.

Furstenberg, F. F., Jr., & Nord, C. W. (1985). Parenting apart: Patterns of childrearing after marital disruption. *Journal of Marriage and the Family, 47,* 893-904.

Furstenberg, F. F., Nord, C. W., Peterson, J. L., & Zill, N. (1983). The life course of children of divorce: Marital disruption and parental contact. *American Sociological Review, 48,* 656-668.

Furstenberg, F. F., Jr., Sherwood, K. E., & Sullivan, M. L. (1992). *Caring and paying: What fathers and mothers say about child support* (Report on Parents' Fair Share Demonstration). New York: Manpower Demonstration Research Corporation.

Furstenberg, F. F., Jr., & Talvitie, K. (1979). Children's names and paternal claims: Bonds between unmarried fathers and their children. *Journal of Family Issues, 1*(1), 31-57.

Ganong, L. H., & Coleman, M. (1987). Effects of parental remarriage on children: An updated comparison of theories, methods, and findings from clinical and empirical research. In K. Pasley & M. Ihinger-Tallman (Eds.), *Remarriage and stepparenting: Current research and theory* (pp. 94-140). New York: Guilford.

Garfinkel, I. (1992). *Assuring child support: An extension of social security.* New York: Russell Sage.

Garfinkel, I., & McLanahan, S. S. (1986). *Single mothers and their children: A new American dilemma.* Washington, DC: Urban Institute.

Garfinkel, I., Oellerich, D., & Robins, P. K. (1991). Child support guidelines: Will they make a difference? *Journal of Family Issues, 12,* 404-429.

Gasser, R. D., & Taylor, C. M. (1976). Role adjustment of single parent fathers with dependent children. *The Family Coordinator, 25,* 397-401.

Gecas, V. (1979). The influence of social class on socialization. In W. Burr, R. Hill, R. Nye, & I. Reiss (Eds.), *Contemporary theories about the family: Research-based theories* (Vol. 1, pp. 365-404). New York: Free Press.

Gecas, V. (1980). *Identification as a basis for a theory of commitment.* Unpublished manuscript.

Gecas, V. (1981). The contexts of socialization. In M. Rosenberg & R. H. Turner (Eds.), *Social psychology: Sociological perspectives* (pp. 165-199). New York: Basic Books.

Gecas, V. (1982). The self-concept. *Annual Review of Sociology, 8,* 1-32.

Geerken, M., & Gove, W. R. (1983). *At home and at work: The family's allocation of labor.* Beverly Hills, CA: Sage.

Gershuny, J., & Robinson, J. (1988). Historical changes in the household division of labor. *Demography, 25,* 537-552.

Gerson, K. (1993). *No man's land: Men's changing commitments to family and work.* New York: Basic Books.

Gerstel, N., & Gross, H. E. (1987). *Families and work.* Philadelphia: Temple University Press.

Giles-Sims, J. (1984). The stepparent role: Expectations, behavior, sanctions. *Journal of Family Issues, 5,* 116-130.

Gilgun, J., Daly, K., & Handel, G. (Eds.). (1992). *Qualitative methods in family research*. Newbury Park, CA: Sage.

Gilligan, C. (1982). *In a different voice*. Cambridge, MA: Harvard University Press.

Ginsberg, G. (1990). The sons of the sons of the samurai. *Winds, 11*(8), 30-38.

Giveans, D. L., & Robinson, M. K. (1985). Fathers and the pre-school age child. In S. Hanson & F. Bozett (Eds.), *Dimensions of fatherhood* (pp. 115-140). Beverly Hills, CA: Sage.

Glaser, B., & Strauss, A. L. (1967). *The discovery of grounded theory: Strategies for qualitative research*. New York: Aldine.

Goffman, E. (1974). *Frame analysis*. New York: Harper & Row.

Goldscheider, F. K., & Waite, L. J. (1991). *New families, no families? The transformation of the American home*. Berkeley: University of California Press.

Goode, W. (1982). Why men resist. In A. S. Skolnick & J. H. Skolnick (Eds.), *Family in transition* (pp. 201-218). Boston: Little, Brown.

Goode, W. (1992). Why men resist. In B. Thorne with M. Yalom (Eds.), *Rethinking the family* (pp. 287-310). Boston: Northeastern University Press.

Graycar, R. (1989). Equal rights versus fathers' rights: The child custody debate in Australia. In C. Smart & S. Sevenhuijsen (Eds.), *Child custody and the politics of gender* (pp. 158-189). London: Routledge.

Greene, B. (1984). *Good morning, merry sunshine*. Harrisburg, VA: Atheneum.

Greif, G. L. (1985). *Single fathers*. Lexington, MA: Lexington.

Greif, G. L. (1987). A longitudinal examination of single custodial fathers: Implications for treatment. *American Journal of Family Therapy, 15*, 253-260.

Greif, G. L. (1990). *The daddy track and the single father*. New York: Macmillan/Lexington.

Greif, G. L. (1995). Single fathers with custody following separation and divorce. *Marriage and Family Review, 20*(1/2), 213-231.

Greif, G. L., & DeMaris, A. (1989). Single custodial fathers in contested custody suits. *Journal of Psychiatry & Law, 17*, 223-238.

Greif, G. L., & DeMaris, A. (1990). Single fathers with custody. *Families in Society: The Journal of Contemporary Human Services, 71*, 259-266.

Greif, G. L., DeMaris, A., & Hood, J. (1993). Balancing work and single fatherhood. In J. Hood (Ed.), *Men, work, and family* (pp. 176-194). Newbury Park, CA: Sage.

Grief, J. B. (1979). Fathers, children, and joint custody. *American Journal of Orthopsychiatry, 49*, 311-319.

Griswold, R. L. (1993). *Fatherhood in America: A history*. New York: Basic Books.

Gross, P. (1988). *An analysis of the information in the official guardian files* (Report No. 2, Ontario Divorce and Custody Project: Phase One). Toronto: Ontario Institute for Studies in Education.

Gutman, H. G. (1977). *The black family in slavery and freedom 1750-1925*. New York: Vintage.

Gutmann, D. (1987). *Reclaimed powers: Towards a new psychology of men and women in later life*. New York: Basic Books.

Haas, L. (1988, November). *Understanding fathers' participation in child care: A social constructionist perspective*. Paper presented at the National Council of Family Relations meetings, Philadelphia.

Haas, L. (1992). *Equal parenthood and social policy*. Albany: State University of New York.

Haas, L. (1993). Nurturing fathers and working mothers: Changing gender roles in Sweden. In J. C. Hood (Ed.), *Men, work, and family* (pp. 238-261). Newbury Park, CA: Sage.

Hanson, S. M. (1985). Single custodial fathers. In S. M. Hanson & F. Bozett (Eds.), *Dimensions of fatherhood* (pp. 369-392). Beverly Hills, CA: Sage.

Hanson, S. M., & Bozett, F. (Eds.). (1985). *Dimensions of fatherhood.* Beverly Hills, CA: Sage.

Hanson, S. M. H., & Bozett, F. W. (1987). Fatherhood: A review and resources. *Family Relations, 36,* 333-340.

Hanushek, E. A., & Jackson, J. E. (1977). *Statistical methods for social scientists.* New York: Academic Press.

Hardesty, C., & Bokemeier, J. (1989). Finding time and making do: Distribution of household labor in nonmetropolitan marriages. *Journal of Marriage and the Family, 51,* 253-267.

Harris, K. M., & Morgan, S. P. (1991). Fathers, sons, and daughters: Differential paternal involvement in parenting. *Journal of Marriage and the Family, 53,* 531-544.

Hartmann, H. (1981). The family as the locus of gender, class, and political struggle: The example of housework. *Signs, 6,* 366-394.

Haskins, R. (1988). Child support: A father's view. In A. J. Kahn & S. B. Kamerman (Eds.), *Child support: From debt collection to social policy* (pp. 306-327). Newbury Park, CA: Sage.

Hawkins, A. J., & Belsky, J. (1989). The role of father involvement in personality change in men across the transition to parenthood. *Family Relations, 38,* 378-384.

Hawkins, A. J., & Eggebeen, D. J. (1991). Are fathers fungible? Patterns of coresident adult men in maritally disrupted families and young children's well-being. *Journal of Marriage and the Family, 53,* 958-972.

Henderson, J. (1988, May 10). Two are better than one: The fact that a husband and wife break up doesn't make either of them less a parent. *Globe and Mail,* p. A7.

Hernandez, D. J. (1988). The demographics of divorce and remarriage. In E. M. Hetherington & J. D. Arasteh (Eds.), *Impact of divorce, single parenting, and stepparenting on children* (pp. 3-22). Hillsdale, NJ: Lawrence Erlbaum.

Hess, R. D., & Camara, K. A. (1979). Post-divorce family relations as mediating factors in the consequences of divorce for children. *Journal of Social Issues, 35,* 79-96.

Hess, R. D., & Handel, G. (1959). *Family worlds: A psychosocial approach to family life.* Chicago: University of Chicago Press.

Hetherington, E. M. (1987). Family relations six years after divorce. In K. Pasley & M. Ihinger-Tallman (Eds.), *Remarriage and stepparenting: Current research and theory* (pp. 185-205). New York: Guilford.

Hetherington, E. M. (1989). Coping with family transitions: Winners, losers, and survivors. *Child Development, 60,* 1-14.

Hetherington, E. M., Cox, M., & Cox, R. (1976). Divorced fathers. *Family Coordinator, 25*(6), 417-428.

Hetherington, E. M., Cox, M., & Cox, R. (1978). The aftermath of divorce. In J. H. Stevens & M. Matthews (Eds.), *Mother/child, father/child relationships* (pp. 149-176). Washington, DC: National Association for the Education of Young Children.

Hetherington, E. M., Cox, M., & Cox, R. (1979). Family interaction and the social, emotional and cognitive development of children following divorce. In V. Vaughn & T. B. Brazelton (Eds.), *The family: Setting priorities* (pp. 89-128). New York: Science and Medicine Publishing.

Hetherington, E. M., Cox, M., & Cox, R. (1982). Effects of divorce on parents and children. In M. E. Lamb (Ed.), *Nontraditional families: Parenting and child development* (pp. 233-288). Hillsdale, NJ: Lawrence Erlbaum.

Hetherington, E. M., Cox, M., & Cox, R. (1986). Family relations: Six years after divorce. In K. Pasley & M. Ihinger-Tallman (Eds.), *Remarriage and stepparenting today: Current research and theory* (pp. 27-87). New York: Guilford.

Hill, R. (1993). *A research on the African American family.* Westport, CT: Auburn House.

Hiller, D. V., & Philliber, W. W. (1986). The division of labor in contemporary marriage: Expectations, perceptions, and performance. *Social Problems, 33,* 191-201.

Hobart, C. W. (1987). Parent-child relations in remarried families. *Journal of Family Issues, 8,* 259-277.

Hochschild, A. (with Manning, A.). (1989). *The second shift: Working parents and the revolution at home.* New York: Viking.

Hochschild, A. R. (in press). Understanding the future of fatherhood: The "Daddy Hierarchy" and beyond. In G. A. B. Frinking, M. van Dongen, & M. J. G. Jacobs (Eds.), *Changing fatherhood: An interdisciplinary perspective.* Amsterdam, the Netherlands: Thesis Publishers.

Hoffman, L. W. (1983). Increasing fathering: Effects on the mother. In M. E. Lamb & A. Sagi (Eds.), *Fatherhood and family policy* (pp. 167-190). Hillsdale, NJ: Lawrence Erlbaum.

Hoffman, L. W. (1989). Effects of maternal employment in the two-parent family. *American Psychologist, 44,* 283-292.

Hoffman, L. W., & Manis, J. D. (1979). The value of children in the United States: A new approach to the study of fertility. In G. McDonald & F. I. Nye (Eds.), *Family policy* (pp. 123-136). Minneapolis, MN: National Council on Family Relations.

Holtrust, N., Sevenhuijsen, S., & Verbraken, A. (1989). Rights for fathers and the state: Recent developments in custody politics in the Netherlands. In C. Smart & S. Sevenhuijsen (Eds.), *Child custody and the politics of gender* (pp. 51-76). London: Routledge.

Hood, J. A. (1983). *Becoming a two-job family.* New York: Praeger.

Hood, J. (1986). The provider role: Its meaning and measurement. *Journal of Marriage and the Family, 48,* 349-359.

Horna, J., & Lupri, E. (1987). Fathers' participation in work, family life and leisure: A Canadian experience. In C. Lewis & M. O'Brien (Eds.), *Reassessing fatherhood.* London: Sage.

Horowitz, I. L. (1967). Consensus, conflict, and cooperation. In N. J. Demerath & R. A. Peterson (Eds.), *Systems, change and conflict* (pp. 265-279). New York: Free Press.

Huber, J., & Spitze, G. (1983). *Sex stratification: Children, housework and jobs.* New York: Academic Press.

Hudson, W. W. (1982). *The clinical measurement package: A field manual.* Chicago: Dorsey.

Hyde, J. S., Essex, M. J., & Horton, F. (1993). Fathers and parental leave: Attitudes and experiences. *Journal of Family Issues, 14,* 619-641.

Ishii-Kuntz, M. (1992). Are Japanese families "fatherless"? *Sociology and Social Research, 76,* 105-110.

Ishii-Kuntz, M. (1993). Japanese fathers: Work demands and family roles. In J. C. Hood (Ed.), *Men, work, and family* (pp. 45-67). Newbury Park, CA: Sage.

Ishii-Kuntz, M., & Coltrane, S. (1992a). Predicting the sharing of household labor: Are parenting and housework distinct? *Sociological Perspectives, 35,* 629-647.

Ishii-Kuntz, M., & Coltrane, S. (1992b). Remarriage, stepparenting and household labor. *Journal of Family Issues, 13,* 3-57.

Isogai, Y. (1972). Difference in social class and images of the father. *Child Psychology, 26,* 21-30.

Issacs, M. B. (1988). The visitation schedule and child adjustment: A three-year study. *Family Process, 27,* 251-256.

James, L. R., & Brett, J. M. (1984). Mediators, moderators, and tests for mediations. *Journal of Applied Psychology, 69,* 307-321.

Jencks, C. (1990). Is the American underclass growing? In C. Jencks & P. E. Petersen (Eds.), *The urban underclass* (pp. 28-100). Washington, DC: Brookings Institute.

Jencks, C., & Petersen, P. E. (Eds.). (1991). *The urban underclass.* Washington, DC: Urban Institute Press.

Johnson, C., & Sum, A. (1987). *Declining earnings of young men: Their relation to poverty, teen pregnancy, and family formation* (Adolescent Prevention Clearinghouse Report). Washington, DC: Children's Defense Fund.

Johnston, J. R., & Campbell, L. E. G. (1988). *Impasses of divorce: The dynamics and resolution of family conflict.* New York: Free Press.

Jones, L. (1991). Unemployed fathers and their children: Implications for policy and practice. *Child and Adolescent Social Work, 8,* 101-116.

Kelly, J. B., & Wallerstein, S. (1977). Part-time parent, part-time child: Visiting after divorce. *Journal of Clinical Child Psychology, 2,* 51-54.

Kennedy, G. E. (1989). Involving students in participatory research on fatherhood: A case study. *Family Relations, 38,* 363-370.

Kessler, R. C., & McRae, J. A. (1982). The effect of wives' employment on the mental health of married men and women. *American Sociological Review, 47,* 216-227.

Kessler, R., & Neighbors, H. (1986). New perspectives on relationships among race, social class and distress. *Journal of Health and Social Behavior, 27,* 107-115.

Kimmel, M. S. (Ed.). (1987a). *Changing men: New directions in research on men and masculinity.* Newbury Park, CA: Sage.

Kimmel, M. S. (1987b). Rethinking "masculinity": New directions in research. In M. S. Kimmel (Ed.), *Changing men: New directions in research on men and masculinity* (pp. 9-24). Newbury Park, CA: Sage.

King, V. (1994). Nonresident father involvement and child well-being: Can dads make a difference? *Journal of Family Issues, 15*(1), 78-96.

Kitson, G. C., & Morgan, L. A. (1990). The multiple consequences of divorce: A decade review. *Journal of Marriage and the Family, 52,* 913-924.

Klinman, D. G. (1986). Fathers and the educational system. In M. E. Lamb (Ed.), *The father's role: Applied perspectives* (pp. 413-428). New York: Wiley.

Knijn, T. (in press). Towards post-paternalism? Social and theoretical changes in father-hood. In G. A. B. Frinking, M. van Dongen, & M. J. G. Jacobs (Eds.), *Changing fatherhood: An interdisciplinary perspective.* Amsterdam, the Netherlands: Thesis Publishers.

Kohn, M. L. (1959). Social class and parental values. *American Journal of Sociology, 64,* 337-351.

Kohn, M. L. (1976). Social class and parental values: Another confirmation of the relationship. *American Sociological Review, 41,* 538-545.

Kohn, M. L. (1977). *Class and conformity: A study of values* (2nd ed.). Chicago: University of Chicago Press.

Krampe, E. M., & Fairweather, P. D. (1993). Father presence and family formation: A theoretical reformulation. *Journal of Family Issues, 14,* 573-593.

Kreppner, K. (1989). Linking infant development-in-context research to the investigation of life-span family development. In R. M. Lerner & K. Kreppner (Eds.), *Family systems and life-span development* (pp. 33-64). Hillsdale, NJ: Lawrence Erlbaum.

Kruk, E. (1991). Discontinuity between pre- and post-divorce father-child relationships: New evidence regarding paternal disengagement. *Journal of Divorce & Remarriage, 16*(3/4), 195-227.

Kuhn, M. H. (1960). Self attitudes by age, sex, and professional training. *Sociological Quarterly, 1*(1), 39-55.

Kumagai, F. (1981). Filial violence: A peculiar parent-child relationship in the Japanese family today. *Journal of Comparative Family Studies, 12,* 337-349.

Kurdek, L. A. (1986). Custodial mothers' perceptions of visitation and payment of child support by noncustodial fathers and families with low and high levels of preseparation interparent conflict. *Journal of Applied Developmental Psychology, 7,* 307-322.

Kurdek, L., & Sinclair, R. (1986). Adolescents' views on issues related to divorce. *Journal of Adolescent Research, 1,* 373-387.

Kvale, S. (1992). Introduction: From the archaeology of the psyche to the architecture of cultural landscapes. In S. Kvale (Ed.), *Psychology and postmodernism* (pp. 1-16). Newbury Park, CA: Sage.

Lamb, L. (1987, January/February). Involuntary joint custody: What mothers will lose if fathers' rights groups win. *Herizons,* pp. 20-31.

Lamb, M. E. (1981). *The role of the father in child development.* New York: Wiley.

Lamb, M. E. (1986). The changing role of fathers. In M. E. Lamb (Ed.), *The father's role: Applied perspectives* (pp. 3-27). New York: Wiley.

Lamb, M. E. (1987). Introduction: The emergent American father. In M. E. Lamb (Ed.), *The father's role: Cross-cultural perspectives* (pp. 3-25). Hillsdale, NJ: Lawrence Erlbaum.

Lamb, M. E. (1994, May). *Paternal influences on child development.* Paper presented at the Conference on Changing Fatherhood, University of Tilburg, the Netherlands.

Lamb, M. E., Pleck, J. H., Charnov, E., & Levine, J. A. (1985). Paternal behaviour in humans. *American Psychologist, 25,* 883-894.

Lamb, M. E., Pleck, J. H., Charnov, E. L., & Levine, J. A. (1987). A biosocial perspective on paternal behavior and involvement. In J. B. Lancaster, J. Altmann, A. S. Rossi, & L. R. Sherrod (Eds.), *Parenting across the lifespan: Biosocial dimensions* (pp. 111-142). New York: Aldine de Gruyter.

Lamb, M. E., Pleck, J. H., & Levine, J. A. (1985). The role of the father in child development: The effects of increased paternal involvement. In B. B. Lahey & A. E. Kazdin (Eds.), *Advances in clinical child psychology* (pp. 229-266). New York: Plenum.

Lamb, M. E., Pleck, J. H., & Levine, J. A. (1987). Effects of increased paternal involvement on fathers and mothers. In C. Lewis & M. O'Brien (Eds.), *Researching fatherhood* (pp. 109-125). London: Sage.

Lamb, M. E., & Sagi, A. (1983). *Fatherhood and family policy.* Hillsdale, NJ: Lawrence Erlbaum.

Landers, R. K. (1990). *Child support: Payments, progress and problems* (Editorial Research Reports). Washington, DC: Congressional Quarterly, Inc.

LaRossa, R. (1986). *Becoming a parent.* Newbury Park, CA: Sage.

LaRossa, R. (1988). Fatherhood and social change. *Family Relations, 37,* 451-458.

LaRossa, R., Gordon, B. A., Wilson, R. J., Bairan, A., & Jaret, C. (1991). The fluctuating image of the 20th century American father. *Journal of Marriage and the Family, 53,* 987-997.

LaRossa, R., & LaRossa, M. M. (1981). *Transition to parenthood: How infants change families.* Beverly Hills, CA: Sage.

LaRossa, R., & LaRossa, M. M. (1989). Baby care: Fathers versus mothers. In B. J. Risman & P. Schwartz (Eds.), *Gender in intimate relationships: A microstructural approach* (pp. 138-154). Belmont, CA: Wadsworth.

Larson, J. (1992, July). Understanding stepfamilies. *American Demographics,* pp. 36-40.

Lempers, J. D., Clark-Lempers, D., & Simons, R. (1989). Economic hardship, parenting and distress in adolescence. *Child Development, 60,* 25-39.

Lerman, R. I., & Ooms, T. J. (1993). *Young unwed fathers: Changing roles and emerging policies.* Philadelphia: Temple University Press.

Lerner, R. M. (1986). *Concepts and theories of human development.* New York: Random House.

Lerner, R. M., & Kreppner, K. (1989). Family systems and life-span development: Issues and perspectives. In R. M. Lerner & K. Kreppner (Eds.), *Family systems and life-span development* (pp. 1-14). Hillsdale, NJ: Lawrence Erlbaum.

Leslie, L., Anderson, E., & Branson, M. (1991). Responsibility for children: The role of gender and employment. *Journal of Family Issues, 12,* 197-210.

Levant, R. F. (1988). Education for fatherhood. In P. Bronstein & C. P. Cowan (Eds.), *Fatherhood today: Men's changing role in the family* (pp. 253-275). New York: Wiley.

Levant, R. F. (1991). Toward the reconstruction of masculinity. *Journal of Family Psychology, 5,* 379-402.

Levine, J. A. (1991, June 11). *The invisible dilemma: Working fathers in corporate America.* Testimony at the hearing, Babies and Briefcases: Creating a Family-Friendly Workplace for Fathers, U.S. House of Representatives, Select Committee on Children, Youth, and Families.

Levine, J. A., Murphy, D. T., & Wilson, S. (1993). *Getting men involved: Strategies for early childhood programs.* New York: Scholastic.

Levinson, D. J. (1986). A conception of adult development. *American Psychologist, 41,* 3-13.

Levinson, D. J., Darrow, C. N., Klein, E. B., Levinson, M. H., & McKee, B. (1978). *The seasons of a man's life.* New York: Knopf.

Levy, R. (1993, September). Panelist for Fathers' Rights at the National Academy of Sciences meeting, America's Fathers: Abiding and Emerging Roles in Family and Economic Support Policies, Washington, DC.

Lewis, C. (1986). *Becoming a father.* Milton Keynes, UK: Open University Press.

Lewis, C., & O'Brien, M. (Eds.). (1987). *Reassessing fatherhood: New observations on fathers and the modern family.* Newbury Park, CA: Sage.

Lewis, R. A., & Salt, R. A. (Eds.). (1986). *Men in families.* Newbury Park, CA: Sage.

Lewis, R. A., & Sussman, M. B. (Eds.). (1986). *Men's changing roles in the family.* New York: Haworth.

Loewen, J. (1988). Visitation fatherhood today. In P. Bronstein & C. Cowan (Eds.), *Men's changing role in the family* (pp. 195-213). New York: Wiley.

Lorber, J., Coser, R. L., Rossi, A. S., & Chodorow, N. (1981). On the reproduction of mothering: A methodological debate. *Signs, 6,* 482-514.

Losh-Hesselbart, S. (1987). The development of gender roles. In M. B. Sussman & S. Steinmetz (Eds.), *Handbook of marriage and the family* (pp. 535-563). New York: Plenum.

Lowery, C. R. (1986). Maternal and joint custody: Differences in the decision process. *Law and Human Behavior, 10*, 303-315.

Lund, M. (1987). The non-custodial father: Common challenges in parenting after divorce. In C. Lewis & M. O'Brien (Eds.), *Reassessing fatherhood: New observations on fathers and the modern family* (pp. 212-224). Newbury Park, CA: Sage.

Maccoby, E. R., Depner, C. E., & Mnookin, R. H. (1988). Custody of children following divorce. In E. M. Hetherington & J. Arasteh (Eds.), *Impact of divorce, single parenting, and stepparenting on children* (pp. 91-114). Hillsdale, NJ: Lawrence Erlbaum.

Maccoby, E. E., & Jacklin, C. N. (1974). *The psychology of sex differences.* Stanford, CA: Stanford University Press.

Maccoby, E. E., & Mnookin, R. H. (1992). *Dividing the child: Social and legal dilemmas of custody.* Cambridge, MA: Harvard University Press.

MacDermid, S. M., Huston, T. L., & McHale, S. M. (1990). Changes in marriage associated with the transition to parenthood: Individual differences as a function of sex-role attitudes and changes in the division of household labor. *Journal of Marriage and the Family, 52*, 475-486.

Management and Coordination Agency. (1981). *Shakai seikatsu kihon chosa* [Basic survey on life in society]. Tokyo: Author.

Management and Coordination Agency. (1986). *Kodomo to chichioya ni kansuru kokusai hikaku chosa* [International comparative survey on children and fathers]. Tokyo: Author.

Markus, H., & Nurius, P. (1986). Possible selves. *American Psychologist, 41*, 954-969.

Marsiglio, W. (1987). Adolescent fathers in the United States: Their initial living arrangements, marital experience and educational outcomes. *Family Planning Perspectives, 19*(6), 240-251.

Marsiglio, W. (1991a). Male procreative consciousness and responsibility: A conceptual analysis and research agenda. *Journal of Family Issues, 12*, 268-290.

Marsiglio, W. (1991b). Paternal engagement activities with minor children. *Journal of Marriage and the Family, 53*, 973-986.

Marsiglio, W. (1993a). Adolescent males' orientation toward paternity and contraception. *Family Planning Perspectives, 25*(1), 22-31.

Marsiglio, W. (1993b). Contemporary scholarship on fatherhood: Culture, identity, and conduct. *Journal of Family Issues, 14*, 484-509.

Marsiglio, W. (1995). Young nonresident biological fathers. *Marriage and Family Review, 20*(3/4), 325-348.

Marsiglio, W. (in press). Artificial reproduction and paternity testing: Implications for fathers. In G. A. B. Frinking, M. van Dongen, & M. J. G. Jacobs (Eds.), *Changing fatherhood: An interdisciplinary perspective.* Amsterdam, the Netherlands: Thesis Publishers.

Martin, L. G., & Tsuya, N. O. (1991). Interactions of middle-aged Japanese with their parents. *Population Studies, 45*, 299-311.

Mason, K. O., & Lu, Y.-H. (1988). Attitudes toward women's familial roles: Changes in the United States, 1977-1985. *Gender and Society, 2*, 39-57.

Massey, D. S., & Denton, N. A. (1993). *American apartheid: Segregation and the making of the underclass.* Cambridge, MA: Harvard University Press.

May, K. A. (1982). Factors contributing to first-time fathers' readiness for fatherhood: An exploratory study. *Family Relations, 31,* 353-361.

Maynard, R. (1988, November). Fathers' rights: Now, it's men who call for parental equality. *Chatelaine,* pp. 61-64.

McAdams, D. P. (1985). *Power, intimacy, and the life story.* Homewood, IL: Dorsey.

McAdoo, J. L. (1986a). A black perspective on the father's role in child development. *Marriage and Family Review, 9* (3/4), 117-133.

McAdoo, J. L. (1986b). The role of black fathers in the socialization of their children. In H. McAdoo (Ed.), *Black families* (pp. 257-269). Newbury Park, CA: Sage.

McBride, B. A. (1989). Stress and father's parental competence: Implications for family life and parent educators. *Family Relations, 38,* 385-389.

McClure, M., & Kennedy-Richardson, K. (1987). *Mr. Mom is alive and well in Kitchener-Waterloo.* Unpublished manuscript, Provincial Court, Kitchener, Ontario, Canada.

McCracken, G. (1988). *The long interview.* Newbury Park, CA: Sage.

McGuire, W. J. (1986). The myth of massive media impact: Savagings and salvaging. *Public Communication and Behavior, 1,* 173-257.

McKie, D., Prentice, B., & Reed, P. (1983). *Divorce: Law and the family in Canada.* Ottawa: Statistics Canada, Research and Analysis Division.

McLanahan, S. S., Seltzer, J. A., Hanson, T. L., & Thomson, E. (1994). Child support enforcement and child well-being: Greater security or greater conflict? In I. Garfinkel, S. S. McLanahan, & P. K. Robins (Eds.), *Child support and child well being* (pp. 239-256). Washington, DC: Urban Institute Press.

McLeod, J., & Shanahan, M. (1993). Poverty, parenting and children's mental health. *American Sociological Review, 58,* 351-366.

McLoyd, V. (1990). The impact of economic hardship on black families and children: Psychological distresses, parenting and socioemotional development. *Child Development, 61,* 311-346.

McPhee, D., Benson, J. B., & Bullock, D. (1986, April). *Influences on maternal self-perceptions.* Paper presented at the Biennial International Conference on Infant Studies, Los Angeles.

Mederer, H. J. (1993). Division of labor in two-earner homes: Task accomplishment versus household management as critical variables in perceptions about family work. *Journal of Marriage and the Family, 55,* 133-145.

Medrich, E. A., Roizen, J. A., Rubin, V., & Buckley, S. (1983). *The serious business of growing up: A study of children's lives outside of school.* Berkeley: University of California Press.

Menaghan, E. G., & Lieberman, M. A. (1986). Changes in depression following divorce: A panel study. *Journal of Marriage and the Family, 48,* 319-328.

Menard, S. (1991). *Longitudinal research* (Series No. 07-076). Newbury Park, CA: Sage.

Mendes, H. A. (1976). Single fathers. *The Family Coordinator, 25,* 439-444.

Meyer, D. R. (1992). Paternity and public policy. *Focus, 14,* 1-14.

Meyer, D. R., & Garasky, S. (1993). Custodial fathers: Myths, realities, and child support policy. *Journal of Marriage and the Family, 55,* 73-90.

Miller, J. B. (1976). *Toward a new psychology of women.* Boston: Beacon.

Miller, L. F., & Moorman, J. E. (1989). Studies in marriage and the family (Series P-23, No. 162; U.S. Bureau of the Census). *Current Population Reports.* Washington, DC: Government Printing Office.

Mills, C. (1959). *The sociological imagination.* London: Oxford University Press.

Ministry of Education, Japan. (1991). *Gakko kihon chosa hokokusho* [Report from basic surveys on schools]. Tokyo: Author.

Ministry of Labor. (1989). *Statistics on Japan*. Tokyo: Author.

Minuchin, S. (1974). *Families and family therapy*. Cambridge, MA: Harvard University Press.

Mischel, W. (1966). A social-learning view of sex differences in behaviour. In E. Maccoby (Ed.), *The development of sex differences* (pp. 56-81). Stanford, CA: Stanford University Press.

Mitchell-Flynn, C., & Hutchinson, R. L. (1993). A longitudinal study of the problems and concerns of urban divorced men. *Journal of Divorce & Remarriage, 19*(1/2), 161-182.

Moen, P., & Dempster-McClain, D. I. (1987). Employed parents: Role strain, work time, and preferences for working less. *Journal of Marriage and the Family, 49,* 579-590.

Morgan, S. P., & Harris, K. M. (1991). Fathers, sons, and daughters: Differential paternal involvement in parenting. *Journal of Marriage and the Family, 53,* 531-544.

Morgan, S. P., Lye, D. N., & Condran, G. A. (1988). Sons, daughters, and the risk of marital disruption. *American Journal of Sociology, 94,* 110 129.

Mott, F. L. (1990). When is a father really gone? Paternal-child conduct in father-absent homes. *Demography, 27*(4), 499-517.

Mott, F. L. (1993). *Absent fathers and child development: Emotional and cognitive effects at ages five to nine* (Report for National Institute of Child Health and Human Development). Columbus: Ohio State University, Center for Human Resource Research.

Mott, F. L. (1994). Sons, daughter and fathers' absence: Differentials in father-leaving probabilities and in home environments. *Journal of Family Issues, 5,* 97-128.

Mulkey, L. M., Crain, R. L., & Harrington, A. J. C. (1992). One-parent households and achievement: Economic achievement of school children. *Sociology of Education, 65,* 48-65.

Murray, C. (1984). *Losing ground*. New York: Basic Books.

Muthén, B. O. (1988). *LISCOMP: Analysis of linear structural equations with a comprehensive measurement model*. Mooresville, IN: Scientific Software, Inc.

National Center for Health Statistics. (1990). *Vital statistics of the United States, 1988, Vol. 1: Natality* (DHHS Publication No. PHS-90-1100, Public Health Service). Washington, DC: Government Printing Office.

National Urban League. (1987). *Adolescent male responsibility: Pregnancy prevention and parenting program*. New York: Author.

Nock, S., & Kingston, P. (1988). Time with children: The impact of couples' work-time commitments. *Social Forces, 67,* 59-85.

O'Connell, M. (1993, September). *Where's papa: Fathers' role in child care*. Washington, DC: Population Reference Bureau.

Office of the Prime Minister, Japan. (1981). *Gendai no wakamono: Junen mae to no hikaku* [Today's youth: A comparison with those 10 years ago]. Tokyo: Author.

Ornstein, M. (1983). *Equality in the workplace: Accounting for gender differentials in job income in Canada: Results from a 1981 survey* (Series A, No. 2). Ottawa: Women's Bureau.

Osherson, S. (1986). *Finding our fathers: The unfinished business of manhood*. New York: Free Press.

Oshman, H., & Manosevitz, M. (1976). Father-absence: Effects of stepfathers upon psychosocial development in males. *Developmental Psychology, 12,* 479-480.

Palkovitz, R. (1984). Parental attitudes and fathers' interactions with their 5-month-old infants. *Developmental Psychology, 20*, 1054-1060.

Parke, R. (1981). *Fathers*. Cambridge, MA: Harvard University Press.

Parke, R. D. (1985). Foreword. In S. M. H. Hanson & F. W. Bozett (Eds.), *Dimensions of fatherhood* (pp. 9-12). Beverly Hills, CA: Sage.

Parke, R. D., & Tinsley, B. (1984). Fatherhood: Historical and contemporary perspectives. In K. A. McCloskey & H. W. Reese (Eds.), *Life-span developmental psychology: Historical and generational effects* (pp. 429-457). New York: Academic Press.

Parsons, T., & Bales, R. (1955). *Family socialization and interaction process*. New York: Free Press.

Pasley, K. (1985). Stepfathers. In S. M. H. Hanson & F. W. Bozett (Eds.), *Dimensions of fatherhood* (pp. 288-306). Beverly Hills, CA: Sage.

Pasley, K., & Healow, C. L. (1987). Adolescent self-esteem: A focus on children in stepfamilies. In E. M. Hetherington & J. D. Arasteh (Eds.), *Impact of divorce, single parenting, and stepparenting on children* (pp. 263-277). Hillsdale, NJ: Lawrence Erlbaum.

Peacock, D. (1982). *Listen to their tears: How Canadian divorce law abuses our own children*. Toronto: Douglas & McIntyre.

Pedersen, F. A. (1985). Research and the father: Where do we go from here? In S. M. H. Hanson & F. W. Bozett (Eds.), *Dimensions of fatherhood* (pp. 437-450). Beverly Hills, CA: Sage.

Perry-Jenkins, M., & Crouter, A. C. (1990). Men's provider-role attitudes: Implications for household work and marital satisfaction. *Journal of Family Issues, 11*, 136-156.

Peters, M. F., & Massey, G. (1983). Mundane extreme environmental stress in family stress theories: The case of black families in white America. In H. McCubbin et al. (Eds.), *Social stress and the family: Advances and developments in family stress theory and research* (pp. 193-218). New York: Haworth.

Peterson, J. L. (1987, August). *Post-divorce events and the provision of child support payments*. Paper presented at the 35th Annual Conference of the National Child Support Enforcement Association, Washington, DC.

Peterson, J. L., & Nord, C. W. (1987). *The regular receipt of child support: A multi-step process*. Final report prepared for the Office of Child Support Enforcement, Child Trends, Washington, DC.

Peterson, R. R., & Gerson, K. (1992). Determinants of responsibility for child care arrangements among dual-earner couples. *Journal of Marriage and the Family, 54*, 527-536.

Pirog-Good, M. A. (1993). In-kind contributions as child support: The teen alternative parenting program. In R. I. Lerman & T. J. Ooms (Eds.), *Young unwed fathers: Changing roles and emerging policies* (pp. 251-266). Philadelphia: Temple University Press.

Pleck, J. H. (1983). Husband's paid work and family roles: Current research issues. In H. Lopata & J. Pleck (Eds.), *Research in the interweave of social roles* (pp. 251-333). Greenwich, CT: JAI.

Pleck, J. H. (1984). *Working wives and family well-being*. New York: Garland.

Pleck, J. H. (1985). *Working wives/working husbands*. Beverly Hills, CA: Sage.

Pleck, J. H. (1987). American fathering in historical perspective. In M. S. Kimmel (Ed.), *Changing men: New directions in research on men and masculinity* (pp. 83-97). Newbury Park, CA: Sage.

Pleck, J. H. (1993). Are "family-supportive" employer policies relevant to men? In J. C. Hood (Ed.), *Men, work, and family* (pp. 217-237). Newbury Park, CA: Sage.

Pleck, J. H., Lamb, M. E., & Levine, J. A. (1986). Epilog: Facilitating future change in men's family roles. *Marriage and Family Review, 9*(3/4), 11-16.

Polikoff, N. (1983). Gender and child-custody determinations: Exploding the myths. In I. Diamond (Ed.), *Families, politics, and public policy: A feminist dialogue on women and the state* (pp. 183-202). New York: Longman.

Presser, H. (1988). Shift work and child care among young dual-earner American parents. *Journal of Marriage and the Family, 50*, 3-14.

Presser, H. (1989). Can we make time for children? The economy, work schedules, and child care. *Demography, 26*, 523-543.

Pruett, K. (1987). *The nurturing father.* New York: Warner.

Pyke, K. (1994). Women's employment as a gift or burden? *Gender & Society, 8*, 73-91.

Radin, N. (1982). Primary caregiving and role-sharing fathers. In M. E. Lamb (Ed.), *Nontraditional families: Parenting and child development* (pp. 173-204). Hillsdale, NJ: Lawrence Erlbaum.

Radin, N. (1991, June 11). *Babies and briefcases.* Hearings of the 102nd Congress (pp. 78-85). Washington, DC: Government Printing Office.

Radin, N., & Goldsmith, R. (1985). Caregiving fathers of preschoolers: Four years later. *Merrill-Palmer Quarterly, 31*, 375-383.

Radin, N., & Sagi, A. (1982). Childrearing fathers in intact families in Israel and the U.S.A. *Merrill-Palmer Quarterly, 28*, 111-136.

Rains, P. M. (1971). *Becoming an unwed mother.* Chicago: Aldine-Atherton.

Rainwater, L., & Yancey, W. L. (1967). *The Moynihan report and the politics of controversy.* Cambridge: MIT Press.

Rasch, G. (1966). An individualistic approach to item analysis. In P. F. Lazerfeld & N. W. Henry (Eds.), *Readings in mathematical social science* (pp. 89-107). Cambridge: MIT Press.

Rauhala, A. (1988). Women alarmed by male activists. *Jurisfemme, 8*(3), 11-14.

Ray, S., & McLoyd, V. (1986). Fathers in hard times: The impact of unemployment and poverty on paternal and maternal relationships. In M. Lamb (Ed.), *The father's role: Applied perspectives* (pp. 339-383). New York: Wiley.

Reischauer, E. O. (1981). *The Japanese.* Cambridge, MA: Harvard University Press.

Rexroat, C., & Shehan, C. (1987). The family life cycle and spouses' time in housework. *Journal of Marriage and the Family, 49*, 737-750.

Richardson, J. (1988). *Court-based divorce mediation in four Canadian cities: An overview of research results.* Ottawa: Minister of Supply and Services, Canada.

Risman, B. J. (1986). Can men "mother"? Life as a single father. *Family Relations, 35*, 95-102.

Risman, B. (1989). Can men "mother"? Life as a single father. In B. J. Risman & P. Schwartz (Eds.), *Gender in intimate relationships: A microstructural approach* (pp. 155-164). Belmont, CA: Wadsworth.

Risman, B. J., & Schwartz, P. (1989). Being gendered: A microstructural view of intimate relationships. In B. J. Risman & P. Schwartz (Eds.), *Gender in intimate relationships: A microstructural approach* (pp. 1-9). Belmont, CA: Wadsworth.

Robertson, I. (1987). *Sociology* (3rd ed.). New York: Worth.

Robinson, J. (1975). *Americans' use of time project.* Ann Arbor: University of Michigan, Survey Research Center.

Robinson, J. (1988). Who's doing the housework? *American Demographics, 10*, 24-28, 63.

Roman, M., & Haddad, W. (1978). *The disposable parent.* New York: Holt, Rinehart & Winston.

Rosaldo, M. (1980). The use and abuse of anthropology. *Signs, 5*, 389-417.

Rosenberg, M. (1986). *Conceiving the self.* Malabar, FL: Robert E. Krieger.

Rosenthal, K. M., & Keshet, H. F. (1981). *Fathers without partners.* Totowa, NJ: Rowman & Littlefield.

Ross, C. E., Mirowsky, J., & Huber, R. (1983). Dividing work, sharing work, and in-between: Marriage patterns and depression. *American Sociological Review, 48*, 809-823.

Rossi, A. S. (1985). Gender and parenthood. In A. S. Rossi (Ed.), *Gender and the life course* (pp. 161-191). New York: Aldine.

Rotundo, E. A. (1985). American fatherhood: A historical perspective. *American Behavioral Scientist, 29*(1), 7-25.

Ruddick, S. (1984). Maternal thinking. In J. Trebilcot (Ed.), *Mothering: Essays in feminist theory* (pp. 213-220). Totowa, NJ: Rowman & Allanheld.

Ruggles, S. (1994). The origins of African American family structure. *American Sociological Review, 59*(1), 136-151.

Russell, G. (1983). *The changing role of fathers?* St. Lucia: University of Queensland Press.

Russell, G. (1986). Primary caretaking and role sharing fathers. In M. E. Lamb (Ed.), *Fatherhood: Applied perspectives* (pp. 29-57). New York: Wiley.

Salamon, E. D., & Robinson, B. W. (1991). Doing what comes naturally? Theories on the acquisition of gender. In E. D. Salamon & B. W. Robinson (Eds.), *Gender roles: Doing what comes naturally?* (pp. 5-38). Nelson, Canada: Scarborough.

Sampson, R. J., & Laub, J. H. (1994). Urban poverty and the family context of delinquency: A new look at structure and process in a single study. *Child Development, 65*, 523-540.

Santrock, J. W., Warshak, R. A., Lindberg, C., & Meadows, L. (1982). Children's and parents' observed social behavior in stepfather families. *Child Development, 53*, 472-480.

Savage, B. D. (1987). *Child support and teen parents.* Washington, DC: Adolescent Prevention Clearinghouse, Children's Defense Fund.

Scanzoni, J., & Marsiglio, W. (1993). New action theory and contemporary families. *Journal of Family Issues, 14*, 105-132.

Scanzoni, J., Polonko, K., Teachman, J., & Thompson, L. (1989). *The sexual bond: Rethinking families and close relationships.* Newbury Park, CA: Sage.

Schaeffer, N. C., Seltzer, J. A., & Klawitter, M. (1991). Estimating nonresponse and response bias: Resident and nonresident parents' reports about child support. *Sociological Methods and Research, 29*, 30-59.

Schwartz, M., & Stryker, S. (1970). *Deviance, selves and others* (Rose Monograph Series). Washington, DC: American Sociological Association.

Schwebel, A., Fine, M. A., & Renner, M. A. (1991). A study of perceptions of the stepparent role. *Journal of Family Issues, 12*, 43-57.

Seccombe, K., Marsiglio, W., & Lee, S. R. (1991). *Social class and fathers' socialization values: Does class really matter?* Unpublished manuscript, University of Florida, Gainesville.

Segal, L. (1990). *Slow motion: Changing masculinities, changing men.* New Brunswick, NJ: Rutgers University Press.

Seltzer, J. A. (1990). Legal and physical custody in recent divorces. *Social Science Quarterly, 71,* 250-266.

Seltzer, J. A. (1991). Relationships between fathers and children who live apart: The father's role after separation. *Journal of Marriage and the Family, 53,* 79-101.

Seltzer, J. A. (1994). Consequences of marital dissolution for children. *Annual Review of Sociology, 20,* 235-266.

Seltzer, J. A., & Bianchi, S. M. (1988). Children's contact with absent parents. *Journal of Marriage and the Family, 50,* 663-677.

Seltzer, J. A., Schaeffer, N. C., & Charng, H.-W. (1989). Family ties after divorce: The relationship between visiting and paying child support. *Journal of Marriage and the Family, 51,* 1013-1031.

Sevenhuijsen, S. (1986). Fatherhood and the political theory of rights: Theoretical perspectives of feminism. *International Journal of the Sociology of Law, 14,* 329-340.

Shelton, B. (1990). The distribution of household tasks: Does wife's employment status make a difference. *Journal of Family Issues, 11,* 115-135.

Shelton, B. A. (1992). *Women, men, time.* New York: Greenwood.

Shwalb, D. W., Imaizumi, N., & Nakazawa, J. (1987). The modern Japanese father: Roles and problems in a changing society. In M. E. Lamb (Ed.), *The father's role: Cross-cultural perspectives* (pp. 247-269). Hillsdale, NJ: Lawrence Erlbaum.

Silverstein, L. B. (1993). Primate research, family politics, and social policy: Transforming "cads" into "dads." *Journal of Family Psychology, 7,* 267-282.

Simon, W., & Gagnon, J. H. (1986). Sexual scripts: Permanence and change. *Archives of Sexual Behavior, 15,* 97-120.

Smith, H. L., & Morgan, S. P. (1994). Children's closeness to father as reported by mothers, sons and daughters: Evaluating subjective assessments with the Rasch model. *Journal of Family Issues, 15,* 3-29.

Snarey, J. (1993). *How fathers care for the next generation: A four-decade study.* Cambridge, MA: Harvard University Press.

Snarey, J., Son, L., Kuehne, V. S., Hauser, S., & Vaillant, G. (1987). The role of parenting in men's psychosocial development: A longitudinal study of early adulthood infertility and midlife generativity. *Developmental Psychology, 23,* 593-603.

Sofue, T. (1981). A cultural-anthropological examination of the father. In H. Katsura (Ed.), *The paternal role* (pp. 125-147). Tokyo: Kaneko Shobo.

Sonenstein, F. L., & Calhoun, C. A. (1990). Determinants of child support: A pilot survey of absent parents. *Contemporary Policy Issues, 8,* 75-134.

Spitze, G. (1986). The division of task responsibility in US households. *Social Forces, 64,* 689-701.

Spitze, G. (1988). Women's employment and family relations. *Journal of Marriage and the Family, 50,* 595-618.

Sprey, J. (1979). Conflict theory and the study of marriage and the family. In W. R. Burr, R. H. Hill, F. I. Nye, & I. L. Reiss (Eds.), *Contemporary theories about the family* (Vol. 2, pp. 130-159). New York: Free Press.

Stack, C. (1974). *All our kin: Strategies for survival in a black community.* New York: Harper & Row.

Stanley, S. C., Hunt, J. G., & Hunt, L. L. (1986). The relative deprivation of husbands in dual-earner households. *Journal of Family Issues, 7,* 3-20.

Starrels, M. E. (1994). Gender differences in parent-child relations. *Journal of Family Issues, 15*, 148-165.

Statistics Canada, Household Survey Division, Canadian Centre for Health Information. (1993). *Earnings of men and women, 1991.* Ottawa: Minister of Industry, Science and Technology.

Stephen, E. H. (1989, October). *Where have all the fathers gone?* Paper presented at the annual meeting of the Southern Demographic Association, Durham, NC.

Stewart, J. R., Schwebel, B., & Fine, M. A. (1986). The impact of custodial arrangement on the adjustment of recently divorced fathers. *Journal of Divorce, 9*(3), 55-65.

Stier, H., & Tienda, M. (1993). Are men marginal to the family? Insights from Chicago's inner city. In J. Hood (Ed.), *Men, work and family* (pp. 23-44). Newbury Park, CA: Sage.

Stone, G. P. (1962). Appearance and the self. In A. M. Rose (Ed.), *Human behavior and social processes* (pp. 86-118). Boston: Houghton Mifflin.

Strauss, A. (1988). *Qualitative analysis for social scientists.* Cambridge: Cambridge University Press.

Strauss, A., & Corbin, J. (1990). *Basics of qualitative research.* Newbury Park, CA: Sage.

Stryker, S. (1968). Identity salience and role performance. *Journal of Marriage and the Family, 4*, 558-564.

Stryker, S. (1980). *Symbolic interactionism: A social structural version.* Menlo Park, CA: Benjamin/Cummings.

Stryker, S. (1981). Symbolic interactionism: Themes and variations. In M. Rosenberg & R. Turner (Eds.), *Social psychology: Sociological perspectives* (pp. 3-29). New York: Basic Books.

Stryker, S. (1987). The vitalization of symbolic interactionism. *Social Psychological Quarterly, 50*, 83-94.

Stryker, S., & Serpe, R. T. (1982). Commitment, identity salience, and role behavior. In I. W. Ickes & E. Knowles (Eds.), *Personality, roles and social behavior* (pp. 199-218). New York: Springer-Verlag.

Suitor, J. J. (1991). Marital quality and satisfaction with the division of household labor across the family life cycle. *Journal of Marriage and the Family, 53*, 221-230.

Sullivan, M. (1989). Absent fathers in the inner city. *Annals of the American Academy of Political and Social Science, 501*, 48-58.

Sullivan, M. L. (1990). *The male role in teenage pregnancy and parenting: New directions for public policy.* New York: Vera Institute of Justice.

Sweet, J. A., & Bumpass, L. L. (1987). *American families and households.* New York: Russell Sage.

Sweet, J. A., & Bumpass, L. L. (1989). *Conducting a comprehensive survey of American family life: The experience of the National Survey of Families and Households* (NSFH Working Paper No. 12). Madison: University of Wisconsin, Center for Demography and Ecology.

Sweet, J., Bumpass, L., & Call, V. (1988). *The design and content of the National Survey of Families and Households* (NSFH Working Paper No. 1). Madison: University of Wisconsin, Center for Demography and Ecology.

Takeuchi, K., Uehara, A., & Suzuki, H. (1982). A study of fathers' child-rearing consciousness. *Proceedings of the 24th Meeting of the Japanese Association of Educational Psychology* (pp. 302-303). Tokyo: Association of Educational Psychology.

Tallman, I., & Gray, L. N. (1990). Choices, decisions, and problem-solving. *Annual Review of Sociology, 16,* 405-433.

Tallman, I., Gray, L., & Leik, R. (1991). Decisions, dependency and commitment: An exchange based theory of group development. *Advances in Group Processes, 41,* 154-162.

Teachman, J. D. (1991). Contributions to children by divorced fathers. *Social Problems, 38,* 358-371.

Thompson, L. (1991). Family work: Women's sense of fairness. *Journal of Family Issues, 12,* 181-196.

Thompson, L. (1993). Conceptualizing gender in marriage: The case of marital care. *Journal of Marriage and the Family, 55*(3), 557-569.

Thompson, L., & Walker, A. (1989). Gender in families: Women and men in marriage, work and parenthood. *Journal of Marriage and the Family, 51,* 845-872.

Thompson, R. A. (1994). The role of the father after divorce. *Children and Divorce, 4*(1), 210-235.

Thomson, E. (1993). Work schedules and time for children. *Proceedings, Social Statistics Section, American Statistical Association.* Alexandria, VA: ASA.

Thomson, E., Hanson, T., & McLanahan, S. S. (1994). Family structure and child well-being: Economic resources vs. parent socialization. *Social Forces, 73,* 221-242.

Thomson, E., McLanahan, S. S., & Curtin, R. B. (1992). Family structure, gender, and parental socialization. *Journal of Marriage and the Family, 54,* 368-378.

Thorne, B., with Yalom, M. (1992). *Rethinking the family: Some feminist questions.* Boston: Northeastern University Press.

Thornton, A. (1989). Changing attitudes toward family issues in the United States. *Journal of Marriage and the Family, 51,* 873-893.

Trotter, B. B. (1989). *Coparental conflict, competition, and cooperation and parents' perception of their children's social-emotional well-being following marital separation.* Unpublished doctoral dissertation, University of Tennessee, Knoxville.

Tschann, J. M., Johnston, J. R., Kline, M., & Wallerstein, J. S. (1989). Family process and children's functioning during divorce. *Journal of Marriage and the Family, 51,* 431-444.

Tschann, J. M., Johnston, J. R., & Wallerstein, J. S. (1989). Resources, stressors, and attachment as predictors of adult adjustment after divorce: A longitudinal study. *Journal of Marriage and the Family, 51,* 1033-1046.

Tsuya, N. O. (1992, August). *Work and family life in Japan: Changes and continuities.* Paper presented at the meeting of the American Sociological Association, Pittsburgh, PA.

Turner, R. H. (1978). The role and the person. *American Journal of Sociology, 84,* 1-23.

Umberson, D., & Williams, C. L. (1993). Divorced fathers: Parental role strain and psychological distress. *Journal of Family Issues, 14,* 378-400.

U.S. Bureau of the Census. (1986). Child support and alimony: 1985 (Series P-23, No. 152). *Current Population Reports.* Washington, DC: Government Printing Office.

U.S. Bureau of the Census. (1987, July). Money income and poverty status of families and persons in the United States: 1986 (Series P-60, No. 157). *Current Population Reports.* Washington, DC: Government Printing Office.

U.S. Bureau of the Census. (1991). Child support and alimony: 1989 (Series P-60, No. 73). *Current Population Reports.* Washington, DC: Government Printing Office.

U.S. Bureau of the Census. (1992). Household, families, and children: A 30 year perspective (Series P-23, No. 181). *Current Population Reports.* Washington, DC: Government Printing Office.

U.S. Bureau of the Census. (1993). Household and family characteristics: March 1992 (Series P-20, No. 467). *Current Population Reports.* Washington, DC: Government Printing Office.

U.S. General Accounting Office. (1992). *Unemployed parents and evaluation of the effects of welfare benefits on family stability.* Briefing report to the chairman, Committee on Finance, U.S. Senate, Washington, DC.

Valentine, C. A. (1968). *Culture of poverty: Critique and counter-proposals.* Chicago: University of Chicago Press.

Visher, E. B., & Visher, J. S. (1978). Common problems of stepparents and their spouses. *American Journal of Orthopsychiatry, 48,* 252-262.

Vogel, E. F. (1963). *Japan's new middle class: The salary man and his family in a Tokyo suburb.* Berkeley: University of California Press.

Vogel, E. F. (1979). *Japan as number one: Lessons for America.* Cambridge, MA: Harvard University Press.

Volling, B., & Belsky, J. (1991). Multiple determinants of father involvement during infancy in dual-earner and single-earner families. *Journal of Marriage and the Family, 53,* 461-474.

Wallerstein, J., & Blakeslee, S. (1989). *Second chances.* New York: Ticknor & Fields.

Wallerstein, J. S., & Corbin, S. B. (1986). Father-child relationships after divorce: Child support and educational opportunity. *Family Law Quarterly, 20,* 109-128.

Wallerstein, J. S., & Huntington, D. S. (1983). Bread and roses: Nonfinancial issues related to fathers' economic support of their children following divorce. In J. Cassetty (Ed.), *The parental child support obligation* (pp. 135-155). Lexington, MA: Lexington.

Wallerstein, J. S., & Kelly, J. B. (1980a). Effects of divorce on the visiting father-child relationship. *American Journal of Psychiatry, 137,* 1534-1539.

Wallerstein, J. S., & Kelly, J. B. (1980b). *Surviving the breakup: How children and parents cope with divorce.* New York: Basic Books.

Weiss, R. (1984). The impact of marital dissolution on income and consumption in single-parent households. *Journal of Marriage and the Family, 46,* 115-127.

Weitzman, L. (1985). *The divorce revolution: The unexpected social and economic consequences for women and children in America.* New York: Free Press.

Wells, L. E., & Stryker, S. (1988). Stability and change in self over the life course. In P. B. Baltes, D. L. Featherman, & R. M. Lerner (Eds.), *Life-span development and behavior* (pp. 191-229). Hillsdale, NJ: Lawrence Erlbaum.

West, C., & Fenstermaker, S. (1993). Power, inequality and the accomplishment of gender. In P. England (Ed.), *Theory on gender/Feminism on theory* (pp. 151-174). New York: Aldine de Gruyter.

Whitbeck, L. B., Simons, R. L., Conger, R. D., Lorenz, F. O., Huck, S., & Elder, G. H., Jr. (1991). Family economic hardship, parental support and adolescent self-esteem. *Social Psychology Quarterly, 54,* 353-363.

White, L. K., Brinkerhoff, D., & Booth, A. (1985). The effect of marital disruption on child's attachment to parents. *Journal of Family Issues, 6,* 5-22.

White, S. W., & Bloom, B. L. (1981). Factors related to the adjustment of divorcing men. *Family Relations, 30,* 349-360.

Wilkie, J. R. (1993). Changes in U.S. men's attitudes toward the family provider role 1972-1989. *Gender & Society, 7,* 261-279.

Wilson, W. J. (1978). *The declining significance of race: Blacks and changing American institutions.* Chicago: University of Chicago Press.

Wilson, W. J. (1987). *The truly disadvantaged.* Chicago: University of Chicago Press.

Woodhouse, B. (1993). Hatching the egg: A child-centered perspective on parents' rights. *Cardozo Law Review, 14,* 1747-1865.

Zill, N. (1993, April). *Analysis of Census Bureau data.* Paper presented at the Children's Rights Council National Conference, Bethesda, MD.

Author Index

Acock, A., 265
Adams, P. L., 24
Agnostinelli, J., 42, 51
Ahlburg, D. A., 1, 4, 78, 89, 119, 211
Ahrons, C. R., 71-72
Albrecht, S., 250
Allan, K., 14, 256
Allen, W. R., 122
Allison, P. D., 2, 58, 60
Allport, G., 23
Alwin, D., 150-151, 171
Amato, P. R., 196
Ambrose, P., 252-253
Anderson, E., 102, 129, 131
Antonucci, T. C., 47
Ardelt, M., 150
Arditti, J. A., 2, 87, 94, 96-97
Arendell, T., 58, 71, 176, 231, 250, 252-253
Armstrong, P., 252
Armstrong, H., 252

Babcock, G., 71, 74
Backett, K., 18, 22, 170, 191
Bahr, K. S., 47

Bairan, A., 4, 22
Bales, R., 23, 50
Bandura, A., 16, 47, 48
Barnett, R. C., 41, 50, 72, 259
Bartz, K. W., 151, 197
Baruch, G. K., 41, 50, 72, 259
Baumrind, D., 149, 152
Bay, R. C., 167
Becker, G. S., 263
Becker, H. S., 61, 64-65, 68
Beer, W. R., 171
Belsky, J., 50, 54
Bem, S. L., 262
Benin, M. H., 42, 51
Benson, J. B., 70
Berger, P. L., 25
Berk, S. F., 41-42, 52
Berman, P. W., 22
Bernard, J., 22, 166, 257
Berry, V. T., 14
Bertoia, C. E., xi, 3, 94
Betz, P., 73
Beutler, I. F., 47
Bianchi, S. M., 72, 121, 168, 170-171, 190
Biller, H. B., 257
Blair, S. L., 41

Blakely, M. K., 56
Blakeslee, S., 250
Blanton, P. W., 2, 8, 79
Bloom, B. L., 195
Blumberg, R. L., 264
Bly, R., 52
Bokemeier, J., 41
Bolton, F. G., 22
Booth, A., 215
Bose, C. E., 262
Bowen-Woodward, K., 215
Bowman, M., 72, 151
Boyd, S., 231, 237
Bozett, F. W., 2, 22, 79, 81, 83
Brand, E., 214-216
Brandreth, Y., xi, 2, 13
Branson, M., 102
Braver, S. L., 167
Bray, J., 212, 226
Brett, J. M., 74
Brinkerhoff, D., 215
Brinton, M. C., 116
Brod, H., 1
Broderick, C., 32
Brody, G. H., 152
Bronfenbrenner, U., 42, 46
Brooks-Gunn, J., 122-123
Buckley, S., 171
Buehler, C., xi, 2, 73, 85, 92, 192
Bullock, D., 70
Bumpass, L. L., 1, 78, 119-120, 153, 167-
    168, 172-173, 216
Burke, P. J., 2, 6, 7, 16, 58, 61, 63-68
Burr, W. R., 47
Buss, T. F., 152

Calhoun, C. A., 167
Call, V., 153, 172, 216
Camara, K. A., 60, 73, 171
Campbell, L. E. G., 194
Caspi, A., 150
Cazenave, N., 151
Chafetz, J., 258, 262, 264
Chambers, D., 95, 231
Chang, P., 197
Chapman, M., 212
Charng, H. W., 94, 183
Charnov, E., 27, 51, 55, 104

Cheal, D., 38
Cherlin, A. J., 1, 5, 81, 87, 99, 119, 122,
    137, 139, 140, 167-169, 212, 214
Chiba, A., 116
Children's Defense Fund, 152
Chodorow, N., 21, 24, 36, 48, 257, 262
Christiansen, S., xi, 7, 84, 267
Cicourel, A., 27
Clark-Lempers, D., 150
Clingempeel, W. G., 214-215
Cohen, T. F., 24, 53, 267
Coleman, M., 194, 212, 214
Collins, R., 259
Coltrane, S., xi, 3, 14, 17, 20, 54, 94,
    103, 104, 250-251, 253, 256-260,
    262-266, 269, 273
Condran, G. A , 102, 170
Conger, R. D., 150
Conine, J., 231
Cooney, T. M., 17, 54, 84
Coontz, S., 262
Corbin, J., 26, 33, 81
Coser, R. L., 24
Coverman, S., 41
Cox, M., 60, 72, 171-172, 215, 252-253
Cox, R., 60, 72, 171-172, 215, 252-253
Cowan, C. P., 42, 48-50, 52, 54, 260
Cowan, P. A., 42-43, 48-50, 52, 54, 260
Crain, R. L., 11
Crean, S., 230
Crockett, L. J., 9
Crouter, A. C., 42, 49, 50
Crowell, N. A., 120
Curtin, R. B., 171
Cutright, P., 79, 83
Czapanskiy, K., 94

Daly, K. J., xi, 15, 22-23, 26, 83
D'Andrea, A., 96
Daniels, P., 45, 49, 265
Danziger, S. K., 145
Darrow, C. N., 44
Da Vanzo, J., 211
Dawson, B., 230
Deaux, K., 262
DeFrain, J., 197
Deinard, A. S., 197
DeMaris, A., xi, 197, 199, 202, 204

Demo, D., 265
Demos, J., 22
Dempster-McClain, D. I., 42
Denton, N. A., 122
Depner, C. E., 166, 212
Deutsch, M., 73
DeVault, M., 259
De Vita, C. J., 1, 4, 78, 89, 119, 211
Dickie, J. R., 22
Dinnerstein, D., 48
Doeing, S., 5
Doherty, W. J., 22, 49
Doi, T., 103-104
Downey, D. B., 11
Drakich, J., xi, 2-3, 94, 230-231, 233, 240
Dudley, J. R., 71
Duncan, G. J., 152, 250

Edwards, S. R., 92
Eggebeen, D. J., 9-11, 98
Ehrenreich, B., 2, 5, 100, 257
Ehrensaft, D., 273
Eichler, M., 243
Eirick, R., 197
Ekeh, P., 19, 83, 213
Elder, G. H., 84, 150
Ellwood, D., 152
England, P., 264
Entwisle, D. R., 5
Erickson, R. J., 89
Erikson, E., 42, 44-45, 48, 84
Essex, M. J., 2

Fairweather, P. D., 7
Farkas, G., 264
Farley, R., 122
Farrell, M. D., 145
Fein, R., 148, 256
Fenstermaker, S., 265
Fenstermaker-Berk, S., 258-260, 265
Ferree, M. M., 41-42, 52, 260, 264-265
Fine, M. A., 5, 72, 212
Fineman, M., 231, 253
Fishkin, J. S., 88
Fitzpatrick, P. J., 167
Flinn, M., 213
Fogas, B. S., 167

Foster, M., 150
Fox, G. L., 2, 8, 79
Franz, C., 45
Furstenberg, F. F., Jr., xi, 2, 5, 8-10, 12,
    18, 58, 60, 72, 74, 79, 81-82, 87,
    89-91, 99-100, 120, 122-123, 131-
    132, 136-137, 139-140, 145, 167-
    171, 176, 190, 212, 214, 231, 252,
    256-257

Gagnon, J. H., 79
Ganong, L. H., 194, 212, 214
Garasky, S., 10, 12, 25, 52, 197
Garfinkel, I., 10, 99, 145, 167, 191
Gasser, R. D., 197
Gecas, V., 64-65, 89, 150
Geerken, M., 37, 263
Gershuny, J., 260
Gerson, K., 2-3, 42, 79-81, 84, 87, 93,
    256, 263-264, 269
Gerstel, N., 213
Giles-Sims, J., 212
Gilgun, J., 23
Gilligan, C., 262
Ginsberg, G., 117
Giveans, D. L., 22
Glaser, B., 26, 232
Goffman, E., 27
Goldscheider, F. K., 257, 261
Goldsmith, R., 72
Goode, W., 88, 121, 267
Gordon, B. A., 4, 22
Gove, W. R., 37, 263
Gray, L., 64-65, 77
Graycar, R., 251, 253
Greene, B., 46
Greif, G. J., xi, 81, 96, 193, 196-199,
    202-204
Grief, J. B., 71, 96
Griffith, J., 167
Griswold, R. L., 1-5, 7, 20, 78-79, 81,
    83, 89, 93, 96, 121, 256
Gross, H. E., 213, 252
Gutman, H. G., 122
Gutmann, D., 45

Haas, J., 18, 91, 215, 264-265

Haddad, W., 231, 241
Handel, G., 23, 25
Hanson, S. M. H., 2, 22, 25, 79-80, 83
Hanson, T. L., 11, 150
Hanushek, E. A., 110
Hardesty, C., 41
Harper, J., 252-253
Harris, K., 2, 8-9, 41, 50, 104, 111, 121, 212
Hartmann, H., 264
Haskins, R., 95, 167, 176
Hauser, S., 45
Hawkins, A. J., xi, 7, 9-11, 54, 84, 93, 267
Healow, C. L., 215
Henderson, J., 240
Hernandez, D. J., 6, 211
Herrin, D. A., 47
Herrington, A. J. C., 11
Hess, R. , 25, 60, 171
Hetherington, E. M., 60, 71-73, 76, 171-172, 212, 215, 226-228, 252-253
Hickman, N., 3, 94, 250-251, 253
Hill, E., xi, 7, 84, 267
Hill, R., 122
Hiller, D. V., 41
Hobart, C. W., 226
Hochschild, A. R., 41-42, 50, 52, 88, 104, 135, 240, 257, 259, 263-264, 269
Hoffman, L. W., 25, 50, 171, 250, 261
Holtrust, N., 253
Hood, J. A., 103, 197, 257, 259, 263-264
Horna, J., 149
Horowitz, I. L., 73
Horton, F., 2
Huber, J., 50
Huber, R., 50, 258
Hudson, W. W., 201
Hunt, J. G., 50
Hunt, L. L., 50
Huntington, D. S., 169
Huston, T. L., 49-50
Hutchinson, R. L., 195
Hyde, J. S., 2, 17

Ihinger-Tallman, M., xi, 2, 6, 15, 85-87, 192
Imaizumi, N., 106

Indelicato, S., 17, 54, 84
Ishii-Kuntz, M., xi, 15, 17, 103-105, 112-113, 262-263, 265
Isogai, Y., 105
Issacs, M. B., 73

Jacklin, C. N., 25
Jackson, J. E., 110
James, L. R., 74
Jaret, C., 4, 22
Jencks, C., 82, 122
Johnson, C., 91
Johnston, J. R., 73, 194, 196
Jones, J., 93

Kaufman, M., 1
Kelly, J. B., 60, 72-73, 169, 171, 195-196
Kelly, M., 87, 96-97
Kennedy, G. E., 29
Kennedy-Richardson, K., 237
Keshet, H. F., 197
Kessler, R. C., 50, 152, 258
Kimmel, M. S., 1, 22
King, V., 2, 9, 11, 121
Kingston, P., 2, 149
Kite, M. E., 262
Kitson, G. C., 194
Klawitter, M., 167
Kleine, E. B., 44
Kline, M., 73
Klinman, D. G., 22
Knijn, T., 2, 4, 18, 83
Kohn, M. L., 150, 216, 219
Krampe, E. M., 7
Kreppner, K., 43, 46
Kruk, E., 58, 71
Kuehne, V. S., 45
Kuhn, M. H., 61
Kumagai, F., 106
Kurdek, L. A., 73, 212
Kvale, S., 38

Lamb, L., 230
Lamb, M. E., 7, 19-22, 27, 51, 55, 79, 90, 96, 102, 104, 106, 257, 259
Landers, R. K., 79

LaRossa, M. M., 23, 37
LaRossa, R., 2-4, 15, 21-23, 37, 42, 48,
    53, 80, 103, 256-257
Larson, J., 211
Laub, J. H., 150
Lee, S. R., 219
Leeper, E. M., 20
Legg, B. H., 73
Leik, R., 64
Lempers, J. D., 150
Lerman, R. I., 79, 82
Lerner, R. M., 43, 46
Leslie, L., 102
Levant, R. F., 22, 53
Levine, J. A., 17, 19, 21, 27, 51, 79, 90,
    97, 102, 104, 106, 151
Levinson, D. J., 44
Levinson, M. H., 44
Levy, R., 96
Lewis, C., 22, 29, 39-40, 46, 54
Lewis, R. A., 22
Lichter, D. T., 41
Lieberman, M. A., 194-195
Lindberg, C., 215
Loewen, J., 252
Lorber, J., 24
Losh-Hesselbart, S., 25, 39
Lowery, C. R., 169
Lu, Y. H., 172
Luckmann, T., 25
Lund, M., 169, 172
Lupri, E., 149
Lye, D. N., 102, 170

Maccoby, E. R., 25, 166, 212, 237
MacDermid, S. M., 50
Management and Coordination Agency,
    105, 107
Manis, J. D., 171
Manosevitz, M., 212
Markus, H., 46
Marsiglio, W., 2, 5-6, 8, 11, 14-19, 22,
    59, 79-83, 85-87, 89, 104, 120,
    133, 145, 168, 170-171, 213-214,
    219, 256-257, 259, 263, 265, 267
Martin, L. G., 117
Mason, K. O., 172
Massey, D. S., 122

Massey, G., 152
May, K. A., 17
Maynard, R., 230
McAdams, D. P., 45
McAdoo, J. L., 5, 151
McBride, B. A., 22
McCarthy, J., 167
McClelland, D., 45
McClure, M., 237
McCracken, G., 27
McGuire, W. J., 4
McHale, S. M., 49-50
McKee, B., 44
McKie, D., 237
McLanahan, S. S., 10-11, 150, 167, 170
McLeod, J., 151, 153, 165
McLoyd, V., 93, 150-151, 153
McPhee, D., 70
McRae, J. A., 50, 258
Meadows, L., 215
Mederer, H. J., 42
Medrich, E. A., 171
Menaghan, E. G., 194-195
Menard, S., 193
Mendes, H. A., 197
Meyer, D. R., 10, 25, 52, 79, 197
Mikus, K., 47
Miller, J. B., 48
Miller, L. F., 211
Mills, C., 234
Milner, J. R., 24
Ministry of Education, Japan, 108
Ministry of Labor, 105
Minuchin, S., 208
Mirowsky, J., 50, 258
Mischel, W., 25
Mitchell-Flynn, C., 195
Mnookin, R. H., 94, 167, 212, 237
Moen, P., 42
Moorman, J. E., 211
Morgan, L. A., 194
Morgan, S. P., 2, 14, 41, 50, 58, 60, 102,
    104, 111, 121-122, 170
Mott, F. L., 2, 8-12, 57, 120, 133, 168,
    171, 212
Mulkey, L. M., 11
Murphy, D. T., 79
Murray, C., 122
Muthén, B. O., 154

Nakazawa, J., 106
National Center for Health Statistics, 168
National Urban League, 92
Neighbors, H., 152
Nock, S., 2, 149
Nord, C. W., 2, 58, 60, 74, 167-168, 170, 177, 231, 252
Nurius, P., 46

O'Brien, M., 22, 39
O'Connell, M., 8, 257, 261, 264
Oellerich, D., 99
Office of the Prime Minister, Japan, 104
Ooms, T. J., 79, 82
Ornstein, M., 252
Osherson, S., 21, 24
Oshman, H., 212

Palkovitz, R., 17, 21, 54, 84
Parke, R. D., 23, 256, 259
Parsons, T., 23, 32, 50
Pasley, K., xi, 2, 85, 192, 215
Peacock, D., 231
Pedersen, F. A., 7, 17, 22, 54, 84
Pemberton, R., 252-253
Perry-Jenkins, M., 42, 49
Peters, M. F., 152
Petersen, P. E., 122
Peterson, J. L., 58, 73, 168, 170, 177, 231
Peterson, R. R., 42, 264
Philiber, W. W., 42
Pirog-Good, M. A., 91
Pleck, J. H., 2-3, 17, 19, 21, 27, 41-42, 50-52, 55, 79, 90, 102-104, 106, 257-258, 261-262, 264-265
Polikoff, N., 237
Polonko, K., 7, 217
Powell, B., 11
Prentice, B., 237
Presser, H., 8, 261
Pruett, K., 257
Pyke, K., 259, 265

Radin, N., 72, 106, 145, 148-149, 257, 263
Rahman, M. O., 211

Rains, P. M., 131
Rainwater, L., 122
Rasch, G., 14
Rauhala, A., 230
Ray, S., 93
Redburn, F. S., 152
Reed, P., 237
Reischauer, E. O., 104
Reitz, D., 2, 6-7, 16, 63-64, 66-67
Renner, M., 5, 212
Resnick, G., 73, 92
Rexroat, C., 41
Richardson, J., 237, 250
Risman, B. J., 23, 25, 96, 100, 257
Robertson, I., 76
Robins, P. K., 100
Robinson, B. W., 25
Robinson, J., 104, 259-260
Robinson, M. K., 22
Roizen, J. A., 171
Roman, M., 231, 241
Rosaldo, M., 262
Rosenberg, M., 65
Rosenberg, S. D., 45
Rosenthal, K. M., 197
Ross, A. S., 50, 258
Rossi, A. S., 7, 24
Rotundo, E. A., 2
Rovine, M. , 50
Rubin, V., 171
Ruddick, S., 46, 48
Ruggles, S., 122
Russell, G., 7, 42, 50, 106, 257
Ryan, C. M., 73

Sagi, A., 79, 96, 106
Salamon, E. D., 25
Salt, R. A., 22
Sampson, R. J., 150
Sandler, I. N., 167
Santrock, J. W., 215
Sargent, K., xi, 7, 84, 267
Savage, B. D., 92
Scanzoni, J. H., 7, 19, 83, 213, 217
Schaeffer, N. C., 94, 167, 169, 183
Schrepf, N. A., 24
Schwartz, M., 65
Schwartz, P., 23

Schwebel, A., 5, 212
Schwebel, B., 72
Seccombe, K., 219, 228
Segal, L., 2, 4, 18, 79, 95, 267
Segal, S., 214
Seltzer, J. A., xi, 2, 8, 10-11, 13, 72, 94,
    120-121, 167-168, 170-171, 183,
    190, 212
Serpe, R. T., 2, 61-67
Sevenhuijsen, S., 253
Shanahan, M., 151, 153, 165
Shehan, C., 41
Shelton, B., 41, 260-261
Sherwood, K. E., 123, 167
Shwalb, D. W., 106
Silverstein, L. B., 100
Simon, W., 79
Simons, R. L., 150
Sinclair, R., 212
Smith, H. L., 14
Snarey, J., 45
Sofue, T., 105
Son, L., 45
Sonenstein, F. L., 167
Spitze, G., 50, 264
Sprey, J., 73
Stack, C., 213
Stanley, S. C., 50
Starrels, M. E., 2, 7
Statistics Canada, 252
Stephen, E. H., 169
Stewart, J. R., 72
Stier, H., 165
Stone, G. P., 61
Strauss, A. L., 26, 33, 232
Styker, S., 2, 6, 61-67, 85, 213
Suitor, J. J., 50
Sullivan, M. L., 2, 82, 123, 145, 167
Sum, A., 91
Sussman, M. B., 22
Suzuki, H., 105
Sweet, J. A., 120, 153, 167-168, 172-
    173, 216

Takeuchi, K., 105
Tallman, I., 64-65, 77
Talvitie, K., 131
Taylor, C. M., 197

Teachman, J. D., 7, 94, 217
Thompson, L., 7, 21-22, 41-42, 52, 135,
    217, 257-260, 262-265
Thompson, R. A., 79, 81, 94-96, 99, 100
Thomson, E., xi, 2, 11, 149-150, 165, 171
Thorne, B., 262
Thornton, A., 267
Tienda, M., 165
Tinsley, B., 256, 259
Trotter, B. B., 58, 73
Tschann, J. M., 73, 196
Tsuya, N. O., 117
Tully, J. C., 58, 61, 65-68
Turner, R. H., 47

Uehara, A., 105
Uhlenberg, P., 98
Umberson, D., 196
U.S. Bureau of the Census (1986), 67, 74
U.S. Bureau of the Census (1987), 199
U.S. Bureau of the Census (1991), 10,
    168
U.S. Bureau of the Census (1992), 119,
    256
U.S. Bureau of the Census (1993), 193
U.S. General Accounting Office, 90

Vaillant, G., 45
Valdez, E., 264
Valentine, C. A., 122
Van Nguyen, T., 150
Verbraken, A., 253
Visher, E. B., 212, 214
Visher, J. S., 212, 214
Vogel, E. F., 104, 117
Volling, B., 50

Waite, L. J., 257, 261
Walker, A., 21-22, 41-42, 257-260, 262-
    265
Wallerstein, J. S., 60, 72-73, 81, 169,
    171, 195-196, 250
Warshak, R. A., 215
Weinberger, J., 45
Weingarten, K., 45, 49, 265
Weiss, R., 74

Weitzman, L., 10, 231, 237, 250
Wells, L. E., 66
West, C., 265
Whitbeck, L. B., 150
White, L. K., 215
White, S. W., 195
Wilkie, J. R., 3
Williams, C. L., 196
Wilson, R. J., 4, 22
Wilson, S., 79
Wilson, W. J., 122
Witcher, W. C., 197

Wolchik, S. A., 167
Woodhouse, B., 140

Yalom, M., 262
Yancey, W. L., 122
Youngblade, L., 50

Zill, N., 11, 58, 168, 231
Zvetina, D., 167

Subject Index

Adult development, 7, 12, 45
Adult male development, 53
AFDC regulations, 90

Biological children, 18

Census data, 10
Child care:
    among dual earners, 261
    future patterns of, 270
    men's involvement in, 41, 55, 93, 103,
        135-136, 197, 258, 272
    perceptions of, 240, 242
    See also Child-rearing activities
Child custody, 96
    best interest of the child doctrine
        regarding, 243, 254
    Canadian laws about, 237
    contested, 204, 207-208, 237
    dispensation policies for, 211
    fathers' perceptions of, 240-242, 245,
        249
    joint legal custody, 96, 253
    judicial descretion in cases of, 99

Child-rearing activities:
    father-daughter, 113, 115-116
    father-son, 113, 115-116
    men's involvement in, 21, 51
    See also Child care; Father-child inter-
        action; Paternal conduct; Pater-
        nal involvement
Children:
    commitments involving, 123
    consequences of divorce on, 196
    development, 7
    economically stressed, 150
    fathers' role in the development of,
        244
    home environment of, 10
    outcome measures for, 9, 154
    perceptions of father, 110-111
    problem behaviors of, 11, 60, 159-163
    role of fathers in the lives of, 124-127
    self-esteem, 60
    well-being of, 1, 10-11, 15, 57-58, 60,
        91, 93, 97, 152, 159-163, 209,
        212
Child Supplement of the NLSY, 9, 11
Child support system, 94, 167
    collection, 145-146
    guidelines for, 99

310

policies for, 95
Chodorow's theory, 24
Clinical Measurement Package, 201
Comparative analysis, 26
Conflict theory, 73
Congress, 99
Constabulary model, 32
Coparental relationship, 72-73, 96, 230,
    240-241
  power issues in, 99
Current Population Survey, 169

Daddies, 82, 124, 139-140, 142
Daddy track, 270
Demographic trends, 98, 268-269
Developmental perspective, 7, 42-43, 50
Developmental transitions, 43
Divergent developmental trajectories, 7,
    48, 55
Division of labor in family life, 3, 50,
    120, 262
  theoretical explanations of, 262-265
  See also Gendered family system;
    Gendered perspectives on
    parenthood
Divorce, 4, 166-167, 194-196
Domestic labor (work), 41, 50-51
  economic trends related to, 266-267
  See also family work
Domestic routine, 135

Erikson's theory of human development,
    42, 45
Europe, 1

Family policy debates, 1
Family role behavior, 48
Family transitions, 8, 122
Family work, 28, 42, 51-53, 260, 271
  See also Domestic labor
Father absence, 9-10, 57
  Japanese, 106. See also Japanese,
    fatherless
Father-child interaction, 17
Fatherhood:
  conduct of, 103

cultural images (scenarios) of, 5-6, 14-
    15, 21, 78-79, 80-83, 100, 103,
    128, 213
definition of responsible, 90
future of, 269-274
identity, 23
ideologies of, 2, 89
late-timed, 54
symbolic representations of, 2, 12
timing of, 54
Fatherhood identity:
  construction of, 22, 27, 34, 39
  male models for, 25
  microstructural theories of, 23
  psychoanalytic, 23-24
  socialization theories of, 23
  social learning theory, 23
  symbolic presentations for, 24, 39
  transitions, 98, 133
Fatherhood images:
  deadbeat father, 3-4, 257
  good dad-bad dad, 3-4, 27, 82, 88, 90,
    121, 124, 257
  inner-city, 128-129, 134
  moral overseer, 3, 22
  new father, 4-5, 103, 148, 255-257
  nurturer, 3, 22, 150
  polarization, 4
  sex role model, 3, 22
  social construction of, 3
Fathering:
  good, 67-68
  ideals, 37-38
  nonprovider aspects of, 17
  postdivorce, 60
  quality of, 76
  responsible, 89. See also Fatherhood,
    definition of responsible
  shadow, 133
  social initiatives to promote responsi-
    ble, 100
  style, 15
Fatherlike perceptions, 19, 215-216, 221-
    223, 226-227
Father (paternal) models, 15, 21
  fragmented, 34-37
  modeling, 29
Father (paternal) roles:
  adjustment to, 200-204

biological, 9, 19, 185-189. *See also* Fathers, biological
breadwinner (financial provider), 6, 12, 16-17, 40, 92, 102-103, 256
companion, 6, 63, 67
commitment to, 6, 15, 19
disciplinarian, 15
good provider, 22, 63, 67, 257
nurturer, 6, 15, 22, 63
playmate, 12, 49, 63, 67
Father role identities, 2, 59-60, 68-72, 85-86
commitment to, 2, 12, 15-16, 59, 63-64, 69, 76, 85, 87, 96, 121, 128, 213
conditional commitment to, 87, 93, 131, 137
identity salience, 12, 59, 62, 65, 68-69, 76
salience hierarchies, 62, 85-86, 92
Fathers:
African American, 82, 122, 128-129, 151. *See also* Black
black, 4-5, 8. *See also* African American
biological, 11, 80, 83. *See also* Father roles, biological
caregiving behavior of, 47-48
caring of newborns by, 49
child support, 10, 12, 19, 63, 74, 87, 90, 97, 135, 167-172, 177-183, 245-246, 248. *See also* Child support system
closeness with child, 12, 14, 223-224
coresident, 79-80
custodial, 96
dating, 197
developmental position in relation to his partner's, 54
direct attachment to children by, 93
disengagement from children, 145-146
divorced, 6
economically disadvantaged, 5, 89, 121, 150. *See also* Fathers, unemployed
economic well-being of, 73-74
education, 171-172
emotional stability of, 71
employment opportunities for, 19
expressive cognitive structures for, 46

financial obligation of, 83
Hispanic, 82
household structures for, 55
ideal images of, 3-4, 80, 82
interpersonal resources, 11
Japanese, 15, 102, 115-117
life course patterns, 15, 78, 98
modeling of, 46-47
noncustodial, 96, 250. *See also* Fathers, nonresident
nonresident, 2, 4, 6-7, 8-14, 67, 80, 82, 87-88, 90, 94-95, 167, 176, 191. *See also* Fathers, noncustodial
nontraditional, 83
North American, 15
possible selves, 46
resident, 2, 87
responsibility of, 2, 19, 127
self-identity of, 208
self-image of, 114
self-report data from, 13
sexual abuse of children, 4
single fathers, 11, 15, 23, 25, 52, 81, 87, 193-194, 196-198, 205
socialization of, 47, 51
socialization values of, 216, 227
stereotypes of, 3, 12, 80, 82-83
transitional experiences of, 17, 24, 87
unemployed, 92-93. *See also* Fathers, economically disadvantaged
visitation patterns of, 94
visitation rights, 10, 95
well-being of, 208
working class, 49
young unwed, 82
Fathers and Children Survey, 107
Fathers' Day March, 233
Fathers for Justice, 230
Fathers' rights groups, 3, 14, 94, 230
reverse discrimination charges by, 238
rhetoric of, 231, 233-237, 250-251
vocabulary of motives of, 253
Feminist movements, 20

Gay/Lesbian organization, 20
Gender:
social construction of, viii

Gendered family system, 51-52
    erosion of, 273-274
    See also Division of family labor in
        family life; Household division
        of labor
Gendered perspectives on parenthood,
    12, 14, 129, 149, 252
Gender role:
    attitudes, 17, 83
    ideologies, 42
Generativity, 12, 42, 44-45, 48-49, 50-
    52, 54, 79, 84, 91, 93, 97
Government income support programs,
    271
Grounded theory, 26

Household division of labor, 1, 260
    See also Gendered family system;
        Division of labor in family life
Housework:
    men's participation in, 104, 149, 259,
        271
Human Equality Action Resource Team
    (Heart), 230

Identity, 61
    significant others influence on, 65-66
Identity theory, 27, 58-59, 61-67, 79, 85
Index of Parental Attitudes (IPA), 201
Individualism, 5
In Search of Justice, 230
Interpersonal negotiations, 86

Japanese families:
    behavioral outcomes of children in,
        106
    fatherless, 103. *See also* Father
        absence, Japanese
Japanese youth:
    images of fathers and mothers, 104
Joint custody, 10-11

Levinson's concepts of adult develop-
    ment, 43-44
Liberal feminists, 8

Life course perspective, 79, 83
Life structure, 44

Mandatory salary withholding, 99
Manhood:
    meaning of, 81
Masculinity, 5, 53
Maternal employment, 24
Media, 4, 14-15
Mediation, 96-97
Men:
    caregiving, 98
    sensitivity to children, 97
    young inner-city, 92
Men's movement, 52
Men's perceptions of marital relation-
    ships, 50
Men's perceptions of paternal roles, 110,
    116
Men's rights organizations, 20
Methodological issues, 12-14, 53
Moral labor, 93
Mothers:
    employment status and work schedule,
        8
    gatekeepers, 137, 215
    mediating role of, 117. *See also*
        Women, role in mediating men's
        relationships with children
    perceptions of fathers, 17
    preferences for father-child contact,
        71
    relationship with children with step-
        father present, 228
Mothers' reports of paternal conduct, 13-
    14, 182

National Health Interview Survey, 72
National Longitudinal Study of 1988, 11
National Longitudinal Survey of Labor
    Market Experience (NLSY), 8
National Survey of Children (NSC), 8-9,
    60
National Survey of Families and House-
    holds (NSFH), 5, 8, 13, 153, 165,
    172, 216, 228

National Urban League's Male Respon-
    siblilty Project, 92
Negotiation issues, 18
New right, 20
Nonmarital births, 89
    See also Out-of-wedlock childbearing
North America, 1, 20

Profeminist:
    men, vii
    perspective, 99
PromiseKeepers, vii
Psychosocial health, 44-45
Public policies:
    mediation, 96

Object relations and self-psychology
    theory, 7
Ontario Support and Custody Enforce-
    ment Branch, 233
Out-of-wedlock childbearing, 4
    See also Nonmarital births

Parental control, 155, 162, 164
Parental rights and obligations, 89, 94
Parental roles postdivorce, 58
Parenthood:
    contested, 130-131
    meaning of, 60
    negotiated, 130
    responsibility of, 134, 184
Parenting role identity, 58, 62
Parents Without Partners (PWP), 198
Paternal absence, 60
    See also Father absence
Paternal conduct, 2, 6-8, 19, 79
    See also Father-child interaction;
        Paternal involvement
Paternal (fathers') involvement, 12, 16,
    55, 58-59, 70-74, 90-91, 103, 116,
    154, 164, 168, 177
    interventions to promote, 93
    Japanese fathers, 105, 110-115
    measurement of, 108
    pilot program to enchance, 91
    See also Child care; Child-rearing
        activities; Paternal conduct
Paternity:
    commitment to, 133
    establishment procedures, 99
    out-of-wedlock, 80
Postdivorce families, 231, 252
Postmodernist analyses of families,
    38
Postseparation child rearing, 173

Rasch's measurement model, 14
Reflected appraisals, 6-7, 15
Reinforcement, 46-47
Reproductive technologies:
    modern, 81
Responsibility for housework, 17
Role ambiguity, 60, 96
Role identities:
    masculine male, 16, 18-19
    partner, 16
    worker, 16-17
Role identity, 59
Role identity theory, 2, 6, 14
    identity setting, 6
    identity standards, 6
Role performance, 59, 80
Role-person merger, 46-47
Role strain, 96

Sampling biases, 13
Scripting perspective, 6, 79-80, 83
    cultural scenarios, 80
    interpersonal scripting, 80, 82, 87, 97
    intrapsychic scripting, 80, 88
Second shift, 41, 104, 257
Sex, viii
Sex role development, 24
Sex role identity, 24
Sex segregated labor markets:
    Sweden, 91
Sexually based primary relationship, 17,
    217
Single-mother households, 11
Single-parent families, 1
Social constructionist perspective, 3, 25,
    38
Social learning theory, 7, 15, 47
Social policy:
    Sweden, 89

Social trends related to family work, 267
Stepchildren, 18
Stepfathers, 5, 14, 19, 59, 80-81, 86-87,
    99, 170-171, 211
    cultural scenarios of, 88
    perceptions of stepfather role, 212-
        213, 217-219, 221-223
    quality of relationship with children,
        223-226
Structural symbolic interactionism, 2
Surrogate father, 8-9
Symbolic interactionist perspective, 25,
    61, 67, 213

The Ethnograph, 27
Therapist role with children of single
    fathers, 209
The Single Parent, 198
Transition to parenthood, 48-49, 50

Transitions to the involved-parent role, 54

Univocal reciprocity, 19, 79, 83, 86-87,
    90, 97-98

Wives' mentoring role, 52
Women:
    role in mediating men's relationships
        with children, 170-171, 190-
        191. *See also* Mothers, mediat-
        ing role of
    white middle class, 88
Women's labor force participation, 1, 3,
    256
Workplace norms, 17

YM-YWCA, 26

About the Authors

Carl E. Bertoia is a Sessional Instructor in sociology at the University of Windsor, Windsor, Ontario, Canada. He is currently finishing his doctoral degree in sociology at McMaster University, Hamilton, Ontario. In his dissertation, he examines the fathers' rights movement, specifically the threats to fatherhood identity as a major social process. His interests include theories of self and identity, masculinity, family, and qualitative methods.

Yvonne Brandreth is a Ph.D. candidate in sociology at the University of Wisconsin. Her primary areas of interest are family demography and gender. She is Research Assistant on a project exploring demographic and social issues in child support. She is currently working on her dissertation on the psychological and structural determinants of father disengagement from children following divorce.

Cheryl Buehler, Ph.D., is Associate Professor of Child and Family Studies at the University of Tennessee in Knoxville. Her major research interests include the effects of marital conflict on youth and the correlates of divorce adjustment.

Shawn L. Christiansen, M.S., was a graduate student in the Department of Family Sciences at Brigham Young University when his chapter was written. He is now a doctoral student in the Department of Individual and Family Sciences at the University of Delaware. His research interests include fathering, Japanese family life, and parental involvement in early childhood education.

Scott Coltrane, Ph.D., is Associate Professor of Sociology at the University of California, Riverside. His research on gender, families, and social change has appeared in *American Journal of Sociology, Gender & Society, Journal of Marriage and the Family, Journal of Family Issues, Social Problems,* and *Sociological Perspectives.* He is coauthor (with Randall Collins) of *Sociology of Marriage and the Family: Gender, Love, and Property* (fourth edition, 1995). His most recent book, *Family Man: Fatherhood, Housework and Gender Equity* (1995), focuses on the personal, social, and political implications of men's changing family roles.

Kerry J. Daly, Ph.D., is Associate Professor at the University of Guelph. His research on fatherhood is concerned with the meanings of family time for fathers, the gender politics of family time, and the way that fatherhood is socially constructed. He is interested in adoptive kinship and is coauthor (with Michael Sobol) of *Adoption in Canada* (1993). He has also focused on the use of qualitative methods to study families and is coeditor of *Qualitative Methods in Family Research* (1992).

Alfred DeMaris is Associate Professor in the Department of Sociology at Bowling Green State University, Bowling Green, Ohio. His interests include statistical applications and the study of the family. He is the author of *Logit Modeling: Practical Applications* (1992) as well as additional papers on logistic regression. He is the author or coauthor of a number of other articles on premarital cohabitation and its relationship to subsequent marital quality and stability, single fathers, and violence in intimate relationships.

Janice Drakich, Ph.D., is Associate Professor of Sociology at the University of Windsor, Windsor, Ontario, Canada. Her work in the area of the family has focused on child custody issues, fatherhood, and fathers' rights groups. In 1994 she received a 3-year research grant from the Social Sciences and Humanities Research Council of Canada to examine the status of women academics in Canadian universities. Her other theory and research interests are in the areas of social psychology and women's studies.

Frank F. Furstenberg Jr., Ph.D., is Zellerbach Family Professor of Sociology at the University of Pennsylvania. He is the author of a number of books on the family, including *Adolescent Families in Later Life* and *Divided Families*. His current research projects focus on the family in the context of disadvantaged urban neighborhoods, adolescent sexual behavior, and changes in the well-being of children.

Geoffrey L. Greif is Associate Professor at the School of Social Work at the University of Maryland at Baltimore. The author or coauthor of four books on single-parent issues (including *The Daddy Track and the Single Father*, 1990) and two forthcoming books, he has also published numerous journal articles and chapters on group work, family therapy, parental kidnapping, and the impact of AIDS on the family.

Alan J. Hawkins, Ph.D., is Assistant Professor of Family Sciences at Brigham Young University. His research interests include fathering, men's adult development, and the allocation of domestic labor in dual-earner families.

E. Jeffrey Hill is a Ph.D. candidate in family and human development at Utah State University. He is Senior Account Representative in Human Resources Research at Workforce Solutions, an IBM company. His research interests include work/family issues, full-time fatherhood, and the influence of children on their parents. He is the editor of the *DAD/S Newsletter*, in which fathers from 35 states share their parenting ideas. He took a 6-month unpaid paternity leave from IBM and wrote about his experiences in *Good Housekeeping* (1990).

Marilyn Ihinger-Tallman, Ph.D., is Professor and Chair of the Department of Sociology at Washington State University. She has published extensively on the subject of remarriage and stepparenting and sibling behavior in families. A number of her published pieces deal with theory construction and she has developed theories that attempt to explain sibling conflict and norms of equity, sibling/stepsibling relationships, factors influencing the quality of life of single parents, and father parenting identity after divorce.

Masako Ishii-Kuntz, Ph.D., is Associate Professor of Sociology at the University of California, Riverside. Her research on fathers' roles in comparative perspective, and division of household labor and child care, has appeared in *Journal of Marriage and the Family, Journal of Family Issues,* and *Sociological Perspectives,* among others. She is the author of *Ordinal Log-Linear Models* (1994) and recently completed a book manuscript comparing Chinese, Japanese, Korean, and Filipino American families. She was guest editor for a 1994 volume of the *Journal of Family Issues* devoted to international perspectives on work and family. She is presently studying Japanese dual-earner couples who share housework and child care responsibilities.

William Marsiglio, Ph.D., is Associate Professor of Sociology at the University of Florida. His current theory and research interests include men's issues as they relate to sexuality, procreation, contraception, child support, child care, parenting, and primary relationships of men of varying ages. His research on men has appeared in *Journal of Marriage and the Family, Sex Roles, Family Planning Perspectives, Journal of Family Issues, Journal of Sex Research, Marriage and Family Review,* and *Journal of Gerontology,* among others. He was recently guest editor for two volumes of the *Journal of Family Issues* devoted to fatherhood issues. He recently completed a book manuscript, *Families and Friendships: Applying the Sociological Imagination.*

Jane Mosley, M.S., is pursuing her Ph.D. in sociology at the University of Wisconsin—Madison. Her research interests focus on child well-being, particularly the role of poverty in the lives of children.

Kay Pasley, Ed.D., is Associate Professor of Human Development and Family Studies at the University of North Carolina at Greensboro. Her research interests have focused on the marital dyad in remarriage, multiple remarriage, and stress and coping in pregnant and parenting adolescents. Much of her work in the study of remarriage has been in conjunction with Marilyn Ihinger-Tallman. Together they have published three books, a number of book chapters, and various articles on remarriage. Her current attention is directed toward the application of identity theory and social cognition principles to fathering in divorced and remarried families.

Kathryn Pond Sargent received her M.A. in family life education from Brigham Young University. Her primary areas of interest include issues relating to single-parent and remarried families, father involvement in child care, and women and religion.

Judith A. Seltzer, Ph.D., is Professor of Sociology at the University of Wisconsin—Madison. She is interested in the social definition of kinship and inequality within and between families. Her recent publications examine the relationships among legal custody, child support, and contact between parents and children who live apart. She has also written about the effects on children of separation and divorce.

Elizabeth Thomson, Ph.D., is Professor of Sociology at the University of Wisconsin—Madison. She is also a faculty member of the Center for Demography and Ecology. Her current research focuses on the consequences of divorce and remarriage for children, fertility decisions and behaviors, and methodological issues in measurement and modeling with couple or parent-child data. She has served as a member of the design team for the National Survey of Families and Households since its inception.